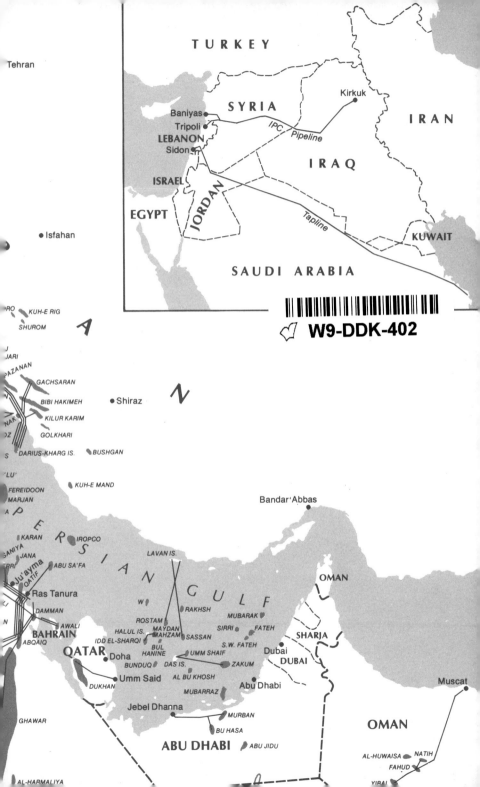

W9-DDK-402

MAKING DEMOCRACY
SAFE FOR OIL

V. Osborne

MAKING DEMOCRACY SAFE FOR OIL

Oilmen and the Islamic East

CHRISTOPHER T. RAND

An Atlantic Monthly Press Book
Little, Brown and Company—Boston—Toronto

FIRST EDITION

T 06/75

LIBRARY OF CONGRESS CATALOGING IN PUBLICATION DATA

Rand, Christopher T.
  Making democracy safe for oil.

  "An Atlantic Monthly Press book."
  Bibliography: p.
  Includes index.
    1. Petroleum industry and trade — Near East.
  2. Petroleum industry and trade — United States.
  I. Title.
  HD9576.N36R35   338.2'7'282   75-1426
  ISBN 0-316-73331-8

ATLANTIC–LITTLE, BROWN BOOKS
ARE PUBLISHED BY
LITTLE, BROWN AND COMPANY
IN ASSOCIATION WITH
THE ATLANTIC MONTHLY PRESS

Designed by Susan Windheim

*Published simultaneously in Canada
by Little, Brown & Company (Canada) Limited*

PRINTED IN THE UNITED STATES OF AMERICA

For Hoda, Leila and Camilla

Contents

Author's Note

THOUGH OIL COMPANIES have often changed their names with the passage of time, evolving circumstances, or new owner-ship, this book, without exception, refers to them by the names they possessed in 1974. For instance, British Petroleum Corpora-tion is always British Petroleum (or BP) here, although it started out in the world as D'Arcy Petroleum, a venture in southern Iran, then became Anglo-Persian Oil Company after the British government bought into it, then stayed Anglo-Persian after it went into Iraq, then became Anglo-Iranian (and Benzin-e Pars, or "Persian Gasoline") with changing circumstances in Iran — only, in fact, assuming the title "British Petroleum" when it was thrown out of Iran, decisively but temporarily, in 1951. This has been much the case with Exxon — known as Standard Oil of New Jersey for most of its life — and Mobil, known through half its life as Socony (Standard Oil Company of New York, a state which lies across a river from New Jersey), then Socony-Vacuum.

Some Arabic and Persian words and names appear in the book. The transliteration of Persian names here is consistent with the standard speech of modern Iran — not that of Afghanistan or some period in the Middle Ages beloved of scholars who to this day transliterate Persian as if it preserved the sounds of the Arabic from which it borrowed half its vocabulary a millenium or so ago. By contrast, the book's rendition of Arabic names and words is most chaotic. Standard written Arabic is a sort of dead language, like Medieval Latin, low on idiom, high on vocabulary, used for writing and for speech between people whose dialects are very different. There is no single acknowledged standard Arabic dialect — just a number of regional dialects — and different individuals can render their names differently into English even if they speak the same dialect. This is probably due for the most part to the subtle and complicated consonant structure of Arabic — in comparison with which that of Persian is very simple.

For most of what is in this book, I am indebted to the scholars who have written on the various related fields in depth; I apologize if I have omitted any of their works from the bibliography. It is impossible to thank, by name, at the present time, those other persons who, however unconsciously, in an amorphous and collective sense delegated this author to commit the fruits of their knowledge and experience to writing here, but I hope they know that I am sincerely grateful to them.

MAKING DEMOCRACY
SAFE FOR OIL

1

From the Eshratabad Garrison

On the morning of the twenty-eighth of Mordad 1332 — August 19, 1953 — one of the most important episodes in the history of the Cold War and international oil unfolded in the northeast of Tehran, capital of Iran.

Iran is one of several predominantly Moslem states, grouped together around the Persian Gulf, which possess vast and very accessible resources of crude oil. Its government, under its Shah and the popular, nationalist Prime Minister Mohammad Mosaddegh, had expropriated the producing and refining properties of its opulent guest, British Petroleum Company, about two years before, in March, 1951. In the two years that followed, the nation passed through much turmoil and suffering. Yet while the Iranian people experienced a period of asceticism and denied themselves the bounties of the foreign world which BP's sterling taxes had once enabled them to procure, the economy itself held up. The oil nationalization became an accomplished fact which most Iranians accepted along with its hardships. Their internal dilemma was, rather, political: whether or not their nation should exchange its Shah, and the institution of the monarchy, for a republic of sorts under Mosaddegh.

It was a hard decision to make. Through 1952 and 1953, the Shah's power eroded at the skilled hands of his premier. Mosaddegh had already started with a broad mandate from Iran's religious right and non-Communist left in 1951; the Shah appointed him prime minister largely against his will. In 1952, the Shah tried to remove him but failed.

Then, in 1953, Mosaddegh began to lose the mandate. By the summer of that year, he had become somewhat dependent on the indigenous Communist party, the Tudeh, for support on the streets of Tehran — where a good many of Iran's political conflicts were resolved. In mid-August the Shah, in alarm, once again sought to dismiss Mosaddegh and replace him with the loyalist general Fazlollah Zahedi. He sent a colonel to inform Mosaddegh of this action and the premier forthwith arrested the courier. Communist-led throngs swept the streets of Tehran. Zahedi went into hiding and the Shah left the country.

The Tudeh raged out of control, tearing down statues of the Shah, besieging American information centers. Mosaddegh's foreign minister, Hossein Fatemi, just recovered from a gunshot wound in the abdomen, pitilessly lashed out at the monarchy in a mass meeting and the Tudeh called for a people's democratic republic of Iran.

But the crowds had got out of hand. Mosaddegh, in apprehension, passed the order to the chief of staff to bring the army across from Eshratabad, to restore order in the streets and protect the American embassy, a little over one mile to the west.

To that time, the public had not known at all of the Shah's order dismissing Mosaddegh and appointing General Zahedi in his stead. The Shah had availed himself of his constitutional prerogatives in taking this action, but Mosaddegh expressed doubt that the dismissal order had come from the Shah himself. Now, however, as the army's I-4 tanks and armored personnel carriers squealed out into the hot midday glare from the garrison, their treads nicking grooved bars into the soft asphalt of Takhtejamshid Avenue, a group of loyalists moved against the premier. They took over the radio station and General Zahedi emerged from hiding in the outskirts and drove toward it.

In later years, sympathizers of the Tudeh claimed that the Communist leader Lenin used to admit that revolution was not always an inevitable occurrence, an "objective manifestation" of the will of the masses; sometimes, the leader had conceded, a good break here or there could turn the tide of events and bring on revolution. For instance, Zahedi's chauffeur belonged to the Tudeh. Had he shot his passenger, he might have saved the day for his party. But the driver did not act. Zahedi reached the station safely, broadcast the Shah's order dismissing Mosaddegh, and declared himself premier.

A resurgent counterwave of loyalist crowds broke over Tehran, perhaps aided by American agents, who had been covering the events of the past weeks and days — perhaps supplemented by an American airlift of military supplies and police expertise to Iran. The crowd swept parts of the capital city and joined forces with the detachment from Eshratabad, which went on past the embassy and rumbled on toward Mosaddegh's place of refuge a mile or so beyond.

One witness to the events described the following scene thus: "All morning Mosaddegh's house had been thrown into a state of flurry as reports of defections by the security forces poured in and pro-Shah gangs made headway and occupied government offices by noon. . . . But the commander of Mosaddegh's house stood his ground. It was reported that he had betrayed the preponderantly Royalist wing of the army, leaving himself no choice but to fight to the end. He commandeered a house two blocks away from Mosaddegh's at the key Kakh-Shah intersection and mounted machine-gun nests on the roof and the balconies. The battle for Mosaddegh's house was joined at 4:30 PM. . . . It was a bitter, senseless fight. Mosaddegh's tanks after a brief duel with Royalist tanks capitulated. As Mosaddegh's defenders abandoned positions, tanks battered the walls of his house and reduced the defenses. Behind tanks came soldiers and the crowd of riff-raff and looters. Nobody knows how many were killed; it is said to be between 30 and 300. . . .

"The only things left behind were home-made heaters, certainly not tempting objects in the mid-summer heat. Soldiers with fixed bayonets stood on the steps leading to the once high command rooms on the upper floor. Someone in the crowd broke the silence and pointing at the house exclaimed, 'The ruins of Mosaddegh!'

"Just a hundred yards south of the house stood the Shah's Palace, without scars, intact. The contrast could not be more brutal."[1]

In a day, the nationalist leader had fallen: the Shah returned to the country in triumph. Slowly, Iran's economy regained life. With Zahedi as premier, the security forces very largely extirpated the Tudeh. The oil industry came back to the country, in a modified form, a "committee," or consortium, in which the old British Petroleum held a powerful minority position — along with the other major oil powers of the world, mostly American. In just over a year, Iran's new guests had the oil flowing out to the world market again. Over the years to follow, the Western press printed little about the twenty-eighth of Mordad and the march from Eshratabad. Peace returned to the international oil industry and its great heartland, the Moslem Middle East, for twenty years.

During these two decades, the oil industry expanded virtually without impediment, until, by late 1974, the world was producing and consuming 55 million barrels of oil a day — about 20 billion barrels a year. Of this volume, 10 million barrels a day originated, and mostly remained, in the Communist world; another 11 million was produced and consumed in North America; and most of the rest, almost half the world's total, or 25 million barrels a day, passed from the Islamic Near East to the major consumers of the world. In turn, the overwhelming bulk of this, or 22 million barrels, came from the Persian Gulf, and the seven major oil companies controlled 90 percent of it.

During these two decades, furthermore, the Middle Eastern

peoples very largely kept the Cold War out of oil, and for this the West has given them precious little acknowledgment. If the price of oil has now gone outlandishly out of control, the blame belongs not so much with the Iranians and Arabs as with the Nixon and Ford administrations and the international oil industry.

There are at least two explanations for this twenty-year lull. One is that the Near Easterners scarcely had better or more ingenious ideas for disposing of their oil than did the companies themselves, so they largely let the companies be; the industry's position was assured, by default. For outsiders do not know much about the oil industry, in the Near East as in the West. Most schemes Arabs or Iranians propounded for reforming or replacing the international industry were quite naïve, and the more extreme they were, generally the more unrealistic.

Another reason is that deep down, whatever bitterness and vindictiveness Near Easterners did harbor at times toward the companies did not arise from Marxist theory, nationalist dogma, or other partisan bias so much as it grew from the genuine knowledge that the companies were not treating their hosts as full men, as equals. Although the Arabs and Iranians have at times made outrageous demands on the industry, in a spirit of frivolity, contempt, or arrogance, they have never seriously pursued a claim against the industry which did not fundamentally represent a legitimate long-standing grievance. Almost never have they acted with the spite of a Castro, forcing a company from malice to accept a humiliating condition — such as refining Soviet oil — on pain of immediate expropriation.

For its part, the oil industry in the Middle East has continuously conducted itself with deafness and bad faith toward outsiders, on a few occasions committing what in the United States would be prosecuted as felonies, and quite often perpetrating wrongful acts against nature. The story shows the limitations of putting faith and trust in the oil industry when it is not negotiating from a position of real rather than feigned weakness — from a position of real hunger.

Seen in this bleak light, stripped to these stark essentials, the story of oil in the Islamic East is thus quite a simple one. However, the lessons to be drawn from it are complex in the extreme. It is a tale of willful incompetence and avarice more than of conspiracy or malevolence, and there are few clear-cut villains in it. While teaching that the bigger the company is, the richer and less trustworthy it is, it also shows that no one passed bribes as profligately as the arrant newcomer Armand Hammer. Nor did anyone raid other companies as ruthlessly: in America, one firm, Texaco, took Hammer's company, Occidental Petroleum, to court for engaging in this practice and Shell, in its southern California operations, would give its geologists half a day to empty their desks and leave the company if they were found so much as talking to an Occidental representative.

Yet Hammer, in 1970, made an honest appeal to his counterpart in Exxon, Chairman James Jamieson, for a guarantee of cut-rate crude oil, which would help him make a firm and honorable stand in Libya, where the government seemed about to expropriate his oil production. Since Hammer had also raided the far more powerful Exxon of one of its top Libyan negotiators and had offered the Peruvian government to operate the oilfield which it had expropriated from an Exxon subsidiary,[2] Jamieson turned the appeal down. So, blame for the subsequent decline of the industry's position in Libya lies as much with the biggest company in the business as with its most flamboyant and reckless actor.

In turn Exxon's history in the Near East — in the Persian Gulf and Libya alike — displays much naked arrogant power; many concessions in which Exxon played a part have produced fields either too slowly or too fast. Still, there is much more to Exxon's role than that. In Iraq, Iran, and Saudi Arabia, this giant was a key instrument in a system of oligopoly which had a restraining effect on prices, regional squabbles, and countervailing cupidities. Exxon, along with the other six of the Major Seven, was partner to a structure which worked to the advantage of all direct participants for a long time.*

---

* Much reference will be made to these seven throughout the book. They dominate the international oil industry. All but two, British Petroleum and Royal Dutch/Shell, are American: Exxon, Texaco, Gulf, Mobil, and Standard of California (SoCal). Three of the American companies — Exxon, SoCal, and Mobil — were spun off from the Standard Oil Trust in 1911.

The very fact that it took a company like Occidental, which practiced a corrupt and devious brand of business, to carve a position of importance for itself within the Near Eastern oil system by 1965 indicates how tightly the oligopoly held the concession rights in the area under control.

The other companies, of varying size, ambition, and wealth, between Exxon and Occidental were actors whose roles were flawed more by their own philosophical and commercial limitations than by any presumed innate evil. In turn, the representatives of our Justice and State departments and our congressmen and senators — even the state of the postwar world, which bestowed near immunity on all American enterprises abroad for the duration of the Cold War — deserve much criticism and blame for the fact that these actors enjoyed such freedom of movement. Nonetheless, since the conclusion of the Cold War on terms acceptable to this nation was the top priority in our foreign actions for twenty-five years in the eyes of the majority of the American people, it was difficult for criticism of the oil industry — or of any multinational enterprise based in this country — to gain a hearing until the public came to see that America had truly achieved détente with the Soviet Union and China.

Now the Cold War is dead or dying. The world sees that ex-President Nixon had, perhaps out of simple fear and weakness, made more concessions to the international oil industry than it deserved. The industry in turn has not been subtle in its acceptance of these concessions and is finally coming within the range of public scrutiny and criticism.

Let us begin the story by moving ahead of it, to its outcome, the massive price rises and shortages of oil products in the United States in the winter of 1973–1974, when, in the space of four months, the price of gasoline rose 25 percent and the cost of domestic crude oil doubled and then tripled. The cause for this oil industry counterrevolt — which most people labeled a "crisis" at the time — does not lie with the Arab oil embargo that accompanied it. The embargo was the excuse by which the companies, and the American government, sought to explain the *coup* in the marketplace.

As this narrative proceeds, the many reasons for this contention will emerge. But public comprehension of the matter has already grown a great deal since the outset, in November, 1973, when the American people stood ready to accept in silence, if not total credulity, anything the oil industry told it; was willing to accept in its entirety the myth that the Arabs would want to starve the Western world of its oil, or could do so.

President Nixon set the climate for this mass suspension of disbelief in November, 1973, by removing the pliant and mild John Love from directorship of federal energy activity and replacing him with the no more knowledgeable but ruthless and ambitious William Simon, a crack investment banker, who was, in the coming months, to demonstrate a lack of skepticism about industry figures and a sublime ignorance of the structure of the world petroleum trade which were at total variance with his training and discipline, and a strict unwillingness to discuss substantive issues on this industry with public spokesmen except in very controlled, structured circumstances. For instance, he would not appear on the Dick Cavett television show, although Interior Secretary Rogers Morton did. There were numerous other forums on which he would not appear either. He would not bring critics of the industry into the Federal Energy Office. By New Year's, he was feeling free to announce flatly that the price of gasoline was going to rise to 60 cents a gallon within two months — as indeed it did. It was a real surprise to observers to note that his deputy, John Sawhill, became an occasional critic of the industry when he fell heir to the post on Simon's elevation to secretaryship of the treasury.

Simon's temper became shorter and shorter as the winter wore on, prices duly rose, the voices questioning the veracity of the Arab embargo — or any shortage — became louder and shriller, and the rumors began to proliferate that tankers were wallowing out beyond America's three-mile limit and distributors were secretly emptying and filling abandoned gas station tanks in the dead of night. At one point in February Roy Ash, Director of the Office of Management and Budget, remarked that the gasoline shortage would be short-lived and would not recur. Simon erupted, suggesting that Ash "keep his cotton-pickin' hands off" energy.[3] Later that month Simon flew into a rage against the Shah of Iran — head of a friendly foreign state — for doubting on American television that the embargo had really harmed America; venting his anger before Congress, Simon branded the Shah's statements "irresponsible."

The Simon interlude is striking because in several respects it gives room for suspicion that the federal government had a vested interest in maintaining the illusion of shortage and might have been protecting the industry in its endeavor to raise prices drastically. Simon's refusal to meet with critics; his refusal — most out of character in a banker — to show curiosity about the industry's various protestations of shortage and need for drastically raised prices; the tolerance which President Nixon showed him; the fact that Nixon appointed him Secretary of the Treasury as soon as the embargo ended; Simon's tenacious adherence to the full body of oil industry claims — all indicate that the government was not willing to help the public get at the facts bearing on the state of the international industry.

In retrospect, one can sympathize with one motive for this, which was to prepare American public opinion for a rapprochement with the Arab world. Convince America that the Arabs hold a knife at its throat and it will be easier to win public endorsement of a more even-handed official attitude toward the Arab-Israeli struggle; win this acceptance and it will be possible to move toward real peace in the Middle East. This is fair enough; for a generation American Middle East policy has been hobbled by Zionist pressure. But when the price for this transformation is the strengthening of the oil industry, the most powerful concentration of private wealth in America — the closed state within an open society *par excellence* — it becomes clear that this strategy has begun to fall afoul of the deepest public interest.

In fact, many congressional voices did question whether or not there was a real shortage of crude oil and gasoline in the country. Senator Henry Jackson, for instance, had often been a valuable foe of governmental endeavors to enrich the industry, such as

Nixon's campaign to deregulate natural gas piped in interstate commerce — which would shift 2 to 5 billion dollars per year from the consumer to the industry, giving the former nothing in exchange except the industry's temporary assurance that supplies were no longer tight. Jackson has since performed a further public service by probing into the relationship between the major oil companies and the United States military. In late January, 1974, though, he brought vice presidents of major American oil companies before a long table, made them swear in in unison, and berated them for the excesses of their companies at length without really explaining to the public what these excesses were, without getting these executives to reveal much of real substance about their profession. Then he declared, "We have opened the books of the oil industry."

Dozens if not hundreds of energy reform bills emerged in Congress only to be emasculated, voted down, or vetoed. Political figures were in total disarray on the question of what national oil and gas policy to formulate; their position often depended on their constituency's self-sufficiency in energy or indeed its proximity to the ice-blown borders of Canada.

From Congress, in the Nixon-sanctioned, industry-dictated energy price counterrevolt of winter 1973–1974, some faint light did shine forth to touch the issue with a small spot of warmth, a pale arctic glimmer. For instance, there was Representative John Dingell's Select Subcommittee on Small Business and Senator Frank Church's Foreign Relations Subcommittee on Multinational Corporations.

It was the latter which, established in the wake of a previous international scandal, the history of ITT's actions in Latin America, spearheaded investigation into the international operations of the oil industry. At this writing, it seems that much of what the subcommittee has achieved stands out because of comparison with the previous congressional investigations into the industry — the 1957 hearings on the emergency oil lift program and related oil problems, the 1969–1970 inquiry into governmental intervention in the market mechanism of the petroleum industry, and the Federal Trade Commission's 1952 study *The International Petroleum Cartel.*

However, Church's subcommittee came closer than any body inside or outside government at that time to the central fact of the 1973–1974 price disasters: the industry did not struggle against the Arab embargo and the international price hikes; it welcomed them, nurtured them, perhaps helped inspire them, and certainly gained handsomely from them.

2

A Couple of Rounds in Washington

I have had good relations with the companies all the time
I was in the office and one of the main reasons was that we
never quoted companies specifically by name. I frequently
talked about the industry doing this or even Aramco taking this position but to single out a single company or
even worse talk about an individual would certainly have
soured my relationships or the relationships of the State
Department with the companies.
— Ambassador James Akins,
before the Church Subcommittee

THE CHURCH SUBCOMMITTEE'S efforts were enclosed in a
small chamber, Room 4221, narrow, possessing roughly the size
and shape of an ample indoor tennis-court, on the fourth floor of
a Senate office building, one of the lesser prides of the New Deal.
The walls of this hearing room were of pale yellowish-nicotine
wood, flanked on both sides by columns, little Brunnhilde breast-
plates of the Eastern and Western Hemispheres in relief, and
mammoth aluminum lighthorns protruding from chevroned wall
fixtures.

At the end, the chamber hosted a horseshoe table overseen by
high-school wall maps facing press tables and armless leather
chairs. The acoustics — like those in any indoor tennis court —

were very good and very irksome at the same time. One could hear any speaker clearly, from any corner of the room, unless a television camera was working in the middle distance, churning the testimony into incoherence. It was rather like attending an international conference on Dante at the entomology wing of a provincial agricultural school.

Earlier, in January and February, 1974, the subcommittee had held hearings, but they had gnawed at the edges of power, exploring peripheral areas such as the law and the federal government and hosting witnesses from lesser companies like Bunker Hunt — an independent firm named after a son of the Texan H. L. Hunt, who had had the good fortune, in his one foreign venture, to hit the biggest known oilfield in Africa, Sarir of Libya. John McCloy had taken the stand — it turned out that this elder statesman, as well as pursuing a distinguished diplomatic career, had also been representing the major oil companies before the Department of Justice for over a decade — and the subcommittee had called up several ambassadors and antitrust lawyers.

Now, in late March, at the end of the 1973–1974 oil price counterrevolt, this chamber witnessed a historic event: the panel finally brought forward some men from the epicenter of the international oil industry. No such a group had spoken in public hearing for almost two decades, and now, after much jousting, cross-questioning, and grilling, the subcommittee managed to entice its honored guests into admitting to the American public that the international market — though now in ruins, of course — had, to a certain extent, been their creation, that a structural design of sorts governed it, in part. Some newspapers carried this revelation on their fifteenth or twentieth pages.

On the surface, this apparently banal, prolonged two-day tournament between Frank Church's Subcommittee on Multinational Corporations and the men who for two decades had produced Arabian Light crude oil for a dime a barrel and kept its price (at the terminal) to the public between $1.75 and $1.98 was a draw, a skirmish which seemed as immediately important as the Battle of Jutland. Its climax was the hour-long recitation of an arcane and archaic Justice Department brief by an oil company counsel — successful in its purpose, which was to drive spectators from the room in exasperation and ennui.

However, it did enable the public to discover a few new things. One was that the dominant figures of the oil industry did not always wear top hat and tails and walk with cigar clenched in teeth while clutching twin bags of gold. One witness, Exxon's George Piercy, a senior Middle East coordinator and one of the top practitioners of the trade, began the hearings like a soft-spoken Glenn Ford and came more and more to resemble Edward Teller, his eyes growing increasingly sunken as the round wore on. Continental sent its Iranian representative, Elby "Smokey" Shafer, elegantly clad and endowed with a crisp Oklahoma bass and blazing silvery hair. SoCal's representative was Dennis Bonney, who spoke with an articulate, close-cropped Midlands British accent. Then there was Joseph Johnston, the ponderous, monosyllabic director of financial affairs for the non-Communist world's biggest oil enterprise, Aramco of Saudi Arabia. And finally there were the retired senior statesmen, George Parkhurst of SoCal and Howard Page of Exxon, short, truly unyielding men with ample hair only slightly less silvery than Shafer's. The hearings had got into gear.

On the first day, they scrutinized two subjects: the mechanism, as intricate and impregnable as the breastworks of a great flood-control dam, whereby the Iranian producing company, the Consortium, controlled that nation's oil output for twenty years — while at all times guaranteeing that it would operate smoothly for decades to come if left untouched. This system is so complex that it will be covered in a later chapter.

The second subject, less exotic, more to the point of the hearings, was an analysis of the financial workings of the immense Arabian-American firm Aramco.

The discussion commenced with a statement by a government auditor, Shirley Ward, who showed that Aramco is a profit-making corporation which sells to its parent companies at the artificial, high tax-reference price which is known in the trade as the "posted price."

The "posted price" is an inflated and fictitious price, a hold-over from the price at which all oil-producing firms, up to fifteen years or so ago, used to offer their oil on the world market. Though these firms no longer sell oil to outsiders at this high price, but (except on rare occasions) offer it at a lower market price — an open price of sorts — the companies still sell their oil to their own subsidiaries as close to the posted price as they can. Furthermore, the taxes and royalties they pay to their host governments are based on the posted price.

Since the posted price is no longer close to an open market price, it is a doubly fictitious number — not only is it an oligopolistic sales price; it has for some time not even been the *real* oligopolistic sales price. The first move in its evolution toward artificiality came after World War Two: till that time, it reasonably reflected prices at the Gulf of Mexico, which dominated prewar international oil pricing, as it was the center of the petroleum export trade in that era.

After World War Two, though, the center of this trade gravitated eastward, following the initial development of the prolific fields in Kuwait and Saudi Arabia and the extension of the longer-established province in Southwest Iran. However, in those days the seven major companies had an even bigger slice of the world oil trade than they have now; they were selling almost exclusively to themselves and to each other, in Europe and America, and could at the very least prevent the price of oil from slipping in any but minor, local ways.

They proceeded to do this, in a most thorough manner. Although the cost of the new, cheap, voluminous Persian Gulf oil was far below the fictitious international quotations even then, the exporting companies, to keep the price of oil high throughout the world, refused to price it in conformity with its own cost. They priced it, rather, on the basis of the old Gulf of Mexico rates, which applied to much costlier oil. Thus a company would ship the barrel of oil which it could produce in Saudi Arabia for less than 30 cents a barrel — *including all costs, depreciation, and capital investments* — and sell it to a subsidiary or independent client as if it were the most expensive barrel of that kind in Texas; that Saudi barrel, when it arrived in the United Kingdom, for instance, would not undercut the Texas barrel in the same port. The exporting companies took the price of a barrel of

Texas crude, which was around $1, added to that the 15 or 20 cents it would cost to get that barrel of Texas crude to the United Kingdom, and subtracted what it would cost to ship that barrel from Saudi Arabia to the United Kingdom; what remained was the "posted price" for Saudi crude at the terminal in Saudi Arabia. This posted price bore no relationship whatsoever to the cost of producing oil in Saudi Arabia.

So Middle Eastern oil came out of the Persian Gulf with the force of a tidal wave and reached Europe in ripples.

Exxon and Mobil, which had just bought into 40 percent of Aramco, gain much of the credit, or blame, for keeping the price of Persian Gulf oil so far above its cost. SoCal and Texaco, the two other Aramco parents, had thought they would be able to bring the price of Saudi crude down, perhaps to 90 cents or less, since they owned the majority of the venture; but then the two newcomers threatened to sue them for breach of fiduciary responsibility if they did not agree to raise the price to the Gulf of Mexico level. The threat succeeded, and the result was a cost, to the consumer, of billions of dollars over the next generation.

The companies liked this arrangement, and kept it. In 1961 the United States Department of Justice could observe that this pricing was consistent with another industry principle — that "surplus production in a given area shall not be used to upset the price structure in any other area." The Justice Department concluded that "foreign oil, as a general rule, only entered the United States at United States prices."[1] Another reason for this, as Chapter 4 will seek to show, is that the United States government also liked this arrangement; it kept small independent American oil producers from rising up in revolt.

So the posted price is not really a price at all, but a figure used as a basis for calculating tax.

Still, artificially high though the posted price always has been, and despite the prodigious rise in the posted price of all foreign oils since October, 1973, this tax reference price remained static at much lower levels for a generation. In 1946 Arabian Light sold, at the terminal, for about $1.20 a barrel; then, after the removal of price controls in America at the end of World War Two and the absorption of Exxon and Mobil into Aramco, it rose to about $2.20 a barrel in 1948. But then it dropped; and although it rose again, it started dropping again, and ultimately came to rest at $1.80 in 1960. There it remained, untouched, until 1971, when it went up to about $2.40 — and then spurted up by stages to $3.01. At last, it began a very steep ascent with the 1973 Arab-Israeli War, eventually shooting up to $11.65 by January, 1974.

During this era, the actual cost of producing this oil kept dropping, consistently, so that by the late 1960's the total cost of getting a barrel of Arabian Light into a tanker at the eastern Saudi port of Ras Tanura — *all depreciation and capital investments included* — had dropped to about 15 cents.

During this interim, Aramco had been paying a tax to the Saudi government which was equal to 50 percent of this artificial high price (less costs, depreciation, and, until 1965, royalties). Aramco kept a little bit of the remainder for itself, to cover operating expenses and investments, and distributed the rest to its four parents in the form of dividends.*

It so happens that if American interests own 40 percent or more of a company operating abroad, United States tax laws look upon the venture favorably. They exempt all but 15 percent of the dividends received from such a company from payment of tax to the United States federal government. In fact, Aramco's four American parents owned 100 percent of the Saudi venture until mid-1973, when, after some struggle, the Saudi government bought into 25, then 60, percent of it. To this writing, 85 percent of the dividends they receive from Aramco are exempt from United States tax; the Saudi government purchase of Aramco's remaining shares will presumably end this benefit.

Now, in the hearings of late March, 1974, Senator Church began to question his witness, the government auditor Shirley Ward, by wondering if the companies which owned Aramco had really worked to check this recent prodigious rise in the posted price. For the available figures showed that as the posted price rose, so did the money accruing to Aramco as profit. Aramco would still, presumably, sell as many barrels as it had before the

* Aramco's parents are four of the big seven, all American: Mobil, Exxon, Texaco, and Standard of California.

increase (as long as the price for all other oils in the international trade rose by the same amount). What incentive, therefore, could there be for Aramco to keep this tax-reference price down?

Miss Ward endorsed the validity of this question by pointing out that in 1973 Aramco had made a profit of $3.2 billion. This was an increase of more than 350 percent over its profits in 1969. During the same period, the posted price rose by an almost identical percentage. So Aramco's profit on its crude oil exports rose, between 1973 and 1974, from 70 cents to about $4.50 per barrel.

Senator Edmund Muskie, also on the subcommittee, reacted sharply to this. "It seems there is no reason for the companies to resist any increase in the posted price," he stated somewhat censoriously.

Miss Ward again agreed. Senator Church, continuing his inquiry, pointed out another phenomenon: while Aramco imposed deterrents to any partner's taking more oil than his investment in Aramco entitled him to, this penalty seemed to decrease between 1971 and 1973. Furthermore, it seemed to be less stringent than that which Mr. Shafer was to demonstrate the Consortium had imposed on its members in Iran. This meant that the companies in Aramco had themselves worked out an arrangement which financially obligated them to increase their liftings from Saudi Arabia at the expense of other concessions in which they had an interest. It was during the 1971–1973 period, too, that Aramco began substantially to increase its investments in expanding capacity.

The long and short of all this was that the Aramco parents had had no choice, over the past two years, but to increase their production in Saudi Arabia at the expense of the other countries. They had worked it out that way.

Aramco's treasurer, Joseph Johnston, then took the stand and made a brief statement in partial rebuttal to Miss Ward's testimony.

The staff followed this, too, with considerable questioning. For instance, Church read off a list of Aramco dividends to stockholders: $666 million in 1970, rising to $2.59 billion in 1973.

Mr. Johnston agreed that those were not fictitious dividends.

Muskie went back to the point he had raised with Miss Ward. He broke in to ask Johnston if he thought the companies were likely to argue very hard with the Saudi Arabian government to keep the posted price down, then. Johnston replied in the affirmative.

"What *is* the incentive to keep that price down?" Muskie pressed him.

"Well," Johnston muttered, "I think it'd be better to direct that question to stockholders who have familiarity in the market area of the pressures and other factors that are exerted on them in order to move."

One vignette which the public witnessed three months later, in a television documentary on Occidental Petroleum, would have underlined Muskie's point. It showed Occidental's chairman, Armand Hammer, walking along with the oil billionaire J. Paul Getty and exulting in a gravelly voice, "Did you know the price of oil has gone up to fifteen dollars a barrel in Nigeria?" Getty wheezed a long, rich laugh. But now, Muskie could do little to make his point. Johnston seemed to know virtually nothing about the industry. For instance, as was well known throughout the industry, all big oil companies had economics and planning departments, which put out annual brochures on supply and demand forecasts. SoCal's annual document, being blue, was known as "the blue book"; Senator Case had asked Johnston if he had ever seen that. He shook his head in bewilderment. What about Exxon's compilation, known as "the green book"? No, he hadn't seen that either. Gulf put out an orange book — again, Johnston claimed never to have seen that either — reasonably enough, as Gulf owned no shares in Aramco. Nor had he ever set eyes on any red books. Muskie could only repeat the question: "What is your incentive as a negotiator to get the Saudis to keep the posted price down? Don't you know? . . . You haven't given me that incentive. What *is* the incentive to keep the posted price down?"

Clifford Case of New Jersey, the third senator on the panel, broke in by reassuring Johnston that he wanted to get the facts, not assess blame.

"What persuasive arguments do you have for the American consumer?" Muskie went on and on, relentlessly: "Do you have any bargaining tool? . . . What kind of negotiators are you in the interests of the American consumer?"

"Today," Johnston finally conceded, "while I don't believe we have any major negotiating strength left, we still have some."

The discussion went on: the staff observed that Aramco for a long time had maintained a cushy excess capacity so that it could produce more than the Aramco parents had forecast they would need in a given year, in case sudden demand should arise for supplementary crude. This excess capacity used to be perhaps 20 percent more than normal demand. Although no outsiders had direct access to this, the Aramco parents would be happy to sell it to all comers at a mutually agreeable price if they really needed it. But over the past two years even this excess capacity had dwindled almost to nothing.

Muskie raised his eyebrows over this too: the only weapon which had given Aramco any bargaining power was its control over production rates, he said; once it lost that, it in a sense lost its own raison d'être. Without coming out and saying so, he was indicating that the Aramco parents, at least by their inaction, had acquiesced in a tightening supply situation which could not but have a strengthening effect on prices.

The staff counsel, Jerome Levinson, asked why Aramco indeed existed at all — "Aramco really is a device for maximizing tax credits for the parent companies," he said. Johnston didn't want to talk about that. The associate counsel, Jack Blum, asked if the parent companies paid an intercompany dividend tax of 15 percent.

"You'd have to ask the companies," Johnston said.

After a little more of this, George Piercy, Exxon's Middle East coordinator, who was to serve as a full participant in the next day's tournament, took the glove from Johnston and after a few knucklers and sliders on postings and Aramco, served up the number of the day: 34.

This delivery stymied all players. It seemed to hang over the plate, yet no one could get the fat of his bat on it. Church at once pronounced it statistical legerdemain and disputed its relevance. In the back of the room, a copy of the morning's *Platt's Price Service* slapped to the floor. "I thought they retired that number with Koufax," grumbled an antitrust attorney.

Piercy reached down to the mound, though, and produced a thick binder with a slick blue cover, looked for the number in the binder — though it was not one of the mythical blue, green, or red company planning books, which Johnston claimed never to have seen — and found it.

Obviously, this binder must have contained most if not all the numbers one could possibly need to determine how much money Exxon really earned, and where, and how in its operations all over the globe. The number was there. Sure enough, Piercy read, Exxon's net profits on sales of oil from Aramco in 1973 were a mere 34 cents a barrel.

His near-namesake Charles Percy, last senator on the panel, wondered if he too might have a look at the book.

"I'd rather keep this to myself," Piercy replied. And he did, although, just before the luncheon break, Jack Blum asked if he had numbers on operations besides Aramco, and Levinson declared, "Surely you have to keep that bookkeeping. They've got to be someplace, got to show up as $2.4 billion [Exxon's net profits for 1973]. Where are they? We'll Xerox that blue book after the meeting."

There was a little more riffling and shuffling through pages. More fruitless inquiry: what did Exxon earn from Aramco in 1973? Dividends of $789 million, as Aramco's books said? Or earnings of $265 million, as the slick blue binder reputedly stated? This wasn't the green book he was quoting from, was it? Or the orange book? Piercy would not provide per-barrel profit figures for production in other areas of the world — though he did make one slight admission. On the average, he said, Exxon's profits on oil production in the rest of the Eastern Hemisphere were 25 cents a barrel.

"You keep two sets of books," Blum proclaimed. "One for tax purposes, one for profitability."

Piercy said that was misleading.

The next day, the hearings went on, in the same vein, in circles, achieving, apparently, not much. But there was a difference; the subcommittee was treated to a historical overview of the Near East by an almost legendary figure, Howard Page.

Page had worked with the Middle East for Exxon upward of twenty years, from 1950 to late 1970, following a stint in the government's Petroleum Administration for War, where many oil executives established their contacts and reputations. On the face of it, Page had the most illustrious career of any oilman in America. He served as a director of Exxon, Iraq Petroleum Company, and Aramco almost the entire time; he had participated in the big negotiating campaigns in Iran (1954) and Iraq (1951–1952). He was in on all the big events of the past decade: the royalty expensing negotiations of 1964 and — after retirement — the Tehran negotiations of 1971, at the express invitation of BP's chairman Lord Strathalmond. He was one of the main architects of the structure within which the international industry grew to greatness in the postwar generation.

The staff had been viewing this day's session with real trepidation, because of Page's prestige and fame as a negotiator. They weren't sure how to handle him. One member said, "In our conversations it was always I, I, I. The King and I, the Shah and I. He's going to get up and instead of an opening statement he is going to say, 'My name is Howard Page.' "

"We'll have to go for his ego," averred one of the other members.

When they entered the hearing room in the morning, newsmen took photographs of Church and Levinson standing with their arms around Page. Church was almost embarrassed to request that Page swear in — he asked him, rather, to go through the formality they used. When they sat down to business Church remarked, "I've heard it said that you were the Kissinger of the oil industry."

Page was a most distinguished-looking man, short but trim and endowed with well-groomed silvery hair and an exquisite diamond-shaped face, but his delivery, the gist of his testimony, turned out very different from what one was expecting. The audience was treated not to the performance of a kingmaker, a high-rolling international speculator, entrepreneur, or archtransactor,

but to a dazzling exposition of control, method, concealment —
of hypocrisy, ultimately. With every comment and response, Page
demonstrated how vital it was to Exxon, or indeed to any major
international company, never to concede any point to any adversary, opponent, or even observer. He showed masterful refusal to
betray the least sign of self-interest, profitmindedness, ruthlessness
in his pronouncements. Everything he did in the service of his
company had been tinged with rationality, higher ethos, and supreme commercial justice. Piously, to prevent the adversary from
gaining the least moral advantage and to demoralize and paralyze,
to prevent him from challenging the industry's right to absolute
dominance of international energy policy, he would use any
method — including a determination to speak for the American
consumer, the Shah of Iran, or small independent oil companies:
any party outside the major industry.

Apparently he succeeded, for twenty years, as his testimony indicated. His delivery went on for quite some time and was impressive — he spoke more rapidly and compactly than any of the other
witnesses.

It appeared that Page, and a few others, had a special function
in the Middle East, which one could compare to that of a brigade
commander combatting an insurrection of swelling yeast within
the New York sewage system: most of the time his immediate
task was to keep the lid on an infinite number of simultaneously-
rising manhole covers. Take the case of the proud, ancient land of
Iran — commonly pronounced "Yronne" among the cognoscenti,
though Senator Church steadfastly referred to it as "Eye-ran."

All during the fifties and sixties, when consumers were being
told and made to feel, as they always have been, that oil is as
precious and potentially scarce as ambergris, that they are being
allowed to have it for a bargain price which could shoot up at any
time, Page, and the industry he represented, had to keep this commodity, the second most abundant fluid on earth, from becoming
so available that its price would drop. This meant that Exxon,
and the other majors, had to curb excess capacity — had, ultimately and repeatedly, to take decisions contrary to the interests
of the consumer.

One of the most important aspects of Middle Eastern oil history during the past generation was the arrangement whereby the industry, in 1954, got Iran back into production after the traumatic period of Mohammad Mosaddegh, who nationalized the previous concession-holder, BP, then fell after twenty-eight months of severe economic and political turmoil, as we saw in the previous chapter. Page told the subcommittee that not only had Aramco, in Saudi Arabia, always been a better oil property than southwestern Iran, but his company Exxon hadn't wanted to go into Iran at all, back in 1954. Exxon went in only at the behest of the American government, to help clean up the wreckage. Later, he claimed that the move into Iran in 1954 probably has not produced a financial advantage for Exxon to this day. "We knew when we went into the [Iranian] Consortium," he remarked, "that as a business deal, a straight business deal, it was for the birds. . . . We lost money with every barrel we produced. . . . We went in there to save the situation. It was in the interests of the U.S. and Britain at the time."

He stated, in fact, that Exxon would not have gone into Iran at all without the United States government. "We had no interest in this whatever as a commercial proposition," he said. ". . . This could not possibly have been set up without the assistance, if you like, of the U.S. government. It was more than assistance, it was the request of the U.S. government." To illustrate the unattractiveness of the venture, he said he had a bodyguard with him all during his negotiations with the Iranian Finance Minister, Ali Amini, and received threats against his life all the time — as did Amini, later, for a brief period of time, a reformist prime minister hated by left and right alike.

In fact, according to Page, not only did Exxon not much want to go into Iran, it subsequently turned out that the Iranians kept trying to get the Consortium to expand production "by more than the agreement called for." Not that the agreement actually called for anything — Page had deliberately kept a specific growth rate out of that document.*

---

* The final document just said, "It would be the policy of the Consortium members . . . to adjust the quantity so attained in such a manner as would reasonably reflect the trend of supply and demand for Middle East crude oil." (Article 20B)

Again and again, the question arises in this chronicle: was Iran really such a liability? Why did the four American majors prefer Saudi Arabia to Iran? Was it because of costs? Political risks? International politics? The answer is complex. What is of concern here is that in 1954, after the traumatic period of Mosaddegh and his downfall, and the two-year shutoff of oil, Iran wanted its oil back on badly. It could not let BP, the former owner — which had maintained a perfect boycott against Iran — return to the area except in a low profile, as a minority stockholder. Thus, other companies had to be invited in. The American majors had too large a slice of the world market to be ignored or excluded. In fact, they could view their acceptance of a share in the Consortium as a special favor. Over the years they extracted a very high price for this favor.

Page talked about the other countries of the Gulf area in which Exxon had a share in much the same way as he talked about Iran. Exxon, through IPC, kept production down in Iraq too — had it expanded capacity there, it would have had to cut back, or "back up," Iran and Saudi Arabia. The subcommittee read a CIA report which stated that Iraq Petroleum Company had plugged some wells capable of producing 50,000 barrels a day, just to keep the Iraqis in the dark about their country's real production potential.

"They knew the well was there," retorted Page. Muskie reminded him of the last paragraph in the CIA report, which indicated the opposite. Page muttered, "I don't know who is giving you this information but it doesn't sound right to me."

And Oman, south of Arabia: Senator Percy had heard that an Exxon geologist had talked of finding ten billion barrels down in that sultanate. Page said he had told the Exxon executive committee, "I am absolutely sure we don't want to go into [Oman] and that settles it. . . . We are liable to lose the Aramco concession, our share of the Aramco concession, if we are going to back up any further on it by going into new areas." Facetiously he remarked, "I might put some money in it if I was sure we weren't going to get some oil."

This policy, understandable in normal times, faces collapse when there comes a fear of real scarcity. Such a day came in October, 1973, with the Arab embargo. The oil companies worked very hard to portray this embargo as a serious event, fraught with woeful consequences — for the consumer. Yet it was the companies which, over the preceding seven years, had failed to make the investments they could have made to minimize the effects of this embargo. What did Page say to this? What did Page say to a question from the panel on Iran: suppose that non-Arab state had had substantial spare capacity, say a million barrels or two a day, in October? Page sat shaking his head; it wouldn't have done any good.

His successor, George Piercy, was sitting to his left, still unlimbering with sliders. He now volunteered that the Shah had told the Consortium that he did not want more than eight million barrels a day capacity built in the Consortium area — neglecting to point out that the Consortium had told the Shah that that was all that *could* be produced in the area.*

Page, and Piercy, touched on one final area of the Islamic East: Libya. Piercy admitted that Exxon had brought its Libyan oil on as fast and furiously as it could.† Libya, Page averred, had been the exception (with Saudi Arabia, the jewel) : the independents went into Libya rather than Iran because they were sure of finding oil and sure of finding outlets; Libya was very close to Europe.

Levinson didn't buy that explanation. He reminded Page of the Consortium's lush acreage in southern Iran: didn't the independents want access to that too?

Unfortunately, this question got lost in the hectic atmosphere of the hearing room. Page didn't get a chance to fence with it. But he made one more point before he left. When Senator Case asked him if output wasn't determined by "a conscious effort by

---

* Anyway, the Consortium's own documents, the crude capacity development plans, tell a different story. Between the lines, they indicate that Iranian Consortium production could go up to ten million barrels a day and stay at that level for a decade. This subject will be covered in detail subsequently.

† Again, he left something out. This was not true of one field in which Exxon had only half-interest, Mabruk. This respectable property, close to water, has never gone onstream. As the endpaper map of Libya shows, no pipelines lead from it.

intelligent men," he replied, "No sir, it was done by the people in the field. When the tanks got full, they shut back."

Case found that hard to believe: the outlying operations just ran by themselves, like liberated republics within a decadent Roman Empire? "But the input was the demand estimated by the four companies," he protested.

"No," replied Page. "It was the ships that came in to load the oil."

The two-day hearings ended in the afternoon with two men from Standard of California — George Parkhurst, now retired, and Dennis Bonney, the Britisher. They had also been Middle East coordinators, and they talked mostly about the same subject Page had handled — how they coped with the worldwide surplus of crude oil, especially in the late 1960's. In addition, they fended off the question of where the greatest profits lay in the international industry — whether they lay "upstream" or "downstream." ("Upstream" operations mean the process of finding crude oil and getting it out of the ground and the country which hosted it; "downstream" means the process of getting the crude oil — once "onstream" — into refineries and out to the general public in the form of products.)

Parkhurst and Bonney, like Page before them, admitted that they had faced a real problem coping with the glut of oil in the 1960's. Unlike Page, though, they used little righteous argumentation to defend the process of coping with glut and keeping prices high. No one was beholden to them; they appealed more to the senators' sense of fair play, to their instinct for pathos even.

The point of departure for this session was a modest memorandum which Standard of California's Economics Department had prepared late in 1968. In essence, the memo said that there was going to continue to be a crude oil surplus in the world for the following few years and that SoCal was going to have a hard time meeting Saudi Arabian and Iranian demands for production increases during this period. While expressing indignation that the subcommittee had not told them it was going to release the memo to the press, Bonney and Parkhurst maintained that this memo was largely a think-piece, not a product of SoCal's actual planning process. However, its overall projections for 1969 supply and demand were accurate to within 1 percent. Furthermore, it formed the basis for a letter which SoCal executives subsequently delivered to the State Department in defense of their reluctance to increase production in Iran. So, modest as it was, it was not just a piece of busywork either, an irrelevant project aimed only at keeping economists out of trouble.*

But Bonney and Parkhurst did not come out and say that they had worked to keep production down in the way that Exxon must have, to go by Page's complicated logic. Parkhurst, while pointing out that Iran had not been a commercial windfall for his company, either, added that SoCal had suffered economic hardship in Saudi Arabia too. It rarely wanted to lift as much from Aramco as it could and had to pay a penalty for under-lifting — it had to contribute money to facilities which it did not need, and was reimbursed for this at a rate of only 15 percent a year. For a high-risk area like Arabia, Parkhurst indicated, this was terribly low.

He went on to plead that SoCal had had to work very hard to sell what it had been lifting. It couldn't just sell to its own refineries, because their capacities and outlets were limited. So it had to sell to outsiders, at discounts. "We were selling to every independent company we could possibly sell to," Parkhurst said. "Finally about 22 percent of our sales were to independents. . . . I was responsible for our crude oil sales and I know how hard we fought to sell every drop."

Bonney pointed out that in 1973, one million barrels a day, or 40 percent, of SoCal's Eastern Hemisphere production went to such third parties — at big discounts.

The subsequent badinage raised two corollary questions. First was the matter of where profitability lay in integrated oil operations — the question which Piercy had fended off the previous day by refusing to let Levinson Xerox his thick blue binder.

---

* In fact, it must have relied on some unpublished "inside" material since it imparted what the outside world hardly could know: how much oil Aramco, the Consortium, and probably the other producers on the Gulf would be exporting in 1969, as well as later years.

Now SoCal's men raised it by saying their "downstream" capability, their ability to refine and market crude oil, was limited.

Yet they seemed to be doing all right. So the truth of the matter was a little complex — or was it? For the truly big companies, the seven majors which dominate international trade, profitability lies in having access to large volumes of crude oil, at cost, which their companies can sell to their own refineries at fictitiously high prices and then retail in closely protected markets.

But Messrs. Parkhurst and Bonney were not enlightening on the subject of where profitability in their integrated operations lay. When Jack Blum raised the question, Parkhurst asked him to repeat it, then answered, "Well, I think the profit is where you find it, sir."

Blum insisted: "Is it not a fact that [upstream] is where it is for SoCal?"

Parkhurst thrashed about a moment, and Levinson asked him, "Where do you show it on your books?" Again, Parkhurst had the question repeated. Then he said, "Well, it shows on the books as upstream," but attributed that to government reporting practices. Blum pressed him further:

"You are taking advantage of that upstream profitability."

Parkhurst answered that in the negative, then, under further prodding, gave a more obscure and confused answer. Blum addressed the question to Bonney.

"I think it is impossible to generalize," Bonney claimed. "I think it depends entirely on who the company is, what its business is, where its refinery is and where its market is."

"In the case of SoCal," Blum reminded him.

Bonney said he was certain that the companies which had bought crude oil from SoCal would not have done so if they had not thought they could make money by refining it.

"You agreed that the profits are shown upstream in your company," Levinson asked Parkhurst, and Bonney conceded that the net on SoCal's crude ventures was "probably rather more attractive" than on the company's various refining and marketing ventures.

A short while later, another member of the staff, Bill Lane, asserted, "You were reluctant to state that your profits accrued at the crude end of the business," and wondered if that was not because in the industry oil in the ground was essentially worthless, could not be moved unless a market could be found for it.

"The basic reason why I was reluctant or hesitated to answer that question was because I do not know," Bonney replied, and went on to state that he would be happy to discuss the matter "at great length on another occasion," but thought it risky to generalize on the subject at this point.

Lane prodded him anyway: "But is it not generally true without refining, without the marketing . . . the crude is essentially worthless in the ground to a company like yours?"

"That is not at all the case," said Bonney. "The oil is worth what you can sell it for. . . . The real answer to the question if we reduce the prices would buyers have come flocking to our door is that we did and they did."

In a few moments, Levinson summed it up: "What is very puzzling . . . is just this. Mr. Lane began a line of questioning of Mr. Bonney in which he put to him the proposition that really your crude was worthless unless you could get it out through a marketing, refining outlet, and Mr. Bonney says, 'not at all. . . .' Now Mr. Parkhurst comes along and tells us that we are destroying a great American enterprise because it has got an assured outlet." He concluded his query: "What is the inherent economic necessity of the integrated operation when you answer us. . . . 'The crude was just as valuable to us in selling it to anybody.'"

"I didn't say we needed to be an integrated operation to sell the oil to anybody," opined Bonney — by implication doing the subcommittee the courtesy of failing to insist that output depended entirely on the fortuitous appearance of ships at Middle Eastern berths.

That was as close as the subcommittee got that day to one of its objectives, which was to demonstrate that if the United States government broke up all the major oil companies into several specialized firms, these new pieces would still, like the several sections of a chopped-up worm, function well by themselves. In fact, the rest of the inning went to SoCal.

One could even say that it was Bonney's day: he used the best argument oilmen have to defend their actions and this is the personal one, the appeal to human respect for the man who labors, suffers, and holds firm against high odds — only to lose in the end anyway. For, although the major oil companies rarely lose any contest of importance, and have not been driven off an important diamond for forty years, their representatives take a lot of abuse for them sometimes. Sometimes a representative can be seen pressing a demand to the hilt on orders from his superiors, while, unbeknownst to him, the superiors are quietly retreating from their public intransigence. So, when Church suggested that there was no incentive for the companies to negotiate to keep the posted price down, Bonney received a beautiful opportunity to beg the question by relating some vivid personal experiences of negotiation with the Libyan government:

"I spent over a hundred days away last year, 200 days in 1972, and about 200 days away in 1971," he declared, "working as hard as I could on behalf of my company, its customers and in support of the continued supply of oil at reasonable prices in many different cities around the world and in very uncomfortable circumstances around the world.

"I have been so many times, so many times I have lost count, verbally lashed and taken to task for taking the part of the consumer by our opposite numbers on the other side of the OPEC table. I have been, again more times than I can remember, threatened with the nationalization of my company's assets, with production cutbacks and restrictions, with unilateral actions to determine prices eventually as you know, which came to pass, all with the object of intimidating me and the other negotiators into a more pliant attitude with regard to the demands of the OPEC nations.

"I think the most dramatic occasion of those I mentioned took place in the 1971 negotiations themselves but which you have heard extensively from others when my company and our associates in Libya were chosen by the Libyans for extreme treatment, extreme pressure.

"I personally had more than thirteen, I think approximately thirteen, meetings with Libyan government officials, including senior ministers. On one evening my colleagues and I were sum-

moned at short notice to the Ministry where we delivered a
proposal in writing, and we were told to go away and they would
think about it. And we had not gone back to our offices when the
phone was ringing and they called us over, and once again we
went up to the Ministry which incidentally was on the fifth floor
and the elevator was not working. This was the third time, five
flights of stairs. We walked into the room and the Prime Minister
threw the papers at us and told us to get out; we understood him
to mean we should get out of Libya.

"We left, went back to our office and tried to go and get some
dinner. We just arrived at the restaurant when the phone rang
again. We went back to the Ministry on demand, fifth time up
the stairs, where we were told in very formal terms that the
Revolutionary Command Council was going to meet that night
at midnight, it was then after 11 o'clock, and if we did not, my colleague, representing my own company, and the representatives of
our associates, if we did not bow to the demands for much increased posted prices beyond those that we had proposed and
suggested, my company and the company of our associates will be
nationalized that night.

"Mr. Chairman, we said we were very disappointed to hear
that, there was nothing further we could say, we could only stand
firm because we did not believe that their demands were justified.
So in some disappointment and distress we left and we went
down those five flights of stairs again.

"Mr. Chairman, that night, after we reported all these events
to our companies, as many as twenty different companies, I think,
and we had a good deal of company agonizing over that night,
Mr. Chairman, it would have been the easiest thing in the world
for my colleague and I and our associates to say to the Libyan
government, 'Well, in the face of the extreme step we are prepared to accede to your demand or to make a further proposal.'

"We did not do that. Why did we not do that? We did not do
that because we were a part of a company group dedicated to
minimizing the posted price increases that the Libyan government was trying to force upon us. We were doing this with the
full knowledge and the full daily knowledge of the chairmen of

our boards and with many of the boards of directors of our companies.

"It is incredible to me that anybody should think that people, that human beings, would go through this kind of stress, agony and turmoil if all the time we had an incentive to agree with the governments that the prices should go up," Bonney concluded his statement.

Church backed down from his charge, on the strength of this account. He even tried to ingratiate himself with Bonney and Parkhurst by asking their help in devising a federal energy policy and by keeping off the touchy subject of some earlier negotiations, when the company men hadn't stood up quite so well against Jalloud and his tantrums. Those who remained in the chamber long enough after that to hear SoCal's general counsel, James O'Brien, drone on monotonously from an amazingly prolix and obfuscated twenty-year-old legal statement — well after the television lights had been shut down — realized that Standard of California had carried that day.

Still, the subcommittee's question remained. The companies were too powerful for the good of America and many other countries — the hearings had helped underline that; so, if one took punitive measures against the companies — for instance breaking them up into various firms engaged only in exploring and producing, or refining, or transporting, or marketing — that would reduce their power. Good. But would it also disrupt the worldwide flow of energy and create chaos? Or would it create the foundation for a more efficient and ultimately fairer system?

The question remained, and so did other facts. The hearings had established that no matter how hard individuals might have strived, the companies gave way at many crucial points, allowed the posted prices for crude oil to rise all over the world by 350 percent over the few previous months — and enriched themselves accordingly.

More important information began to emerge, too. For instance, that day, in the San Francisco *Chronicle,* the main paper in SoCal's home town, the first of several articles appeared which gave further details on how SoCal managed to participate in this bonanza. The source of these details was Standard of California's

1971–1972 financial performance and forecast for the coming years — a thick sheaf of papers which had spread out to various places, sometimes in plain brown envelopes, sometimes bearing the legend "Material for a Good Story" in the kind of awkward script used by right-handed people when they write with their left hand. No one knew who had sent them — but it quickly turned out that they were authentic.

One thing these documents showed was that if SoCal was stripped of all its foreign activities and became merely a domestic firm, operating only in America, it would still be a very prosperous enterprise. This is the subject of the next chapter.

3

On Industry Costs and Profits

Few large [oil] firms rely significantly on their shareholders for new funds. . . . Many, if not most, prefer what is
called "self-financing," which means that they raise their
money through the prices charged to their consumers.
— Edith Penrose, *The International
Petroleum Industry*

STANDARD OIL COMPANY of California is a massive enterprise by any criteria except those which prevail in the international oil industry. In value of assets, SoCal ranks twelfth among
all the private industrial firms in Christendom; in oil it is only
Number Seven — the Seventh Sister, Enrico Mattei would undoubtedly have labeled it.

Still, it is a magnificent cash-generating mechanism, almost as
good as any of the other six. In 1972, the firm sold two and a
quarter million barrels of petroleum products a day throughout
the world — at 42 gallons to the barrel, this is equivalent to
94 million gallons a day, or 34 billion gallons for the year. In
that year, the firm registered gross revenues of nearly seven

billion dollars and claimed a net income of almost six hundred million. *

Though the company's published documents do not break down the company's earnings by country, the 1972 forecast shows that SoCal made almost 50 percent of its sales in the United States itself. It also shows — in conjunction with other general published information about the industry — that SoCal must have pocketed at least $185 million for the effort, a conclusion discussed later in this chapter. Finally, the forecast does show that SoCal, in the same year, paid, to the United States municipal, state, and federal tax collectors, a total of $33.1 million.

Furthermore, the company is extremely solvent; this is public knowledge. Between 1956 and 1973, according to SoCal's annual reports, the firm's net income grew threefold, from $176 to $547 million — *but this is not as much as the company actually pocketed* — and the book value of the stockholders' equity also tripled.

The point which one eminent scholar of the big oil firm, Professor Edith Penrose, has raised — to wit, that "the primary objective of large firms is to maximize their own retained funds in order to ensure the survival and continued growth of the organization" — is apposite here.[1] A giant company like SoCal desires fiscal autonomy; accountability and indebtedness to no one on the outside. Even the stockholder is a liability, an outsider, to the management of such a company, unless he is the power behind the management. (In the case of a company like SoCal, it is hard to find out if such powers exist. We now know, as a result of Nelson Rockefeller's 1974 vice presidential confirmation hearings, that the Rockefeller family owns 3.5 million shares, or 2.06 percent, of SoCal — as well as 2.3 million shares, or 1.07 percent, of Exxon and 1.78 million shares, or 1.75

---

* Its 1973 performance, of course, was far better — worldwide, it registered a net income of over $800 million on sales of $8.9 billion, as the 1973 *Annual Report* states. However, since the forecast, accurate as it is, was written before the start of that year, the breakdowns it provides for 1972 which are not to be found in the annual reports must be considered the most up-to-date reliable ones. Thus we will have to content ourselves with discussing that earlier year — seeking meager consolation in the likelihood that it was a more typical one anyway, as far as the major oil companies are concerned.

percent, of Mobil.) [2] As Penrose said, "Were it not for traditional notions about the relationship between shareholders and firms, we might as well have found dividends also recorded as costs, since a dividend payment is a loss of funds to the firm. . . . Dividends have to be paid, sometimes on a handsome scale, but these payments are the cost to the firm of maintaining its financial reputation as a good investment."*

SoCal does have a large long-term debt, totaling more than a billion dollars as of 1972. However, this sum is not as formidable as it sounds, for it was only twice the year's net earnings, about one-seventh of total 1972 revenues, and one-eighth of total assets as listed in the firm's annual report. The company's 1972 annual report shows that none of the company's borrowings carried an interest rate greater than 8¾ percent, and most were less: about one-quarter of this long-term debt was in 7 percent sinking fund debentures due in 1996. With such low-interest debts, SoCal could almost go into the banking business.

SoCal is a potent factor in an excellent business — probably the best in the world today. Because the major international oil companies are so rich in cash, they are uniquely independent of such outside influences as banks or insurance companies — in a way that airlines (most notoriously), other transportation firms, utilities, steel, aircraft, automobile and machinery manufacturers, and big construction companies are not. Frank Ikard, the president of the American Petroleum Institute, estimated in 1971 that the major oil firms traditionally generate about 90 percent of their own funds. In 1973, Congressman Les Aspin estimated this figure at about 85 percent.[3] Naturally, since the international oil business is so lucrative, it is now well-nigh impossible to get into it. Even a highly charged magnificently connected international entrepreneur like Armand Hammer of Occidental has had his moments of humiliation endeavoring to join this elite group — as did Enrico Mattei, Nelson Bunker Hunt, J. Paul Getty, and many other rich men.

However, the industry is not only indifferent toward the wealthy; it cares very little for the public treasury or the ordinary

---

* Page 7 of SoCal's 1972 *Financial Forecast* does note dividends as a cost, since it subtracts them from the company's total cash income.

citizen either. Certainly, the major oil companies do not provide many jobs; in the year 1956, as an example, SoCal had 42,000 employees; by 1973, despite the massive growth in the American population — and SoCal's own revenues — this number had actually declined slightly, to 39,267.

Furthermore, in each big company, no more than a few dozen people, carefully groomed and trained over the years, have real control over the enterprise's global activities or indeed any under-standing of them. This holds for the other six as well as for SoCal — for the Americans Exxon, Mobil, Texaco, and Gulf, and the two foreign firms British Petroleum and Royal Dutch/ Shell. Through the operations of these seven firms, in the aggre-gate, flow about two-thirds of the oil moving in the world outside the Soviet bloc and Communist China.

In the closed enterprise of international oil, then, very great power is concentrated within the control of a few men, who have great latitude in picking their subordinates and successors and in withholding or providing information and energy from the public, as they see fit.

The reason for the exclusivity and impregnability of this seven-cornered fortress — one could almost call it a Heptagon — is simple; it lies in two attributes. First, the major company has access to large volumes of crude oil for which it pays cost, or very close to it — in either case a privileged price not available to outsiders. Second, the company moves this low-cost crude oil through its own operations as much as possible, down to the final point of sale (on a lucrative, stable market, of course); at all intermediate points of sale and transfer along the way, it strives to sell its own wares to itself, at as high a profit as possible where taxes are low, and as high a loss as possible at those points where taxes are high. And it does all it can to control output and suppress surplus — in order to keep prices high all down the line.

SoCal's 1972 *Financial Forecast* offers many examples of where SoCal makes money and where it "loses" it. Its biggest earnings came from its biggest source of crude oil, Saudi Arabia, where its 1972 earnings, *after taxes,* totaled $534.7 million. (At about 1.5 million barrels of liftings per day, as listed in Appendix

7, it received dividends of 75 cents a barrel, though its forecast implies that it earned 95 cents a barrel — in either case, much more than George Piercy's 34 cents a barrel.) SoCal's earnings from its next biggest foreign sources of crude oil, Indonesia and Iran, totaled $139.7 and $104.7 million, respectively. Profits from SoCal's oil exploration and production in the Western Hemisphere totaled $267.2 million that year. The firm's refining, marketing, and pipeline operations — again in the Western Hemisphere — were profitable too, "functionally" earning $102.5 million that year. Again, this was not the same as the cash SoCal actually generated and retained.[4]

But other areas of SoCal's operations — all of them "downstream" — sustained heavy paper losses. For example, its European affiliates, Chevron Oil Europe and Caltex Mediterranean, suffered a loss of $121.7 million in crude purchases alone, and SoCal, in its Eastern Hemisphere "trading operations" — its sales of crude from one subsidiary to another — incurred a loss of $381.7 million. This is precisely because it would have been financially damaging, if not devastating, for SoCal to have done otherwise, to have earned its profits in such high-tax countries as Japan, France, Great Britain, or The Netherlands. There, the taxes are higher than in America, which favors the oil industry, as we shall see, with several kinds of benefit almost unknown elsewhere in the world.

These downstream losses in consuming countries, however, are half-illusory. Most, if not all, of the crude oil which Chevron Europe and SoCal's half of Caltex Mediterranean purchase at a loss, they purchase at a very high price, near the posted price — from Standard of California's trading companies, which buy it from Standard of California's holding companies, which purchase it from Aramco, Amoseas, or National Iranian Oil Company (which buys it from the Consortium). Were SoCal's European subsidiaries to buy their crude oil from other suppliers on the open market, the money they paid would not go to the coffers of the mother company but to those of some other rival organization. Then the mother company, SoCal, would lose interest in these subsidiaries and sell them, or let them dry up. However, SoCal's subsidiaries, by buying from other subsidiaries at the posted price, can reap a tremendous tax loss. Hence the convenience and usefulness of the posted price: you can charge it to yourself in many areas where you would rather lose money than earn it.

This simple, basic procedure holds for the other six major companies as well, in greater or lesser degree. True, Mobil and Royal Dutch/Shell are "crude short" — meaning that they produce less crude oil than their refining and marketing organizations need. However, they make up for most of their deficit by purchasing from two of the other major seven, the crude-long Gulf and British Petroleum, at privileged terms, which in fact reduce the earnings of the last two. Gulf and British Petroleum thus have a less illustrious history of profit-making than the other five majors because they have not managed to build up refining and marketing networks which are capable of absorbing their massive production — much of which, incidentally, comes from the state of Kuwait.

Thus, to repeat, it is not enough for a company simply to have massive inventories of crude oil which it can easily bring up from the ground and sell on the international market. There is always the possibility that crude oil prices will drop on the open market — as indeed they have, in the recent past — and the international market for crude will not pay much by itself, in most times. Other crude-long companies such as Amerada and Occidental have demonstrated this dramatically through the vicissitudes of their earnings from sales of their oil, which comes almost exclusively from Libya. The axiom holds true even for SoCal; as Messrs. Bonney and Parkhurst said, it has had to sell increasingly large amounts of its own crude to outsiders, at discounts.*

---

* Amerada, in fact, sold out half its interest in Oasis of Libya to Royal Dutch/ Shell and eventually merged with the New Jersey marketing firm of Hess, while Occidental has generally registered low profits of late from its Libyan operations, and a poor stock performance, although it has managed to survive in the business. Beginning in January, 1972, it observed a three-year moratorium on common dividends, and the Securities and Exchange Commission has subjected its Libyan production and earnings figures to intensive scrutiny, resulting in two consent decrees — wherein Occidental denied committing fraud and promised not to do so in the future.

What does pay is the sale of refined products — but only if a company refines them from its own crude oil in good markets. The oil companies with the least impressive growth rates of all have been essentially crude-thirsty manufacturing concerns such as Sun Oil or Ashland or Citgo in America, Petrofina in Belgium, Antar in France, or Veba in Germany. These companies will rarely appear in the pages of a book like this, which is a success story; they belong rather in the chronicles of a Joseph Conrad, with his frustrated ivory-peddlers and North Europeans beached in Borneo. However, one outcome of the oil counter-revolt of 1973–1974 has been, in fact, an oil industry uprising against this state of affairs, the industrial equivalent of a "police riot." Now that prices of petroleum products in the fertile industrial crescents of the Northern Hemisphere have risen, over a few weeks, by 25 or 30 percent, we can confidently expect the profits of such refining and marketing concerns to surge as the seventies wear on.

To recapitulate the rule: the more crude oil you produce yourself — or just have privileged access to, now that many major oil exporting states are "nationalizing" the old concessions — the more oil you have "tied up" and can sell to your own refining and marketing concerns, the more impregnable your position in international oil will be.

It is possible, and necessary, to engage in considerable review of costs, prices, and taxes to do this. Superficially of interest only to accountants, entrepreneurs, and students of the Dismal Science, these details are nonetheless so central that they merit general study. The reader willing to read through the following pages may well find his patience rewarded by moments of surprise, awe, envy, some outrage, and much sense of self-unimportance.

Let us start at the source, the search for oil in virgin territory.

The first important point to bear in mind is that the international majors carry out little exploration for oil in the United States. They drill a lot of wells in America, but the great majority of these are on properties where oil has already been discovered. These are *not* wildcats but "development" wells —

wells drilled to develop a known field so it can produce more oil. As a result, the percentage of successful wells which any major company drills in the United States will be high. In 1971, in the Western Hemisphere, Standard of California, according to its 1972 *Financial Forecast*, completed 448 producing wells but drilled only 55 exploration wells. Exxon, in 1973, was even less ambitious, drilling only 35 wildcats in the United States, while during the same year Mobil and Texaco, respectively, drilled 28 and 37 exploratory wells in America.[5]

It is not the big companies, but the independents, which take the bulk of the risk and do most of America's exploratory drilling — often on "farmouts," on land leased from the big companies in the first place, sometimes with cash from the majors, in the form of "dry-hole money" for rights to the records or "logs" to any well the independent might drill, so that the big company can add to its own knowledge of the area's geology at no great expense to itself. The independents are experienced in their own regions, know local prospects, and are willing to take risks with them, but do not possess the massive inventories of acreage which the big firms hold.

Conversely, the big companies are reluctant to pour money into regional prospects on mere hunch, no matter how enlightened. The majors, for instance, will not drill into an area unless it has been covered beforehand by seismic survey, and the survey shows identifiable underground formations. But it is impossible to make seismic surveys in some oil-rich areas because the rough countryside will not permit it, will distort the shots. One example is the Santa Ynez Valley behind Santa Barbara, where much oil is produced and a great deal undoubtedly still lurks. Major oil company investment in this area has simply dried up, though a few independents sink a drill into it occasionally. Thus the two groups — the hungry independents and the risk-shy majors — naturally pool their interests, in the United States.

Furthermore, the big companies explore little in the United States because they know that a modest outlay will enable them to continue finding the new oil they will require to maintain their position in the industry. The big company's exploration costs are quite predictable and increase only gradually with time. An internal SoCal memorandum released by the Church Subcommittee is straightforward about this: "Western hemisphere forecast," it relates, is "based on discovery rate of 200 million barrels per year assuming expenditures continue to increase at about 3 percent this year. During last ten years, SoCal has demonstrated the ability to discover about 200 million barrels a year [in the Western Hemisphere]."[6]

This symbiotic relationship between major and independent does not carry overseas. Few independents can afford to venture abroad, and no big international firm will farm out promising foreign acreage to an independent — certainly not acreage in Saudi Arabia, Iran, or Iraq — even when the big companies are unwilling to drill on the acreage themselves. Abroad — most markedly in Libya — farmouts go the other way: from the small company to the big one, not owing to limited funds so much as to limited markets. In Libya, for example, the Libyan American group let in Exxon for half its concession, Nelson Bunker Hunt ceded half its rights to British Petroleum, and Clark let in SoCal and Texaco for 50 percent.

The freezing by the big companies of good foreign acreage is one of the biggest charges which can be leveled against their activities abroad. Legalistic quibbling by the Pages and Parkhursts of the last chapter notwithstanding, it is a fact that in Iraq, for instance, where the government fought long and hard for part ownership of the concession and relinquishment of some concession acreage — and the promising portions of it, at that — and eventually, in sheer exasperation with the unyielding spirit of the companies, expropriated exploration and production rights to 99.5 percent of its own territory, no American firm dared for a decade to come in and explore against IPC's wishes. The IPC parents threatened legal action against them if they did so. As Howard Page told the Church Subcommittee hearings in March, 1974, "We don't deal in stolen property and people who do sometimes get lawsuits." At the end of the decade, a French firm, ERAP, which was virtually immune from such reprisals because it was a government-owned company, finally ventured onto some of this acreage, in the wilderness of southeastern Iraq, and located 14 billion barrels in Buzurgan, a structure which IPC had discovered long before through seismic surveying.

The major companies do spend a great amount of money in one area of exploration within America: on bonuses paid to acquire leases to federal acreage in Northern Alaska and off-shore California, Texas, and Louisiana. President Lyndon John-son accelerated this trend with the Santa Barbara lease sale of February, 1968, most probably so he could acquire additional funds for the Viet Nam war effort without increasing taxation: the government received $600 million in cash for this acreage. And, here, as elsewhere, the big spenders reaped the big awards. Exxon paid $194 million for property just off Point Conception which turned out to include a four-billion-barrel structure, chris-tened Santa Ynez, which will yield billions of dollars for Exxon. It should be pointed out that many of the best prospects off-shore Santa Barbara were well known to quite a few companies, as they had previously conducted drilling tests in the area. Many companies knew of the presence of the Dos Cuadras structure, a shallow "play," or formation, containing at least half a billion barrels, for which the Union Oil group — perpetrators of the famous Santa Barbara Spill — paid $202 million.

The companies newly entering the international arena also pay bonuses in many cases for foreign exploration rights, but these vary from country to country. Leaving bonuses aside, since they are essentially an arbitrary expense, it is clear that foreign exploration costs then consist of only two elements: surveying and drilling. Contrary to many people's belief, these costs are not large at all, compared with the companies' revenues.

Surveying is the first step. It generally consists of mere seismic tests. Modest explosive charges in long lines, about eight to a mile, are detonated. Seismographs record the echoes from under-ground strata. Ripples, bumps, warts, or lumps on the records of seismic shots betray the presence of rock structures likely to provide suitable traps for oil. It may take a day to run off twenty or twenty-five such shots. At the end of the line, the explorer returns and repeats the shots down a parallel line a mile or so to the left or right, until he has covered a broad area with a grid of shots.

Occidental, in Libya, carried out such a survey on its two concessions throughout 1967. It spent between $170 and $200 a shot, or between $1330 and $1550 a mile. Within ten months the company, after spending about one and a half million dollars, had learned where it would be most opportune to start drilling. Though it started with poor luck at Concession 102, four of the first five spots it selected in 103 from seismic tests turned out to be prolific in the extreme.

The Iranian Consortium, with much more extensive acreage to cover, maintains a more complex and permanent surveying capability. In 1973 this enterprise maintained two full-time seismic parties, with portable equipment and a helicopter-borne party, for nine months of the year, though it employed only one such party in 1970, 1971, and 1972. (The parties always take the summer off, when it is blistering hot in southern Iran). The Consortium, to maintain its inventory of promising prospects for wildcat drilling, thus invested in eighteen "party months," which still cost only about 4 million dollars, or less than 3 percent of its total investment for the year 1973.

Incidentally, there are other methods of seeking petroliferous structures, less expensive but also less widely employed than seismic surveying. One is by gravimetric survey, whereby variations, or "anomalies," in the density of underground formations, mostly in the Persian Gulf area, indicate vertical pillars of salt. The Gulf area is riddled with such salt pillars, or "domes," which have broken through overlying formations. As they rose, or pressed up beneath formations, they collected oil on their flanks and created "structural highs" up to which oil in the higher formations often flowed. On the Iranian mainland, these domes have risen to the surface in some places, where the rains erode them and contaminate the groundwater; to the south, they generally lie far below the surface, although it has been said that one such dome lies beneath the site selected for the tank farm at Jebel Dhanna in the sheikhdom of Abu Dhabi, and, since it is close to the surface and rises an inch or so a year, has made it unnecesary for the builders to drive piles under the tanks. Aramco has occasionally used gravimetric surveys because geologists believe that the original cause of the great oil accumulations in Saudi Arabia was salt flows so deep they have never been reached by the drill.

The second half of the exploration process, drilling, is a considerably greater expense than surveying, but even this represents only a small part of a firm's ultimate expenditures. It is no financial burden for a major company which annually sells from $3 to $5 billion worth of petroleum products throughout the world to drill dozens of wells abroad in the same period; it is, however, an expense which the larger, more established firms seek to avoid. Aramco's total exploration expenditures, for instance, came to less than $200 million over a ten-year period between 1963 and 1973 — or an average of less than $20 million per year. The Iranian Consortium budgeted $11.7 million for exploration in 1971, $13.1 million in 1972, and $21.5 million in 1973 — 11.9, 9.4, and 10.8 percent, respectively, of total budgeted capital expenditures for those years. During the preceding decade Aramco drilled about fifty wildcats, sometimes only two or three per year. The Consortium had actually drilled more exploratory wells in this period than Aramco, sinking seven to ten wildcats a year recently and devoting two to four rigs full-time to the effort. It kept three exploratory strings active in its territory in the years 1970–1972, then put in a good 4.5 "string years" in wildcatting in 1973.

Drilling costs of course vary greatly in the Near East, ranging from $50,000 to $1.5 million per well. The average lies around half a million dollars and the cost depends largely on the depth of the well and the penetrability of the formations through which it passes.

However, companies which have been active in a given province for a long period of time become very familiar with its geology and in time virtually cease drilling into anything surprising. In the Consortium area of southwestern Iran, for instance, the main unknown in exploratory activity seems to be the depth at which the well will strike oil. Since it costs the Consortium about $15,000 a day to operate a rig, depth is the critical factor in whether or not to pursue a prospect, and the firm's area is rich in prolific fields which the Consortium has considered too deep to develop. There are two main oil-bearing strata in southwestern Iran: the Asmari (an Oligo-Miocene formation) and the older Bangestan, from the mid-Cretaceous era. Generally, the Consortium can hit the Asmari within two months, for $800,000 or much less. In many fields, especially those toward the northeastern boundary of the concession, close to the Zagros mountain range, the Asmari and Bangestan are for all intents and purposes part of one reservoir system. However, in many other fields which are closer to the Persian Gulf coast, they are not. Especially at Marun, Ahvaz, Mansuri, Binak, Rag-e Safid, and Ramshir, it can take three to four months to get down to the much deeper Bangestan and may cost $1.3 to $2 million to do so.[7] As a result, the Consortium has not, in general, taken the trouble to develop Bangestan reserves, although some of them are very great.

The Consortium's development well drilling costs indicate the range of expenses the firm faces. In computing these, oilmen use the concept of the "daily barrel." For example, the construction of facilities with a capacity of 5,000 daily barrels will handle a flow of 5,000 barrels a day, steadily, over a long period of time — years, during which they will generally require only minor repairs or improvements. So when oilmen say it costs a certain number of dollars to develop a "daily barrel" of capacity, they do not, of course, mean that it will cost this amount to produce each barrel, but rather that this investment will enable them to produce a barrel of oil a day, or 365¼ barrels a year, or 3,653 barrels a decade. Though they pay for the investment at or near the outset, they can pay off the investment quite rapidly; naturally, since an investment is more lucrative the more rapidly it pays out, it is apparent that the prospects which pay out slower are less worth making than those which return the money invested in them quickly. In the Consortium area, as elsewhere, it costs more money to develop some fields than others. In such shallow, prolific fields as Paris and Karanj, the cost of developing wells to produce oil run about 14 dollars per daily barrel; in the deeper and less prolific fields at south Rag-e Safid, the Bangestan zone of Ahvaz, or Cheshmeh Khosh, the costs of drilling the wells and installing the facilities at the well to handle the oil will run from $50 to $65 a daily barrel; and in such prospects as

Ramin and Kupal, they run $100 per daily barrel or a little more.* Obviously, the Consortium has made haste to develop Paris, has dawdled at Ramin, and has ignored Cheshmeh Khosh for a long time because the costs of developing the first are so much less than for the latter two.

In Libya, during the boom years, the breakdown of payment for rigs was somewhat different, because of the large number of concession holders in close proximity to one another. A firm would be likely to contract a rig for one or more wells, let the rig go to a neighboring company, then bring it back again: in the Near East, as elsewhere in the world, the producing companies do almost no drilling at all with their own equipment, but farm it out to contractors such as Sedco, Loffland Brothers, Santa Fe Drilling, or Reading and Bates. Therefore, in Libya, moving costs constituted a large part of the cost of drilling a well. However, ultimate costs of drilling wells in Libya were much the same as those in the Persian Gulf area. Occidental in 1968, for instance, paid between $1,400 and $3,000 a kilometer for moving charges (with lower unit rates for greater distances) and paid another $15,000 to $25,000 for "teardown," or dismantling charges, each time it released the rig to go to another site. For the actual drilling, Occidental would pay between $3,300 and $3,600 a day and an additional $10 to $11 a foot. A well which took four months to drill and penetrated about two miles would incur actual drilling costs of about $600,000, and this, in general, is what the wells in Concession 103 did cost Occidental. Well A1–103 cost about $630,000; well C1–103, almost $700,000; and well D1–103, about $570,000. These were all prolific wells. † Some wells in Libya, in "rank wildcat" acreage — that is, acreage very remote from other exploration or production — cost much more: for instance, Mobil's wells in Concession 11 and a wildcat in Libyan American's Concession 16 required almost three months of drilling and penetrated serious

---

* This material is broken down in detail in Appendix 9.
† These computations, of course, omit the salaries of the geological staff and other experts back in the home office, with their backup crew of draftsmen, secretaries, and the like, and also the unofficial but real cost of bribing someone in order to procure the concession in the first place.

lost circulation zones (that is, porous or even cavernous underground strata which soak up expensive drilling mud), with the result that the wells ended up costing about $900,000. However, they were exceptionally tough.

Exploration is the only really unpredictable aspect of a producing company's operations in normal times, of course, but in the Near East it has constituted only a small part of the cost, maybe 10 to 12 percent as a rule. We have seen that the Consortium has spent between 9.4 and 11.6 percent of its capital investment on exploration drilling in recent years. For this partial risk payment, the companies are very well rewarded, for the remainder of their operations are quite routine. Companies spend the bulk of their money drilling and tying in development wells — wells which are almost sure to find oil and which, once tested, turn out to be highly productive.

The Consortium, for instance, in 1972–1973, was running seven to fourteen rigs in this low-risk endeavor, at a cost of between $35 and $70 million a year. Occidental, to develop its three fields in Concession 103, drilled about seventy development wells.

When one gets beyond the drilling stage, the development of a field is comparatively inexpensive, though complex on the surface. It entails the placement of valve systems, or "wellheads," on the wells, the attachment of pipes, or "flowlines," to the wellheads, and the erection of various installations for removing undesirable matter from the oil. Briefly, the sequence in the field production facilities is this: oil comes up through the wellhead, flows through a gathering line past rock traps which remove sand and other debris, then passes through various separators, usually horizontal, usually sausage-shaped — about the size of a mobile home — which strip water and salt from the oil by electric plates and separate the gas from it by baffles. The oil then churns through further gas-oil separators to tanks, meters, and pumps, which in turn usher the oil into a large-diameter crude oil pipeline, which either transports the oil directly to a tanker terminal, as with Occidental's 103A field in Libya, or to intermediate booster stations and other main lines, as with all the fields in the Consortium (except Kharg, which is at the terminal). And in most cases that is the sum total of the operation.

On a barrel-for-barrel basis, these installations are not very expensive. A wellhead costs about as much as a Cadillac El Dorado — from $10,000 to $15,000 — and handles from 3,000 to 30,000 or 40,000 barrels a day in the Near East. Flowlines to handle this quantity generally go for about $25,000 a mile and are usually less than that in length. A separator tank capable of handling 80,000 to 100,000 barrels of oil a day will cost around a quarter of a million dollars, perhaps a little more. Sometimes a producing company will install two or three such tanks in a row, rather than just one, for more thorough depressurization and removal of foreign matter from the oil, in which case the cost of the separators will double or triple. Tanks to store the oil after it has emerged from this process cost between $3 and $6 per barrel — thus, a 100,000-barrel tank might cost around $400,000. The other facilities to handle this volume of oil consist of meters, flares, gauges, electric generators, valves, and the requisite barracks, offices, sewers, water lines, and electricity — perhaps all this will come to another million dollars, rarely much more. Thus, adding up these finite components of the cost of putting oil reserves into an export system, one arrives at a figure totaling no more than $25 a daily barrel and generally much less.

For example, in the Iranian Consortium, in recent years, new production facilities have ranged in cost from $17 to $28 a barrel a day — except for the test facilities, which always cost more because they are placed in a new location and handle small volumes. The expansion of existing facilities in southwestern Iran was even cheaper than the installation of new ones, running in the narrow range of $7.50 to $17 per daily barrel — depending on the pressure at which the oil emerged and the amount of salt, water, and gas it contained. In Libya, the expansion of capacity generally costs around $7 to $10 per barrel per day.

There remains, in this process, one other very large expense: that of pumping the oil through the main line, down to the export terminal, and onto a ship. Terminal operations are generally the trickiest and most expensive in the chain, like shepherding a large amount of excess baggage onto one of several competing airlines. They entail moving the flow of the commodity, oil, from one medium to another, from stable land onto water which is subject to the vicissitudes of the weather at sea.

Terminal costs vary, naturally, from country to country. In fact, sometimes the proximity of deep, sheltered water to the coast is among the main factors major oil companies will consider in determining, if not whether to proceed to export oil from a country in the first place, at least how much to favor expansion in one country over another.

The oil facilities at Ras Tanura in Saudi Arabia, Mina al-Ahmadi in Kuwait, and Jebel Dhanna in Abu Dhabi were easy to construct. Deep water was close to shore, so the facilities required little dredging and the companies could build piers out to where the tankers could moor, or the tankers could moor by sealines in sheltered water. At Khor al-Amaya in Iraq, however, and off the Gulf of Sirte in Libya, water near the coast is too shallow to accommodate big tankers. It would be prohibitively expensive to build piers out the long distance to deep water in these places, so the companies found it necessary instead to build sealines out to mooring buoys — in the case of Khor al-Amaya, more than fourteen miles out, beyond the Shatt al-Arab, the massive estuary encumbered with millenia of detritus from the Tigris and Euphrates rivers. But sealines, since they can easily snap while they are being laid on the sea bottom, are expensive to construct, and since the loading takes place in open water, which can be turbulent even in the Persian Gulf, this mode of operation is more expensive and hazardous than that of loading off piers. Furthermore, the lines often snap after they have been laid, under the pressure of stormy water.

To get the oil down to the terminal entails construction of a large-diameter pipeline, which in the Middle East generally costs between half a million and a million dollars a mile. This depends on the diameter: since the volume of the pipe increases geometrically with the square of the diameter, the bigger the pipe the lower its cost, per barrel capacity. (In Iran, however, where smaller crude streams lead to the main gathering stations at Ommidieh and Gorreh, the construction of main oil lines has been relatively cheap, because in general the pipes are narrower than most. Although they sometimes cover rough terrain — which adds to construction costs — they are inexpensive to lay, since the terrain over which they pass has already been cleared.) To move the oil along these lines, of course, requires pumps, but these are a minor component of the total cost. A 10,000-horsepower pump which, depending on elevation and assistance from other pumps, can move along from 100,000 to 500,000 barrels a day, will cost between two and two and a half million dollars, or from $4 to $25 a daily barrel, that is, for each barrel it can handle in one day.

The terminal, the last point along the line, requires several facilities — enough tanks to hold four or five days' worth of exports (for instance, the Iranian Consortium, at Kharg Island, had a capacity of 15 million barrels, or enough tankage to hold three days' production, in 1973) , then jetties or underwater mooring facilities — or both — along with several launches and tugs, buildings, pumps, and firefighting equipment. The tanks, as upstream, cost between $3 and $6 per barrel of capacity; thus, a tank which could hold 100,000 barrels of oil might cost $300,000 or $400,000. In the early 1970's, it cost the Iranian Consortium between $65 and $90 for each daily barrel of throughput capacity to expand all its downstream facilities — including the main pipeline, booster pump, and terminal facilities — that lay between the Gorreh station and the tankers off Kharg Island.

This, in turn, means that the total cost, to the Consortium, of developing new production has ranged, in recent years, from $100 to $200 per daily barrel of capacity, depending, of course, on the numerous variables. In general the cost lies closer to the latter figure.

The figure of $200 a daily barrel is a significant number, though the mere quotation of it seems a recitative in a vacuum: one may get a sharper idea of how low this figure is by considering what a daily barrel of capacity can provide for its owner. It can enable him to produce 365 barrels of oil a year. Each barrel, in early 1974, was selling for about $8 on the Persian Gulf, and facilities to produce a barrel a day could thus gain their owner a gross income of $3,000 a year (leaving out calculation of the interest the owner would sacrifice by collecting some of the money later in time) . This is a fifteenfold return on investment, within one year.

Most of it, to be sure, now goes to the producing states, and the 1974 figures are absurdly high. Still, taking a low sales price, say $1.30, which was the free market price until 1971, and assuming that this would give the owner a profit of 40 cents, his investment of $200 per daily barrel would pay out in about 500 days, or about a year and a half. This is what makes international oil one of the most lucrative businesses in human history.

There are usually only three unknown elements in an oil company's development activities. One is inflation — but that is everyone's curse. The second is that at times there can be a long "lead time," or delay, in having equipment shipped in and installed once it has been ordered. This problem is generally a minor one for such reliable long-standing clients as the major international oil companies.

The third unknown is accident. Accidents occur often. Occidental, for example, installed several large, expensive jet engines, to inject gas in its fields in order to keep the pressure up in the oil zone. They were to be the most modern installations of their kind in the world, and the company intended to give them great publicity. However, they proved ill-suited to the desert environment, collected sand, and had to be shut down much of the time. Occidental also ordered, from a European firm, several other pumps which developed rotor trouble, and the supplier spent months and tens of thousands of dollars attempting to rectify this problem. Other engineering mishaps crop up from time to time. These are not always mere accident, as the history of Aramco's problems with its massive water-injection pumps will shortly show. Lines leak or snap, tanks collapse or rupture, pumps break down, every once in a while a pump is sabotaged. The Iranian Consortium purposely erected some of its main-line booster pumps away from the main station at Gorreh "to provide security against catastrophic destruction of the entire export booster pumping system," in the words of one Consortium development plan. Sometimes gas emerges from a well, as happened at Masjed-e Soleyman, Iran; workers drive tractors over oil lines; welders start accidental fires; conflagrations break out in separators. Bechtel Corporation, alone, lost at least fifteen men in Libya in the 1960's through fire and explosion.

These mishaps sometimes cost lives; they always cost money. In general, though, the operating companies, and their subcontractors, are insured. At any rate, the wells themselves are safe. They are almost invariably outfitted, in the Middle East, with "storm chokes" — valves down a well, which can shut the well off at once if someone detonates the valves on the surface in the effort to make the well blow wild.

What is expensive, then, is not so much the unsuccessful quest for oil as the discovery of it, which requires the drilling of numerous further wells and construction of facilities for exporting the oil. It is here, precisely, where the heavy investment decisions are made, in the producing end of the oil industry. The companies always find the oil they want, once they determine to go looking for it. They are not, as some people imagine, engaged in desperate, quixotic quests to avoid running out of the commodity. The choices confronting a successful international oil operation lie in selecting the cheapest of numerous different alternatives for expanding.

These alternatives vary, are apt to grow more expensive, and are watched very carefully. The cheapest capacity increases about a decade ago lay in Saudi Arabia and cost about $40 per daily barrel, in the Abqaiq and Qatif fields. Some options in Iran, at Gachsaran and Marun, were just as attractive. In 1967 the Consortium itself stated that it did not consider it worthwhile developing a prospect which entailed total costs greater than about $185 a daily barrel, or $70 a daily barrel excluding terminal and pump station costs.[8] Time has driven this up, through inflation, devaluation, and exhaustion of the cheapest, lushest prospects, to the $200 per daily barrel noted just above.

To reiterate, in Iran, the costs of developing new capacity vary as follows: development drilling ranges from $14 to $100; field facilities and branch pipelines, from $5 to $25; and costs from the Gorreh station on down run about $85 per daily barrel. As of this writing, $200 is the Consortium's absolute ceiling. It will not develop a field for export if the three main costs of developing it come to more than this figure. The only exceptions to this ceiling, which continues to creep up, year by year, are the test facilities, constructed to measure the potential of a field and to see whether it is economic to develop it further — that is, whether it can be developed on a large scale for less than $200 a daily barrel.

The figure of $200 a daily barrel does not just apply to Iran. It is the yardstick by which the companies in the Iranian Consortium judge many other investments in the expansion of oil production for the international trade. Many members of the Consortium use it to decide whether or not to opt for expansion in Iran or in other countries where they have an interest. Even the Aramco parents, as we shall see, are guided by it. Interestingly, this firm will have to incur costs far greater than $200 a daily barrel if it is to expand production much above its present level. Aramco's budget planning for 1975 onward, as released by the Church Subcommittee, included prospects ranging from two to five times the cost of traditional ones: development of the Zuluf and Marjan offshore fields would cost $455 a daily barrel, the inland field of Khurais would require $810 a daily barrel, and Shayba, south of Abu Dhabi, would require investments of $1070. Remoteness from a terminal, and water injection in some cases, would account for the bulk of this high cost, but it was a cost which Aramco would be obligated to incur, in order to satisfy the Saudi government, if it wished to increase production at a rate of two million barrels a day per year.

Furthermore, since the low figure of $200 a daily barrel is creeping up in all areas, and since the lushest fields in the Middle East are being developed and gradually depleted — ceding place, with the passage of time, to smaller, more expensive prospects — the Middle East, too, is very slowly ceding place to other oil producing areas in the world — the North Sea, Alaska, offshore Indonesia, the Amazon Basin, perhaps someday soon the waters off the American Northeast as well. For this reason, we can expect, over the next decade, a real dropoff of exploration and perhaps development activity in the most prolific areas of the Middle East: Saudi Arabia, Iran, and Libya. We can also expect further concerted activity on the part of the seven major firms — dominant in the Middle East — to keep the successful newcomers in other areas from carving out powerful positions for themselves in the world's big retail markets.

Of course the oil companies do not pay anything close to $200 a daily barrel for all their capacity. This is because the development of new capacity soon becomes but a small part of the company's total operation, accounting, in time, for perhaps 10 to 25 percent of the total capacity being exploited in a given year. The Iranian Consortium, for instance, at the beginning of 1972, had the capacity to produce 5.8 million barrels a day. It wanted to close out the year able to produce 6.5 million barrels a day. This would require about 700,000 barrels of new capacity per day. Furthermore, the wells already on production would decline somewhat in output — say by 500,000 barrels a day, or less than 10 percent of capacity. The company would not have to pay so much to compensate for this decline, however; it could make up for it with engineering modifications, replacement wells, and workovers of existing wells. As a result, the Consortium would have to pay much less than $200 per daily barrel in order to reach its new target: a total of about $140 million for the year, or about $100 a daily barrel, to replace and upgrade existing capacity.

Dividing the total investment for the year, $140 million, by the total number of barrels the Consortium produced during the year, which would be about 1.67 billion, the Consortium's total investment in maintaining and expanding capacity that year would be about 8.7 cents a barrel.

To keep this capacity running, it costs the Consortium another nickel or so a barrel. This is the operating cost. Add to this depreciation and amortization — which are not costs, but credits against Iranian tax — totaling about 4.2 cents a barrel, the total expenses and expenditures of the organization come to about 18 cents a barrel. In the United States, by contrast, operating costs run about 75 cents a barrel, on the average, capital investments 90 cents or so, and exploration from 30 to 50 cents.

The following table shows the actual per-barrel investment and operating costs in the Iranian Consortium and Aramco over most of the past six years:

	1968	1969	1970	1971	1972	1973
Aramco:						
Operating cost	4.6	4.7	8.0	7.1	8.0	7.1
Depreciation and amortization	3.6	3.6	3.3	3.4	3.1	3.5
Investment	3.6	5.5	5.3	10.4	20.3	23.4
Total	11.8	13.8	16.6	20.9	31.4	34.0
Consortium:						
Operating cost	6.6	6.3	6.0	5.6	5.5	5.0
Depreciation and amortization	4.2	4.2	4.2	4.2	4.2	4.2
Investment	6.0	7.2	3.4	6.8	8.7	10.0
Total	16.8	17.7	13.5	16.6	18.4	19.2

(All figures are cents per barrel.)

These totals — less the depreciation and amortization — are what the supplier has to pay out of his own pocket to keep the massive volumes of oil flowing from the Persian Gulf to the consumer in Europe and the United States. On top of this sum, of course, one must add what Edith Penrose calls "monopoly rent" — the taxes and royalties which the host governments charge, and which are many times greater than costs and investments; now around $10 a barrel, although, for the previous two decades, around 90 cents.

(But suppose the host governments ran the entire operation themselves, had to face real competition, and were willing to sell oil to any vessel which might call to procure it, at a markup of 100 percent? They would charge the buyer not $9.50 or $10 for it, but 30 to 50 cents — and could still keep their business running. The dangers which would accompany such a development are apparent. Everyone would lose money except the consumer, and even he would be hard pressed to resist the temptation of surrendering entirely to the use of oil for his energy needs.)

Companies producing oil in the Moslem East expend great effort to keep the grand total of 12 cents, 15 cents, 18 cents, or whatever it might actually be, from rising even by a cent or two a barrel. Sometimes emergencies arise and destroy their plans. This has happened recently with Aramco; the company has had to make very large, rapid investments in pumping equipment to expand its water injections into the Ghawar, Khursaniya, and Abqaiq fields, in the effort — perhaps futile — to keep pressure in these fields from declining fatally.

In a sense, this is the price of avarice. Considering that operating and investment costs are maybe ten times greater in America than in the Middle East, and that the smaller companies have to pay the greater costs, one wonders why a rich company should be so obsessed with pennies. Part of the answer is, of course, that a penny saved on each barrel is $22 million earned a year — for the firm, not the stockholders, as Professor Penrose has noted — if one is producing 6 million barrels a day. So, while the consumers in America and Japan fret that the world is on the verge of running out of oil, the companies operating in the Middle East fret about keeping down the hypothetical 10,000 manholes rising above the Manhattan-sewerful of rampantly expanding yeast, and do not even begin to consider the possibility that the area's oil resources might, some day, begin to dwindle.

Most of the oil produced in the Middle East finds its way to Europe or Japan; the rest goes to divers poorer countries of the world, and, to a small but increasing extent, to the United States. Most of the oil at any rate stays within the channels of the big companies, which, in foreign operations, held 67 percent of the non-Communist world's proven crude reserves, 69 percent of its crude oil production, and about 70 percent of its petroleum sales.[9] A significant amount, about 30 percent, thus bypasses the system or jumps it and passes from crude-long exporters to refiners who produce less crude than they need, if they produce any at all.

Surprisingly, the major companies cannot sell oil at the posted price to their refining subsidiaries to any appreciable extent — except in the United States. This is because the United States, through negligence or design on the part of energy planners, is virtually the only country in the world which has not sought to protect its own crude-short refiners or to gain substantial tax monies from the big oil-importing firms.[10] Nonetheless, as appears earlier in this chapter, the European subsidiaries of Texaco, Standard of California, and the other majors generally operate at a loss and therefore lighten their tax burdens in these countries substantially.

A small example of this practice lies in the history of Lebanon's Mediterranean Refining Company (Medreco), in which Mobil and Exxon have an interest and which has purchased crude oil from Iraq Petroleum Company at or near the posted price for many years — costing Lebanon, in the estimation of its own government, 115 million Lebanese pounds, or about $35 million, between 1955 and 1970.[11]

The tax treatment which the United States affords American oil companies, domestic and international, is a subject which has drawn wide discussion, but it merits review here. The public has vented much indignation over the depletion allowance; the deduction of intangible drilling costs has attracted some public discussion; debate over the propriety of the foreign tax credit has been gaining momentum. Commentators have said little about more esoteric points, such as exemptions for dividends from partly-owned foreign subsidiaries in which American firms hold at least a 40 percent interest, or foreign tax shelters of different types. Standard of California's figures on the subject will help put these points in perspective.

International oil companies may use one of two different systems to calculate their overall foreign earnings and set them off against United States taxes, but they may not use both. One method is to pool all foreign earnings, the other is to calculate them on a country-by-country basis. Three American oil companies, Exxon, Mobil, and Getty, use the former system; the rest use the latter. Exxon paid $333 million in domestic taxes in 1973, or 13.6 percent of its worldwide profit.[12] Exxon's foreign activities, however, are so vast that it is hard to imagine how it could manage to pay much less than that, no matter how it sliced its foreign earnings; the company has hundreds of affiliates and subsidiaries. Mobil paid much less United States tax in 1973 — about $50.4 million — and SoCal paid only $41.5 million. SoCal paid $33.1 million in 1972, according to its *Annual Report* and *Financial Forecast;* of this, $14 million went to the federal government, the rest to state and municipal authorities. Meanwhile it posted United States earnings of at least $185 million on its basic oil operations.

As its 1972 *Financial Forecast* shows, SoCal managed this feat largely by offsetting foreign *losses* against foreign earnings which are taxable in the United States, and then offsetting foreign *gains* with domestic tax credits. It is liable for tax, in America, on only 15 percent of its dividends from Aramco, by virtue of the 85 percent tax exemption for dividends from partly owned foreign subsidiaries. However, when Chevron Oceanic, that subsidiary of SoCal's which holds part ownership of Aramco, buys oil from Aramco then sells it to another Chevron subsidiary, a trading company named Chevron Overseas, it incurs losses which swallow up that taxable 15 percent.*

Another procedure which SoCal and the other majors follow scrupulously is to insure that as much of the actual profit as possible from these interchanges devolves upon their shipping subsidiaries, which for the most part are based in Liberia or Panama — low-tax havens for "flags of convenience."

In 1972, SoCal's functional earnings from its major foreign crude operations — in Saudi Arabia, Indonesia, Iran, and Libya — totaled $831.3 million. Its crude oil losses in Europe, its trading operations, and its activities through Chevron Europe partly swallowed these gains. On the books, these losses totaled $510 million.

The resulting profit — $283.5 million — represented the company's Eastern Hemisphere earnings after foreign taxes, with a few relatively small adjustments.

SoCal's foreign tax credit, however, did amount to $197.8 million. For each barrel it lifted from its Eastern Hemisphere sources, SoCal paid 54 percent, or more, of the profit on the posted price. Since the United States treasury considered this a tax, it allowed SoCal to credit it against its worldwide consolidated earnings, as follows:

---

* Other oil concessions in which SoCal has an interest — the Consortium, for example — do not give dividends. The Consortium sells its oil to the participants' subsidiaries — or rather, collects operating costs in proportion to its "deemed" offliftings from said subsidiaries, and one shilling per ton in addition.

Consolidated earnings before tax	$940.0 million
Adjustment for partly owned or foreign subsidiaries and dividend credits	482.1 million
Audit adjustments	202.6 million
Subtotal	$660.5 million
Less various other tax adjust- ments, mostly domestic	250.0 million
United States taxable income	410.5 million
United States gross tax, at 48%	197.0 million
Less United States foreign tax- credits	197.8 million
Total tax liability	−$ .8 million

In fact, Standard of California paid more tax than this; it added a minimum tax of $12.7 million, and tax contingencies, to this sum and paid the United States government a total of $14 million for 1972.

These computations of foreign earnings, and their effect on a multinational's United States taxes, bring us back to the original point of this chapter, which is that SoCal, although a global firm active in scores of countries, is an American firm and flourishes under the American flag — along with Texaco, Mobil, Gulf, and Exxon. Its domestic achievements and earnings rival, if not outweigh, its foreign gains. The significant element in this is the figure for the various domestic tax adjustments. This is the figure SoCal is able to deduct from its worldwide consolidated income *after* the $482.1 million adjustment. This figure would hold if all SoCal's foreign operations vanished.

Were the company unable to deduct the domestic tax adjustments, its 1972 taxable United States income would have been much higher, and its federal tax bill would have been about $120 million greater. The components of this 250-million-dollar figure consist mostly of the depletion allowance, allowances for intangible drilling costs, depreciation, amortization, and abandonments of unproductive leases.

At the very least, SoCal pocketed 48 cents for every barrel of refined products it sold in the United States in 1972 — and as we shall see later, this computation leaves out much or most of its profits for natural gas and all its chemical and asphalt sales. It also leaves out all sales to the United States military. The firm refined about 937,000 barrels a day and on top of that sold another 110,000 barrels of products a day, which it did not refine domestically, but this could not have cost it more — in fact probably cost less — because SoCal refined this volume itself, for the most part, from its own foreign crude in its own foreign refineries. But assume it cost the same. Thus SoCal, by pocketing 48 cents for every barrel it sold, and by selling 1.049 million barrels a day in the United States, in 1972, actually earned, from its domestic operations alone that year, at the very least $185 million in cash. This is what remained after deduction of all the company's operating costs, royalties, and capital expenditures; it is on this that it paid the total of $33.1 million in taxes (exclusive of severance taxes, which are only deductible as an expense) to all municipal and state authorities in the country as well as to the federal government, which received less than 15 million dollars. This is no more than 8 percent of SoCal's total earnings, and probably less, since the sum of $185 million is a minimum estimate and, as noted above, represents only refined products and natural gas produced in association with oil.

The 1972 *Forecast* does not break down the firm's domestic tax benefits or its earnings within the United States. However, from the data available, it is possible to estimate them with some accuracy, say to within 5 percent. Furthermore, it is important to make this estimate, because within this process lies part of the secret of what SoCal actually had to pay to get these 1.049 million barrels of refined products to the American public each day in 1972. After all, the 1972 *Forecast* gives the general range of the prices it charged the public for these products: on page 6, there appears a graph which shows that SoCal earned between 18½ and 19½ cents a gallon, wholesale, for gasoline, and between 11 and 14 cents a gallon wholesale for gasoil. Since these two products represent about 53 percent of SoCal's total 1972 civilian sales to the public, and can be said to be representative of the upper and lower limits of SoCal's revenues from products that year, SoCal's total average realizations per gallon of product sold probably came to around 16½ cents, and since each barrel contains 42 gallons, a barrel, at 16½ cents a gallon, would sell for $6.93.

As it turns out, it cannot cost SoCal more than $6.45 a barrel to get these products to the American public. The first component of the domestic tax benefits which the federal government allows oil companies to charge in their books as costs, although they do not represent out-of-pocket costs at all, is the so-called "intangible" drilling allowance. This comes from costs "incident to and necessary for the drilling and preparation of wells for the production of oil and gas."[13] According to the tables in the 1972 *Forecast*, SoCal's total allowance for intangible drilling costs came, that year, to $68.5 million. Since this allowance is always an overwhelmingly domestic one, SoCal probably earned an allowance of about $60 million, or 35 cents for each barrel of oil it produced in the United States, for domestic intangible drilling costs in 1972.

We should pause a moment to consider the definition of "intangible" in this context. In theory, the expression means not only intangible services — contributions which one cannot touch, like labor and engineering expertise — but also any material which the company cannot salvage. In reality it embraces a number of eminently salvageable and reusable materials: not only expendable items such as water, drilling mud, and cement, but also goods which last, like drilling rigs, pumps, electrical logs. The oil company can expense all these costs at once as long as it does not own them but just rents or contracts for them. In general, the only part of the drilling operation which an oil company cannot expense immediately as an "intangible" is the casing, the pipe which remains in the well after it has been drilled. This remains the property of the oil-producing company.*

* Therefore, intangible costs run from 85 to 90 percent of total drilling costs. In considering that SoCal earned an allowance of only $60 million, we have made the generous assumption that only 80 percent of SoCal's actual domestic drilling costs in 1972 were intangible. According to the 1972 *Forecast*, the company spent $75.4 million drilling in the United States that year. It paid another $100 million for bonuses to acquire leases offshore Louisiana in the same year. Therefore, its 1972 domestic exploration expenditures came to $175.4 million, or $1.03 for each barrel it produced. Besides receiving a handsome allowance for "intangibles," it was able to amortize the bonus payments quite rapidly, at 20 percent per year.

The second element in SoCal's domestic benefits comes from oil production, the second phase of the company's operations. This is the notorious, celebrated, or venerated depletion allowance, a figure which is also easy to calculate although the 1972 *Forecast* does not break it down either. Federal tax law permits an oil producer to compute depletion at the rate of 22 percent of the market value of the oil (after deducting royalties), provided that the depletion allowance does not exceed 50 percent of the net profit per barrel, which remains after deduction of costs. During 1972, Standard of California produced about 465,000 barrels per day, net, in the United States; this was about seven-eighths its gross production, and the remainder constituted royalty payments. Three different areas accounted for this production: California and Southern Alaska, where its subsidiary Western Operations, Inc., produced 155,000 barrels a day net; the Rocky Mountain area, through Chevron West, which accounted for 85,000 barrels a day, net; and Texas and Louisiana (mostly offshore), through the California Company, which yielded up 225,000 barrels a day. The company's net production profits, according to the *Forecast*, averaged $1.48 a barrel before tax and exploration expenses. The depletion allowance could have averaged as much as 58 cents a barrel, or $98.9 million for the year.*

The third and final category of domestic tax benefits open to SoCal is depreciation and amortization. This covers all areas of the business, refining, marketing, and transportation as well as

---

* SoCal's gross revenues per barrel were $2.82 for Western Operations, $3.38 for Chevron West, and $3.52 for California Company. Its profits per barrel — including natural gas credits — were, respectively, 80 cents, $1.74, and $2.02. The depletion allowance comes to 22 percent of the market price for each barrel, or about 65 cents a barrel for Chevron West and 68 cents for California Company — though only about 40 cents a barrel for Western Operations, since this is one-half its net profit of 80 cents a barrel. The *Forecast* offers no explanation for these discrepancies in profit. One explanation for the low profits in California is, perhaps, that its fields yield less gas. Another is that operating costs there are quite high onshore, since some fields require secondary recovery through steam injection. SoCal's onshore operating costs rose from 33 cents a barrel in California in 1961 to 45 cents in 1967, and the costs of producing oil there by secondary recovery almost doubled — from 64 cents a barrel to $1.43. SoCal's offshore lifting costs, though, were quite low — about 32 cents a barrel in 1967. This helps explain why companies are so anxious to explore for oil offshore.

production. These benefits are the toughest to break down. Indeed, one can only make an intelligent guess at them, based on past performance and a certain proportion of the company's various investments — say, 7 percent for production and 15 percent for the others, which have a shorter life in general. In 1972, SoCal's investments in production facilities in the United States came to $148.1 million, while its "downstream" investments — in refining, marketing, and transportation — came to about $177 million. Deductible amortization of leases came to about $12 million, abandonments of unproductive properties to $38 million. So total production allowances, except depletion, came to about 35 cents a barrel: 6 cents for depreciation, 7 cents for amortization, about 22 cents for abandonments. Depreciation and amortization in downstream operations are assumed to be about $25 million, which would be 15 percent of the company's investments for the year in domestic refining, marketing, and transportation facilities. (In all likelihood, this is an extremely conservative figure, since it does not take accelerated depreciation into account.)

When these three domestic benefits are added up, they show that SoCal received tax writeoffs of about $1.28 a barrel, or $218 million, for its oil operations in the United States during 1972. At a tax rate of 48 percent, this alone would be a loss, to the United States treasury, of about 60 cents a barrel, or $105 million.

Thanks to the above figures, one can estimate quite closely what it actually cost SoCal to find and produce its own crude in America — and from there one can estimate the rest of SoCal's costs in getting a gallon of products to the public.

The company's costs in providing its refineries with its own crude oil in America came to about $3.12 a barrel, or 7.6 cents a gallon — *all expenses included*. The company's exploration expenses, totaling $175 million, came to $1.03 for every barrel produced. Its production costs were 72 cents a barrel; this is simply the market value ($3.26 on the average) less severance taxes (which come to about 20 cents), production investments (which according to page 22 of the *Forecast* came to $148 million, or 87 cents a barrel), and net profit ($1.48), including gas credit of perhaps 10 to 20 cents. The only other out-of-pocket costs would be the severance taxes, overhead, and production investments listed above. Proceeding downstream, the company's costs of transporting the crude from the field to the refinery are assumed to be about 17 cents a barrel, though the *Forecast* does not mention this figure and it is hard to calculate precisely.*

Of course, the foregoing calculations are only a shade less than half the story, since SoCal refined about 937,000 barrels of oil a day in the United States, though its net production totaled just 465,000 barrels a day.[14] It had to get the remaining oil, an equivalent amount of approximately 470,000 barrels a day, from other sources.

SoCal, like other companies, makes up a good portion of this deficit — at the very least, 120,000 barrels a day — by importing its own crude oil and swapping foreign crude of its own with others in exchange for their domestic crude. It received this crude, in its domestic refineries, at cost plus transportation. In 1972 foreign crude was landed at American ports for about $2.60 a barrel on the average — in those days, it was cheaper than domestic crude.

SoCal presumably had to pay the market price for the rest of the crude it refined in the United States, about 350,000 barrels a day. Again, this is a generous assumption: there is much evidence that it was paying as much as 50 cents a barrel less in some instances, especially in California.† This assumption means that for about 37 percent of the crude it refined domestically, SoCal paid about $3.43 a barrel, which is the market price plus 17 cents a barrel transportation.

---

* *Petroleum Intelligence Weekly* of November 22, 1971, gives the cost of piping oil from the Gulf of Mexico to Chicago as 22 cents. But this is a distance of over 1,000 miles, and SoCal's domestic crude rarely travels half as far. From its Gulf of Mexico fields to the Pascagoula refinery is only 150 miles, from California's Central Valley to the Richmond refinery less than 350 miles, from the valley to Los Angeles much less. Assume it costs SoCal 12 cents a barrel on the average to ship this oil domestically and add to that 5 cents in "gathering costs."

† See the *Wall Street Journal*, August 10, 1973, last page. One reason why California crude was selling below the national price in 1972, and other years, was that the pricing system prevalent in California penalized the heavy, viscous crude common to that state more severely than such crudes were penalized almost anywhere else in the world.

One general figure remains in computing what it cost SoCal to get a barrel of refined products to the American public in 1972: this is the money SoCal actually paid to process all the crude it received at its refineries, then to get it to wholesalers, and the money it spent on investments in these operations. Its investments in refining, marketing, and transportation were, simply, 46 cents a barrel in 1972, or $177.3 million, according to the 1972 *Forecast*. The total cost, to SoCal, of operating the facilities to refine, market, and transport this volume of products was at most $2.83 a barrel — a figure obtained by elimination, since it does not appear anywhere in the 1972 *Forecast*.*

Hence, what it really cost SoCal to get a barrel of refined products to the American public in 1972 was $6.45 a barrel. This is a maximum figure: an average of $3.16 for all purchased, owned, and imported crude oil, delivered; 46 cents for investments in all downstream facilities; and $2.83 for all downstream operating costs.

This leaves 48 cents a barrel, straight cash, in the company's pocket. Of this, not very much went out again to pay tax. One will recall the tax benefits the federal government bestowed on SoCal for its owned crude: 35 cents for intangible drilling costs, 59 cents for the depletion allowance, and 35 cents for production depreciation, amortization, and abandonments — a total of $1.28 a barrel, or 60 cents in money saved, at a tax rate of 48 percent.

Thus, to return to the original observation: if SoCal sold 1.049 million barrels of oil in the United States each day in 1972, it pocketed at least $185 million from its domestic operations alone.

What this figure means, ultimately, is simply the following: SoCal does all right for itself in America. The success of its domestic operations is not dependent on its foreign activities. The

---

* By elimination thus: SoCal, in the 1972 *Forecast*, claimed a profit of 17 cents, before tax, on United States refining, marketing, and transportation operations; it paid 46 cents for downstream investments and claimed 15 cents for downstream depreciation and amortization; and it charged itself $3.32 per barrel of crude delivered — even when it delivered this crude from its own fields at a much lower cost. In other words, SoCal charges itself for the profits it realizes on its own crude production. These four figures total $4.10. When subtracted from the market price of $6.93, they leave $2.83.

company's United States operations pull their own weight and did so even when crude oil sold, in America, for $3.26 a barrel rather than $7. So if the company were to be divested of all its foreign operations, it would still turn a very nice profit; it would have done so even before the 1973–1974 price hikes. Thus the price hikes are indefensible; they served no purpose of value to society as a whole. They only further enriched companies which were already doing well. For, although prices for crude oil have risen drastically in the United States — as elsewhere — the cost of producing the oil has hardly risen. Only royalties and sever-ance taxes have gone up, and this is because they are pegged not to costs but to the market "price."

In addition, this minimum figure of $185 million for SoCal's profit from its United States operations omits several considerable sources of profit: chemical earnings, other minor products — and much if not most of its natural gas.

On the eleventh page of the 1972 *Forecast,* there is a list of the earnings of the company's various domestic subsidiaries; this as-cribes profits of $9 million to the company's Western Hemisphere chemical operations and $20 million to its asphalt sales. It does not, however, offer any breakdown of the company's natural gas earnings.

A serious struggle is taking place in the United States at this writing as to whether or not federal price controls on natural gas piped in interstate commerce should be lifted. Beginning early in 1973, President Nixon, his former energy chiefs John Love and William Simon, and even their successor John Sawhill — not to mention Interior Secretary Morton and Duke Ligon of the Office of Oil and Gas — repeatedly called in public and before Congress for deregulation of natural gas prices. The industry's appeals on the subject diminished somewhat in early 1974, with the an-nouncement of massive industry profits for the year 1973 and the first quarter of 1974, but they picked up again by winter. Presi-dent Ford has already put deregulation near the top of his energy agenda.

The stimulus for this intense activity is, in a word, money. There is a great deal of that substance at stake in the natural-gas question. According to the 1972 *Financial Forecast,* SoCal sold, in the United States, about 1.4 billion cubic feet of natural gas a day, or in all about 500 billion cubic feet for the year. The market price for this gas, even though it was regulated for the most part, came to 120 million dollars. This was largely profit; the gas was largely a by-product of oil exploration and production activity which would have taken place in any event. Over the years So-Cal has drilled about five time as many wells for oil as for gas in America.

A company such as SoCal — indeed, any company which produces oil and gas in America — would profit immensely from the elimination of federal price controls on gas. Such a removal of price control would be a massive sellout of the American consumer. Were this one control which the federal government exerts directly on energy prices in the United States to be lifted, SoCal would probably earn another $120 million a year from the sales of natural gas alone, and perhaps a lot more. But its costs would scarcely rise. It is worth the while of a big company like SoCal to spend a few million dollars a year lobbying and advertising to have this price control removed. It would even be worthwhile, under less favorable circumstances, to sacrifice the depletion allowance for it. As we have seen, this saved the company only about $47 million in 1972 (or 48 percent of $98 million). Some of America's biggest oil companies, such as Mobil and Atlantic Richfield, have actually come out in favor of eliminating the depletion allowance; their quid pro quo, which the companies never state directly to the public but voice through the administration, is the deregulation of natural gas.

Although SoCal's 1972 *Financial Forecast* does not furnish a breakdown similar to the foregoing, it offers a list of earnings for separate Western Hemisphere subsidiaries (on page 11) which very largely corroborates it. The earnings of Western Operations, California Company, and the refining and marketing arms Standard of Kentucky and Chevron East came to $300 million in 1972, but then the company subtracted from this most of its general overhead, interest, losses from trading companies, and corporate supply arrangements, which came to $112.7 million. This would account for earnings of perhaps $200 million, maybe a little more, to which the company would add most of its Western Hemisphere asphalt and chemical earnings of $29 million. In no place does the forecast list the company's earnings from natural gas in the United States. Another very profitable area of activity for the company is Canada, where its various subsidiaries earned about $62 million in 1972.

Yet even these figures are misleading. SoCal's domestic overhead most probably includes millions of dollars for foreign accounting, tax, legal, engineering, and other efforts which should not be deducted from the United States tax even though they are incurred on American soil. Much of the company's costs of borrowing money, though credited against United States tax, have helped free money for foreign investment.[15]

Naturally, much of the company's earnings from the United States went to stockholders. Since the Western Hemisphere earnings accounted for about half the total, they presumably accounted for half the dividends, and maybe two-thirds of the company's Western Hemisphere dividends of about $122 million would have come from the United States, or around $80 million. Therefore, of the $185 million which the company earned, as an absolute minimum, from its domestic product sales, $80 million went to stockholders and $34 million to state, federal, and municipal taxes. This left at least $70 million. This is more than the sum by which the company, according to its annual report, reduced its worldwide debt. In other words, not only did SoCal earn enough in America to pay for all its domestic operations and investments, as well as dividends and taxes, it had enough left over to pay for some of its foreign obligations as well.

The year 1973 was even better for SoCal than 1972. The firm registered an increase in working capital of only about $120 million in 1972, but this rose to $477.6 million in 1973. Cash accounted for $37.4 million of this latter sum and the rest took the form of marketable securities. Standard Oil of California, therefore, even if it were to be broken up into smaller companies, were to be divested of all foreign operations and allowed only to operate within the United States, would still be clearing at least $185 million a year, and most probably $220 million or more, on its domestic operations alone, thanks to its ownership of extensive crude resources within the United States, the right to import some crude oil and products from abroad, and the various tax benefits which the United States federal government grants to the United States oil industry.

So far this book has discussed one of the major issues of energy policy in America with only little reference to its main subject, which is the industry in the Near East and North Africa. This should indicate the obvious: the oil industry in the Near East and North Africa is almost *irrelevant* to the direct interests of the American people. Were American interests totally banished from the Moslem world — or indeed from everywhere outside North America — the American oil industry, as SoCal's figures show, could still function smoothly. America still receives, in mid-1974, over 80 percent of its crude oil and refined products from North America and Venezuela. The industry could still minister to the needs of the American consumer and operate at a profit. What holds true of SoCal, furthermore, is very largely true of Exxon, Gulf, Mobil, and Texaco also. Domestically, Exxon and Texaco are even stronger and better balanced than SoCal.

It also holds true for the larger American "independents" — Standard of Indiana, Phillips, Continental, and Atlantic Richfield, which cannot rely much on foreign operations for tax relief within the United States, since their foreign operations constitute only a small proportion of their total effort.

Proof of this assertion lies with the American company Shell. This firm is largely owned by the great British-Dutch enterprise Royal Dutch/Shell, but it operates exclusively within the United States. Although Shell's profit record over the seven-year period 1967–1973 has been much lower than that of other companies mentioned above because it could not avail itself of foreign tax credits, it too has paid its own way in America and has been a mainstay of its mother company.*

Further proof is that foreign oil companies have worked hard to enter the American market, particularly through the oil-producing end. Shell came to America in the 1920's. For a long time

* See Appendix 2 for figures on the 1967–1973 profit performance of this and the other top fourteen American oil firms.

no other foreign company followed because the capital required for admission was too great, although the Belgian Petrofina and the French CFP made entries in modest ways. Then, in the early 1960's, British Petroleum acquired a number of leases in a highly speculative area, the North Slope of Alaska. It turned out that massive deposits of oil lurked under these leases, and British Petroleum gained access to what has very conservatively been estimated at 7 billion barrels of crude oil. The British firm proceeded at once to buy out the Eastern refining and marketing properties of one big American independent, Sinclair, and the majority of shares in another, Standard Oil of Ohio.

The lush profitability of the domestic American petroleum business inevitably leads to a further consideration: perhaps if the Middle East and North Africa are not relevant to the direct interests of the American people, then it is not essential to the well-being of the oil companies, either, that they be involved there. In other words, they are not in the Middle East for reasons related to American requirements or security — or even prosperity. To find areas and peoples which really need Middle Eastern oil one must look a little farther, to western Europe and Japan.

But American control over the supply of oil to these lands implies some American control over the lands themselves. Would the ejection of American interests from the Near East jeopardize American hegemony in Europe and Japan, then? Is it acceptable to allow American international oil companies the freedom of action they enjoy in the Near East, to help ensure that Europe does not turn Communist? Or neutral? To what extent should the American people, the federal government, allow any private group in the country to strive after wealth abroad, to dominate foreign activity? The history of the past generation has shown what a hard question this is to answer in the context of the Cold War.

Although the history of the past generation has shown the merit of influencing Western Europe and imposing safeguards to ensure that this influence continues, what price is it worth to maintain that influence from now on? Perhaps the price becomes exorbitant when, as happened in late 1973, during the last year of the Nixon administration, one of the major instruments of this influence — here, the five major American oil companies — drifted out of the control of the American people, abetted by "a president who was weak and under attack," in the words of a former aide, Charles Colson, and "scared as hell to alienate the military and foreign policy establishment."

The year 1973 showed that it is becoming politically impossible for the American electorate to impose changes on the oil industry, if the industry does not want such changes and has the backing of the executive branch of government in addition to large numbers of congressmen.

In the past fifty years, the depletion allowance has remained almost untouched. Other tax advantages have remained intact — in many cases unnoticed — for decades. The oil companies are under no legal obligation to make available to the public any meaningful information on costs, allowances, profits, or assets, broken down country by country and state by state. It was simply by fluke that Standard of California's 1972 *Financial Forecast,* for instance, came into the light of day.

The oil companies, similarly, forbid the public access to accurate information on the nation's inventory of oil and gas. After a series of catastrophic oil spills offshore Santa Barbara, and much hard effort by enraged citizens, the United States Geological Survey, supported by the American taxpayer although obviously in the thrall of the oil industry, finally, and with much ill humor, allowed select members of a conservation group to look at the survey's information on Exxon's Santa Ynez field, a mammoth collection of pools in federal waters which contains at least four billion barrels of recoverable oil. Nonetheless the USGS would not allow these conservationists — including some retired oilmen — to review the records on hand in Santa Barbara; they had to go down to the regional office in Los Angeles, at their own expense, to do so, and even then they were not allowed to take notes on what they saw — and this material, in turn, was lacking some key information, such as electric logs — and that for a field which was on property belonging to the American taxpayer.

In late 1973 and 1974, Congress ratified this immoral state of affairs by proving itself, in an emergency which called for alacrity of judgment, incapable of forcing crude or oil products price rollbacks even down to double the figure of a few months before, although the executive branch had the ability to impose a rollback and make it stick. Officials in the "weak," "scared" executive branch, from President Nixon and William Simon on down, made with impunity the demands on the public which the oil companies, having recorded staggering profits, were for the moment squeamish about making themselves. The judiciary, the Department of Justice, the Federal Trade Commission, a handful of lawyers, most by background and conviction prohibited access to direct working experience in the oil industry (which is a closed shop) and very short of funds and support from Congress, suffered, too, from the burden of the cowardice and complaisance of the Nixon administration.

Since it is now clear that the American oil industry will survive and prosper if it is banished from the Middle East, is the industry deeply concerned about its future in the Near East? This brings us to the next subject: to what degree is the Middle East dependent on the oil industry? Is it or the industry the more dependent party? How do Middle Easterners feel about the industry? Do they fear it, tolerate it, hold it in contempt? What strategies and policies have they designed to control it or eliminate it? How do they behave toward it? The next chapter will seek to examine some of these questions and our perceptions of them as Westerners.

4

A Glance at Near Eastern Oil Politics

There remains no other course for the national and progressive forces except that of struggle in all its forms, even
if this were to lead to the cutting off of oil supply lines
. . . and the closing down of oil wells in order to deprive
the monopolist, the embezzler, the despot of this oil.
— al-Ba'ath newspaper,
Damascus, 1966

The money flowing to the Arab countries from petroleum
gives them — in the sphere of material resources — more
than is obtained by Israel from the money of America and
world Jewry. . . . Will the Arab nation become a nation
of value in the existing civilization whose progress is ad-
vancing at a terrifying pace, or will it squander its money
and remain bogged down in the swamps of backwardness?
— Ahmad Baha el-Din, al-Ahram
newspaper, Cairo, 1972

WHEN ONE PROCEEDS from the subject of oil industry
bookkeeping to that of Near Eastern oil negotiating history, one
leaps into a void of less fathomable depth. As American citizens,
our deficiencies lie not so much in failing to understand the cold
matters — the United States government's tax treatment of oil
as it passes over the rail of a tanker off Mina al-Ahmadi, the
Iranian Consortium's APQ system, the changes in Aramco offtake policies — as they lie in our attempts, generally futile, to
assess the true relationships between the company men and the
Near Easterners; in understanding the psychological tension, or
balance, that lies between the two.

This is because little is known in the West about Near Eastern attitudes toward the industry and the men who run it. For the most part, all one can do in attempting to shed further light on this subject is to have faith in the dictum that "action is character": to proceed through our knowledge of what the Arabs and Iranians have been saying about the industry over the past twenty-five years or so and how much of what they have been saying they have actually put into practice; and to hope that the actions to follow in the future will be consistent with those of the past.

The Near Easterners' capacity to inflict damage on the West by denying it oil has certainly grown since the 1950's, and perhaps since the 1960's as well, but it is absurd to be swept up in nightmares over it. One needs to think more about what they would *want* to do, and why. Often a Middle Easterner's position on a point will apparently not facilitate such an undertaking. Consider "the Palestine Question": an American with no strong opinions on this explosive issue asks an Arab for his true feelings on it because he wants to include, in his assessment, some feeling that the Arab's ultimate goal, or desire, goes beyond the merely destructive. However, until lately few Arabs were willing to discuss the matter with Westerners at all; Arabs would certainly refrain from discussing terms of future negotiations with Israel, or entertaining the notion that the George Habashes and Nayef Hawatmehs of the world should discuss it with a little humility — indicating that they preferred instead to defer discussion of "a just and honorable solution" until they could do so from a position of real strength. Of course, one might maintain the option of displaying generosity, magnanimity, but within limits; to this day the most articulate of Palestinian spokesmen elect to state that they condemn terrorist activities only "at the proper time and place" — that is, before Arab audiences. Thus, many Westerners have been left with the apprehension that generosity is an archaic, feudal virtue after all.

However, 1973 has also showed that the mere desire to be in a position to dictate terms is not enough by itself to motivate the Arab to win his way into this enviable position by the force not only of thrift and hard work but also of intense self-discipline, asceticism, and fanaticization. Over the past twenty-five years, most Arabs who have rarely been willing to admit that they were willing to coexist with a Jewish state have certainly realized that the price in self-sacrifice and disorientation of social priorities, to say nothing of money, perhaps lives, indebtedness to foreign sympathizers, and conversion to a deadening fanaticism, all of which were requisite for mounting a convincing threat to the existence of the Jewish state (founded after all by an application of much the same qualities), was a high price for them to pay personally; let others pay it if they wished — the others being largely the misfits and psychopaths of which every society has its quota. This conclusion rarely goes announced, of course, except indirectly.

Mention of Arab feelings on the Palestine issue, and on Westerners, is apropos here, because the Arab attitude toward Israel and Zionism is not a unique, bizarre phenomenon. Many citizens of other underdeveloped lands understand the Arab attitude full well and appreciate that it can answer many questions, for it is a product of long-standing frustrations, vindictiveness, and the knowledge that one has suffered and been humiliated for accepting terms which an outsider enjoying a temporary advantage has imposed. This knowledge is a commonplace among many people in the underdeveloped world as a whole.

For it was the Zionists, not the Arabs, who actively sought to determine the course of development of Palestine, infiltrating, in the manner of the Viet Cong, in numbers greater than those the British authorities and the Arab majority of the region had accepted, and setting up "parallel hierarchies" which were able to assume the functions of state after the colonial powers hastily withdrew in 1948. The few times anyone asked them, the Arabs readily declared themselves opposed to the establishment of a Jewish state in Palestine as far back as World War One. All Emir Faisal told Chaim Weizmann in 1917 was that he was willing to accommodate Jewish immigration to the Holy Land on a moderate scale; few other Arabs said as much. But, in the generation between the two world wars, the Zionists gained the upper hand in Palestine; they were truly more united and stronger than the Arab majority. This is probably the fact the Arabs have the toughest time coming to grips with.

Much of the experience of the oil industry in the Middle East is explicable in similar light. An example of this is the history of a promise which the governments of Britain and France made to the yet-aborning government of Iraq in the San Remo Agreement of 1920. Through this accord, the British and French — besides working out an arrangement whereby they could both participate in the development of Iraq's oil — declared that in the future the Iraqi government would have the option to acquire 20 percent of the shares of Iraq Petroleum Company, if the firm ever went public. Five years later this government, when offered the option, declined to exercise it, choosing instead to take a 12½ percent royalty on the oil produced. Why it did so is not clear to this day. Subsequent generations of Iraqis did not forget this lost right, though, and struggled to regain it. They lost their early battle, in 1961 — but the campaign to gain 20 percent participation then spread, within a decade, first throughout the Persian Gulf, then over the whole world — ultimately to succeed in the acquisition of 60 or even 100 percent.

Another campaign which governments in the Middle East, not only that of Iraq but also those of Iran and even Libya, have waged has been one to regain rights to territory which oil companies have held but not used. This struggle is similarly explicable by a universal sentiment: a sense of rage at having once been cheated, no matter how little, no matter how far in the past.

But this is not to say that Middle Eastern oil states have in general wanted to withhold their prime commodity from the Western world or that they will be inclined to do so in the future. Westerners, in their often outmoded feelings of guilt over past injustices, have imputed a much deeper instinct for vindictiveness and destructiveness to Near Easterners than generally exists.

Consider the most basic question of all: have Near Eastern states received fair payment for their oil?

True, this is not an easy question to answer because it is hard to put a fair value on crude oil. Is it worth what it costs to produce it, plus a reasonable profit (10 percent, 100 percent)? Is it worth any price the seller can get? Is it worth just one cent less per gallon, barrel, or British thermal unit than any other fuel competing with it — say coal, hydroelectric power, or wind? Is it worth the cost of turning it into the most expensive of refined products — again plus a reasonable surcharge — or, as often seems the criterion nowadays, is it worth exactly what everyone else is selling it for, a sort of universally sanctified price which no seller would dare betray?

The recent history of the pocket calculator in America shows what hopeless questions these are to answer. Once a dozen entrepreneurs competing out of different garages within a ten-mile radius of Stanford University devised a way to manufacture a "chip," or light-emitting diode, for two or three dollars, the value of a simple eight-digit pocket calculator, once priceless, dropped by late 1972 to about $100; a year later, such an instrument would gather dust on the shelves at $30.

Similarly, it took innumerable breakthroughs in science and the development of the internal combustion engine, the spread of colonialism, and many brilliant hunches for man to reach the point, about the turn of this century, where he had finally learned, and decided, to seek profit by sinking a drill on an elevated plot of rugged Near Eastern landscape seeping asphalt, stinking of sulphur, and plagued with permanent fire.

It is true that from the first discoveries in Iran, Iraq, Kuwait, and Bahrain until about a generation ago — shortly after World War Two — the Near Easterners received little money for their oil, which companies in any event did not produce in great quantity. Till that time, a Near Eastern government or ruler would receive a flat four shillings a ton, gold or silver, as royalty for his oil. Even before the first devaluation of the pound, that came only to about 12 to 18 cents a barrel. In Saudi Arabia, the legend goes, Aramco would fly this gold to King Abdel Aziz at his palace in Riyadh every month.

However, the times changed. In Mexico, in 1938, a left-wing government simply expropriated the properties of foreign companies producing oil there and left them without recourse. During World War Two the major oil companies, damaged by this experience, entered into an arrangement with Venezuela which they hoped would prevent a recurrence of this expropriation; they agreed to split their profits from oil with the government. This formula rapidly moved, under the urging of the United

States government and with modifications, to Saudi Arabia and other countries of the Near East. In fact, the United States government made it very worth the companies' while to accept the split, since it gave them total exemption from United States tax rather than a partial write-off, as had previously been the case. The one country where the concession holder refused to implement the profit split promptly was Iran, where British Petroleum held sway. BP soon came to grief as a result of its refusal. By 1966, the fifty-fifty split was in effect in every oil-producing state outside the Communist world.

As this change was taking place, Near Eastern rulers and officials also became more sophisticated about the international industry, became more aware of what their oil really sold for on the tightly controlled world market. They embarked on a campaign, which has registered unbroken success to this day, to get more and more money from the companies for each barrel they exported. As a result, the Near Easterners, who once received 12 cents, are now uniformly collecting about $10 a barrel — although it still costs only 10 to 20 cents to produce this oil in the Middle East, including all possible components, capital expenditures, fixed costs, depreciation, and amortization.

This is because of the weird institution of the posted price, which we described in Chapter 2: the artificial price which the companies used as the base on which they paid taxes to their host governments. This price was high, and the companies kept it high, in the face of terrific surplus. Though this price, as we have seen, has experienced some fluctuations since the end of World War Two — more than doubling, then dropping, by degrees, to $1.75 a barrel or so — there is little doubt that it would have gone down farther in the 1960's, if allowed. The companies exerted almost no effort to bring it down; to keep the price high would be to buy the allegiance of the Arabs and Iranians to the international system, as well as to protect the profits of the companies themselves. The host countries were getting such great monopoly rent from the major oil firms that it would be sheer folly for them to seek to change the system. The governments of the United States and most western European nations were in favor of preserving the posted price, and keeping it at a high level, also, to protect their more inefficient indigenous energy industries. Only the consumer suffered from this artificial pricing system, but he was disorganized, ignorant, and unconcerned, so he posed no threat to the system.

There is little doubt that the posted price would, in the 1960's, have gone down much farther than it did had it been permitted to do so. Professor Morris Adelman of MIT, who has chronicled the peregrinations of this price through the postwar generation in detail, has demonstrated that this evolution of prices showed that the Persian Gulf "did no more than supplement the consumption of the area it served" during World War Two and that later the companies producing gulf oil would have proceeded to bring this price down, too, more than they did (though they prospered by keeping it high) ; what stopped them was governmental intervention in the market. Imports of oil into the United States came to be restricted as early as 1950. (Of course Exxon, Mobil, and Shell did their part to keep the Persian Gulf price up too, as we shall see.)

Adelman stated that it was futile for a company to contemplate a price reduction in the United States, because of actual, if not formal, import restrictions: it could not significantly expand its share of the market, and, since everyone would follow, the reduction would benefit nobody. However, although the price of oil increased somewhat in America in 1953 and 1957, "the price increases of 1957 marked the zenith of postwar control of the market. After 1957 it was all downhill until 1971, but even that is a lower peak."[1]

In other words, again in Adelman's words, in the late 1950's "the price began to gravitate toward cost."[2]

When the fifty-fifty split was first established, the guests simply paid taxes on the real sales prices anyway in most countries. Then Sheikh Abdullah Tariki, Saudi Arabia's director of petroleum and minerals at the time, discovered this and raised an outcry which forced Aramco — and the other companies — to mend their ways and pay taxes on the artificial price exclusively.

Since the posted price had become sanctified, although it was fictitious, the companies now had no recourse but to lower it. This they proceeded to do, by about 18 cents a barrel, or almost

10 percent, in early 1959 and August, 1960. Their effort in doing so was simply to bring the tax-reference price closer to what a Persian Gulf barrel would actually fetch if they tried selling it to an outside customer — such as the government of Ceylon, or an independent refiner in Italy, or the state oil firms of Argentina and Brazil (which enjoy a strong bargaining position because their winter, or peak fuel consumption season, corresponds to summer, a time of slack demand, in the other big consuming areas).

The price cuts of 1959 and 1960 backfired in two ways. One, the American government, under the pressure of alarmed domestic producers, imposed a mandatory quota on oil imports — thus sealing America off from international oil price fluctuations for fourteen years. Then, the governments of the big exporting states — Venezuela, Iran, Kuwait, Iraq, and Saudi Arabia — raised screams of protest. As the prices dropped after 1957 so did the revenues accruing to these oil-rich states for each barrel their guests exported. They engaged in intense diplomatic activity among themselves to stop this downward spiral. In September, 1960, they held a crude oil price conference in Baghdad, demanding that the companies maintain prices and calling for a coordinating organization.[3] In October, the Second Arab Petroleum Congress met in Beirut and resounded with denunciations of the price cuts and calls for a restriction of crude output to maintain the price.

The five big oil states then formed their coordinating organization, which they named OPEC (the Organization of Petroleum Exporting Countries). This organization quickly succeeded in gaining the acquiescence of the companies in halting the downward progress of the posted price in the Persian Gulf and Venezuela.

There have been instances when the companies really negotiated hard with Middle Eastern states, really resisted their demands — for instance, Iraq Petroleum Company struggled very hard in 1958–1961 with the Iraqi government over the latter's demand for a 20 percent share of IPC's oil producing properties and for the right to select the acreage IPC was committing itself to relinquish. No struggle of this kind marked the stabilization of the posted price.

If the producing companies put up any opposition to this price stabilization, it was feeble, pro forma; there was no incentive for them to resist the oil states' orders then, any more than there was for them to resist massive price increase in 1973–1974. They could simply pass the hikes on to the consumer, since they were all subject to them in equal measure.

Within five years, all the crude-exporting states in the world outside the Communist Bloc came to adhere to this stabilization and a principle was established which the companies never challenged in public: the tax-reference price on Persian Gulf (and other) oil can never drop. That is, the per-barrel revenues which the companies pay to the governments of Saudi Arabia, Kuwait, Iraq, Iran, Venezuela, and the others can never drop; they can only rise.

At any rate, since about 1950 the oil-producing states have received at least six times more, for every barrel of oil they allowed to exit from their territory, than it actually cost the companies to find that barrel, produce it, and move it out of the country. As Professor Edith Penrose has pointed out, this condition "significantly encouraged the development of new supplies, not only by existing producers but also by those users of crude who lacked adequate supplies of owned (that is, 'cost') crude and had to buy from others."[4] In other words, not only did this system allow the oil-producing states handsome revenues; it also guaranteed that these revenues would rise handsomely, thus inspiring outsiders to flock in, find more of the same resources, and develop the nations' endowments still further.

Near Easterners contend that the revenues they received — then perhaps 70 or 80 cents a barrel, now upwards of $10 — were nothing compared to the taxes charged on oil and oil products by European governments. This was true but beside the point: if the Near Easterners could only get 30 cents for a barrel now and for the foreseeable future, and they produce the oil themselves, it will still be worth their while to sell it if it only costs them 10 cents to produce it and expand production. Cost *is* a relative matter. It is scarcely worthwhile to mine gold in the United States for $35 an ounce but undoubtedly profitable in nonunion South Africa, where gold reserves are enormous and concentrated.

Now, the Near Eastern oil-exporting states are largely encumbered with masses of capital which they cannot readily absorb; so they cannot contend that the industry is shortchanging them.

But, again, they have reached this stage only recently. A generation lies between the present and the time they started to enter the oil business in a big way. In the meantime they passed through two crises which resulted in partial cutoffs of oil to the outside world, and twenty-five years of flirting with the political weapon of nationalization. Before we proceed to survey the history of the industry in each of several major states — Saudi Arabia, Iran, the poor stepsister Iraq, Kuwait, Algeria, and Libya — let us discuss these two points in time in some detail, bearing in mind the twin subjects of Near Eastern attitudes toward the oil industry and the Near Easterners' proclivity to take vindictive action against the Western consumer.

The two crises were the two earlier large-scale embargoes of Middle Eastern oil history, in 1956 and 1967. It was war with Israel which preceded both these embargoes — in fact, aggression which Israel initiated or in which it took part.

Slightly different circumstances surrounded the two embargoes. The Arabs had not developed the concept of withholding oil as a weapon for influencing the outcome of the struggle with Israel as fully in 1956 as they had by 1967, so they had less time to plan the execution of an embargo in the former instance. President Nasser of oil-poor Egypt, the most widely respected leader of Arab opinion, had only been talking of this weapon since his accession to power in 1952, and then only in vague terms; in fact, Arab states had only been exporting oil on a large scale for less than a decade.

By 1967, however, the notion of using oil embargo as an indirect weapon against Israel had taken firm root in Arab minds. Sheikh Abdullah Tariki, Saudi Arabia's former oil minister, had been broadcasting his slogan of "Arab oil for the Arabs" through his oil magazine for two years, the states of Iraq and then Kuwait had been engaged in confrontation politics with the oil companies for the better part of a decade, and President Nasser had been embroiled in the civil war in Yemen for almost five years — largely with the objective of establishing a foothold in the oil-rich Arabian peninsula.

In spite of the differences between these two points of time, however, one can argue that the Arab oil cutoff was little more severe in 1967 than in 1956: that although the Arabs had become far more aware of the power of their weapon during that decade than they had been before, they had not in general become more convinced of its utility.

The role of the Suez Canal should help illustrate this. The artery — vital, of course, for the shipment of oil from the Persian Gulf to Europe — was shut down for less than a year after the 1956 war, and for more than seven years after 1967. This was because the Israelis withdrew from the east bank of the canal in early 1957 but stayed there for six and a half years after 1967 — not withdrawing until the Egyptian army mounted a full-scale crossing to dislodge them in October, 1973.

Nonetheless, Persian Gulf oil continued to flood west after 1967. Five years later a senior Egyptian commentator on oil affairs, Mahmoud Amin, could write, in Cairo's *al-Ahram,* "It would be wrong to think that the closing of the Suez Canal would affect supply of Arab oil to Europe. We say this now because it did indeed have an effect in the past. It had a violent effect when the canal was closed for the first time, in 1956. At that time Europe, in spite of its reserves, lost 65 percent of its supply. But the effect did gradually decrease. Likewise, the canal's second closing in 1967 had an effect on Europe. But it was less severe because the petroleum industry had anticipated it and taken a number of precautions. For example, it began to build giant tankers and it began to open new oilfields west of the Suez Canal. Therefore the effect of the canal's closing in 1967 was not as severe in Europe as it had been in 1956."[5]

In fact, the events of 1956 and 1967 underlined a constant element: the oil-producing states are much less prone to cut off their oil exports than are those states, themselves poor in oil, through which much of the oil transits. Paramount in the latter category is Syria. In 1956, Syrian army units destroyed pumping stations along the pipeline from northern Iraq to the eastern Mediterranean, cutting off Iraq's main export channel for almost half a year and reducing that country's production for the year by 22 percent.

The Syrians took even sterner action in late 1966 — half a year before the 1967 war. In August, 1966, they asked Iraq Petroleum Company to renegotiate the arrangement governing the transit of the oil which the company pumped from Kirkuk and other fields in northern Iraq across the Iraqi and Syrian deserts to its terminals at Baniyas, Syria, and Tripoli, Lebanon.

Kirkuk and adjacent smaller fields accounted for 70 percent of Iraq's oil exports. The remainder of Iraq's oil, also produced by the IPC group, came to Europe the long way around the Arabian peninsula from the southern Iraqi port of Basra on the Persian Gulf. Since Kirkuk was only 300 miles from the Mediterranean by pipeline, but the sea voyage from Basra to the eastern Mediterranean took about 3,500 miles, it was far more advantageous to IPC to ship crude westward from Kirkuk than from Basra. Syria, meanwhile, was not nearly as dependent on revenues from the line as Iraq was on revenues from the oil which went through the line. Iraq had been getting about $300 million a year for its Kirkuk oil, or about ten times Syria's transit receipts.

Thus, the Syrians' position was very strong, and *The Economist's* statement at the time, that "it is always easier for a transit government to make itself unpleasant than, say, a host government, if only because there is so much at stake," was quite accurate.[6]

By that time the oil companies, as well as Near Eastern governments, had become accustomed to renegotiating contracts, but in this instance matters quickly moved beyond the talking stage. Ruling Syria at the time was a small group of extremists (some would say Maoists) from the left wing of the Arab Socialist Baath Party: Yusuf Zoayen, Ibrahim Makhus, and Nureddin al-Attasi, three doctors who had performed volunteer service in Algeria during the war of liberation against the French there, then General Salah Jadid and (in the wings) Hafez al-Asad, minister of defense.* The Arab Socialist Baath Party was also strong in Iraq, but out of power; partly underground.

---

* The party is known for short as "the Baath," or "renaissance."

Over the following three months, the negotiations between
Syria and IPC proceeded fitfully. The Syrians wanted greater transit royalties, on the argument that in 1955, when the latest transit
agreement had been reached, IPC had promised them a fifty-fifty
split of the savings it gained by shipping oil to the Mediterranean
from Kirkuk rather than from Basra via Suez. According to the
1955 accord, the Syrians were to receive 9.5 cents a barrel, or 1s.
4d. per 100 ton-miles. The Syrians now contended that this tariff
in fact represented only about one-quarter of IPC's savings. They
requested that IPC double it — then raised their request another
11 cents a barrel. This further demand for 11 cents represented a
retroactive payment dating back eleven years, to 1955. The Syrians
did not specify the total sum of this payment, but it came to between $70 and $112 million.

The company, for its part, claimed that it owed no retroactive
payments: part of the pipeline passed through Iraq, it claimed, so
Syria was not entitled to royalties for use of the entire line.

In time, the Syrians threatened to take "unilateral measures"
against the line if IPC did not comply with their demands. They
did promise that they would not shut the line down; but IPC
stood firm, so, on December 13, 1966, Syria forbade the company
to load oil at the Mediterranean terminal of Baniyas. The tanks
at Baniyas filled up; the company had to shut the line off to keep
the tanks from rupturing.

Of course, it quickly turned out that this cutoff was more harm-
ful to Iraq than to the companies. At that time, there was a serious
threat of oil surplus on the international market. The companies
with the biggest interests in IPC were also represented in the
Iranian Consortium as well (and in Kuwait Oil Company and
Aramco in some cases), and they were embroiled in a serious
running controversy with these other states, which also wanted
their exports to increase substantially.

At first, the Iraqi government placed the blame for the stoppage
squarely on IPC, and the rumor spread through Baghdad that it
would nationalize the northern fields unless the company settled
with Syria. From all accounts, this is what Syria wanted. It appears, in fact, that the Syrian authorities had fulfilled two objectives by forcing IPC to shut down the line: confronting the "West-

ern monopolies" and embarrassing the government of Iraq. In essence, they wanted to pressure the latter to change its attitude toward the Baath, if not actually to take Iraqi Baathists into its cabinet.[7]

Time passed. The Syrian government indicated that it would not up the tariff on Iraqi oil if Iraq simply nationalized the fields. But the Iraqis pulled back from nationalization, and Syria hardened its stand, refusing to accept the company's offer to go to arbitration unless the company first paid the extra royalties for 1966, which it assessed at $10.5 million, then upping its demands for immediate payment.* IPC countered with an offer to pay the $10.5 million if the Syrians would allow pumping to resume.

Though the consultant Sheikh Tariki came out in favor of the Syrian position, and the Kuwaiti government joined him, the Arab states in general maintained silence on the issue and the position of the president of Iraq, Abdel Rahman Aref, began gradually to change. This unimposing, lugubrious-looking, mild fellow, who had actually attained his position through inheritance after his brother Abdel Salaam died in a helicopter crash the preceding year, only stayed in power another year and a half after this period anyway; discredited by his successors as a traitor and a spy, he now languishes in exile in England. His lack of forceful personality notwithstanding, there was probably as much personal freedom in Iraq under his regime as at any time since 1958, and although Aref may not have been a natural leader of men, he did realize that it was vital to his country to keep exporting oil; the Syrian action probably stunned him.

In all likelihood, he decided that there was only one way to get the Syrians to allow the pumping to resume. This was by showing the world that Syria's real intention was to harm Iraq, not IPC. If a scandal were to erupt, if open strife were to develop between Syria and Iraq — two sister states — the appearance of Arab unity would be shattered and this in turn could embarrass others, pri-

---

* Makhus also offered to let the company's French parent, CFP, continue to ship its share of oil through the line, as a gesture of esteem for General de Gaulle (who had been pursuing a policy of sympathy for the Arabs in their conflict with Israel), but the French elected not to accept the offer this time.

marily Egypt's President Nasser, the unchallenged leader of Arab political thinking then. Nasser had committed himself to making the Arabs believe that their states, fragmented by the Ottoman Empire and set against one another by Western imperialism, in reality formed one indivisible nation and were destined to reunite. Aref probably thought that by showing that no one could automatically take this unity for granted and that loyalty to a larger entity implied protection from the larger entity in exchange, it would be possible to persuade other Arabs to influence Syria to reopen the line. Aref did not possess the strength or inclination to send troops into Syria; he could only hope to make it seem that anti-Syrian feeling was ripening within Iraq, as a result of the shutdown. So he proceeded to allow Iraqi citizens to speak their minds on the pipeline struggle.

Some came down hard on IPC: three ministers who favored nationalization resigned from the cabinet and Iraqi Baathists sent telegrams of support to the Syrian government. Other individuals, however, openly expressed conservative nationalist viewpoints within Iraq which did not take Arab unity for granted and were critical of Syria — and of Aref's pusillanimous stand toward Syria. The most outspoken of these persons was the president of the Iraqi Lawyers' Association, Fayek Samarrai, who proposed a scheme to replace the old pipeline through Syria with a new one from Kirkuk to southern Iraq and the Persian Gulf.

This drew fire. Syria's Premier Zoayen immediately discounted rumors that the Iraqi government was contemplating such a scheme. At graduation ceremonies at the Syrian Military Academy, one Syrian minister called for a "scorched-earth" policy of sorts: he spoke of converting IPC's pipeline facilities into pumps for bringing water up from the Euphrates River to irrigate the neighboring dry countryside, and President al-Attasi proclaimed, "What we have done thus far is only the starting signal for a war against foreign oil cartels in all Arab countries. This battle will stop at no limit until the entire resources of the Arab world become the property of the Arab people and in the service of the Arab people's interests."[8]

The protests within Iraq mounted. Samarrai and others went further, complained to President Aref that the Iraqi government had not agreed on the Syrian measures with the Syrian government in advance. An Iraqi newspaper, *Sawt al-Arab,* published this protest in the form of a memorandum which also called for public disclosure of talks between the Iraqi government and IPC — as well as for removal of restrictions on the press and the establishment of an elected parliament.

The Syrian government, from its embassy in Baghdad, upped the severity of its comments a notch: this battle was now "the battle of the Arab nation as a whole, and nobody would cast doubt on the significance of this battle — unless, of course, he be an incorrigible foreign agent, conspirator, and hireling."[9] Meantime other Iraqis, while not following Samarrai's lead, asked other questions, among them: why had the Syrians taken their stand against IPC (and Iraq) but not against Tapline, which passed through Syria also — but from Saudi Arabia? Was this to be interpreted as a Syrian campaign against Iraq, specifically?

In early February, after the line had been closed almost two months, President Aref finally paid a visit to Nasser in Egypt. He presented the leader with his government's position on the Syria-IPC controversy and asked Nasser to influence the Syrians to drop their demand that the Iraqi Baath Party be legalized. It is also likely — though there is no public record of this — that he indicated to Nasser how anti-Syrian feeling had grown in Iraq. Nasser gave Aref his backing, and called for a resumption of the oil flow through Syria. Apparently he asked the Syrians to negotiate with IPC before taking up the status of the Baath in Iraq, because Syria's ambassador to Cairo issued a statement announcing that Syria and IPC had come to agreement on resuming the oil flow.

But this was premature. The Syrian government repudiated the statement and the ambassador retracted it at once. The following day, in fact, the Syrian government came out with fierce statements against Aref and called for the formation of a "progressive front" in Iraq. The Baath international leadership in Damascus branded the *coup* which had toppled a Baath regime in Iraq in 1963 — bringing Aref's brother to the fore — a "criminal reactionary movement." Defense Minister al-Asad declared that there were no differences between the Baath Party in Syria and the "leaders of the revolution." (Some of whom he threw out, in the

November, 1970, Emendation Movement.) He reiterated that "not one drop of oil will cross Syrian territory until the people's rights are satisfied in full."

As a further riposte to the Syrians' riposte to its counterriposte, the Iraqi government then cracked down on domestic Communists. Iraqi Premier Taleb went to Damascus for more talks in late February, and Premier Zoayen responded to these, too, with a strong public statement against IPC.

Then, on February 22, on the anniversary of the defunct 1958 union between Syria and Egypt, President Nasser made a speech on the IPC pipeline controversy. He declared that he supported the rights of both the Syrian and the Iraqi governments. Abruptly, at 4 P.M. on March 2, about two and a half months after it went off, the flow of oil from Kirkuk resumed. Suddenly the crisis was over.

The settlement was cordial enough. The Syrians and IPC met just about halfway. IPC agreed to up its payments to Syria from 9.5 to 14.6 cents a barrel, retroactive to January 1, 1966, and Syria, for its part, agreed to return to IPC all the holdings it had seized during the crisis and in effect put its $75 to $112 million claim in abeyance, insisting only that it "review" IPC's transit payments over the past ten years. This payment rate remained in effect until mid-1971. More than one observer at the time remarked that Syria could have gained that much simply by negotiating.

President Nasser of Egypt was probably the key to the settlement. Once he saw that there was real danger that conflict between Syria and Iraq might flare out into the open, where the world could see it, he moved to dampen it. Certainly the imminent convening of an important oil forum, the Sixth Arab Petroleum Conference, scheduled to begin March 6 in Baghdad, was an inducement to both sides to end the quarrel. So Syria backed down from its earlier claims that its demands were nonnegotiable, and the Arab press in general called the final agreement a historic victory. Abdullah Tariki stated that Syria had "succeeded in forcing the neo-imperialist foreign monopolies, as represented by IPC, to bow to the will of the Arab nation as represented by the valiant Syrian people."[10]

One observer pointed out, "Even before the increases, the payments to Syria were regarded as perhaps the best transit fees in the world."[11]*

So the question remained: had Syria, through the cutoff, sought to punish the oil companies, or the West? Or had it striven to gain political concessions from a fellow Arab state? The mere fact that one can ask such a question casts doubt on the severity of Arab resentment against the oil industry and Arab willingness to use the oil weapon against the West.

The Syrians, in the meantime, had been engaging in other acts of militance in the region. Mostly, these were against Israel: the border between Syria and Israel had been relatively quiet for a long time, but now, in 1966 and 1967, more incidents occurred along it than in any other year since 1956. Syria's relations with Jordan deteriorated also. In late May, 1967, a truck loaded with explosives crossed from Syria into Jordan, where it blew up, killing fourteen and wounding twenty-eight. The two neighboring Arab states broke off relations — two weeks, as it turned out, before joining forces again in war.

In April, the Syrians lost some MiGs in a serious and costly dog-fight with Israelis over the Golan Heights, and in May they charged that the Israelis were massing eleven to thirteen brigades along the Syrian border, preparatory to full-scale invasion. Independent sources never verified the presence of these brigades. United Nations observers claimed not to have detected them, and the Soviet Ambassador to Israel, while relaying the charge to the Israeli government, refused an invitation to visit the border and see for himself whether or not the charge was accurate.

The Russians relayed the charge to President Nasser, though, and he elected to accept it as fact and mobilize his army. Then, under goading and taunting from the Jordanians and Syrians, partly because he had not come to Syria's aid in the April dog-fight, Nasser felt pressed to remove the United Nations buffer forces which had stood between Egypt and Israel over the past

---

* It is also worth noting that the oil press pointed out the obvious at the time — that the added 5 cents or so a barrel which the settlement entailed were significant and did weaken the competitive strength of Iraqi oil. This point will come up again in this study.

decade. The United Nations felt obligated to withdraw all its forces, including those at the entrance to the Gulf of Aqaba, if it were asked to withdraw any at all; this total departure, in turn, made Nasser feel obligated to close the Gulf of Aqaba to Israeli shipping. Although there is evidence that Nasser might eventually have reopened Aqaba, under Western pressure, the Israelis treated his action as a cause for war and mounted their attack on Egypt two weeks later, on June 5.

The Syrian regime at the time thus bears a large amount of responsibility for more than a mere tiff with an oil company; its real enemy, of course, was not IPC, or BP, or "monopolists and despots," but Israel — and opposing Arab political ideologies.

The Arab world quickly forgot whatever quarrels it had with the oil industry. Nonetheless, as a contribution to the June 5 war, most Arab states slowed down their oil production or even halted it for a while. Saudi Arabia shut down for six days, Iraq for three weeks, Kuwait for four weeks. Libya stayed off even longer.* The cutback spread; by June 10, after the war had ended, the shutdown had come to 9 million barrels a day. In Kuwait and Saudi Arabia, June production was 37 percent below the May level; in Iraq it had dropped 72 percent, in Kuwait 79 percent.

The main motive for the cutbacks was not hatred of the companies, though. The conservative exporting states of Libya, Saudi Arabia, and Kuwait shut down less out of solidarity with the states combatting Israel than out of real fear of reprisals by indigenous radicals and labor unions, under prodding from President Nasser's propaganda apparatus. *Petroleum Intelligence Weekly* wrote, "Most of the six million barrels a day shutdown in Arab countries was apparently caused by civil disorder and a desire by Arab governments to avoid the destruction of oil facilities."[12] Some demonstrations occurred in Tripoli, Libya; in Saudi Arabia's Eastern Province, about one hundred persons, including numerous Aramco employees, were arrested for disorderly conduct; workers threatened oil installations in Kuwait and refused to load oil into

---

* Kuwait did not go off completely. Since a total shutoff of oil would have meant a total cutoff of the gas produced with this oil, this would have been extremely damaging to that state, where gas is literally the country's lifeblood, as it generates the electricity and provides the energy to desalinate the water.

American tankers. However, many people overreacted to these disturbances. American oil company personnel went in droves to Wheelus Air Base, near Tripoli, in an atmosphere of panic, and were strongly encouraged, if not ordered, onto evacuation craft by the military personnel there — while many who stayed on in Tripoli saw little violence of any kind.

One indication that it was fear of hostile and militant Arabs rather than hatred of the West which motivated the conservative states was that there was a certain ambiguity and secretiveness to their actions. Saudi Arabia's oil minister was more concerned that Aramco not publish its real production figures than that it cut back its production. Libya's oil minister, who had sent the companies written orders to cut production, gave them permission to resume in time but would not commit this permission to writing. Several days after the war began, a new premier took over in Libya, Abdel Kader Badri. He put down the demonstrations, and a short time later the court, anticipating a public reaction against his tough measures, replaced him in turn with the urbane Abdel Hamid Bakkush; but the peace prevailed.

In July, Saudi Arabia tried to get around the Arab-wide embargo of the United States, Britain, and West Germany, Israel's assumed accomplices in the June war. The Egyptian press and radio denounced this attempt. So did the International Confederation of Arab Trade Unions, which stated that "the Arab nation does not consider Saudi oil as fuel for the Sixth Fleet or for British and West German planes to enable them to kill the sons of the Arab nation." The Saudis were obliged to stick to the embargo.

Another indication that the embargo was to some extent an imposed one is that other countries, less vulnerable to Nasserite pressure, did not cut back appreciably, if at all, during this period. The militant Algeria is one example. One country, Oman, even started exporting oil earlier than scheduled as a result of this war.

Then again, although Nasser prompted the Arab-wide embargo of the United States and Great Britain by accusing them of helping Israel invade Egypt on June 5, he nonetheless did not seriously interfere with American oil companies operating in Egypt. Phillips and Pan American (a Standard of Indiana subsidiary) continued to drill in Egypt during the war and directly after it. In fact Egypt's biggest field, El Morgan — a property which the government produced with Pan American — went onstream right at that time.

In the end, in spite of the growing politicization or even radicalization of the Arab world, the effects of the embargo in 1967 were hardly more severe than those in 1956. The difference was that the embargo of 1956 was not so well organized — was, in fact, occasioned more by accident and sabotage than fear.

In 1967, it was not for three months that most — but not all — of the Arab states agreed, at the Khartoum Summit Meeting, to rescind the embargo against Great Britain and the United States. In exchange for this concession, Kuwait, Libya, and Saudi Arabia agreed to give massive grants-in-aid to Egypt and Jordan, totaling 378 million dollars a year. Iraq, whose government was more hostile to the West than this conservative trio, did not really underwrite the agreement, but it was not requested to contribute to the fund either. The other three states, in turn, gained some control over the fund, by winning the right to pay in quarterly rather than annual installments.

Nasser made some other generous concessions to the conservatives as well. He unfroze perhaps $100 million worth of Saudi funds and investments in Egypt and promised King Faisal of Saudi Arabia that he would withdraw his army from Yemen. All parties to the summit conference agreed that the Arabs would unite in their political efforts to "eliminate the effects of the Israeli aggression" and would cease their internal propaganda warfare. The summit's final communiqué stated that this unification of efforts would "take place within the general framework of the political principles to which the Arab states adhere, namely: no peace with Israel; no recognition of Israel; no negotiation with Israel; insistence on the rights of the Palestinian people to their homeland."

The communiqué explained thus the apparent sacrifice of national principles which the decision to allow oil to flow again to Israel's "allies" implied: ". . . after careful study of the matter, the summit conference concluded . . . that Arab oil represents an Arab asset which could be used to strengthen the economies of those Arab states which were directly affected by the aggression, thereby enabling them to stand firm in the battle. The conference therefore decided to resume oil pumping operations *on the grounds that this is an Arab asset which can be put to use in the service of Arab aims* and in contributing toward enabling those Arab states which were subjected to aggression and a consequent loss of economic resources to stand firm in their resolve to eliminate the effects of the aggression."*

The outcome of the 1967 war, then, was that Arab oil production was stopped only for a short while — mostly to prevent its export to those states accused of having helped Israel. More important, the war concluded with a political shift advantageous to pro-Western interests in the Arab world, which gained some control over their radical and militant brethren at considerable cost. Elsewhere the communiqué "approved the proposal presented by the Kuwait government for establishing an Arab economic and social development fund."

To be sure, the events leading from the Israeli attack of June 5 to the issuance of this declaration on September 1 were complicated and riddled with disagreement and animosity. Considerable debate in the United Nations and three other conferences preceded the agreement at Khartoum. (The conferences will be familiar to students of the recent impeachment drive in America as exercises in shunting and transferring responsibility and initiative to those parties least adroit at avoiding them.)

The first of the parleys, the Foreign Ministers' Conference at Khartoum from August 2 to 5, merely ended with a decision to devote careful study to projects for economic warfare against the West. The Iraqis proposed a total denial of oil to all parties, without exception, for three months, and recommended that oil be shipped thereafter only to those countries which were deemed not to have assisted Israel in its successful aggression. This of course was a hopelessly unreasonable appeal and was undoubtedly propounded as such. Other proposals included the withdrawal of all Arab funds from American, British, and West German banks and

---

* See Appendix 5 for the full text of this communiqué. Emphasis supplied.

the "nationalization and Arabization" of all these nations' interests in the Arab world.*

The second conference, which took place in Baghdad on August 15 among economics, finance, and petroleum ministers from various Arab states, did not end conclusively either, but it marked a subtle turning point: now the Arab conferees in general started to express readiness, through their communiqué, that "those Arab oil exporting countries for whom oil constitutes the main source of revenue should meet to decide what effective and appropriate measures should be taken."[13]

As it turned out, the Arab foreign ministers met one more time, in Khartoum, to prepare the ground for the eventual summit.

The termination of the 1967 embargo was therefore a drawn-out, painful process. Many Arabs were opposed to any reconciliation with the United States and Britain and even those who had sought it felt obligated to apologize and rationalize their stand. Radio Cairo, on September 3, stated that a total embargo would have harmed the Arabs more than the West. Egypt's Minister of Economy and Foreign Trade stated that customers who would have been denied Arab oil would simply have turned to Venezuela or Iran, and anyway the embargo would have hurt friends like France and India as much as enemies. The Algerians (who had hardly cut back at all) atoned for their inaction by putting their few American guests, all small operations, under their control and nationalizing the retail outlets of Exxon and Mobil.† President Aref of Iraq crisply declared that the Arabs had agreed to end the embargo because they needed "the money to strengthen their armies and renew their military efforts against their enemies."[14] One pro-Egyptian newspaper in Lebanon summed it up: the summit resolutions were "better than nothing."

For their part, the radicals, such as the Syrian leaders, Iraqi Communists, and various trade union leaders, were crestfallen at the outcome of Khartoum. They complained that Nasser had become a moderate, that the Khartoum signatories had "weakened before the imperialist oil monopolies." In fact, the oil policies of

---

* Incidentally, even these proposals were more sweeping than those which the various producing states set forth in 1973. So was the extent of the cutback.
† The Iraqis did the same in 1973: they nationalized American oil interests, but allowed production to increase to the maximum.

the Iraqi government did harden because it passed a law, Number 97 for the year 1967, which gave all the acreage it had previously confiscated from IPC to the national oil company and effectively torpedoed a compromise agreement hammered out in the past two years. Some Arab nationalists such as Abdullah Tariki and the Egyptian editor Muhammad Hassanein Heykal, however, became somewhat better disposed toward conservative Arabs than they had been. The conservatives, they maintained, were capitalists, true — and among doctrinaire Nasserites this was almost an insult. But they were rich in funds and they were patriotic. The Arabs must not become the satellites of the Soviet Union any more than of the Western powers, said Tariki: the conservatives had balked in the past at investing money in some Arab states because they did not enjoy guarantees against expropriation. Arab socialists, Tariki wrote, had to offer such guarantees and "create a new atmosphere of trust by engaging in frank, sincere dialogue with Arab groups which are, first and last, Arab groups," in order to attract the billions of dollars which oil-rich Arabs had on tap in Western banks.

Since the 1967 war, Syria has engaged in another form of cutoff: six times it has closed its borders to commerce with Lebanon, most adamantly in May, 1973, as a protest against Lebanese government policies toward Palestinian paramilitary groups. The country hosted one other oil shutdown as well, and this turned out to be crucial. In April, 1970, a saboteur damaged Tapline, the half-million-barrel-a-day aorta which passes to the eastern Mediterranean from Saudi Arabia by way of Syria; the Syrians would not allow repairs on the line for 270 days. Like the closure of Suez three years earlier, this benefited the countries to the west, especially Libya, whose crude, coming to water just 800 miles off Italy, gained in value. The closure of Tapline helped pave the way toward oil company capitulations to Gaddafi's demands for a steep rise in prices that same year. When the Syrians finally agreed in January, 1971, to allow the line back on, the breach was repaired in twenty-seven hours.

Now Tapline and the IPC line often run below capacity, and the supertankers' share of trade, which of course received a tremendous boost from the 1967 war — tantamount to the techno-

logical spinoff which results from every war — has made the reopening of Suez somewhat irrelevant to the oil industry.

What was the lesson of the 1956 cutbacks and disturbances and
the 1967 embargo? Arabs themselves disagree on this matter. The
"extremists" — the governing group in Syria, certain trade union
leaders, various Communist party members, and many others —
considered that its specific purpose was to inflict damage on Western interests. But this does not hold for most of the others. They
believed that Israel, not the West, was the ultimate enemy, that
embargo would be fruitless unless it succeeded in driving a wedge
between Israel and its Western supporters. Nasser himself probably did not have a clear notion of the ultimate function of this
weapon. The Arabs would not have debated the subject at such
length if they had enjoyed a consensus on how to apply the
embargo.

The Egyptian petroleum analyst Mahmoud Amin obliquely
summarized this absence of an Arab-wide oil policy when he
wrote: "For the British and American companies operating in the
Arab world, their strained relations with their host governments
are a grave danger. . . . The Arab states should collectively stop
all oil shipments to Western Europe, with the exception of
friendly states like France, which has already clarified its position
vis-à-vis the Israeli aggression [by withholding arms and spare
parts from Israel] and others whose position becomes clear in the
course of the U.N. General Assembly deliberations."[15]

Oil embargoes rarely work, in either direction. Iran, under
Mosaddegh, does not seem to have made it work in 1951–1953,
and the British did not succeed in making it work against the
secessionist state of Rhodesia in the mid-sixties, either. Britain's
Prime Minister Wilson managed to keep oil from Rhodesia for a
short while, during which the Rhodesians rationed their supplies;
but in the end the United Kingdom had to pay them transit fees,
in dollars, to allow Zambian copper through to Mozambique and
the open water. From then on the Rhodesians got all the gasoline
they wanted — at $1.21 a gallon.

Few countries suffered from the Arab embargo of 1967. Several,
though, have suffered badly from the closure of Suez: the Sudan
and South Yemen, dependent on ports just to the south of the

waterway; Malta with its shipyards a short distance to the north-west; and Italy and Greece. Even the big oil states which had to contribute $378 million to Egypt and Jordan in the wake of the Khartoum Conference made up about half their pledge simply by phasing out the 6½ percent marketing discount off posted prices which they used to grant exporting companies.

Conversely, some non-Arab oil exporting states profited from the embargo: Venezuela certainly, Canada, Iran, the Soviet Union to some degree, even American states, primarily Texas and Louisiana, where output restrictions were relaxed in the summer. In the second half of 1967, the United States' oil production rose by an unprecedented million barrels a day, or about 12 percent. The Western consumers of Arab oil were in such a good position to weather the embargo that few were willing even to declare that they were confronted with an oil supply emergency — which the United States government wanted them to do, since only through an official declaration of emergency could American oil companies gain immunity from antitrust prosecution in the United States and feel free to draft cooperative supply plans.

In 1973, Arabs were much more united in their conception of the gains they could win by using the oil weapon — or, more precisely, by threatening to use it. The history of the 1973–1974 embargo, and the resulting ascendancy of American influence in the Arab world, Secretary of State Kissinger's bravura peacemaking efforts, the tumultuous reception the Egyptians gave President Nixon in June, 1974, indicate that the Arabs, in the main, did not consider the elimination of the American presence to be such a gain. Thus, the 1973 embargo was milder and better focused even than that of 1967.

Let us attempt, at this juncture, to take a somewhat closer look at specific relations between Near Eastern countries and the oil companies themselves.

5

Aramco

To me it is an appalling suggestion that you would want
to destroy this great American enterprise.
— George Parkhurst, former
Vice President and Director,
SoCal

BAHRAIN IS A SMALL ISLAND in the Persian Gulf which
lies within eyesight of Saudi Arabia's eastern coast. In the early
1930's, geologists with an aggressive American firm new to the
international industry, Standard Oil of California, drilled into
a simple domelike structure on that island, found modest oil
there, looked across the water, and saw a similar structure on the
Saudi mainland — topped, in fact, by a small village named
Dhahran, "that which is prominent," "a dome." SoCal's men
assumed oil would lie beneath Saudi territory too, and set about
acquiring a concession there.

This was in 1932. Companies had already started to develop,
and even export, oil from two major Near Eastern states, Iran

and Iraq. But British interests were dominant in both ventures. British Petroleum in fact had a 100 percent interest in southwestern Iran; it held almost 25 percent of the rights to the great Iraqi field at Kirkuk, and other British interests, minority holders of Royal Dutch/Shell, possessed another 10 percent of the Kirkuk concession. American companies, Exxon and Mobil, held only about another 25 percent of the rights to this great resource. Saudi Arabia was to become the American pride.

Aramco's history, among those of all important ventures in the Islamic East, is the easiest to grasp, since it has been the smoothest. It is fitting, therefore, to start a review of industry relations with specific Near Eastern countries in Saudi Arabia, although that land was a bit slow to come onto the stage of world oil.

Nineteen thirty-two, the year of SoCal's move toward Arabia, was also four years after two momentous and related events in oil history. One of these was signature of the Red Line agreement, the other — as we shall see shortly — the pact of Achnacarry.

The Red Line agreement, like Achnacarry, was binding on the four majors which controlled Iraq Petroleum Company, whose oil rights extended over some of the Eastern Arab portions of the defunct Ottoman Empire. The Red Line agreement went beyond their joint venture in Iraq and prohibited all signatories from extending their dominion individually into any of the remaining old Ottoman Arab lands, which lay inside a "red line" around all the Arabian peninsula except Kuwait.[1] Those participants in the Red Line pact who did not want to go into areas still up for bid within the old Ottoman Empire prevented those who did from doing so. For instance, British Petroleum could not gain permission from the others to go into Bahrain, even though Bahrain was a protectorate of BP's main shareholder, the British government. SoCal, which was not an international power at the time and held no interest in IPC, had not of course signed the pact, so it could go into Bahrain with impunity, and did.

What helped SoCal toward Saudi Arabia, then, were the checks and balances which the international majors had set up against one another. SoCal went the rest of its journey through commercial aggressiveness. It approached the British

Arabist Harry Philby, a friend of the Saudi royal family.resident in Arabia at the time, for help in getting the concession. Philby — also a close friend of some representatives with British Petroleum — vividly recorded the story of the subsequent interlude in his book *Arabian Oil Ventures*. In exchange for a job for a friend, Philby passed a tip on to a friend with BP in Iraq — offering "for your private ear a piece of information anent a territory, in which I understood from you that your folk might be mildly interested."[2] He thus had managed to provide service to three parties to the same issue, though his loyalties to SoCal soon become stronger, as that firm paid him a retainer.

It turned out that BP was not very interested in Arabia, anyway. This was in the depths of the Depression, and King Abdel Aziz's finance minister, Abdullah Suleyman, demanded an initial payment of fifty thousand pounds, gold, for the concession. Still, BP was somewhat alarmed at SoCal's progress, so decided to make a bid for Saudi Arabia regardless of the consequences to its Achnacarry obligations, and sent a high-level emissary, Brigadier Stephen Longrigg, to negotiate with Suleyman. Longrigg behaved in an overbearing manner. As Philby said, he seemed to think that the concession would fall into BP's lap anyway, and made it obvious to the Saudis that BP was "not out for full development as much as for the prevention of competition with its production in Iraq." For his part, Philby — now committed to SoCal — really did state, "It seemed that I was batting on an easier wicket than Longrigg." In the end SoCal agreed to pay the Saudis thirty thousand pounds down — as a loan — and won out, as BP would only offer five thousand.

SoCal's first efforts to develop its new concession were difficult and unrewarding. It took the company seven wells to find oil in Dammam, the promising structure it had originally spotted from Bahrain. However, by 1934 it had discovered more oil in Bahrain than it could market on its own. Therefore, it found that it had to consider bringing other partners in on its ventures.

This was where the second historic agreement of 1928, Achnacarry, came into play. This pact was essentially a market-sharing agreement which the Red Line companies, the sole international oil powers of the time, made among themselves in a Scottish grouse-hunting manor. These firms were, again, not American for the most part, the main parties to Achnacarry being British Petroleum and Royal Dutch/Shell, in addition to Exxon. Representatives of other firms, some American, also attended this meeting. The ambience at the Achnacarry manor was most genteel, to be sure, and the parties which met there observed rigid standards against the use of violence which the persons who met a generation later in upstate New York to mediate between warring sects of the Mafia did not share. The purpose of Achnacarry, however, was much the same as that of Apalachin: to put an end to a futile death-struggle between a group of firms who were accountable to almost no one but a few select competitors in a most lucrative enterprise. Prior to Achnacarry, the three main forces in the international oil industry — BP, Shell, then Exxon — had been engaged in a cutthroat price war in Asia and Europe which had exhausted all parties but destroyed none. One skirmish in the war, in India, had Exxon selling kerosene it had procured from the Soviets — who were refining it in plants they had expropriated from Shell.[3] In a word, Exxon had been trafficking in "hot oil" — an activity for which it remorselessly threatened to penalize small companies severely during the next forty years.

Now the discovery of large reserves in Bahrain posed another problem for this band, and its members courted SoCal royally for its fortune. "SoCal spurned the early advances of StanVac, Exxon, Mobil and the IPC group," said a Justice Department attorney, Barbara Svedberg, recording the subsequent ruttings of the Achnacarry participants, "but succumbed to the wooing of Texaco, which offered an outlet through its five wholly owned marketing subsidiaries in the Far East. The marriage took place in 1936."[4] SoCal let Texaco into both Bahrain and Saudi Arabia as a half-partner, in exchange for half its spouse's Eastern marketing outlets, and rechristened the Saudi enterprise Aramco. Almost everywhere else, the two firms named their joint venture Caltex.

Since Texaco already was a member, of sorts, in the extended Achnacarry family, "StanVac, the losing suitor, was not too dismayed by the merger" (again, in the words of Mrs. Svedberg).

This union indirectly gave the established majors control over SoCal's production. The newcomer was being co-opted into the system.

A decade later, with the end of World War II, SoCal and Texaco had begun to learn that Aramco's resources were massive, although the venture was producing at a low rate. Since the two firms had only limited outlets and capital, and were in fact under intense pressure from the Saudi government to expand, they had to consider whether to let the former spurned suitors from Achnacarry, Exxon, and Mobil into Arabia as well, to help expand production and market it. At that time, as Mrs. Svedberg narrates, there was a strong debate within SoCal whether or not to sell part of the concession to Exxon. Proponents of the merger could point out that SoCal, with its limited, vulnerable markets, could not have stood a fierce price war in Europe or Asia, and would have been hard pressed to ship Arabian crude to its big markets on the West Coast of America in the small, inefficient tankers prevalent then. Those opposed to the merger stated that SoCal could raise capital by selling oil to thirsty American companies with strong markets anyway, and retain their independence. To this day a rumor about the venerable gray halls of SoCal has it that those in favor of the merger also possessed shares in both Exxon and SoCal, in the manner of the Rockefeller family.

Exxon and Mobil faced extreme pressure from their partners in Iraq Petroleum Company — especially the French firm CFP — to adhere to the Red Line agreement and stay out of Saudi Arabia. It took Exxon and Mobil seven years to work free of this restriction, and they did so only by threatening to take the matter to court on grounds that the agreement violated American antitrust law: this would have exposed the secret agreement.

The two American giants also compensated, in part, for their abandonment of the Red Line agreement by signing large contracts to purchase Kuwait crude from BP and by supporting CFP's right to lift more oil from Iraq than the IPC agreement had previously enabled it to. This latter concession hardly mollified the French, though; they had also been demanding entry into Aramco since the end of the war, and, as we shall see in Chapter 10, they never forgave Exxon and Mobil for abandoning the Red Line.

In the end, Exxon and Mobil were let into Aramco, for 30 and
10 percent, respectively, in exchange for a total consideration of
about $105 million. In return, they agreed to let Caltex's share
of the market east of Suez — in accordance with the Achnacarry
agreement — expand from the 10 percent the Achnacarry participants had granted them in 1936 (in exchange for a pledge to
keep Aramco production down), to 33⅓ percent by 1966.[5] As
the Federal Trade Commission staff stated in their report *The
International Petroleum Cartel,* Exxon and Mobil "followed the
Red Line agreement for almost twenty years without making any
serious objections, but when they wished to obtain an interest
in Aramco, they described the agreement as one 'in restraint of
trade and contrary to public policy and void and unenforceable
in law.' "[6]

From the vantage point of the final quarter of the twentieth
century, it should seem strange that for a long time — over a
decade following this accommodation — Aramco actually grew
more slowly than its promise warranted, but such was the case.
In fact, Aramco expanded far more slowly, in many years during
the period between 1945 and 1965, than Kuwait, Iran, or Iraq.*
This slow development was due partly to politics and partly
to the offtake policies of the two newcomers, especially the
crude-rich Exxon. In 1947 Exxon and Mobil did not want to lift
much from Saudi Arabia. SoCal and Texaco did, and thought
that since they had a majority of the shares in Aramco, they
could overlift and get a lower offtake price from Aramco for
doing so — as we have seen in Chapter 2. Then Exxon ordered
them to raise their posting for Arabian Light to the world market
price; otherwise, it threatened, it would sue them for a breach of
fiduciary responsibility. They fought back, knowing that a low
price for Arabian oil would disastrously affect Exxon's sales of
Venezuelan crude on the East Coast of the United States — and
even in Europe, where Exxon controlled one-third of the market.
So Exxon and Mobil intensified their pressure. They stopped
lifting products from the Ras Tanura refinery and very nearly

* Appendix 1 gives annual production figures for these countries between
1945 and 1973.

compelled Aramco to shut this facility down — at a time of world oil shortage.

In the end, they won their campaign. By mid-1948 the price went up drastically, and the parents then consolidated their understanding that no party would lose if it failed to take as much as its share of the crude exported (though Exxon and Mobil did agree to "increase" their purchases from Aramco). By this system, Aramco, the profit-making concern, would pay dividends to all parties on the basis of their equity in the concession no matter how much oil any party took. Thus, the only way a party could really profit by overlifting would be by cutting price. (Which is what the parties did, for a while.)

Illustrative of the strong pressures against the expansion of Aramco just after the war was the story of James McPherson, Aramco's general manager at the time. McPherson, a former SoCal man, took personal pride in developing Aramco rapidly and smoothly, but he adopted several measures which irked the directors of the enlarged company. He redesigned the company's structure; the Aramco board vetoed his reorganization. He wanted to expand exploration and wildcatting activities, but the board cut back on them. Through his own initiative, he reached agreement with the Saudi government on a potentially thorny issue — the dollar value of the gold which Aramco was paying Saudi Arabia as royalties — and the Aramco board then vetoed this agreement only to be compelled, later, to accede to a more costly one. Aramco moved its United States headquarters from SoCal's home base, in San Francisco, to New York, which was home to the other three partners.

McPherson, the old hand, finally left Aramco in disappointment, sending ornate letters of farewell to King Abdel Aziz and the senior Saudi officials concerned with Aramco's operations. His resignation also incurred the displeasure of the Aramco directors, who tried to summon him before the board to explain himself.

He refused, and went instead to work for American Independent, a much smaller operation producing viscous crude from the Eocene formation up north in the Neutral Zone, between Saudi Arabia and Kuwait. Later, in the early 1950's, Mc-

Pherson explained to Abdullah Tariki, then Saudi director of petroleum and minerals (and to Frank Hendryx, Tariki's legal advisor), how Aramco really calculated its tax obligations to the Saudi government. This caused quite a furore in its day because, unbeknownst to the Saudis, Aramco had been calculating tax on realized, rather than the much higher posted, prices. An independent accounting firm would vouch that Aramco had averaged out all its figures properly, but would not show the specific figures to the Saudi authorities. When Tariki learned of this practice he went before the Saudi public at once with the claim that he had caught Aramco cheating the Arab people of $17 million — and Aramco settled.

Sheikh Abdullah, holder of the Venezuelan Order of Francisco de Miranda, First Class, and many other honors and accolades, was, in fact, another major cause for Aramco's slow development during the fifties. As noted on earlier pages, he was a contentious nationalist, hostile to Western capital, embittered by experiences as an engineering student in Texas and frustrated in later employment with Aramco. The Aramco directors never knew where their enterprise stood with this man and feared the worst from him.

Tariki was a protégé of Abdullah Suleyman, grand old man of Saudi finance, signatory to the 1933 agreement with SoCal, and minister of finance through the 1940's and 1950's. Suleyman also had a reputation for parsimony and contentiousness,* and the two men filled a sort of oil policy vacuum which opened during the last days of Abdel Aziz and the reign of his son and successor Saud. The revelation that Aramco had shortchanged the Saudi government on taxes was not the only time Tariki caught his guest cutting fiscal corners. In 1961 he mounted a claim for one-half of the money Aramco's parents had been saving for a decade by pumping oil to Lebanon through Tapline rather than sending it around the Arabian peninsula by tanker (a claim which should strike the reader as familiar, from the one Syria presented about five years later). Aramco's parents, for their part, did not want to

---

* For instance, the former oilman Ambassador George McGhee, in his testimony before the Church Subcommittee, indicated that Suleyman was constantly seeking to expropriate the concession.

give Saudi Arabia any share of the money they saved from Tapline's operations outside the borders of Saudi Arabia.

Into this claim Tariki interjected another complaint: Tapline was too short. That is, the section within Saudi Arabia, on which the government collected transit fees, was too short: it did not really begin, Tariki contended, at the far northern town of Qaisuma, as Aramco said it did, but at Abqaiq, 314.7 miles up the line. Therefore, he concluded, Saudi Arabia was also entitled to transit fees for the use of this additional 314.7 miles of line.

Aramco's legal staff had little difficulty demonstrating that some of the oil that passed between Qaisuma and Abqaiq flowed south, away from the Mediterranean — so how could one call that stretch Tapline? — but the larger argument took several years to settle and points up another strategy which the oil companies often use. This writer has heard that at one point the Aramco parents could have settled the dispute over Tapline fees for about $50 million, but elected to stall, investing this sum outside Arabia and earning a return of 30 to 40 percent per year on it, and actually saved by settling for $125 million several years later.

Tariki forced many issues with Aramco, raised many complaints about its policies, tried to get it to industrialize Saudi Arabia, and attempted to turn it into a Saudi corporation (which its parents refused to do, since it had to be at least 40 percent American-owned in order for them to qualify for the 85 percent dividend exclusion allowed by the United States government).

In December, 1960, King Saud elevated Tariki to minister of petroleum and natural resources. Thanks very largely to Tariki's militance, the Saudi delegation was the most outspoken participant in the first two Arab Petroleum Congresses, in 1959 and 1960, odd as that may seem now. Some of the sheikh's rhetoric from those days is memorable. One subject which used to obsess him was the flaring of natural gas. Although there were strong economic reasons why Aramco had to burn off most of the gas it produced with the oil (reasons which also saved money for the Saudi government, because of the tax structure), Tariki could never reconcile himself to this practice, and once declared, after one Arab petroleum congress, "Go to the Gulf and see this crime of

waste making the night sky red. Hear the roar by day — the burning of the blood of the Arabs."[7]

However, Tariki's star descended in time. He did not head the
Saudi delegation to the Third Arab Congress, because the Saudi
government was trying to improve its relations with the West,
especially America. Egypt's President Nasser was directing a campaign against the "reactionaries" of the Arab world at that time,
as a reaction to his own recent bitter disappointment, the dissolu-
tion of his union with Syria — and Saud, as the paramount "reactionary," needed help in outflanking the Egyptian *rayyes*.[8*]

Then, in 1964, after the Saudi government had come close to
bankruptcy, King Saud abdicated. His brother Faisal, who followed him, sent Tariki into exile. For some years afterwards, Tariki dispensed advice to other Arab states, published his oil magazine in Beirut, and called from numerous rostra for the nationalization of foreign, especially American, oil interests. These activities could not have compensated him for the loss of the Oil
Ministry, but many of his ideas bore fruit sooner or later.

There is another, less political explanation for Aramco's slow
growth in the 1950's, and its sudden development after the departure of Tariki.

When Aramco became a four-company partnership in 1947, and
for over a decade afterward, it became financially burdensome, as
noted earlier, for any partner to lift more than its equity share of
oil from Saudi Arabia because the partner had to relinquish 70
percent of Aramco's profit on this sale to the other three partners
(or 90 percent, in the case of Mobil). A company which did not
take even as much of the share of the total oil lifted as it was entitled to take would still receive an equity share of its profits on
all exports anyway. Therefore, no partner enjoyed an incentive
to expand its exports of oil generously from Saudi Arabia.

In 1959 this changed. The full reason why it changed is not
publicly known to this day, and one can only speculate on it.
Across the gulf from Aramco, the Iranian Consortium had been
expanding at a rapid, scheduled rate for three years. In 1957, the
Consortium ceased to adhere to this scheduled growth and agreed

---

* "Rayyes" — "chief," "boss" — is Egyptian argot for the classical Arabic "Ra' is."

only to expand thereafter at a rate which "would reasonably reflect the trend of supply and demand for Middle East crude oil."[9] This, of course, is a hollow, virtually meaningless pledge: the Consortium, if it so desired, could slow its expansion almost to zero, and the Iranian government would be virtually powerless, under normal conditions, to accuse it of reneging on its contract.

However, the four American majors which in concert owned 100 percent of Aramco held only 28 percent of the shares of the Consortium, so they did not control production from the Iranian concession. Furthermore, Mobil, Aramco's junior member, was buying oil from British Petroleum in Kuwait and Iran at a better price than Aramco would give it for overlifting in Saudi Arabia. The parents of the Saudi venture — perhaps under Tariki's prodding — looked around the gulf and saw that production was growing faster in Iran and Kuwait than in Saudi Arabia. They thus set about devising a system which made it more advantageous for them to lift surplus oil from their common venture in Aramco. Up to that time, it had made little difference where one overlifted: one still paid for the excess at the posted price, which was prohibitive. But in 1959, the Aramco parents agreed to reduce their penalty by half. Thenceforth, any party which lifted more than its entitlement would only have to pay *one-half* the difference between actual cost and posted price.[10]

In oil jargon, this is known, understandably, as "the halfway price." It came, in the late 1950's, to about 46 cents a barrel. In Iran, however, one still had to pay the full posted price, or a penalty of 98 cents a barrel — *plus* the ten-cent override to BP — for overlifting. Suppose a company producing in both Iran and Saudi Arabia wanted to lift an additional 50,000 barrels a day from the Persian Gulf; if it elected to take this increase from Saudi Arabia rather than Iran, it would save, at a premium of $1.08 less 46 cents a barrel, or 62 cents, a total of $31,000 a day, or over $11 million a year — so it just could not afford to lift the excess from Iran.

Thus, beginning in 1959, Aramco encouraged its partners to increase production at rates which members of the Iranian Consortium would consider prohibitive.*

* See Appendix 7 for details of the liftings and dividends of Aramco parent companies from 1963 to 1973.

When Messrs. Page and Parkhurst stated before the Church Subcommittee in March, 1974, that they had not really wanted to go into Iran, that it was a money-losing venture for them — that they went in only from patriotic duty, to keep Iran from going behind the Iron Curtain — they related the true history of matters backward. Iran was only slightly less profitable than Saudi Arabia. It was just outside the full control of their companies. Therefore the American companies *made* Saudi Arabia more profitable than Iran, for themselves.

In the mid-1960's, the Consortium caught up with Aramco and reduced the penalty for overlifting to a halfway price, also under pressure from the host government, and one or more partners. However, the Consortium kept this allowance within narrow limits: 15 percent above a production quota, known as the APQ (on which more later). Aramco, meanwhile, had gone to a quarterway system. This made it even more worthwhile for Aramco's partners to export their surplus requirements from Saudi Arabia, rather than elsewhere, because the firm now reduced the penalty from 42 cents to 15 cents a barrel, or one quarter the difference between cost and posted price (which also had dropped).

In fact, Aramco's penalty was even less stringent than quarterway, because, although the overlifter in Saudi Arabia had to pay 15 cents or so to its partners, it also got a rebate of about 5 cents on the capital investment it would have to make to install the capacity which would enable it to produce each extra barrel. Therefore the penalty dropped to about 10 cents, or about fifthway. The table on page 115 compares the Aramco charges for underlifting and overlifting as of the late 1960's, as well as the various allowances Saudi Arabia granted Aramco in keeping with OPEC-wide agreements, for Arabian Light.

Around 1967, when Iran went halfway, a Consortium member leaked the new Aramco arrangement to the Shah of Iran; the Shah went to the Consortium in anger and demanded a similar accommodation for his country. So the Consortium, in 1968, also dropped its overlifting penalty to a quarterway price, but again, within a narrow margin — including only the difference between what the Consortium as a whole had allowed that company to lift beforehand and its share of the Consortium's actual capacity.

	Underlifting	Overlifting
Posted price	$1.800	$1.800
OPEC marketing allowance	.005	.005
OPEC discount	.099	.099
(5½% off posting)		
Gravity adjustment	.023	.023
OPEC tax price	1.673	1.673
Operating costs	.046	.046
Depreciation and amortization	.036	.036
Royalty on posted price	.225	.225
Tax (½ of tax price less costs and royalty)	.692	.692
Overlift penalty	.000	.151
Capital investment charges	.07	.021
Grand total	$1.07	$1.173

It would have to pay the full posting for anything above the latter volume.

Aramco observed no such limit and in fact two years later it lowered the penalty even further, to eighthway. Like Zeno's hare, Aramco was, by stages, halving the distance toward a specific goal line — that where a company would pay no penalty at all for taking more than its share of production. Approaching it rapidly, that is, without ever quite reaching it.

Meantime, in Iran, and also Iraq, Abu Dhabi, and Qatar, the penalty for overlifting remained far more stringent. Only in Kuwait was there no penalty — but Kuwait, with a population of only about 400,000 souls, was ashamed to let its neighbors watch it expand production at their expense and enrich itself egregiously, so it did not pressure Gulf or BP to overlift.

This shift of profitability toward Aramco had an only gradual effect. However, development in Saudi Arabia during the postwar generation was smooth, disturbed only by a few minor shutdowns and a severe workers' strike in 1956. In this period, the nation's oil exports rose from 50,000 barrels a day in 1945 to over 8 million a day in 1974. Saudi production increased every single year during this period. Aramco built its major installation Tapline to transport half a million barrels of oil a day across a thousand miles of desert from the gulf to the eastern Mediterranean. It built and maintains a 400,000-barrel-a-day refinery, one of the world's largest, at the Ras Tanura terminal on the gulf, which is also the biggest and probably most magnificent oil-handling port in the world.

The company is a marvelous instrument for dispensing crude oil and products, in almost any combination. Sometimes it drops a full range of products into crude oil to allow customers to import them into a country of destination at lower tax. Then, when the Ras Tanura refinery produces a product for which demand is slight — such as naphtha — Aramco simply reinjects it into the ground until another day. It was a major supplier of products to the United States military for thirty years, meeting many of the nation's needs in Viet Nam. It was also an excellent arbiter between its parent companies, developing an intricate system for scheduling tanker loadings for each partner, always planning three years ahead yet flexible enough to fluctuate month by month, penalizing the dilatory offlifters by deducting from their future entitlements, rewarding those who took all they asked for by guaranteeing them the right to take 7 percent more the following year, regardless of circumstances short of war or insurrection.

No one can dispute that Aramco has done a lot to provide material prosperity, health, and welfare for the hundreds of thousands of Saudis, Yemenis, Goanese, Californians, Palestinians, and Pakistanis who worked in the Eastern Province of Arabia. It has nurtured a class of Saudi entrepreneurs and contractors and has contributed most extensively to the nation's education. A recent study shows that over 20 percent of the top civil servants in Saudi Arabia have received a Western education, that fourteen ministers and deputy ministers have received advanced degrees in America, and that half the top officials in the major agencies are American-educated.[11] For example, the petroleum minister, Ahmad Yamani, studied at NYU and Harvard; Abdelhady Taher, head of the Petroleum and Mineral Organization, received a doctorate from the University of California; and the head of the planning organization, Hisham Nazer, has an advanced degree from USC.

Aramco knows as much as any oil company in the Near East about the environment it works in. It has the oil industry's best Arab affairs organization — indeed, the only one worth mentioning. Although the quality of this organization may have been declining in recent years, Aramco still spent almost $5 million on government and public relations in 1972. Aramco's staff monitors the daily Saudi and other Arab press and radio broadcasts, closely follows political and economic developments in the Arab world, and employs a large body of Americans schooled in Arabic along with numerous highly trained Arabs.

It has performed meticulous and exhaustive geological, geographical, anthropological, cultural, economic, and linguistic studies of the Arabian peninsula; Arabia, once one of the most obscure areas of the world, is now one of the best-charted. The company produces substantial periodicals and broadcasts and has subsidized the publication of really important works which would never have reached the general public otherwise, such as Harry Philby's memoirs and travel accounts and the English translation of Hans Wehr's German-Arabic dictionary, the only substantial lexicon of modern written Arabic. Its magazine *Aramco World* produces some of the best photography and reproduction of Middle Eastern art, architecture, and calligraphy obtainable anywhere.

Aramco is highly attuned to developments and trends in its environment and is hardly ever surprised by events within Saudi Arabia. This explains why Arabs who have been associated with Aramco generally hold the company in high esteem, even if they are unhappy with America or its policies. It also casts genuine doubt on the common belief that Aramco was not prepared for, was not expecting, and did not easily weather the embargo of October, 1973.

Much remains to come to light on the subject of the 1973 Arab embargo, and Arabia's role in it, but one point is immediately relevant. Every year, Aramco parents convey their respective forecasts of crude oil requirements for the coming year to the company's New York headquarters, which totals up these forecasts, gains the concurrence of all partners to this total, then sets it up as the export target for the following year. This target is usually off the following year's actual exports by one percent or less. In

1973, the year of severe embargo, Aramco's parents nominated liftings of 7.3 million barrels a day; in the end they actually lifted 7.33 million barrels a day. So, despite the embargo, Aramco's production was 20 percent greater than that of the preceding year and its parents were off forecast by four-tenths of one percent.[12]

This point, in turn, has its relevance for one other feature of Aramco's recent history which is of interest here — the general economics of oil production in the Near East.

Saudi Arabia's oil installations, viewed from a distance, are not much different from those in other big Middle Eastern oil states: silvery spheroids with lazy swirls of staircase, long red sausage-tanks, smokestacks, oil lines arranged in parallel like cattleguards — neater perhaps than many in Libya, where they lie haphazardly about like thick black hoses at a catastrophic flash fire. And, in fact, Saudi Arabia's fields are nothing very special by Near Eastern standards, ranging in much the same progression of immensity as those in Iran, Iraq, Kuwait, or Abu Dhabi. There is one exception: the leviathan Ghawar, a unique natural creation, an Everest or Lake Baikal of its kind.

Saudi Arabia is the gift of Ghawar. This accumulation stands out no matter how one looks at it, even on regional economic maps, as a natural wonder. The Persian Gulf Geosyncline plays host to numerous fields which are 20 miles long or so and several miles wide, but Ghawar — of an almost rectangular solidity, shaped like the island of Manhattan but many times larger — is 140 miles long and, except at the beveled southern end and its python-headed northern extension, varies from 13 to 20 miles in width. It is in reality not one but five fields, all, by fluke, interconnected. (Ranging from north to south, these fields, or areas, are named Ain Dar, Shedgum, Uthmaniya, Hawiya, and Haradh; the immense Abqaiq field, only ten miles from Shedgum, is nearly a sixth section.) Furthermore, Ghawar's oil-bearing stratum, a 260-foot section of the Arab D Zone, is remarkably continuous. Hardly a fault or obstruction blemishes its pay; plentiful gas under high pressure used to drive the oil, and the voids between the grains of sand which constitute the pay are so large and consis-

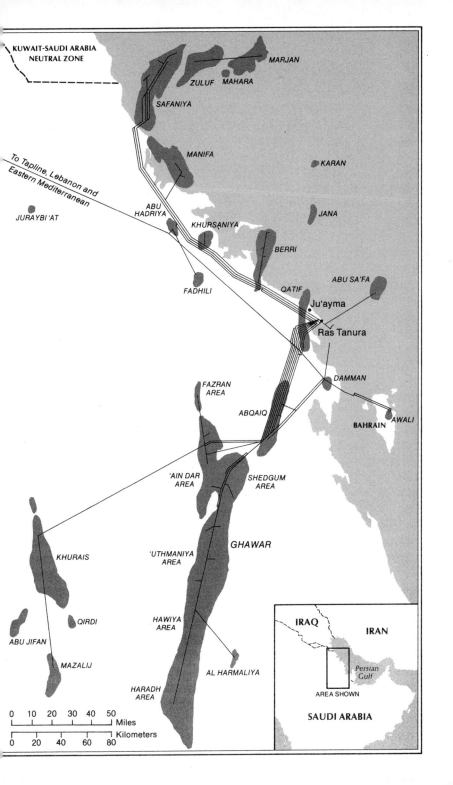

KUWAIT-SAUDI ARABIA
NEUTRAL ZONE

MARJAN

ZULUF MAHARA

SAFANIYA

MANIFA

KARAN

To Tapline, Lebanon and
Eastern Mediterranean

JURAYBI 'AT

ABU
HADRIYA

KHURSANIYA

JANA

BERRI

FADHILI

QATIF

ABU SA'FA

Ju'ayma

Ras Tanura

DAMMAN

FAZRAN
AREA

ABQAIQ

BAHRAIN AWALI

'AIN DAR
AREA

SHEDGUM
AREA

KHURAIS

'UTHMANIYA
AREA

GHAWAR

QIRDI

ABU JIFAN

HAWIYA
AREA

MAZALIJ

AL HARMALIYA

HARADH
AREA

0	10	20	30	40	50	
						Miles

0	20	40	60	80	
					Kilometers

IRAQ

IRAN

Persian
Gulf

AREA SHOWN

SAUDI ARABIA

tent that oil flows through it virtually without effort, almost like air through a harmonica.

When Howard Page told Senator Church's Subcommittee that "Aramco is not something to lose," he was talking specifically of this field; Saudi Arabia has established nothing else that is comparable, not even the other big fields of Abqaiq, Safaniya, Qatif, or Berri — accumulations which are about as big as a dozen others in neighboring countries. Had the Lord in His infinite wisdom placed Ghawar in Egypt, peace might have descended on the Near East a long time ago.

The existence of Ghawar, which, although Aramco has been producing from it for over twenty-five years, still contains perhaps 90 billion barrels of oil, as much as has ever been consumed in the United States, is another reason why the parent companies of Aramco have favored Saudi Arabia above all other oil nations in their long-range planning and short-term production increases. These four companies, as it is, comprise the bulk of the international oil industry.

Aramco's investment policies are as tight as the Iranian Consortium's. The evidence shows that if it costs more than $200 per daily barrel to drill a well in Iran, put it on production, and get its oil onto a tanker, the Consortium would just as soon not develop it. The figure is about the same in Saudi Arabia (though, as we have seen, it will be surpassed in the near future). A good many prospects have remained undeveloped in Saudi Arabia although they would be considered major, even giant, fields in North America.* There are some areas in its concession where Aramco has never drilled at all, in spite of their excellent promise: one thinks of broad areas in the great sand sea to the south, the Rub' al-Khali or Empty Quarter, and of such prospects as the Sanaam Axis, an extension of Qatar's great Dukhan field. (At this writing, Saudi Arabia reached a border settlement with its neighbor Abu Dhabi, acquiring a land corridor to the sea by way of Sanaam — so Aramco has probably begun drilling into this axis and developing Shayba.)

---

* Among the discoveries which Aramco has made but not developed, or developed only with reluctance, one may name Juraybi'at, Marjan, Zuluf, Shayba (with reserves of at least four billion barrels), Khurais/Mazalij (which some consider almost as promising as Ghawar), al-Harmaliya, Karan, and Jana.

Meanwhile, the expansion of other fields in Saudi Arabia, not just Ghawar but also Abqaiq, Berri, and Abu Sa'fa, has occurred at a breathtaking rate. Oil development in the Iranian Consortium has always followed a conservative British system, because British Petroleum's engineering practices have always dominated there, even after it was squeezed out of Iran for good as a majority participant in the operation. When the Iranian Consortium says that its fields have a maximum productive potential of 8 million barrels a day, it means that its fields could produce for years at a rate of 9 or even 10 million barrels a day. But the American venture Aramco, in announcing that its properties could easily put out 20 million barrels per day, was placing them in jeopardy by running them at 8. Furthermore, in the Consortium, a field goes "on probation" — on production test — for a minimum of one year until the company's technical staff decides that it is able to produce at a sustained rate; Aramco has not always waited so long to put all its fields onstream, as the tables in Appendices 3 and 4 show. Aramco's Zuluf, for instance, went on at a high rate immediately.

Why this difference in approach? Why should Aramco develop its fields — and only some of them, at that — so rapidly?

First, again, it costs Aramco much less to develop some properties than others. Like all oil enterprises in the Near East, it seems as if a certain principle of concentric circles of profitability has guided Aramco in this endeavor. One could envision a series of concentric arcs radiating outward from the company's export terminal at Ras Tanura. Assuming that all other costs were roughly equal, that it cost about the same to drill wells in most fields onshore, one could also assume that those fields which lay within the circles closest to Ras Tanura would be the cheapest to develop, those farthest away the most expensive. Naturally, this is because it would be more expensive to bring oil to terminal the more distant the field was — one would have to build extra pipelines, install extra pumps, establish further outlying communities.

Were one to draw such concentric circles radiating outward from Ras Tanura, the first circle would cut through Qatif and Dammam (a field of little current importance); the second through Abqaiq and Abu Sa'fa; the third through Berri; the fourth through Khursaniya, Ain Dar, and Shedgum in north

Ghawar, and a couple of minor properties; the fifth through Manifa and Uthmaniya in central Ghawar; then, on the outside, Safaniya, Khurais, Zuluf, Marjan, Shayba, Sanaam, and southern Ghawar (Hawiya and Haradh). And, as it turns out, Aramco has been developing these properties in almost exactly this order of priority. It has been concentrating its production in the fields closest to Ras Tanura, which are the cheapest. There is one exception, the far northern Safaniya field. This is virtually Aramco's only reservoir of heavy oil, which is in great demand in Europe and Japan for its high proportion of fuel oil; furthermore, since this field has a natural water drive, it has been cheap to expand the production facilities there.[13]

A decade or so ago, Aramco was planning to expand its production of a specific type of crude, "Arabian Medium." It faced three main alternatives in this endeavor: the first was to expand at Khursaniya, whose oil had a low sulphur content. Khursaniya offered the cheapest option, since the initial facilities there cost about $63 per daily barrel.[14] Second was to expand at the more distant and costly Manifa, and third was to introduce a third field, Qatif, and blend its crude with that from Manifa.

Qatif, being very close to Ras Tanura, was the cheapest property to develop in Saudi Arabia at that time, at $40 per daily barrel — with the exception of Abqaiq, a touch farther from Ras Tanura but also a shade shallower and more prolific. Qatif crude was of high enough quality so that, when mixed with the "sour" Manifa, it could provide customers with an adequate substitute for Khursaniya. For Khursaniya had one drawback: Aramco computer studies determined that its reservoir pressure showed a steep decline rate, so it was going to require greater investment in the future.[15]

If the Sierra Club had been running Aramco, it would have let up on Khursaniya for this reason and invested in the more expensive but technically sounder measure of developing the Qatif-Manifa blend. But, since the cheapest option was obviously to exploit Khursaniya, Aramco proceeded to run that property for all it was worth. And the field quickly developed a pressure decline. Production from Khursaniya dropped sharply — from 120,000 barrels a day in 1966 to 30,000 barrels a day in 1968 (see Appendix 4). Then Aramco turned to Manifa, in conjunction with

Qatif, after it had exhausted the cheapest possibility. Then, in turn, with reluctance, it invested in water injection facilities for Khursaniya and brought that field back to its original level by 1972.

Then, in the early 1970's, Aramco turned to Berri; it developed this prospect, along with Ghawar and Abqaiq, to the virtual exclusion of all other prospects. In 1972, for example, Aramco added one million barrels to its capacity. Of this increase, 550,000 barrels a day were in Ghawar, 300,000 in Berri, and 150,000 in Abqaiq. The firm did not expand its other properties at all.[16] These three fields, which had accounted for 75 percent of Aramco's actual increase in production in 1971, accounted for 93 percent of the increase in 1972 and virtually all of it in the first half of 1973.

Berri, Ghawar, and Abqaiq are very big fields, endowed with great potential; especially Ghawar, of course. There could be no risks to opening them full throttle in the short run. For a few years, the company could keep its investments down to an absolute minimum by developing them to the exclusion of other prospects — freeing its parents to invest capital elsewhere, at even higher rates of return than Saudi Arabia offered.

But this policy would be risky over the long range. The main problem lay with the maintenance of pressure in these three fields. This is because they lack a "water drive" — a large body of water under high pressure, within the zones themselves, which can force the overlying oil up through the zones evenly as it is removed and can sustain pressure in the fields.

This deficiency poses potential dangers because the oil also contains a great deal of gas, and, as it loses its pressure, the oil will start "coning" gas — releasing gas within the zone as it flows toward the well bore. Once this has started to happen, the oil is said to have "reached the bubble point" and the well has started "going to gas": in a word, is turning useless. Naturally, the faster oil is produced, the faster pressure will drop; if this keeps up, eventually no oil will rise into the well at all.

The only materials which it is feasible to inject into oil zones to prevent such precipitous and undesirable pressure drops are natural gas and water. Water, being uncompressible, is a far superior medium; it can bolster pressure much more effectively. Even then, in the case of Abqaiq, Ghawar, and Berri, it is not enough simply to inject a volume of water equivalent to the oil taken out, to maintain pressure. This is because the oil "shrinks" as it comes to the surface and releases gas. Engineers with Aramco and its parents estimate that it is necessary to inject as much as one and a half barrels of water to compensate for each barrel of oil extracted from Abqaiq, Ghawar, and Berri because a barrel and a half of oil in the ground will diminish in volume to one barrel at the surface. Thus, for instance, if Aramco were producing 5 million barrels of oil a day from northern Ghawar, it would have to inject at least seven and a half million barrels of water a day into that area to maintain pressure there.

Two factors complicate the procedure of maintaining pressure in these fields even further. First, the companies which buy oil from Aramco's parents demand that it contain very little salt — until recently, no more than four pounds per thousand barrels. This is because an excess of salt in the oil will corrode refinery pipes and vessels. However, since Saudi Arabia is a massive parched land with no rivers, and its people need every drop of decent water they can get for their own purposes, the water injected into the fields must be worthless for residential or agricultural use — hence very saline. There is one major source of low-grade water in northern Arabia, the Wasia zone, which is shallower than the oil zones and under very high pressure. For over a decade Aramco has been injecting Wasia water into Ghawar and Abqaiq either by letting it flow to the surface through artesian wells, or by "dump-flooding" it — that is, letting it flow directly down into the oil zones without coming to the surface first. (To the south, the Wasia disappears, or "pinches out," so, for the Uthmaniya, Hawiya, and Haradh areas of Ghawar, Aramco must use water from a deeper, saltier and less prolific zone, the Biyadh aquifer.)

Second, Aramco must insure that the water not produce large volumes of sand. This is hard to do, since the Wasia consists largely of unconsolidated sand and, because Aramco usually completes its Wasia water wells "barefoot" — that is, without protective screens or pipe in the producing zones — in order to save money and avoid obstructing the flowing pressure of these wells, Wasia water inevitably flushes sand out with it on its rush to the surface or the oil zone. However, the sand can pit, corrode and destroy the injection machinery at the surface and block the pore spaces in the oil zone — effectively sealing it off.

So, in order to keep producing from its best fields, Aramco has had vigilantly to monitor the salt production of the oil and the sand production of the water, and, if either undesirable condition gets out of hand, face the dilemma of saving money by failing to correct it or taking costly and elaborate steps to reduce it.

Aramco seems to have opted for the former alternative, starting sometime in 1971. Obsessed with cost consciousness, it lagged in its water support program. However, it resolutely expanded production. Problems built up to a head — then broke out in the open on January 11, 1974, when the investigative journalist Jack Anderson published a column, syndicated in over 200 newspapers throughout America, which asserted, "The final lifting of the Arab oil embargo, according to secret reports from the Saudi Arabian fields, won't bring forth the promised gush of oil."[17] Without naming sources or quoting documents, Anderson declared that this was because Aramco had been increasing production from existing fields too fast, "without spending any more money than necessary on developing new wells," fearing that "its whole Saudi operation will be taken over by the government." Anderson claimed the "secret reports" told of "huge pressure drops" and "erratic production" and maintained that the Saudis' "suspicions were aroused" but that they were "kept in the dark about the seriousness of the trouble."

The Church Subcommittee, as part of its investigation into international oil firms, set out to obtain the reports Anderson had talked about. Late in January, they took testimony from Anderson at a closed, or "executive," session. Anderson still would not disclose his sources, but claimed "they could be in one of the parent companies" and insisted that they had let him see verbatim notes, and some documents, that "show, or at least appear to show . . . that in 1972, late 1972, or early in 1973, Aramco and its [parents] became aware, probably for the first time, or at least began to believe for the first time, that their wells over there were in jeopardy." He claimed that they wanted to increase production rapidly in Arabia, in order to get as much as they could out of the country before they "lost their fields" there — investing as little money as possible in the process.[18]

In short time, the subcommittee staff determined that Anderson's sources were in Standard of California, one of the Aramco parents. The staff managed to subpoena and acquire some engineering trip reports from SoCal which were similar to those Anderson had described. Ironically, it turned out that the sources knew their Eric Ambler; one of Anderson's key documents, an internal SoCal research division memo, which had triggered the articles and searches, almost certainly had been forged (no one has yet learned by whom or to what end. However, the engineering reports themselves were genuine, and the subcommittee later published excerpts from them, along with transcripts of its open and closed hearings on the matter and the text of the forged document, in part seven of its hearing series.

The engineering reports show quite clearly that in 1972 and 1973 — and by implication during most if not all of 1971 — Aramco so increased production from Ghawar and Berri, and then Abqaiq, that its water injection facilities became outdated and inadequate, pressure in the fields dropped markedly, and production of sand and salt increased — all at alarming speed. In late August, 1973, Saudi government officials complained in a letter to Aramco's Dhahran representative of a severe pressure drop and excessive water encroachment in the area of Abqaiq nearest the Ras Tanura terminal. This disturbed Aramco's President, Frank Jungers, who had discussed the matter with oil minister Yamani, wanted to increase production from Abqaiq, but realized "we are on relatively shaky ground here." He told Aramco's treasurer Joseph Johnston "I had already decided out here that we were not going to push this Abqaiq increment at all on this budget."[19]

Then a high-ranking engineer with SoCal, William Messick, went to Arabia in early November, 1973, to take a closer look at Aramco's production problems. Earlier in the year, he had warned that the ratio of gas produced with oil at Abqaiq "increased rapidly at some point difficult to pinpoint" and that at Berri "injection system corrosion" had been so severe that "injection systems will have to be replaced after only a year or so of

operation." But on the November visit he became more concerned with another set of problems, declining pressure rates in
the great field, Ghawar.

Water injection was lagging badly in the Ain Dar, Shedgum,
and Uthmaniya areas, the sections of this colossus closest to Ras
Tanura. At Ain Dar, oil production, except for two months in
the summer of 1972, had been exceeding water injection for at
least two years. In 1973, Ain Dar water injection was below
800,000 barrels a day, whereas it should have been double that,
or 1.5 million barrels a day. At Shedgum, water injection had also
lagged behind oil production for at least two years; it had then
caught up in the summer of 1973, held at a satisfactory level for
two months, then dropped off sharply by the end of the year. "A
large and growing area in the center of [Shedgum] is below the
bubble point," though free gas had not yet started to form in the
field, Messick wrote, adding, "It has not been possible to maintain the large injection pumping plants in operation." (These
pumps had a capacity of up to 22,000 horsepower, similar to
steam boiler feed pumps, and had developed serious vibration
problems and breakdowns.) He pointed out that before the 1973
embargo Shedgum reservoir pressure had been declining at a
rate of 10 pounds per square inch — or half a percent — per
month. Since the highest pressures in Shedgum, at the edges,
were about 2400 pounds per square inch, and the bubble point
was about 1915 pounds per square inch, this would mean that the
entire Shedgum area of Ghawar would reach the bubble point
in four years at that rate — and it was producing from one-sixth
to one-third the oil of Aramco. Indeed, the overproduction at
Shedgum was almost deliberate: one of the production units in
the center of the area, where pressure was lowest, was producing
oil at twice the rate of the other units. With regard to the
Uthmaniya area, Messick wrote that reservoir pressure had
dropped by 200 to 300 pounds per square inch in less than two
years, in the northern third, and that it was "at the bubble point
in these areas." Oil production was also above water injection
in Uthmaniya.

In addition, Messick affirmed that the water injection pumps
were developing corrosion problems, that salt production was
getting out of control, and that thirty Ghawar oil wells, producing

430,000 barrels of oil a day in all, were producing salt water or taking it in through leaks. Exxon and Mobil executives, in separate communications, signaled that they would accept an increase in salt content to 10, 15, perhaps even 40 pounds per thousand barrels — as much as ten times the former limit — if it took that to increase production in Ghawar. Messick himself recommended that the companies investigate relaxing the subsequent ten-pound limit. Later, at another executive hearing, he told the Church Subcommittee that there had also been a serious lag in drilling water wells for injection into Ain Dar, Shedgum, and Uthmaniya. "We were taken off the hook by the embargo," he told the subcommittee staff.

In another communication which the Church Subcommittee released, one SoCal vice president had written another, "It is my feeling that Aramco has reached the limit of its ability currently to undertake further expansion in an efficient manner and is also now beginning to reach beyond the point of their engineering knowledge." These SoCal vice presidents, when questioned at this executive session, would not directly dispute Messick's statement, though they managed to avoid concurring with it.[20]

The conclusion which these reports and assessments would inspire was that Aramco was on the verge of accomplishing a negative technical feat, willfully damaging if not destroying some of nature's proudest works of their kind. Aramco had extended production as far as it should, if not too far, and it would have to make considerable investments to expand farther: greater investments, per barrel of capacity, than might be necessary to increase production in other oil countries. As a result, when the embargo ended and Aramco was free to increase production again, almost as much as it wished, it faced four obvious choices: it could cease expanding production in the country by more than 5 or 10 percent; it could restrict expansion to other fields, which generally did not produce Arabian Light, though this would be at higher cost; it could take pains to sustain water injection at Abqaiq, Ghawar, and Berri at a high level, which would also be costly; or it could simply go on producing from these three major fields as it had, either severely damaging or ruining parts of them in as little as three years. Just to maintain the pressure would be hard enough; Messick had reported that target production rates in Ain

Dar, Shedgum, and Uthmaniya were 1, 1.5, and 3.3 million barrels a day, respectively, or a total of 5.8 million (Aramco's total 1972 production). While it would take water injection of about 8.8 million barrels a day to maintain pressure in these areas, at this rate of production, actual injection at the time of Messick's visit was at most a total of 3 million barrels a day.

Apparently the company has opted for the first alternative. During the embargo, oil production in Ghawar was cut back to about 3.2 million barrels a day. It has since risen somewhat, but as of this writing, Aramco has cut back considerably in its planning. Expansion has been too expensive, and, given the shortages of water at Uthmaniya and south Ghawar, almost impossible beyond a certain point. Aramco's average production in 1974, forecast at 9.97 million barrels a day, came only to about 8.6 million for the year — and was below this rate for months after the embargo was lifted in March. This meant that Aramco was producing at about 14 percent below forecast; since the company had not been off its planned rate by more than 6 percent in the past decade, this was an unprecedented lapse.

The past and present overproduction of Aramco's properties, though not as rapacious as Jack Anderson claimed, has had two specific short-range effects, if not purposes. One, of course, was to provide the Aramco parents with massive volumes of cash very rapidly. The 1973 production increase, as we have seen, was startling — between January and July the company upped production by 2.5 million barrels a day, or 40 percent. As we have also seen, this of course gained diminishing returns with time, since the Saudi authorities could not condone unlimited increases and Aramco, in its expansion program, found itself compelled more and more to take costly prospects into consideration. Its 1974–1976 budget and program included the development of fields which would be much more costly than those being developed in the Iranian Consortium: Marjan and Zuluf, where capacity additions would cost $455 per daily barrel; the Haradh area of south Ghawar, where expansion would cost $510 a daily barrel; the Khurais-Mazalij prospect, costing $810, and the Shayba field, which would total a prohibitive $1076 per daily barrel. About $150 of this would go for pipelines, in the case of Marjan and Zuluf, and over $200 at Haradh and Khurais would go for water injection. In any event, Aramco could no longer expand production in Saudi Arabia for a mere $200 a daily barrel.[21]

The other purpose of overproduction must have been more immediate and political: to increase the bargaining power of Saudi Arabia and the Aramco parents both, by creating the illusion that they were in control of the only proved area of potential oil expansion in the world. Acceptance of this illusion would give Aramco's parents an acknowledged monopoly over resources of additional oil — in the event of a shortage — and it would give Saudi Arabia a near-monopoly over the power to exert political influence on consumers by denying them extra oil. It was to the advantage of the Saudi government, needless to say, to convey the impression to the world that, if it cut off its production — or even curtailed it — it could easily place the industrial world in parlous straits.

In time, to be sure, the Aramco parents would be able to develop other sources of oil — offshore California, Alaska, the North Sea — but they would rather wait until circumstances were ideal, until the areas became more profitable and the price of oil rose substantially — not just a few pennies or dimes, but four or five dollars a barrel; the prices of petroleum products would have to rise at least 25 or 30 percent. The Aramco parents would have to wait until the industry gained a virtual *carte blanche* to explore for oil in the Western world, free of financial restrictions, to say nothing of environmentalist shackles. They would want other benefits as well, in particular an end to the price regulation of natural gas piped in interstate commerce within America. It simply would not be worthwhile developing oil resources outside the Middle East for anything less, as the industry and its spokesmen indicated on many occasions.

But this is getting ahead of the story — "coning" it, outflanking the rest of the gulf's reservoir, in a drive to reach the wellbore of the 1970's. One must first understand the rest of the industry in the Near East, and central to this is a nodding acquaintance with the twenty-year history of the Consortium which the oil industry founded in Iran after the downfall of Mosaddegh.

6

Black Gold: the Curse of Iran?

No matter how hard we try to change things we'll never get around the fact that basically we are absentee landlords. You can put the nationals in charge but they'll be torn and in the end it'll destroy them because they won't be able to choose between being a company man or doing what the masses demand them to. We're not there in perpetuity and all we can do for the time being is run the company the way we think it ought to be run.

— Major oil company executive

FOR A GENERATION, a fear has haunted the oil companies operating in the Near East: the apprehension that their hosts would expropriate their operations. During this period Middle Easterners encouraged, even nurtured, this fear. Yet, for almost twenty years, between 1951 and 1971, through times of intense political strain and recrimination, intense anti-American feeling, Russian penetration and subversion, growth and acceptance of socialist and state capitalist dogma, and many other symptoms of unrest and disaffection with the power and influence of Western business, no Middle Eastern government nationalized any oil producing properties of consequence. There was one minor exception: after the 1967 Arab-Israeli War, Algeria nationalized several small American holdings.

In 1971–1972, there occurred, in Libya and Iraq, the nationalizations of which we shall speak later in this study. All other acts of "nationalization" since then have not strictly speaking been expropriations, but the buy-out by host nations of crude production facilities and concessions. From the standpoint of financial burdens on the companies, they mean something quite innocuous, for they have been more symbolic than real. Although they were, on the surface, accompanied by price hikes, there is evidence to show that the companies retained the power they had held all through the history of the oil industry in the Near East: control over production rates and the price at which they sell the oil.

The 1973–1974 Arab oil embargo demonstrated that the oil states were in firm control of one power: they could slow production down or cut it off, as they had done in 1967. Furthermore, in many cases they could force companies not to slow down production. But it is very hard for them to force companies to increase production, which would be a far more positive power if they possessed it. Nor will they be able to keep oil up at its present price very long either, without real help from the oil companies. As an example, in early 1974, when the posted price of Arabian Light had gone to $11.65 — after languishing for a generation around $1.80 to $2.00 — some European countries started to bypass the majors, so the majors retaliated by selling some crude in Europe at cut rates.[1]

Even nationalizations in Libya and Iraq, beginning in 1971, were very risky undertakings, not entered into lightly. Nationalization is a tricky measure, especially in the oil industry, where, unlike copper mining, to bring the product out of the ground to usable form requires expensive and complicated processing equipment and cumbersome storage facilities. Oil, unlike copper, is volatile, highly flammable, explosive, and composed of many elements. Even Libya's President Gaddafi expressed reservations about nationalization early in 1973, before he launched an all-out campaign to buy out 51 percent of his guests' concessions, when he stated, at a press conference in Benghazi, "To speak of nationalizing is like asking for war in Egypt. Who would buy the oil? When BP was nationalized [by Gaddafi himself], the Soviets agreed to buy only a very small part of its production from us.* Look at Iraq's difficulties. . . . It is better to proceed very slowly, to set up some refineries, to train staffs."[2]

Gaddafi's subsequent acts do not, therefore, negate the validity of the main question: why, in spite of all the threats, was there such little expropriation of Western oil interests in the Near East during the turbulent postwar generation, with its Cold War, decolonization, and fervent Arab nationalism?

There are at least two major explanations. One lies in the paucity of strong criticism of specific oil industry procedures in the Near East; in general and with important exceptions, Near Easterners, with their conservative, elitist instincts and their lack of more imaginative plans for disposing of their oil themselves, have not had it in their hearts to hate the oil industry in its own right. We will explore this later.

The other explanation lies in the experiences which many interested parties gained from an earlier, serious nationalization campaign which occurred in Iran.

In Aramco, we have seen relations between oil companies and host governments at their very smoothest. The example of British Petroleum in Iran in the years following World War II were quite the opposite.

The nationalization of British Petroleum in Iran, in March, 1951, and the turmoil and suffering which preceded and followed that cathartic act, constituted the most traumatic experience to afflict the international oil industry in the past forty-five years. It comprehended many of the most powerful conflicting forces of our era: the struggle — against the backdrop of the declining European empires — between the Western, Christian civilization which had dominated most of the world, and other perhaps alien civilizations, once proud, now awakening from centuries of stagnation and self-contempt; the confrontation between an America

---

* One should add that the Russians are ill prepared to bail out many producing states by buying oil from them in cases like this, because they need to import little oil and have little foreign currency with which to buy any. In fact, they export a certain amount of oil for the express purpose of raising foreign currency.

once isolated from the world, still very naïve about it, and the hostile, expansionist Communist bloc under the leadership of the arch-paranoid Stalin; and the first painful discovery by the under-developed "third" world that, in a time of increasing interdependence between nations, it had underestimated its own ability to influence this confrontation, and indeed to influence the entire movement and development of the international economy and polity — and that as a result it had been shortchanged, perhaps for decades or generations.

In brief, what happened in Iran after World War Two was that the Iranian people, who had spent the years of conflict under British and Russian occupation and, since 1901, had played host to the Knox D'Arcy, subsequently Anglo-Persian, then Anglo-Iranian, now British Petroleum Company, under majority own-ership of the British government, had become very disenchanted with their guest, for several reasons.

For one thing, the revenues which BP was paying to the Iran-ian treasury in the late 1940's, four gold shillings a ton, were in line with what other companies were paying elsewhere, but the other countries in the area were actually receiving more: Iraq was getting about 22 cents a barrel, Saudi Arabia from 21 to 33 cents, while Iran only received 18 cents. The agreement in force in Iran stipulated that this sum of four shillings would increase in proportion to increases in the price of gold, above a floor of 120 shillings to the ounce. Thus British Petroleum was actually paying the government about $8\frac{1}{3}$ shillings per ton, or about 16 cents per barrel, by 1950. With other payments, this sum came to about 18 cents a barrel in 1949. Iraq was compensated for in-creases in the gold price above 88 shillings per ounce. Mohammad Ali Eghtedari, in his M.A. thesis, "Some Financial Aspects of the Anglo-Iranian Oil Dispute," Department of Economics, Univer-sity of California, Berkeley, 1949, discusses this at length.

Then, the oil industry had already agreed to apply the fifty-fifty formula for splitting profits in Venezuela, in the aftermath of the Mexican expropriations of 1938, and this formula was spreading to the Near East; in December, 1950, Aramco agreed to apply it to its revenues in Saudi Arabia also. This put further pressure on British Petroleum to modify its agreement with the Iranians drastically.

In August, 1948, the Iranian government proceeded to broach, and negotiate, a number of important points on which it was at odds with BP, not just regarding payments to the treasury but also a host of issues governing oil industry control and power. It demanded that the company refine all its crude oil production in Iran, entertained differences over the price of oil (BP had been selling at quite discounted prices to the British navy, Exxon, and Mobil), and asked BP to find a use for the wasted natural gas. It called for access to BP's financial records, suspecting irregularities in the company's computation of depreciation. The Iranians raised several other points. Britain too was in poor straits at the time, so the BP team, with strong backing from the British government, resisted and rejected the fifty-fifty split, anxious as it was to save the company money. The 1948–1949 negotiations culminated rather in the 1949 Supplemental Agreement to the Concession, which, among other things, increased Iran's take to about 31 cents a barrel.[3]

Thanks to strong public resentment, focused in the opposition of a small group of nationalists in the nation's parliament, or *majles*, the Iranian government never ratified this agreement. In fact, it could be said that the agreement "died in committee." The leader of the special oil committee, the parliamentary group that killed it, was the deputy Mohammad Mosaddegh, who had been fighting foreign influence in Iran for years; among his colleagues were the non-Communist leftists Mozaffar Baghai and Hossein Makki.

The nationalization of oil in Iran might never have come about had the Anglo-Iranian Oil Company — now BP — agreed, in 1948–1949, to bring their agreement with the Iranian government in line with the fifty-fifty profit-sharing terms the other major oil-producing nations of the world were coming to acquire. There is much dispute about this, of course, but serious scholars do not categorize the Iranians as simply militants, since BP hardly made any effort to sell the arrangement to the Iranians. Even the Soviets had done that much in 1946, in their bid for a concession in Northern Iran — which the *majles* rejected.[4]

Then, though some people in the *majles* were strongly opposed to any compromise with the British, there was ignorance in their ranks too. Many members of parliament opposed to the 1949 Supplemental Agreement were reported not to know what was in it.[5] The most serious obstacle to a reconciliation with the British would have been Mosaddegh himself, who could have been out to inflict real damage on England. If British Petroleum had capitulated, or done the unthinkable, which was to offer more than the Iranian government itself was asking, that would probably not have satisfied this obstinate nationalist either, but most Iranians could not in all conscience have expected to get more than Iraq or Saudi Arabia, though they were certainly entitled to no less.

There were other reasons impelling Iranians toward a showdown with BP. Iran at that time was in the throes of political turmoil caused by inflation, wartime occupation by allied troops, and a real shift in the structure of urban society.[6] Inflation was probably the most important irritant in the short run. In Iran, like other relatively simple Middle Eastern economies (which have quite traditional, paternalistic employment structures, not mass layoffs or industry-inspired recessions but rather extensive unemployment), sharp increases in the prices of a few basic commodities, rice or sugar or onions, have been known to wreak political havoc. For this reason, most Middle Eastern states now subsidize the prices of these basic commodities in order to keep them stable.

Iran was headed for turmoil. Many elements preferred to have a foreign company, rather than themselves, bear the brunt of this; consciously or unconsciously, they were aware that a campaign against a discernible, vulnerable foreign institution such as BP might be the only way to keep their country from exploding into civil war. Still others, hostile to the West, though perhaps, like Mosaddegh, well-placed in society, wanted to strike out at the company anyway. The final powerful current at work in Iran was the old Communist party, the Tudeh, which had sunk roots under the dictatorial regime of the former Shah and flourished under Soviet wartime occupation.

The company played into the hands of these disparate malcontents and, as a result, Mosaddegh, even as a mere deputy in the *majles*, very rapidly acquired powerful public support for the nationalization of British Petroleum's Iranian assets. Subsequent to the rejection of the Supplementary Agreement, persons within the Iranian government opposed to nationalization were mostly intimidated against taking their stand in public.

Some who were not were assassinated. One man who met his death this way was a former premier, Abdol Hossein Hazhir. Another was his successor, General Ali Razmara.

In fact, the Shah's appointment of Razmara to be prime minister was a tactical error which helped Mosaddegh along; it was a violation of Iranian tradition to appoint a military man to this position. So the shooting of Razmara in March, 1951, accelerated the break with BP. Parliament forthwith passed a nationalization law, with the Shah's approval, and the Shah, who hardly had any choice in the matter, appointed Mosaddegh prime minister.

In the following period, Mosaddegh, who possessed greater experience and aggressiveness, boxed the young Shah further and further into a corner. The Shah either failed to anticipate potentially disruptive currents or was powerless to inhibit them. Certainly he was hard pressed not to punish the xenophobic religious hard-liners who had countenanced the assassinations of Hazhir and Razmara, and he could not extirpate the Communist Tudeh.

Mosaddegh's tenure as premier lasted till August, 1953, with one brief interlude of four days in July, 1952. It was a time of great turbulence and violence. Bloody riots occurred in July, 1951, when the American statesman Averell Harriman came to seek a peaceful resolution to the oil problem; posters sprang up all over Tehran, the capital of the old Zoroastrian state, proclaiming, "Ahriman Go Home." More riots swept Tehran in early 1952, during the elections to the seventeenth *majles,* then in the four-day period in July when Mosaddegh resigned because the Shah would not also appoint him minister of war — then had to take him back on his own terms — and, intermittently, during spring and summer of 1953.

During this period, Iran exported no oil at all. British Petroleum made effective use of its weapon, which was to intimidate foreign buyers, threatening them with lawsuits all over the Western world should they endeavor to lift any. And American firms, among most others, refused to lift Iranian oil. So Iran's oil production, which had been running at about 600,000 barrels a day before nationalization, dropped to about 26,000 barrels a day by 1953. Much negotiation took place between Iran and BP, mostly under American auspices, but the talks foundered — not so much on the issue of compensation to BP as on the question of sovereignty over the company's day-to-day operations. Furthermore, since American companies had refused to lift Iranian oil, and thus were conforming to BP's wishes in the matter, Mosaddegh was naturally suspicious of the State Department's impartiality in the matter. Finally, in mid-1952, the International Court of Justice declined to arbitrate the case, as BP had requested, on grounds that it lacked the jurisdiction to do so: it could only mediate between nations, and BP was a private company. This was a victory of sorts for Mosaddegh, and oddly enough, after this the Iranians, despite the tightening economic conditions in their country, very largely neglected the oil issue, so preoccupied were they with their own internal conflicts. Their economy was bearing up, despite the almost total cutoff of foreign currency.

What did crack under the strain, though, was Mosaddegh's coalition. Baghai and Makki, who were anti-Communist, parted ways with their prime minister as he came to depend more and more on Tudeh support in the streets of Tehran. The religious leader Kashani, speaker of the *majles,* also split with Mosaddegh. A naked several-sided power struggle developed, in which the Shah and the army came to demonstrate that they were aware that their survival was in peril. In August, 1953, on the twenty-eighth of Mordad, there occurred the cataclysmic events summarized at the beginning of this narrative.

After the army overthrew Mosaddegh and the Shah returned in triumph from his three-day flight, a military court tried Mosaddegh and sentenced him to three years in prison. After he served his term, the ex-premier stayed under house arrest virtually the rest of his life, which ended in 1967. At his trial he claimed that he really had wanted to settle with British Petroleum, and would have paid the firm a large compensation, had it not been for political pressures against him.

Now, more than twenty years after his downfall, it is very difficult for the parties to these events rationally to debate whether the demise was a national tragedy, a stroke of national deliverance, a bravura CIA *coup,* or something more ambiguous and hard to define. Certainly the Iranians themselves, the true arbiters to the dispute, have difficulty arriving at any consensus on this; when the subject of Mosaddegh's career is broached at Iranian gatherings outside Iran itself — to this day — the discussion tends to drift to violence and vituperation long before all sides of the issue are aired. It is a very touchy subject.[7] Furthermore, it is complicated by the consideration that, had Mosaddegh endured, the Tudeh might very well have thrown Mosaddegh over and turned Iran into a secular Democratic Republic, "socialist," of course. Some Iranian Communists have acknowledged this — usually after a few drinks. This too is a very touchy subject. The evidence is strong, though, that the Tudeh had infiltrated the government, the army, and other nationalist movements effectively and was building up a large supply of arms. Much of Mosaddegh's countervailing center and right-wing support had evaporated before he fell.

Iran borders the Soviet Union on the north, and this powerful neighbor has attempted not only to debilitate and subvert Iran from within, through the Tudeh, but also to dismember it from without. Russia removed northern Azerbaijan from Iran in the nineteenth century, nearly succeeded in securing the secession of the southern half as well in 1946, and supported a separatist movement in Kurdestan the same year.

As it is, in recent years, the Russians have unquestionably been behind Iraqi-supported movements of national liberation in the provinces of Iranian Baluchestan and Khuzestan, where the oilfields are located. Russia's domination of Central Asia goes back one hundred fifty to two hundred years and its history, in the Moslem areas where it holds sway, is blemished with military measures of a sort which American troops have never carried out in any Moslem land.

In the long run, as long as the Soviet central government remains strong, Iran would have faced risks aligning itself with the Russians; maybe America, twelve time zones away, is a more innocuous ally. Let the Iranians argue that out among themselves.

If Iran had gone Communist, though, the Persian Gulf would have become an area of great political tension. Soviet armed forces could have come right down to the water and posed a real threat to exports from Arab oil states which also front the gulf, and no doubt the Soviets would have spread subversion and perhaps sabotage all through the area.

Maybe this would have benefited Czechs, Poles, and Hungarians. Iran, had the Soviets possessed it, would have given them a base of irresistible strategic importance, perhaps a better situation vis-à-vis America than Cuba itself affords. Such leaders as Khrushchev and the Soviet military would have been very tempted to exploit it. In that event, America would have been very hard-pressed to retaliate — except by opening a second front, fomenting trouble in eastern Europe.

Maybe the Soviets gained by staying out of Iran in 1953, but many Iranians are nostalgic about Mosaddegh now. Perhaps the main reason for this is a strong feeling of resentment over the way events have gone in the past twenty years. Most articulate Iranians believe that their country, for a while at least, was a client state of America, pure and simple.[8] It is a member of the United States–inspired regional alliance, CENTO (formerly the Baghdad Pact) ; the people who hold power in the government largely come from a small, elite segment of the population; the government has received massive American military and intelligence assistance; the nation follows a path of economic development favorable to private (thus largely foreign) capital; and this foreign capital — represented above all by the Consortium, the Iranian Oil Exploration and Production Company, IOEPCO, known formally by its Dutch name Iraanse Aardolie Exploratie en Productie Matschappij NV, and its sister organization Iranian Oil Refining Company — has been very powerful in determining Iran's economic flexibility over the past twenty years.

Again, one asks if Iran would have done better under the Soviets. Had Iran become a Soviet ally or satellite, not much Iranian oil would have moved west until Iranian authorities reached an agreement satisfactory to Eisenhower, Dulles, Eden, and the French, as well as to British Petroleum. Iran could have moved some oil north to Russia, no doubt; but the Soviet Union was not bound to be a large purchaser and was ill-equipped to construct a pipeline of the size and complexity required to transport up to a million barrels of oil a day over 750 miles of plateau and mountain to the Caucasus. For twenty years the Soviets have been carrying out a major campaign to purchase large-diameter pipe from the West, and even when, in the late 1960's, they finally succeeded in arranging for the construction of a line to bring natural gas from southern Iran to their borders, they found it necessary to invite German and American pipe-fabricating expertise into the project. No oil pipeline has yet been built from Iran to the Soviet Union, nor is one seriously being contemplated. Furthermore, it is clear that the boycott which BP mounted in 1951 was effective. Mosaddegh could not get around it, but BP itself replaced Iranian oil in its internal stream with offtake from Kuwait and Iraq.

Thus, British Petroleum and the international oil industry won, against the specter of expropriation of crude oil production in the Near East, a victory which in essence held, with only trivial disturbances, for twenty years. However, the victory had its price. It shocked and traumatized the oil industry to see the depth and bitterness of feeling which could flare up against it. This experience motivated industry leaders further to isolate themselves from the societies in which they worked, introverted them to the point where they hardly wished to continue discussing the realities of Near Eastern politics and problems of development among themselves in truly dispassionate or even meaningful terms.[9] The oil industry vividly saw that its relations with the Arabs and Iranians were bound to be on a hostile and contentious basis. Some Near Easterners contributed to this notion — certainly Mosaddegh, Tariki, to some degree Nasser, later Gaddafi — and the oil company men, with their deep distrust of human nature, rapidly came to believe that these leaders spoke for all their fellows and that one could not survive in the world of Middle Eastern oil without taking sides against them as a group. Best serve one's time in discreet silence, and leave, having done as well by one's chairman and board of directors as one could in the meantime. This writer has talked with a number of oilmen about the Mosaddegh era, and other hard times in the Near East. On this subject, they seem to have bent themselves very firmly to the euphemistic, oblique mode of the Near Eastern host who would rather not communicate than discuss an offensive topic.

The Mosaddegh experience had a debilitating effect on Iran, too. Full repression held sway for several years, to be followed, in 1959 or thereabouts, by a few years of turmoil. This unrest reached its apex between 1961 and 1963 and did bring about some liberalization within Iran. Political agitation against the regime was spirited, fairly overt and often quite sophisticated. Some observers might be inclined to suspect that opponents of the regime had the sympathy if not the support of Western diplomats and intelligence experts, at least as a means for applying pressure on the Shah to carry out various measures of which the country was in dire need, such as agrarian reform, the eradication of illiteracy, improvement in health facilities and income redistribution. The message which this support perhaps sought to convey was that neglect of these reforms would hasten revolution, if not civil war, in the country; that there were many enlightened, well-educated people in Iran, many of them young and unprejudiced, and it would be better to have them than the neighbor to the north take command of a deteriorating situation; and that if the Shah did not stop the deterioration he might find them taking his place.

A major figure during this era was Ali Amini, a brave and broad-minded person who, as premier, did back liberal reforms, did support freedom of speech and expression, and kept the turmoil from exploding — though unfortunately he could do no good in the eyes of the Left because he had headed the delegation which made peace with the oil industry after Mosaddegh, in 1954, and had presided over the creation of the Consortium.

The Shah ended Amini's political career in the mid-sixties — thus writing the postscript to a public career which illustrated the anguish of mediating between nationalist feeling and Western commerce in the Near East. But for his part the Shah never forgot the turbulence of the era, and the threat it had posed to his position. A decade later, when the evolution of the oil industry seemed to be taking a disastrous turn and caused much panic in the West, the Shah made numerous public statements. Most commentators just dismissed these as eccentric mutterings, if not babblings, and made little effort to see what lay behind them — especially when he described his mystic visions to the Italian interviewer Oriana Fallaci or condemned the West for its political riots and miniskirts. Observers seemed little intrigued by his mammoth arms purchases, either, or his obsessive personal supervision over his domestic intelligence network.

But at least one remark he made, haphazardly, at a press conference in January, 1971, should have received deeper scrutiny than it got. Someone had asked him whether or not he was considering cutting Iran's oil off from the West if the companies did not bow to his latest demands for higher prices.

"I am not one of those people who, in the old times, attributed everything happening in Iran to the British, saying these events were a hundred percent their doing — or to attribute whatever happens these days to the doings of the oil companies," the Shah declared.

"But when we ourselves were engaged with them we saw symptoms of such things. . . . In 1959, we found that in Iran, which had been a very stable and quiet country, gradually undercurrents and noises appeared. We saw that those foreign countries which during the war [under the occupation] used to form governments, elect deputies to parliament and ensure the life of their elected governments [in Iran] by exercising martial law, suddenly showed concern for Iran's democracy, and equally suddenly in Britain the confederation and association of Iranian students [a group dedicated to the overthrow of the Shah] was formed, and there were other similar instances. Now all these things may well be nothing more than coincidence. To repeat the subject matter of your question, I wish to say that the question of cutting the oil flow is one of the points which will definitely be surveyed."[10]

7

Iran: the Consortium Era

We know more in public about the CIA and the National
Security Agency than is known about the internal workings
and activities and information of General Motors, Standard
Oil, International Telephone and Telegraph, and so on.
They know very well that if they disclose more informa-
tion, they have to share more power.

— Ralph Nader before the
United States Senate

It is unfortunate but true that most of the public has very
little, if any, understanding of the role of earnings and
reinvestment in our economy. Advocates of sweeping social
and economic change know this, and they are exploiting
it well.

— H. J. Haynes, Chairman of
SoCal, before the Security
Analysts of San Francisco

IN OCTOBER, 1954, slightly more than one year after the
overthrow of Mosaddegh and the restoration of full powers to
the Shah, oil began flowing west from Iran again. The industry
had come back in a new guise. The old Anglo-Iranian had become British Petroleum and it regained only 40 percent of its
original concession — sharing the rest with a group of international companies, in exchange for a cash down payment and an
overriding royalty of 10 cents a barrel, or $510 million in all,
which the other companies finally paid out by 1971.

But the Iranians, notwithstanding the impression all sought to
convey of regained national honor and revindicated national
pride, received the Consortium very much as suppliants in 1954.

The American State Department acted very much as a suppliant, too, toward the international industry, and did not work effectively to grant the Iranian government the strength to change its status. The story of the next twenty years of oil in Iran is, despite the proliferation of details on the surface, a narrative of weak Iranian government efforts to induce the Consortium to increase production and of strong industry efforts to keep it down whenever it saw fit — mostly to the benefit of Saudi Arabia, where the costs of expanding production were sometimes lower and the penalties against expanding far lower, as we have seen.

Iran's ability to influence the Consortium was never strong, for one reason: although the firm's composition was diverse indeed, which made it hard to run, it did function as a unit, a united front, in its dealings with the Iranian government.

The companies which make up this organization are, in descending magnitude of equity, the old nationalized tenant British Petroleum, now holding a 40 percent interest in the property; British Petroleum's old adversary from the days before Achnacarry and the Red Line, Royal Dutch/Shell, holding 14 percent; the five American majors, with 7 percent interest each; the French firm Compagnie Française Des Pétroles, with 6 percent; and a sprinkling of American independents, banded together in one enterprise, Iricon, which took up the remaining 5 percent.

Much struggle and political effort went into the apportionment of these shares. It has been stated, by Howard Page among others, that the parties barely managed to reach agreement on the venture in the first place.[1] First, it was unthinkable to the Iranians that BP should return to their land as the majority owner of the enterprise, and it was unthinkable to BP to accept much less than a controlling interest in an enterprise which it used to own outright; 40 percent was the closest compromise possible between these barely compatible aspirations. The American majors, for their part, would not come in for less than 40 percent of the venture; otherwise, United States tax law would not give the Consortium an 85 percent dividend exemption, should it become a profit-making firm (which in the end it did not). Thus, each of the five Americans was awarded an 8 percent share.

BP also had to show some consideration to its old Achnacarry partners, and of course favored Shell, which got 14 of the remaining 20 percent; the other 6 percent went to the French CFP. It looks like a mere sop, and one can imagine that the French government applied strong pressure to secure even that for its subject.

After the parties had worked out these shares, the five American majors found themselves prevailed upon by Herbert Hoover, Jr., of the State Department, in 1955, to allow a group of solvent American independents into their shares, so that the arrangement would be more palatable to the independent industry in America; thus, each of the five American majors relinquished one-eighth of its share to this new group, Iricon. It must be stated that this accommodation did not arise parthenogenetically from the skull of Mr. Hoover, though. Robert Engler, in his book *The Politics of Oil,* ascribes the acquisition of this share to the efforts of one Ralph Davies, a former SoCal executive who was squeezed out of his old firm after the war. He went to work for American Independent, the small firm in the Neutral Zone, and, after he and several other independent oilmen acrimoniously protested the apportionment of Consortium shares, the State Department saw to it that their companies were granted 5 percent of the venture.[2] But that was the only concession the original parties made to Western public opinion; they excluded at least one applicant, the Italian state firm ENI, in reaction against its unorthodox approach to the international system.

At the Church Subcommittee hearings in March, 1974, Howard Page discussed the manner in which the American independents were granted shares to the Consortium. Senator Church contended that many companies, indeed, would have been happy to get a bigger slice of the Consortium and produce more from it than the majors did. Page managed successfully to avoid coming out and stating the plain truth, which was that the major companies didn't want any of the others in. They wanted to have full control over Iranian oil, even though they had little need for this oil themselves. He said, rather, that the other companies "didn't want as much as they said they did."

Senator Muskie asked him how he knew. Page admitted that he didn't know for sure, but claimed it was only logical that they would ask for more than they got. At any rate, they got a minimum.

Page outwitted the panel on this point. Unbeknownst to him, they had a State Department communication which said that the various American independent firms which applied for membership to Price Waterhouse — the accounting firm which the United States State Department had appointed to carve up the 5 percent — had nominated for 34 percent of the Consortium in 1955. Unbeknownst to the panel, this 34 percent — as Page immediately pointed out — was merely the total nominations of a group of companies which knew they were, in the aggregate, going to get only 5 percent of the Consortium anyway, but wanted severally to get as much as they could at each other's expense. "I think it is like Treasury bills," Page stated. ". . . people go out and put in a bid for a tremendous amount of them, but they couldn't possibly handle [them] if it came down to it, merely because they know they are going to get cut back to one-tenth of what they put in, because there are ten people bidding for the same amount."

The panel dropped the point, but their question remains unanswered: how much could these smaller firms have used if they had been offered more than five percent? Would they have taken more? Eight percent? Fifteen percent? Thirty-four percent? J. Paul Getty, for rights to the Neutral Zone, paid over ten million dollars — which would have bought more than one percent of the Consortium — and he paid it in cash, several years before. Other companies paid similar bonuses for rights offshore Iran several years later. The latter properties, unlike the Consortium's area, were virgin.

The agreement which the Consortium, as a unit, reached with the Iranian government did not obligate the producing firm to increase production by any specific volume or percent, in any year after 1957.* In turn, the agreement among the participants themselves consecrated this inhibition to increase production by

* See above, pages 112–113.

placing control of growth in the hands of parties who would be unlikely to desire a large growth rate. Specifically, these parties included British Petroleum, Shell, and any three of the five American majors.

BP, with massive resources and production in Kuwait, and far more production potential than it needed in Iraq, Qatar, Abu Dhabi, and later Libya, was "crude long," therefore ill-inclined to increase production in Iran beyond the acceptable minimum (except, of course, in times of crisis elsewhere).

Sharing BP's reluctance to increase production dramatically in Iran was Gulf, its partner in Kuwait. Joining them, in turn, was Royal Dutch/Shell, which, though crude short itself, lifted about half of Gulf's Kuwait production (see Chapter 8). Gulf and BP, the most crude-long companies in international oil, could arrange production increases in the two states of Kuwait and Iran jointly, at least in a tacit manner, since they knew what each other's liftings in each country would be, and of course Shell would share in this knowledge to some extent through its familiarity with Gulf's plans in Kuwait.

Then the Aramco parents all knew what each other was lifting from Aramco. With the exception of Mobil, they were also so self-sufficient in crude that they would be unlikely to need to increase their exports from Iran markedly either. In fact, three of the four Aramco parents, SoCal, Exxon, and Texaco, often found their mere entitlement of Iranian oil to be an embarrassment of riches.

Together, BP, Gulf, Shell, Exxon, SoCal, and Texaco accounted for 82 percent of the Consortium's shares, but it did not take all of them to keep production down. Article 10 of the Participants' Agreement, the mechanism which gave the crude-long companies virtual control over Consortium growth, stated that the Consortium could override its own production forecast only if all the members but one, or a "quorum" of at least 70 percent of the members, voted in favor of this increase.

While this agreement did not penalize any party which took less than its share of forecasted production (unless it were really derelict, and took much less, or below 75 percent of its entitlement), it compelled any party which took *more* oil than it was entitled to to pay the prohibitively high posted price for it.

Of course, no party would overlift from the Consortium under such costly conditions unless it were almost desperately thirsty. It would be sure to get crude oil at some discount elsewhere — certainly from a partner in Kuwait, or Aramco, where, as we said, members paid only the "halfway" price for the excess they lifted, beginning in 1959.

The volume of oil which the Consortium entitled its members to lift at cost was a share of the production which the Consortium members agreed upon in advance each year. They called this "the APQ," or "aggregate programmed quantity." This quantity was somewhat less than the Consortium's actual production capacity for each year and was allotted to members on a pro rata basis, in accordance with their percentage ownership in the Consortium.

It was Elby Shafer, an executive with one of the Iricon partners, Continental Oil Company, who explained to the American public for the first time, at the Church Subcommittee hearings in March, 1974, the precise workings of this recondite system, which had been common knowledge in the industry for some years. As he explained it, every member of the Consortium would propose a figure, in barrels per day, which it thought the Consortium's total output for the following year ought to be. This would be that member's "APQ nomination." It could not exceed the Consortium's available capacity for the coming year but could go far below it.

The Consortium would collect all the various nominations, compile a list of them in descending order, and then go down the list until it came to that company whose nomination, when added to all those preceding it, represented a cumulative 70 percent of the Consortium's shareholders. That nomination would then be the APQ nomination which the Consortium as a whole finally settled upon. Mr. Shafer gave, as an example, the nominations for the year 1966, in which the French firm CFP set the volume of the Consortium's output for the following year (as it has done almost half the time since 1957).

Participant	Share in the Consortium (Percentage)	Cumulative Percentage of Shareholders	APQ Nominated by This Participant (Millions of Barrels/Day)
Iricon	5	5	2.030
BP	40	45	2.027
Shell	14	59	2.027
Mobil	7	66	1.964
CFP	6	72	1.945

As one can see, CFP set the APQ in this instance, in 1966, because its share, when added to those of the companies whose nominations were higher, brought the Consortium to a "quorum" of sorts, or a lowest common denominator, of 70 percent. Thus, in 1966, the Consortium determined that it would produce at an average rate of 1.945 million barrels a day in 1967. The four crude-rich Americans made still lower nominations that year. To round out the table:

Participant	Share (Percentage)	Cumulative Percentage of Shareholders	APQ Nominated (Millions of Barrels/Day)
Exxon	7	79	1.890
Texaco	7	86	1.712
Gulf	7	93	1.700
SoCal	7	100	1.644

In 1966, as Shafer also pointed out, the Consortium's expected capacity was 2.126 million barrels a day, or about 5 percent more than the largest nomination, which his company had submitted.

As it turned out, the Consortium almost never lifted as much as it nominated, although a few times it did adjust the APQ upward in the light of sudden developments — especially in 1967, the year of the Arab-Israeli War, when, as Mr. Shafer pointed out in his statement, the Consortium upped it to 2.055 million barrels a day.

In fairness to British Petroleum, the biggest single shareholder, one should note that its nominations were almost always above the ultimate APQ agreed upon, though never by much.

It must also be stated that the crude-long American majors Exxon, Gulf, Texaco, and SoCal were not successful in bringing the APQ down to their low nominations; they, by themselves, did not possess the 30 percent share necessary to do so. Furthermore, during the period 1963–1970, there seemed to be a rough consensus among 70 percent of the Consortium shareholders, because the nominations they agreed upon through this procedure were never more than six percent below the nomination which the venture's most crude-thirsty single member proferred, and generally much less — within an average of 3.6 percent. This is evident from a comparison of the highest nomination with that setting the APQ for each year during this period:

	1963	1964	1965	1966	1967	1968	1969	1970
Highest nomination (company)	1.575 (BP)	1.740 (Iricon)	1.863 (CFP)	2.030 (Iricon)	2.274 (CFP)	2.698 (Iricon)	3.062 (Iricon)	3.547 (Iricon)
Nomination setting APQ (company)	1.521 (Mobil)	1.680 (CFP)	1.836 (Mobil)	1.945 (CFP)	2.178 (Iricon)	2.568 (CFP)	3.014 (CFP)	3.329 (CFP)
Percentage difference between the two companies	3.4	3.4	1.4	4.2	4.2	4.8	1.6	6.1

Thus, the insurance mechanism which the parties to the venture so carefully pieced together in 1953–1954 was not called into service often. Perhaps its mere presence was sufficient to inhibit the Consortium's crude-hungry members from asking for all they wanted.

Also, of greater importance, the major oil companies, in the years 1958–1965, entered into a period of confrontation with Arab oil officials and opinion leaders in general which dictated a policy of prudent expansion outside the Arab world. It was during this period that Sheikh Abdullah Tariki was crying out against the industry from many podiums and Egypt's President

Gamal Abdel Nasser was baring an attitude of hostility toward the Western powers and capitalist development generally which could easily turn upon the oil industry; as we shall see shortly, it was also a period of oil confrontation politics in Iraq and Kuwait.

Thus it happened that the Iranian Consortium increased its oil production more rapidly than Aramco in the period 1958–1965. The growth of oil production in the Consortium and Aramco during this period is as follows, with average daily production, in millions of barrels per day and rate of increase over the previous year (from Appendix 1).

Year	Aramco Production (Millions of Barrels/Day)	Increase (Percentage)	Consortium Production (Millions of Barrels/Day)	Increase (Percentage)
1958	1.0151	2.3	.822	14.8
1959	1.0954	7.9	.925	12.5
1960	1.2471	13.9	1.048	13.3
1961	1.3925	11.7	1.171	11.7
1962	1.5207	9.2	1.301	11.2
1963	1.6290	7.1	1.4443	11.0
1964	1.7161	5.3	1.6554	14.6

One can readily see that Consortium production grew by at least 11 percent in this period, whereas Aramco's growth rate fell below 8 percent twice for two years running.

In fact, in 1964 the Consortium saw itself faced with what it could only have considered an exciting prospect. Right about then, it made a number of oil discoveries to which it gave substantial publicity at the time, at Binak, Bibi Hakimeh, Mansuri, Bushgan, Golkhari, Kupal, Ramshir, Karanj, and the giant Marun. Though the enterprise was actually producing one and a half million barrels or so a day, it had the potential, by its own reckoning, to triple this output, to raise it to 4.6 million barrels a day, just by relying on eight of the old and new fields in its inventory.[3] Of these eight fields only one, Agha Jari, was then producing anywhere near its probable maximum capacity of one million barrels a day. Three of them — Marun, Karanj, and

Bibi Hakimeh, all very large — of course lay idle. The remaining four, Ahvaz, Pazanan, Gachsaran, and Kharg, had gone onstream but were only producing at one-half to one-tenth their ultimate maximum.

To leap ahead of the story a moment, the Consortium's inventory position remained excellent through the following decade. In this period, 1964–1973, the Consortium discovered, in addition to the above, eighteen more fields, most of them endowed with excellent potential, and it increased its ultimate probable maximum capacity to about 10 million barrels a day — or almost double its 1973 production. Yet during this period, it seriously pursued the development of only seven fields, five of which (Ahvaz, Marun, Gachsaran, Karanj, and Bibi Hakimeh) it had already known about in 1964. It put only two of its new fields on flush production. One of them, Paris, had relatively shallow wells, each capable of producing as much as any well in the Consortium, or about 36,000 barrels a day. The other, Rag-e Safid, could put out only about 12,000 barrels a day per well (around one thousand times the output of the average well in America), but it was close to the terminal at Kharg.

Of the five fields which the Consortium had known about, it was still running Marun at only about half its ultimate probable maximum of 1.8 million barrels a day, and Pazanan and Kharg at about one-sixth their maximum, in 1973. The Consortium ran most of Ahvaz and Bibi Hakimeh at their ultimate rates, but even then it never did develop the southeastern third of Bibi Hakimeh (though it had planned to do so at one point), and it developed the northwestern third of Ahvaz with great reluctance, postponing this investment until 1972 because the wells in that area could yield only about 18,000 barrels a day each. Of the twenty-one new fields, fourteen were still not producing by the end of 1973.*

This was mainly because the wind shifted against Iran, about 1965. Aramco further liberalized its offtake regulations and the Arab nationalist wave seemed, in subtle ways, to be receding.

---

* These were Kilur Karim, Cheshmeh Khosh, Sarkan, Maleh Kuh, Shadegan, Sulabedar, Ab Teymur, Kabud, Danan, Halush, Karun, Susangerd, Dehloran, and Gorangan.

Tariki left Saudi Arabia in exile, Nasser bogged down in the civil war of Yemen, the Iraqi government showed that, in matters of oil politics, it did not possess the versatility or strength of its guest, IPC. The Arab-Israeli War of 1967 seemed to radicalize large segments of the Arab population, but in reality it prepared the ground for the opposite: once the dust had subsided, it demonstrated the short-range limitations to the nationalist and progressive strategy of confrontation with Western interests. One will recall that in the summer of 1967 most Arab leaders concurred that for the time being they should encourage the Western industry to expand production from their oil resources, in order to increase their material strength, and should put the battle for national liberation in abeyance for a while; they consecrated this doctrine at Khartoum at the end of August.

Thus it came about that a new battle was joined in the Iran of the late 1960's: that between the government and the crude-rich members of the Consortium over the rate at which Iranian oil exports, and revenues from oil, should grow.

In those years, not even the highest APQ nomination was high enough to satisfy the Iranian government. To begin with, in 1966, it put intense pressure on the Consortium to increase output by 12 to 13 percent in both 1967 and 1968. In 1966, in fact, it wrested two benefits in addition to a good production hike. The first was minor: the Consortium would give Iran a certain small volume of oil above and beyond its own needs, which Iran could sell abroad. However, this volume — only 5 percent of the total, or about 40,000 barrels a day, in 1967 — was to go only to eastern European governments, through barter transactions, and the Consortium forbade Iran to bring any of this crude back to its own soil in the form of refined products.[4]

The Consortium's second concession that year, much more important, was to relinquish 25 percent of its acreage. Naturally, the Consortium had the sole right to choose which acreage it would give up. By then, it had been over most of the terrain in its jurisdiction, and the parcels it returned to Iran were, understandably, the ones it considered the least promising.*

---

* Eventually, the Iranians let out some of this acreage, and adjacent plots, to others — to the French state company ERAP, the Italian ENI (which had

These two sweeteners, in conjunction with the increased production in 1967, when Iranian output, thanks to the Arab-Israeli War, surged not by 12 but by 22 percent, did cool Iranian demands for a time. The relinquishment, however, was only a one-shot expedient, a device whereby the Consortium could satisfy the Shah for a year at no cost to itself. So in late 1967 the Iranians came back with more demands. Now they wanted the Consortium to increase production by 20 percent the following year as well. The Consortium very obviously took the attitude that its greater increase in 1967 had acquitted it of its commitments for *both* 1967 and 1968, and said it was planning on only a 6 to 8 percent increase for 1968.* Now it grumbled about the conditions of doing business in Iran. For instance John Warder, general manager of the Consortium at that time, complained in spring, 1967, about Iranian production costs, in a strong statement before the Central Bank of Iran. He claimed that these costs were much higher in Iran than elsewhere in the gulf — 14 cents a barrel as compared with 6 cents in Kuwait and 8 to 9 cents in Saudi Arabia.[5] He stated that Iran's higher production costs were due mostly to the Consortium's excessively large payroll and claimed that the Consortium could save from 10 to 15 million pounds a year if the government permitted it to remove half its Iranian work force, which was more than twice as large as Aramco's.

Then the major companies used to go to the United States Justice Department and get an antitrust statement from one of its high officials which would forbid the companies from discussing production levels jointly with the Shah.

---

been kept out of the Consortium in 1954), some Japanese firms, and one Consortium member, Mobil. It gained large cash bonuses for this land, and some plots have since yielded up discoveries, such as ENI's find at Doudro. However, none have gone onstream.

* One further wrinkle helped mollify Iran that year. OPEC, the producers' organization to which it belonged, had secured a fiscal benefit from the companies in late 1967: the gradual elimination of a special 6½ percent discount off posted prices for purposes of computing tax. Then Iran won an additional $14 million or so to compensate for devaluation of the pound, a concession attributable largely to the alertness of Iran's Cornell-trained finance minister, Jamshid Amouzegar, who has won many additional spurs (and epithets) in the 1970's.

Naturally, these arguments did not mollify the Iranians. In mid-1968, Manuchehr Eghbal, chairman of the National Iranian Oil Company, sent stiff letters to the Consortium members, who in turn protested that they could not get production up even to a compromise increase of 11.8 percent. Their most common excuse was that the Consortium's existing facilities could not handle that much.

In the end, Iran's actual rate of production increase did come only to 9.6 percent, and another complication entered the Iranian scene. The French firm CFP suffered from the Consortium's low production increases. It was one of the most crude-short members in the venture, was more dependent on Iran than most of the others, and, being French, was an outsider to the "Anglo-Saxon system." So it tried to avenge itself, and informed the Shah that Aramco's penalty for lifting excess crude was less severe than the Consortium's.[6] So now the Shah pressed for a liberalization of the Consortium's offtake agreement.

The Consortium negotiators fought hard and in the end granted him this — with strings. The venture would only charge the overlifter a halfway price on liftings above APQ entitlements, but not above the overlifter's entitlement to total capacity available for that year. (Howard Page, again, has gained much of the credit for this arrangement.)

Late 1968 brought yet another confrontation between Consortium and Shah. This time, the debate was harsher: now the Iranian government stepped up its demands to a flat 20 percent increase per year over a five-year period, and combined the demands with political pressure, launching an attack against former Premier Amini, who had headed the Iranian team which negotiated the agreement with the Consortium in 1954. The press charged Amini with having gained oil company support for a political comeback. The current prime minister, Amir Abbas Hoveyda, stated, in a speech in March, 1969, without actually naming Amini, that the time had passed when the oil companies "could put their friends in power." Amini, the liberal who had assumed the premiership in 1961 and defused a potentially explosive political and economic crisis — thus earning the enmity of left and right alike — had to go to court to answer government charges that he had been guilty of misconduct while prime minister, and he was released on a million dollars' bail.

The Iranians began the 1969 round by demanding that the Consortium raise production by 16 percent and payments by at least 10 percent — to a billion dollars a year. They complained that the Consortium had fallen short of its 1968 revenue commitment by $20 million. Furthermore, they added a new wrinkle. It will be recalled that the Marun field, discovered in early 1964, had languished undeveloped. In 1964 the Consortium, scrutinizing its inventory, considered that Marun had some potential but was not a very desirable prospect for expansion because of its remoteness from the Kharg Island terminal. What usefulness it did have lay in supplying the nearby refinery at Abadan. Marun has since turned out to be the lushest producing property in Iran, although it was still yielding fewer than 500,000 barrels a day in 1969, and the Shah threatened to take it over.

The Consortium apologized for its slow growth and said there was a glut in the world oil market; it countered with a "best endeavor" of $900 million. By that time oil revenues were providing Iran with 50 percent of its national budget, and Iran was building three expensive petrochemical plants, so the Shah suggested that in that case the Consortium should restructure its membership and give outsiders a chance to come in.[7] He stuck to the $1 billion figure as a basic, nonnegotiable demand and his chief negotiator, Reza Fallah, made a tour of Western countries to dramatize the Iranian viewpoint and gain popular support for it — publicizing the greater stability his government enjoyed compared with the less-populated Arab states to the south. The Iranian government even went to the expense of publishing a booklet in London, *Oil at the Service of the Nation*.

The threat to take over Marun had some effect. Again, the Consortium reached a compromise with the Shah by mid-Spring. It so happened that Marun produced a lighter crude, which fetched a higher price than the Consortium's main export, Iranian Heavy; so the Consortium gave in and promised to expand Marun faster than it had wanted to. In turn, the Consortium held back its production of Iranian Heavy — while

Aramco sharply increased production of Arabian Heavy in the Safaniya field by an unprecedented 80 percent (prior to that, Safaniya production had actually been declining). This was a good resolution for the Consortium because now it could increase payments without much increasing production. Iran, in the end, would receive the billion dollars it had claimed, though some of this money would be merely a roll-over of production payments for one month — the month of March, which was the last month in the Iranian calendar year.[8] Production itself would increase by only 10 percent. To the major companies, in other words, it was sometimes even worth sacrificing money to keep production and surplus down.

The Shah said that the advance payment would be repeated "the next year and the next, as long as we really need it to implement our development plans," but he did not succeed in gaining a promise from the Consortium to increase production by the amount he wished in forthcoming years.[9]

In the end, some Palestinian guerrillas sabotaged Tapline, Saudi Arabia's *aorta maxima* to the eastern Mediterranean, so Aramco's 1969 production increased by only 5.6 percent as a result, and Iran's output for the year rose by 14.9 percent. But even that good news bore a flaw: Saudi Arabia's production picked up dramatically in October and November, after the repair of the line. So Iran's opening shots at the Consortium for the year 1970 began well before the end of 1969. Now the government declared that it wanted $1.155 billion in revenues for the year.

This time, for the last time, debate was muted. The Iranians took some solace in the fact that all the gulf states were faced with a common problem, the serious competition from Libya, which had opened up in 1961 and since 1967 had enjoyed an unbeatable competitive advantage through its location west of the closed Suez Canal, eight hundred miles south of Italy.

Furthermore, with the Suez Canal closed, the Iranians felt strengthened in another sense. That spring, the Israelis had opened a pipeline from the Gulf of Aqaba to the eastern Mediterranean, skirting Suez. This line held two great advantages for Iran. First, to ship small volumes of Persian Gulf crude, as Iran was doing, directly to Bulgaria and Rumania, whose shallow Black Sea ports could accommodate only tankers of 20,000 tons or so, it was *necessary* to use this line: such small tankers could not negotiate the stormy route around the Cape of Good Hope easily, if at all. Second, the National Iranian Oil Company was the only significant firm which could use the Israeli line anyway. Mobil and other major Consortium partners competing with Iran for Communist European markets did not dare do so, of course, for fear of losing all they had in the Arab world, so this sharpened the Iranian edge. For a while Iranian use of the line remained an open secret, but then in May, 1972, the Jerusalem *Post* confirmed that NIOC was shipping as much as 50,000 barrels of oil a day to Rumania through it.

There was one further element which temporarily buoyed the morale of the Iranian government, though it turned out to be only a mirage.

By this time the nation was obviously running out of devices to raise its revenues from the Consortium — except for the one the Consortium simply would not go along with, that of increasing oil production drastically. The government was in no position to foresee the price-tax revolution which was to erupt in Libya in just a few months, and once the 6½ percent discount had vanished, Iran could not raise its tax take much either. It had little worthwhile acreage left to reclaim. Furthermore, the Consortium consistently kept the whole story of the production potential of its assets from the Iranian government, so the Iranians probably did not even know the full worth of their own properties.

The Iranians were also limited in their ability to get away from the producing end of the oil business and diversify into refining, distributing, and marketing. Though the state firm did take out a majority share in a refinery at Madras, India, sold jet fuel and aviation gasoline to Afghanistan, and contemplated downstream investments in the United States, this kind of investment policy did not sit well with many Iranians. They remember the time they nationalized British Petroleum's assets and are well able to envision the possibility that Europeans, Americans, or others might choose to do the same to them someday. Then Iran, like most underdeveloped agricultural countries, has a predominantly peasant population which does not understand credit and "leverage" very well, is afraid of being fleeced by those who do, and has a natural suspicion of clever money schemes, no matter how sound they might be. The Shah must have discovered this by early 1960, when he bruited about a project to invest in tankers and many of his compatriots railed against this as a device for moving money out of the country. Iranians generally prefer to see their nation's wealth kept at home, even if in the ground.

It so turned out that there was one ideal way for Iran to invest money while burying it in the ground, and this was to build pipelines to move oil and gas out of the country.

This idea began to take serious form in the mid-1960's. Russia would be an excellent client for the commodities. In fact, a gas pipeline to Russia finally was constructed, in 1970; the Soviets helped approvision it by constructing a steel mill in Iran and Westerners built a plant to roll the steel into pipe.

Iranians concocted further pipeline schemes, potentially more lucrative than this but also more fantastic; one would move Iranian gas through Turkey to the Balkans, up through Yugoslavia, and into the heart of Europe, another would move more gas to Europe by piping Iranian gas to Russia and pushing Russian gas along the line to West Germany — with the end result that the Germans would pay Iran, in marks, for their new Soviet gas.

The day for these plans has yet to dawn, but one other scheme held real promise. This was to build an oil pipeline up western Iran, over to Turkey, and bend it across southeastern Anatolia to a terminal at Iskenderun on the eastern Mediterranean.

On the face of it, this line would have some drawbacks. It would be over a thousand miles long and would cost at least $500 million — and maybe twice as much. It would pass through the earthquake belt of Van in eastern Turkey and other difficult terrain — among the coldest and most impassable in the Middle East. About one third of the route would lie in Kurdish territories, potentially if not actually hostile to the central governments of Iran and Turkey. It would go through two irredentist areas claimed by Arabs: oil-rich Khuzestan and part of central southern Anatolia, the port of Iskenderun itself and its hinterland, which had in fact been Arab territory until the French mandate forces in Syria delivered it up to the Turks in 1937.

The operation of big pipelines in mountainous lands can be very hazardous. The main problem is combatting "surge" — a condition which arises when pipelines passing over high mountains and steep slopes have to be shut down in a hurry for one reason or another. In small pipes, such as airport fuel lines, one can control the resultant sudden pressure buildup with spherical vents containing rubber diaphragms if a fire or explosion necessitates an immediate shutdown, but in big lines, the liquid can build up in both directions down the pipe from the point of cutoff, recoil and rebound to the cutoff point, and recoil and rebound again until the twin shock waves which have surged away from one another come up against obstacles, and return, rupturing the pipe where they meet and wreaking havoc to the environment. The international oil companies had just financed the construction of such a hazardous major line from Trieste to Ingolstadt, over the Alps in Germany. This Transalpine Line ended up costing 50 percent more than originally estimated; it was built under extreme flood conditions and involved much new technology, especially the construction of massive side-tanks to control potential surge. To build the line, the constructors blasted twelve miles of tunnel through rock, crossed 166 rivers and streams, and excavated a twenty-five-mile trench through solid rock north of Trieste. In the end German authorities held up operations for six months anyway.[10]

Naturally, the oil companies were reluctant to involve themselves in another such venture through the politically turbulent Middle East — but the Turks and Iranians didn't ask them to. They made only one request: that the companies commit themselves in writing to move 900,000 barrels a day, or about one quarter of their Iranian production, through this line, so that the Turkish and Iranian governments could secure financing for it from the Export-Import Bank. The two governments would tend to all other arrangements themselves.

The major oil companies, which, in 1971 gave the oil-producing countries in the Near East a price increase of about 30 percent after only two months' quibbling, and acceded to another price hike of 400 percent in 1973–1974 with hardly a murmur — passing every cent of it on to the Eastern and Western consumer — fought against signing this through-put commitment tooth and nail, with every argument, ruse, and device at their command, and in the end the Shah, powerless to influence them, could do nothing to gain their concurrence.*

However, they played the Shah along a little. The pipeline did hold two distinct advantages for the companies. First, it would bypass land under actual control of Arab states — if not actual Arabic-speaking territory. Then it could pick up some oil production in southern Turkey. For the Turks, there was the added advantage that although the line would not pay for itself in years, it would generate considerable economic activity for the port of Iskenderun.

Finally, it would give Iran a real chance to increase its oil exports. Fields which were too far from the Persian Gulf, perhaps, to be worth developing — such as ENI's Doudro, as well as some Consortium properties — would be closer to the line, hence cheaper to develop than many more southerly fields closer to water. Perhaps more dangerously, the pipeline would further strengthen Iran's ability to land its barter oil in Eastern Europe, by offering an alternative to Suez, or the Israeli line. It was precisely for the latter two reasons that the scheme was doomed to fail. In the long run it would have obligated the Consortium to increase production above the level it desired to maintain, and would have enhanced Iranian ability to compete (and drive down price) in a European market, meager though it was.

The first time the companies played with the idea was, naturally, right after the Arab-Israeli War of 1967. Their tentative endorsement of the Iran-Turkey pipeline scheme strengthened their hand in coping with the Arab embargo and gave them an instrument for temporarily placating the Iranian government without increasing actual oil production sharply.

Then, by fall of 1967, they dropped the idea. They used numerous excuses for doing so — one being that Turkey, the only Mos-

---

* There were possible exceptions to this diffidence, especially Gulf Oil, the sole major to have no part of a pipeline from the Persian Gulf to the Mediterranean.

lem state in NATO and one of America's oldest and most steadfast allies, was politically unstable. One representative for
Bechtel, a construction firm which would help build the line,
cabled his home office that the proposal had fallen indefinitely
into abeyance, not for economic reasons or misgivings about
Turkey's political stability but simply because the Consortium
did not "relish being forced to move putthru at expense of members global interests and believe Iranian will force beyond reason" any through-put schedule the companies might offer.[11]

The Shah, for his part, did not even ask Bechtel to provide a
feasibility study for the line. He believed that such a study would
show that the line *was* feasible and would commit him to construct it, but he knew the Consortium would never give him the
commitment he needed either, so he would lose face by giving
the project any endorsement at all.

Then, in mid-1970, Moammar Gaddafi, President of Libya,
cut back oil production in his country, Aramco's Tapline went
down once more, and toward the end of the year a trio of cataclysmic explosions destroyed three supertankers off Africa. Suddenly there was a tanker shortage of critical magnitude. At that
point, the oil industry began to display favor toward the line
again. Industry publications set about actively promoting the
Iran-Turkey project and State Department officials talked seriously of building so many pipelines west from the Persian Gulf
that in fact there might someday be no need to ship any oil out
of the gulf whatever. Bechtel composed its feasibility study and
for a short time the Iran-Turkey line was back in vogue.

In February, 1971, the line lost favor among the major oil companies again, though, with the Tehran price agreements. These
agreements raised the tax-reference prices of Persian Gulf crude
by 30 to 70 percent and again made Iran look like bad territory
for investment to the majors.

At this point it is pertinent to remember that the major oil
companies have never revived the Iran-Turkey pipeline scheme.
They did not even brandish it as a hollow publicity weapon after
the Arabs mounted their oil embargo in October, 1973. This
should offer further suggestion that this embargo did not seriously
perturb the oil companies, that they went along with it most

docilely because it posed no threat to their deepest economic interests.

There are two footnotes to this brief history. One is the following: if this line were built, and if a political rapprochement were to take place between Iran and Iraq — which have been waging a cool war of sorts for the past fifteen years but could easily end it if they saw that a rapprochement would serve their most vital interests — it would become possible, then feasible, and finally necessary to incorporate Iraqi oil into this pipeline system. It would be healthy for peace in the region if such a development occurred — even if it posed a challenge to the financial interests of the majors. As will appear presently, Iraq also has a great deal of oil potential in an area too far north of the Persian Gulf to be attractive to the major companies but of real interest to others. Iraqis have been complaining for decades that the great oil wealth in their south-central area has been largely untapped. If the line were to be built in such a way that it originated in Iraq, picked up oil in Iran, then doubled back through Iraq on its way to Turkey, it would be hard for either party to cut off the line to spite the other party without damaging itself in the process as well.

The other footnote is really just a shard, an Elamite bowl-fragment. At the beginning of 1966 Standard Oil of Indiana, operating jointly with the National Iranian Oil Company, discovered a massive oilfield, Fereidoon, in Persian Gulf waters. As it turned out, a major portion — perhaps the lion's share — of the property lay to the west, beneath Saudi waters. Aramco had rights to this portion, which it christened Marjan. Understandably, this discovery occasioned a sharp border conflict between Saudi Arabia and Iran, in early 1968, after Standard of Indiana and NIOC had begun developing it. The Iranians dispatched a gunboat, which took possession of a drilling rig Aramco was operating near the median line bisecting this field, and it looked as if open warfare could flare out between the two oil states. The crisis faded, though, and in nine months' time the two parties reached a comprehensive border settlement which paved the way for the orderly development of Fereidoon-Marjan.

The mere discovery of this resource, which some industry experts called "another Prudhoe Bay," a 30-billion-barrel field,[12] gave a Persian Gulf government, for the first time in history, access to a great volume of oil totally outside the control of the major oil companies. The Iranian government began promptly to flex this resource by proposing to transfer its equity share in it to a joint Iranian-Pakistani company, thereby gaining a thirty-year monopoly of supply in Pakistan's crude market.[13]

This project never got beyond the stage of exchange of memoranda of understanding. Furthermore, the development of the field lagged strangely. It is quite possible that the Aramco partners, or even the Consortium members, realizing that the Iranian government belonged to neither venture and could be hard to control, managed to forestall the development of this field by giving Standard of Indiana cut-rate access to Saudi or Consortium crude.

Standard of Indiana has hotly denied this, for instance in a piece by Philip Moeller in the Chicago *Sun-Times*.[14] This important independent is, however, uneasy to see the matter discussed in the American press. According to Moeller (who described the story behind this story in the Chicago *Journalism Review*), another local newspaper, the Chicago *Tribune*, had been thinking of running a piece which talked of Fereidoon; one *Tribune* editor asked Standard of Indiana about the reasons for the delay in developing Fereidoon and recounted later that "a Standard executive, he didn't remember who, had said something to the effect that 'he envisioned a lawsuit'" if the *Tribune* mentioned Fereidoon in its piece. In the end, wrote Moeller, the *Tribune* editor "got in touch with Standard, and said the company apologized for any inference that it might file a lawsuit." Moeller concluded that it was four weeks after the *Tribune* piece had appeared — "however, without the offensive material."[15]

Standard of Indiana's "deliberate speed" in developing Fereidoon would be the envy of a segregationist school superintendent in the deepest South. It discovered the field in early 1966 and still had not put it on by late 1974. It ascribed the lag to "a couple of dry wells" and a "delay" in getting rigs, as well as to Iranian government indecision and obstruction in subcontracting out the engineering work on the field. But this does not jibe with Iranian policy. The Iranians, as we have seen, have been aggressive in expanding their oil exports. Moeller, in his original *Sun-Times* article, showed that Standard of Indiana admitted as much by quoting one official of that company who said, "Iran has been steadily boosting its production, and would not tolerate any delay in developing a field." Other offshore Iranian fields, such as Rostam and Sassan, went onstream in three years, not nine, as did other offshore fields elsewhere: Bulhanin off Qatar, Mubarraz in Abu Dhabi, and Ashtart off Tunisia. In addition, since Standard of Indiana is very crude-thirsty, it has never been choosy in what it developed. One example of its willingness to exploit mediocre prospects is the nearby Darius field, which it developed promptly, as soon as it discovered it. Darius is really just the downdip extension of the Consortium's Kharg field; the Consortium has rights to the field within three miles of the island's shoreline, Standard of Indiana's rights extend beyond the three-mile limit. Standard of Indiana hastened to develop its part of the field but the Consortium has always viewed the part of the field under its jurisdiction with great scorn, stating that because of its depth and its "low" well potentials of 5,000 barrels a day its further development was completely unattractive from the financial standpoint.[16] One awaits the discovery of further shards on this subject.

By early May, 1970, the Consortium did agree to provide Iran with $1.155 million in revenues for the Iranian year 1349 — the Christian year 1970–1971 — again, by advancing a month's payment and offering to help Iran get a favorable loan. As it turned out, Iran's production increased by 13.4 percent in the Christian year 1970.

However, the new complication of revolutionary Libya had ripened on the international scene. This state, which had been enjoying a competitive advantage vis-à-vis Persian Gulf crudes, suddenly cut back its production and faced the various companies doing business on its soil, individually or severally, with demands for an increase in the posted price which had been inconceivable for years and unheard-of for a decade — in the course of which the posted price had remained frozen. Hitherto, no nation in the Near East had seriously challenged the companies' rights to set the prices they wished.

Therefore, in the fall of 1970, the Shah of Iran presented the Consortium with some equally stiff demands of his own. Once the companies met those, in early 1971, he proceeded to move against them even more decisively. He was a major participant in the 1973 price explosions.

However, lest one believe that his story is typical, that all Near Eastern states eventually get their guests to meet them halfway, it is essential to look at the neighboring countries of Kuwait and Iraq; Kuwait first, because its history is the simpler and less tragic one.

8

Still Life of a Wild Card

We have not given up by a long shot. We have the international logistics system. Someone may take it away from us, but we have it today.
　　　　　　　— Emilio Collado, Executive
　　　　　　　　Vice President, Exxon

OILFIELDS ARE ALMOST NEVER IMPRESSIVE on the surface, and those in the Near East are no exception. Mostly, they lie under unexceptional terrain and the differences there may be between one set of ground-level installations and another will hardly jolt the untrained eye.

In southern Iran, one can be traveling through the Zagros foothills, by back dirt road, passing only an occasional whitewashed shrine or brilliant shallow creek lined with glittering sycamores, and then see, off to one side, beyond a tribesman with crown-shaped felt hat and baggy black trousers, on a donkey, a thick silvery pipe surfacing into a wire enclosure — then vanishing into the ground once again, drawing no attention to its capacity, which might be in the order of 20,000 to 30,000 barrels a day.

Approaching the Gialo field in Libya's Sirtic Basin, one does feel as if he were drawing toward a landmark of the American past, for there, levitating on an inch of mirage which distorts light like a thick round plastic bar, is a forest of narrow towers, as pointed as San Francisco's fabled Transamerica Pyramid. However, as one draws still closer, these turn out not to be the oil derricks of the heroic days in Spindletop or Signal Hill but mere electric pylons, covering the entire field and conveying 33,000 volts to the electric pumps down each of the field's two-hundred-odd wells. Nothing terribly impressive there either: Gialo's wells themselves look like television camera tripods cluttered with household plumbing and utility meters, though, in the aggregate, they gurgle up about 300,000 barrels of crude a day, which is a little less than the entire oil production of Wyoming.

The same is true of the wells of Burgan, in Kuwait. They are stout and intricate, blazing silver in color, but no taller or wider than a man; all they offer to the imagination are red signs bearing the skull and crossbones and the Arabic word *khatar* — danger. Still, each of these wells produces at least 4,000 barrels a day, as much as the ordinary field in Texas or Oklahoma.

In popular accounts of Near Eastern oil history, the example of Kuwait stands out as the most obviously and gaudily spectacular of all. In reality, though, the state is just a small barren plot of land lying athwart the headwaters of the Persian Gulf, between Iraq and Saudi Arabia, lacking much population or history. Kuwait used to be steeped in poverty. It had virtually no agriculture or fresh water it could call its own; its sparse population lived by its wits, eking out sustenance from pearl diving, shrimp fishing, and occasional trade along the Gulf coast. Its emir was once so poor he did not have a pair of sandals to his name. Even its boundaries seem to be the result of afterthought: for a short distance along its old southern border, its rhomboid shape was disrupted by a bulge which described an arc so perfect it looked very much as if it had been drawn by a compass anchored in Kuwait port fifty miles or so to the north. The assimilation of the Neutral

Zone has flattened out this southern stretch of border, but it remains as artificial as ever.

As everyone knows, oil changed the state completely. After
World War Two, with the development of the underlying Burgan, Magwa, and Ahmadi fields and several less immense petroleum accumulations, among the largest in the world, Kuwait,
man for man, became one of the richest societies on earth. The
citizens of the state enjoy a per-capita income now estimated at
ten thousand dollars a year. Even before the spectacular price
rises of 1973–1974, the nation held at least two billion pounds
sterling in foreign currency. All Kuwait's modern educational
and health facilities and public utilities are accessible without
charge to the public, and the state, hard put after all to find outlets for its surplus capital, dispenses a large segment of its gross
national product as loans or grants-in-aid to other countries,
mostly Arab.[1]

This wealth has not come free of social cost, to be sure. Kuwait
suffers from some problems, foremost of which perhaps are the disintegration of family relationships and the presence of an unas-
similated foreign population — which constitutes the majority in
the state. Many of these foreigners live in shanties, which Kuwaiti
sources themselves estimate at about 100,000 structures, largely
in such places as Mina Abdullah, al-Jahra, and al-Aridiya. A spot
check in several such slums has shown that as few as one-tenth of
their inhabitants are citizens of Kuwait. Many hope to become
citizens — largely by claiming that they don't know where they
were born, being bedouins who were paid to come by National
Assembly candidates seeking votes, or bachelors seeking work.[2]

The breakdown in family relationships among the Kuwaitis
themselves is partly explicable by the sudden wealth, and the need
parents feel to hold several jobs in order to pay for their expensive new life-style. Parents consign their children to Egyptian and
Indian servants, the children go to school speaking several lan-
guages and dialects poorly and none well, and their parents —
fearing the encroachment of foreigners while failing to give their
children a firm upbringing — deprive teachers in schools of their
authority over the Kuwaiti children. The top students in most
classes must be Kuwaiti, and attempts to fail Kuwaiti students
have generated furious protests.

However, the strong hand of the Moslem religion has instilled enough moral discipline in the people of Kuwait to enable them to maintain their equilibrium in the face of these cataclysmic changes, and Kuwait, in terms of freedom of expression and the strength of parliamentary institutions, is the second most democratic nation in the Arab world. Furthermore, the state's economic future is assured. Although the oilfields have yielded up 15 billion barrels of oil to date, they still hold another 60 billion or so, recoverable at very low cost. Kuwait will certainly not be threatened with becoming a ghost town for a long time to come, if its production stays at only a moderate level.

Kuwait's oil history is much less tangled than that of its neighbors. One reason for this is that the firm which developed and until recently controlled all the production from its reservoirs, Kuwait Oil Company, was a joint venture between only two major firms, British Petroleum and the American Gulf Oil Corporation.

The former, BP, although a partner to the Red Line agreement of 1928, had no trouble gaining access to the Kuwaiti concession, since the sheikhdom was a British protectorate and lay outside the old Ottoman Empire — hence outside the Red Line. Gulf did have trouble. For three years from the time Kuwait first attracted the American firm's attention, because its terrain oozed up telltale seeps of asphalt — like areas in Bahrain and northern Iraq — the British Foreign Office resisted Gulf's inclusion in the concession, stating that only a British firm or subject should have the rights to Kuwait.

However, Gulf — and Andrew Mellon, Secretary of the Treasury under President Hoover and a member of the family which dominated Gulf — took the matter up with the United States State Department, which "requested equal treatment of American firms under the open-door policy." Gulf received this — with restrictions — after three years of tedious negotiation.[3] The two applicants came together as equal partners in Kuwait Oil Company in 1934 and forthwith obtained oil rights to the entire state. KOC discovered oil in 1938, but the intervention of World War Two prevented the firm from going onstream, just as it slowed Aramco's development until the mid-1940's. The story goes that in 1945 the United Kingdom used one-quarter of its meager dollar reserves just to get Kuwait onstream. Steel was hard to come by in those days, but KOC brought in the American construction firm, Bechtel, which had had experience in the gulf and mitigated this deficiency by calling on Bethlehem Steel, to which Bechtel had access through a wartime shipbuilding venture in California.

So development forged ahead in Kuwait, and the country's production then rose rapidly — to 300,000 barrels a day in 1950, then more than double that the following year, after Mosaddegh nationalized British Petroleum's properties across the gulf in Iran. By the late 1960's, production in Kuwait had reached about 2.5 million barrels a day and by 1970 it had risen to 3 million. After peaking at about 3.5 million, it dropped slightly in 1972 as the result of a cutback which the Kuwaiti government had imposed in the desire to conserve its gradually dwindling resources.

One aspect of Kuwait's development which is of particular interest here is its role in the anomalous history of Gulf Oil Company.

Gulf is unique among the five American majors in several respects. The company is absent from Libya and Saudi Arabia, where the other four are powerful — but then, those four are not in Kuwait. Gulf is very dependent on Kuwait, furthermore, and it is the only major oil company which does not have a source of oil along the Mediterranean. All the other six majors have a share in Tapline or the IPC pipe from Kirkuk, or both, in addition to Libyan ventures.

In the late 1950's, Abdullah Tariki tried to mobilize company and government support for a million-barrel pipeline which would move Arab oil to the Eastern Mediterranean from Kuwait as well as Saudi Arabia and southern Iraq. Interestingly, this line — like the later Iran-Turkey scheme — would bypass Syria.[4] This project failed for the same reason its successor from southwestern Iran died aborning after the 1967 war: Gulf would be the only important oil company to benefit from it.

After the 1967 war, Gulf made up for its logistical shortcomings in part by pioneering a concept which other majors have since copied: it ordered and chartered six tankers which were about one and a half times as large as any other vessel afloat. These "very large crude carriers" of 325,000 to 375,000 deadweight tons capacity each are too big to squeeze through Suez into the Mediterranean or to slip into any of the world's main oil-receiving ports. Instead, they go to deepwater transit terminals, in Okinawa and southern Ireland, where somewhat smaller craft siphon off their crude — darting, in turn, into the industrial ports where Gulf's refineries are situated.

Though these leviathans would not be able to go through the Suez Canal even if it were open, the unit costs of operating them are so low compared to those for smaller tankers that Gulf will still save money running them all the way around Africa, rather than putting smaller vessels through Suez, once the canal does reopen. Thus Gulf, in the field of crude oil transportation, has pioneered a new concept; many companies are emulating it — thereby slightly lessening their dependence on crude landed in the Mediterranean and the edge they used to enjoy over Gulf.

Another feature of Gulf is that it is by far the most "crude-long" of the American majors. Again, this is because of Kuwait. That state accounts for almost one-half Gulf's Eastern Hemisphere production and Gulf, in turn, produces twice as much oil as it consumes in the Eastern Hemisphere.[5]

Because of these considerations, Gulf's position among the American giants is not enviable. Although rate of growth of net earnings can be a deceptive gauge of an oil company's performance, American oil companies with substantial foreign interests show a compound growth rate of profits between 1967 and 1974 of between 9.5 percent (Texaco) and 14 percent (Mobil) — with one exception, Gulf. This lonesome giant averaged a rate of profit growth of only 5.9 percent during this period. (See Appendix 2.) Furthermore, as the price squabbles of mid-1974 have shown, Gulf is vulnerable to pressure from the Kuwaiti government. When the firm expressed a reluctance to buy crude back from the Kuwaitis at what it considered an excessively high price, the Kuwaitis threatened to cut back production; so Gulf gave in. It is hard to imagine any of the other six capitulating so rapidly to any of their hosts.

However, Gulf's dependence on Kuwait is a recent phenomenon. At the end of World War Two, Gulf saw that it would have real trouble disposing of all the oil it could produce in Kuwait and realized that if it failed to keep pace with its partner BP, it would incur the displeasure of its equal and create friction within the enterprise. As a solution, Gulf and a third firm, the crude-short Royal Dutch/Shell, midwifed by British Petroleum, helped pioneer in the creation of a new kind of business venture which was a cross between a sales contract and a partnership. This agreement gave Shell, the party which would purchase Gulf's oil, great control over the output of the concession and thus allowed a massive amount of this commodity, ostensibly the property of an arrant newcomer, to be "co-opted" by the international trade without disrupting any established markets. In its modified original form of February, 1950, the contract between the two parties stipulated that Gulf would supply Shell a massive amount of oil, at least 175,000 barrels of Kuwaiti crude per day, over a very long period of time.

This was too heavy a commitment to be a mere sales transaction, and in time the parties even expanded the terms: Gulf officials, at a stockholders' meeting in 1960, disclosed that Shell's minimum entitlement had risen to 475,000 barrels a day and that the deal was to last through the year 2026. By the early 1970's, Shell was lifting about three quarters of a million barrels per day from Gulf in Kuwait. In time, this arrangement gradually did expire, beginning in 1973. Finally, in January, 1975, it was officially terminated: as a Gulf oil executive phrased it, "Gulf is no longer long on crude," and Shell is "not as [short] as it was in the past." In fact, Shell had found, with Kuwait's buy-out of 60 percent of KOC, that it could purchase its requirements just as easily from the government as from Gulf. But Shell still bought half a million barrels of Kuwait oil a day from Gulf in 1974.[6]

David Haberman, one Justice Department attorney from the days of the United States government's emasculated suits against the American majors, analyzed the terms of the Gulf-Shell agreement in Kuwait, and the circumstances of its consummation, with painstaking detail in a government memorandum and came to the conclusion that Shell wanted more than mere crude oil from the American newcomer. Shell also sought control over Gulf's penetrations into markets where it already enjoyed a position. Furthermore, as Haberman pointed out, BP shared Shell's aspiration, in view of its allegiance to the Achnacarry market-sharing agreement and its carefully wrought understandings with Shell all over the globe. "The conclusion is inescapable," he declared, "that the consummation of this agreement had the sanction, indeed the blessing," of BP.[7]

Shell did not want a full partnership with Gulf, though; this would have obliged it to tell Gulf more than it wished about its disposition of oil in the world market. Gulf, in turn, had one aspiration: it wanted some guarantee that Shell would not bring any Kuwait oil into the United States, where *it* had markets. But this was empty and futile: even if Shell had granted this guarantee, it could have used Kuwaiti oil to penetrate Gulf's American markets by "backing" its substantial Venezuelan crude out of Europe and into the United States East Coast. Gulf had no chance to penetrate Eastern Hemisphere markets rapidly; by the calculation of its experts, at the end of World War Two the major markets of the world could absorb only about 40,000 barrels of oil a day from outside the established stream.

So the two parties had to reach an agreement which could only be considered a tidy victory for Shell. Put simply, the agreement gave this giant — but not Gulf — some insurance against market penetration by its partner.*

Shell derived one other valuable advantage from this agreement. It did not have to guarantee Gulf a minimum price for the oil it bought. In other words, if the bottom dropped out of the world crude market (which it never did), Shell would be obligated to pay Gulf only the money it cost to produce the crude and deliver it to the ship's rail at Mina al-Ahmadi. This advantage, of course, has remained academic. Shell, as it worked out, was to pay Gulf a halfway price between cost and realized — *not* posted — price.

Even in this arrangement one can see that Shell was shrewd to avoid a partnership. To determine the halfway price in a part-

* Shell gained the right to *decrease* its liftings of Kuwaiti crude for a given market if Gulf increased its share in that particular market, but Gulf failed to gain the corresponding right: to demand that Shell *increase* its offtake, in the event that Shell increased its share of a market where Gulf was also present. The shares used as criteria were probably those in being as of December 31, 1946, though this is not publicly known.

nership, Shell would have had to show Gulf what its refining and transportation costs actually were all over the world. This is very valuable information — generally off limits to most competitors, let alone to the United States government.

In the final agreement, Shell's only obligation was to refer its accounts to a neutral party, the American firm of Price Waterhouse, which would go over the numbers and present Gulf with one average figure. The agreement discouraged Gulf from sending men actually to look at the records themselves.[8]

Gulf, in its original 1933 agreement, had reached a further understanding with BP: if the British firm so wished, it could cut back on *Gulf's* production in Kuwait — provided it gave Gulf an equal amount of oil from Iran or Iraq, at no extra charge to Gulf. BP would be the "sole judge" of when it would be convenient to let Gulf have oil from one of these other sources.[9]

Through these ground rules the three majors turned Kuwait into a sort of "wild card" in the international poker game of oil: a kind of extra valve, or even safety valve, with which to protect the worldwide position of the established majors.

Some observers go farther than this and suggest that other major firms also used Kuwait as a factor in their worldwide supply planning. One such observer is the economist John Blair, head of the group which wrote the 1952 study *The International Petroleum Cartel*. In a statement before the Church Subcommittee in July, 1974, he declared, "According to Exxon's yearly forecasts Kuwait has been used as an 'evener' by means of which actual Mideast output is brought into balance with the supply called for by the overall growth rate. Thus, 'Kuwait production is estimated by difference after reviewing possible company supply positions' (1963) and 'Kuwait output is determined to be the difference between Eastern Hemisphere demand and supplies from all other sources' (1964)." And again, said Blair, "To prevent such [accidental] interruptions from upsetting the smooth and orderly increase in overall supply, production in Kuwait has not infrequently been contracted when supplies from other sources appeared excessive and expanded when they seemed insufficient."

Blair pointed out that Exxon had some influence over Kuwait's production through long-term crude oil contracts with BP which were not nearly as large as that which Shell had with Gulf. In essence, Exxon was an outsider to Kuwait; its insight in Kuwait's role in the international trade thus seems quite uncanny.

As it turned out, then, the established majors brought the emirate into the world petroleum market most smoothly, and Kuwait never posed a meaningful threat of any kind to the industry.

During most of the years between the fall of Mosaddegh and the present, KOC's production grew healthily and all interested parties prospered. The following figures show a robust growth of over 5 percent in all but seven of the years between 1954 and the conservation cutback of 1972, demonstrating that on occasion BP and Gulf — and Shell — would open Kuwait up to compensate for slack production in other countries of the area and would then slow Kuwait down on grounds that Kuwait was not likely to need the extra revenues as strongly, or at least as vociferously, as Iran, Iraq, or Saudi Arabia. This is just the way one would expect a dominant player to use a wild card: if oil were not forthcoming elsewhere under good conditions, one could fall back on Kuwait but it was best not to deplete the emirate rapidly. Furthermore, Kuwait, in its disinclination to complain vociferously about slow rates of increase, "perhaps recognized, reasonably enough, the greater revenue needs of its larger and more populous neighbors."[10]

Circumstances outside the control of Kuwait, and in a sense KOC, may explain the low growth in four of these years. The companies cut back in Kuwait — after reaching agreement with the government to do so — in order to compensate for the abnormal liftings from Iran in 1956–1957, which were necessary to bring that country back into the stream in a significant way after conclusion of the Consortium agreement. KOC probably managed to cut back in 1959 and 1961 on grounds that the growth the preceding two years had been excessive. Then of course in 1967 Kuwait's production remained stagnant because the government ordered a sharp cutback just before summer.

Finally, in 1971, after the National Assembly learned from KOC that the state's oil reserves were being depleted at an alarming rate — that they might not last more than fifteen years at the

Year	Production (Million Barrels per Day)	Increase Over Previous Year (Percentage)
1954	.952	9.0
1955	1.092	14.7
1956	1.093	0.1
1957	1.143	4.6
1958	1.401	22.6
1959	1.383	−1.3
1960	1.624	17.4
1961	1.644	1.2
1962	1.834	11.6
1963	1.933	5.4
1964	2.125	9.9
1965	2.171	2.2
1966	2.275	4.8
1967	2.292	0.1
1968	2.421	5.6
1969	2.576	6.4
1970	2.735	6.2
1971	2.926	7.0
1972	2.999	2.5

current rate of production growth — the Kuwaiti government imposed a ceiling of 3 million barrels a day on exploitation of these reserves. However, it elected to keep the reason for this ceiling a strict secret and declared that this curtailment was part of a gulfwide "prorationing system." Thus the government was able to allow production to rise sharply above 3 million barrels a day in the months immediately preceding the 1973 embargo, apparently to soften the blow of its forthcoming political cutback.

The one real anomaly in Kuwait's rate of development occurred in the mid-1960's, the one time Kuwait made a stand of sorts against the companies.

At that time, all OPEC member states had been demanding a fiscal benefit which would handsomely increase their revenues; in technical jargon this went by the name "royalty expensing."

This was the nations' right to levy royalties on top of the 50 percent tax instead of considering them a credit against this tax, as had been the arrangement since 1950. In 1964, after an OPEC-wide campaign, all major exporting nations acquired this right except Kuwait and its poor stepsister Iraq, where other problems were tied to the royalty-expensing demand.

Kuwait would not ratify the royalty-expensing agreement outright because its National Assembly wanted to give the matter some thought. The state had just gained its full independence from Britain three years before and it had acquired a new institution in the form of this parliament, which had never had to pass judgment on an important oil problem and did not want to commit a blunder on its first assignment.

Gulf and BP pressured the National Assembly to ratify the agreement quickly, stating that if it did not do so by January, 1965, Kuwait would lose rights to the higher payments for 1964. The Assembly bided more time, though. Then the Iraqi government, which had not signed either, sent a delegation to Kuwait which pointed to some disadvantages in the agreement, generally not of a fiscal nature but in essence depriving the state of some valuable prerogatives, such as the right to raise taxes in the future and to assess claims for back taxes on oil exported during the 1959–1960 posted price drops.[11] The negotiations which followed after the Iraqi mission went home became quite acrimonious and went on for two years. Professor Adelman suggests that Kuwait may have had the motive, behind this opposition, of expropriating Kuwait Oil Company, though others suggest simply that Gulf and BP resisted more and more adamantly — for fear of setting contractual precedents which would harm them elsewhere — while the Kuwaiti government, having made a stand, had to stick to it or lose face.[12]

BP and Gulf — and Shell and Exxon, too — used the best defense at their disposal; they slowed down Kuwait's production growth. This promptly incurred the wrath of Sheikh Tariki. In his *Arab Oil and Gas Journal,* the advisor railed at the companies' excuse, which was that refineries were complaining about a rise in the sulphur content of Kuwaiti crude: "When Kuwait, which was the first of the producers and exporters in the Arab

Gulf, whose oil was coveted and desired, resisted agreeing on what she considered was not in the interests of the people in her territory, her oil was found to contain a large amount of sulphur, and this, unfortunately, is the logic of the monopolistic companies."

In the end Tariki counseled the Kuwaitis not to nationalize — though he counseled the Iraqis to do so. This inconsistent stand was to bedevil him at the Sixth Arab Petroleum Conference in 1967. At any rate, in early 1967 the government came to terms with KOC, after the expiration of Kuwait's first National Assembly and the failure of "the radicals" — the Arab Nationalist Movement — to get the representation they wanted in the second assembly. Perhaps the Kuwaitis did so for the reason Adelman cited; they decided that if they expropriated the concession and tried to bring in a new company, the "array of probabilities" would indicate that the new company would not probably "be able to offer as good a deal as the old."[13]

Whether or not the Kuwaitis were contemplating such an action in the mid-sixties, the "risk premium" they may have contemplated certainly is a factor among oilmen. It detracted from the desirability of the southwestern Iranian oil fields in 1954, after the failure of nationalization, as even Mr. Shafer of Continental has attested.

Kuwait could have developed somewhat further than it did had it not been for the vociferous, nationalist minority in parliament, which enjoyed the support of leftist and Palestinian nationals in the state and has on several occasions hindered or blocked a venture which the government wanted to pursue, such as participation in Kuwait Oil Company or the export of natural gas. The National Assembly rejected the latter project, a seemingly lucrative one, because it was not ambitious enough and the Assembly claimed Gulf and BP did not offer much training of Kuwaitis in the project, or an active role for the national oil company in the operation of the gas liquefaction plant.[14] The Assembly held out for a long time, too, against 25 percent participation, and in the end forced the government to accept 60 percent. The minister of petroleum, Abdel Rahman al-Atiqi, even resigned for a time over the Assembly's refusal.

Still, the Kuwaitis did undertake some ventures, and they were not always profitable. The most striking example is that of the National Petroleum Company's new refinery at Shuʻaiba. Originally estimated to cost $95 million, it perhaps ended up twice as expensive, though the real figures have never been made public. Kuwait lost further money on the refinery with the closure of Suez because it could not profitably ship products over to Europe, even for its own marketing firm in Denmark. It offered swaps with major companies on very generous terms. At least one major oil company, offered airplane fuel on excellent terms at Shuʻaiba in exchange for fuel oil in Europe, refused to go along with the deal because it did not want to give Kuwait a hand in penetrating the lucrative European market.

But, since 1967, the history of oil in Kuwait has been relatively uneventful. This is true, as well, of such smaller oil-rich states as Abu Dhabi, Qatar, and Dubai, which have generally taken the lead of the older, larger, established nations and their advisors. It is also largely true of the Neutral Zone between Kuwait and Saudi Arabia, where great oil never was found.

The state verging on the gulf whose oil history merits closer scrutiny as much for its tortuous path as for the larger lessons which emerge from it is Kuwait's poor stepsister Iraq, the ancient land of Mesopotamia, the terrain between the two rivers, the Tigris and Euphrates, which by their very deposits of nutrients into the rich, warm waters of the gulf made the accumulation of oil in the region possible in the first place.

9

The Case of Iraq

Clemenceau,
Lloyd George,
Woodrow Wilson.
Three old men shuffling the pack,
dealing out the cards:
The Rhineland, Dantzig, the Polish Corridor, the Ruhr,
self-determination of small nations, the Saar, League of
Nations, mandates, the Mespot, Freedom of the Seas,
Transjordania, Shantung, Fiume, and the Island of Yap:
machinegun fire and arson
starvation, lice, cholera, typhus
oil was trumps.

— John Dos Passos, *USA*

IN TERMS OF THIS NARRATIVE'S SCOPE — indeed, in terms
of any assessment one could make of oil history in the Middle
East — the role of Iraq has not been central.

The relevance of Iraq here lies, rather, in demonstrating how
deeply embittered relations can become between a company and
a government when industry malpractices nourish governmental
hostility: both qualities have been most conspicuous in the Iraq
of the past forty-five years.

Even the most favorable of commentators on the current
political scene in Iraq are ill-disposed to speak of that nation's
recent regimes with undiluted enthusiasm. The French Marxist
Maxime Rodinson, generally ready to give leftist Arabs a sympa-

thetic hearing, admitted that Abdel Karim Kassem, the anti-Western ruler who held sway in Iraq between 1958 and 1963, was "wild and fantastic," and such liberal observers as Stephen Head, hostile as they might be to the conservative regimes in the region, refer to that country as "a grim police state."[1]

The revolution which deposed the royal family of Iraq in 1958 was indeed a violent reaction against an autocratic regime out of step with the Arab world of its era. There is room to believe that the regime itself was well aware of its unpopularity and was resigned to its own destruction, in the manner of Russia's Czar Nicholas in 1917. The king of Iraq, Faisal, was actually a figurehead — a young descendant of the Sherif of Mecca and grandson of the Emir Faisal whom the British placed on the throne of the new state of Iraq after World War One, as a reward for his aid against the Turks. The real power behind the throne lay with the prime minister, Nuri es Said, and the regent, Faisal's Uncle Abdul Ilah. According to one account by an Iraqi junior intelligence officer who witnessed the revolution,[2] Abdul Ilah had lost confidence in his rule, had stopped acting on the thorough reports of plots against the regime which his intelligence apparatus had been providing for him, and assumed that an indigenous regime would probably do more for Iraq than he could. He assumed that if a revolution struck, insurgents would grant his family safe conduct out of the country, so he seemed to have stopped working to prevent such a revolution.

His calculations were fatal. On Bastille Day 1958, when the army finally revolted and lay siege to the royal palace, Abdul Ilah, though protected by loyal units, capitulated without fighting or attempting to escape. One of the insurgent officers opened fire on him as he was retreating, in single file with the rest of his family, and killed all but the Queen Mother. Nuri es Said was elsewhere at the time and took flight, veiled like an old woman, but a servant turned him in for ten thousand dinars and he met his death the next day.

Demonstrations wracked Baghdad. A senior vice president with the American construction firm Bechtel, George Colley, disappeared in the fray along with some other identifiable Westerners. The story goes that Colley was staying in a hotel with several other Americans and made the error of going down to the hotel lobby to pick up reading matter for a long siege. Accompanying him was a middle-aged woman, the wife of another representative. In the lobby, a group of armed soldiers burst onto the scene and ordered them off for interrogation. The woman asked if she could go up to check her baby, was allowed to do so, and disappeared. Colley was taken off to the radio station with a number of other Westerners, interrogated, then released and sent back to the hotel in an open, unguarded truck. At one point a mob spotted the truck, fell upon it, and killed and dismembered everyone in it except a former SS paratrooper, who escaped, with both arms broken, to tell the tale.

This revolution brought to power a general in the army, Abdel Karim Kassem, who established a government founded on nationalism and nonalignment in foreign affairs, domestic reconciliation, and hostility toward Western capitalism and the Baghdad Pact, of which Iraq was then a member. Kassem brought some Communists into government and effected a rapprochement with the secessionist Kurdish minority that inhabits the hills and mountains in the northeastern third of the country.

Much of Iraq's subsequent history has been marked by struggles and reconciliations among Communists, Kurds, groupings of the Arab Socialist Baath Party, and other nationalists and leftists. Since 1958, Iraq's government has changed hands several times: Kassem was overthrown and killed in 1963, just like his predecessors, and his corpse thrown into the Tigris; moderate Baathists then took power for a brief period, the pro-Nasser Aref brothers threw them over and held sway for four years, moderate Baathists overthrew Abdel Rahman Aref in mid-1968, and Ahmad Hasan al-Bakr with his more intransigent wing of the Baath took power in July, 1968. Though al-Bakr has been incapacitated, probably for life, by a cerebral hemorrhage, his regime, under vice chairman Saddam Hussain, remains in control of the state to this writing. Some members of al-Bakr's government attempted to overthrow him in 1972, though, and his police claim to have found a large sum of fresh American banknotes in the possession of the plotters. Most Iraqi commentators consider that this was a gift of the CIA, though they differ on the motive behind the donation — whether it was to encourage Iraq to make peace with Israel, fight Israel, fight the Kurds, or a combination of the three.

Al-Bakr's regime remains a bit shaky, although he has made moderately successful attempts to bring stability to the country — at a cost which includes some executions and numerous imprisonments. It made peace with the Kurds in March, 1970, after an eleven-year war which had been triggered, oddly, by Kassem's reconciliation, since it brought the Kurdish nationalist Mustafa al-Barzani back from a dozen years of exile in the Soviet Union. Three years later, though, this peace began to crack, since the Kurds claimed that the regime twice tried to assassinate al-Barzani afterwards and launched numerous small operations against Iraqi troops and Baathist civilians from their northern strongholds, primarily in 1973–1974. The government has accused Iran, which also hosts a minority of Kurds in neighboring territory, of abetting and exacerbating this conflict.

There has, in fact, been considerable unrest on the border between Iraq and Iran for some years. It is not obvious what the causes of this unrest might be. One irritant is the fact that the borders themselves are not clearly defined. Another has been controversy over access to the estuary leading to the Persian Gulf from the confluence of the Tigris and Euphrates, which passes the Iranian oil terminal at Abadan. The existing demarcation places the border not down the middle of this estuary, the Shatt al-Arab, but to the Iranian side of it. This has led the Iraqis to demand transit fees from the Iranians, who, rather than pay these fees and consign their exports to the jurisdiction of Iraqi pilots, arranged a fundamental shift in the logistics of their industry by moving their oil terminal, at a cost of about $100 million, from Abadan to Kharg Island in the early 1960's.

Another element in this cool war has been the Cold War. Iran has enjoyed American support, Iraq has aligned itself with the Soviets. The Iranians have given aid to the Kurds, and the Iraqis — according to Iranian, and Arab leftist, sources — have trained and armed some Iranian minority groups to cross back into Iran and mount guerrilla operations in the predominantly Arab province of Khuzestan and in Baluchestan to the east.

Iraq's relations with its Arab neighbors have been strained, too — marked, in the case of Kuwait, with some violence. A spirit of rivalry, if not open hostility, has prevailed between Iraq and its fellow oil state Saudi Arabia, and this has generally militated against the formation of a truly coordinated Arab oil policy over the past fifteen years. For instance, after the 1967 war, the conservative Arab oil states banded together to form an organization within OPEC, which they understandably labeled OAPEC, the Organization of Arab Petroleum Exporting Countries. This was a Saudi-inspired organization probably intended to provide an international body which would support pro-Western Arab oil policies and offer an Arab alternative to Nasserite oil policies. Iraq naturally refused to join it in 1968. Libya and Algeria joined in 1970, after it had shifted its emphasis a little; Iraq still refused to join. Then, in 1971, it tried to join but Saudi Arabia blocked its application.[3] It finally did join in April 1972 — the ninth Arab state to do so.

A similar spirit of mutual hostility has carried over between Iraq and Egypt since the days of Nuri es Said, Abdul Ilah, the Baghdad Pact — and the late President Nasser of Egypt, who died in September, 1970, of fatigue and heartbreak from the fruitless attempt of trying to unite the incompatible Arabs into one nation under his dominance.

Thus Iraq, through its policies, remains geographically and politically isolated from the Arab world to a large degree. Some commentators ascribe the truculence and meanness of its government to its extreme political complexity — the fact that it contains warring ethnic groups, does not enjoy a consensus, and therefore can be ruled only by force. The only tranquil element in the society seems to be the rural population in the lowlands. In the early 1950's, after the creation of Israel, most of Iraq's Jews left under fear if not duress; the nation still contains a large Kurdish minority perhaps a million strong, a few tens of thousands of Turcomans and Yazidis, numerous Shiites (although members of this dissident Islamic sect, whose recent origins are Iranian, have largely left), and Assyrians and other Christians, who have also provoked, and borne, governmental wrath in the past. (In fact it was a Christian who, as a pilot in the Iraqi air force, flew a MiG 21 to Israel in August, 1966. The story has it that he received $300,000 for his defection. Access to this MiG was a key element in Israel's big air victory ten months later, during the June, 1967, war: the Israelis discovered that this craft had a gasoline ignition system and that a direct hit on its gas tank would cause it to explode instantly.)

There is also a substantial Communist movement in Iraq, the Baathists do not always enjoy good relations with their colleagues who rule Syria, and Barzani, leader of the Kurdish insurgents (who by no means represents all the Kurds in Iraq), has hinted to journalists that he is hostile to the Soviets, not the Americans or "the Jews."

Iraq's recent history has been tragic, then. It is understandable that in such unstable circumstances the nation's oil policy, and its relations with the oil companies, should also have been steeped in strain, recrimination, and bitterness. So they have been, for forty years.

The International Petroleum Cartel, the 1952 staff report to the United States Federal Trade Commission, chronicles the first thirty years of this history with a thoroughness which these pages will not duplicate. Suffice it to state that the concession-holder, Iraq Petroleum Company, while enduring some unwarranted abuse from Iraqi authorities, did not adhere to the spirit of the agreement which first brought it into the country, in two important respects.

The first lay within the postwar settlement which the British and French reached at San Remo, Italy, in 1920 to dispose of the territories they had won from the old Ottoman Empire. Among other things, the agreement carved up the eastern Arab world, including Iraq, as mandates between the two European powers. The agreement also said that the Iraqi government, if it so wished, should receive a 20 percent share in any public company which the parents of IPC might form within Iraq.

IPC never granted Iraq this share. Afterward, the company used to claim that it had offered the Iraqi government this option, in the mid-1920's, but that the government rejected it in favor of a 12½ percent royalty on the oil produced. In the strict sense this is true, but it tells one nothing about the circumstances surrounding the rejection. The act created a crisis within the Iraqi government — and the Iraqis lost the option for almost fifty years.

The second serious point at long-standing issue between Iraq and the IPC parents was the same which plagued Iran: the slow rate of petroleum development. Iraq's history proves what the American public did not realize during the artificial shortages of 1973–1974: the oil-rich nations of the world can always force companies to cut back production — and indeed the companies welcome this pressure, in consistent moderation — but it is only with the utmost difficulty and coercion that they can force companies to *expand.*

Iraq, after World War I, was to be an open territory for Western oil interests in general, not the exclusive preserve of one concessionaire. This was largely the result of pressure from the United States government. As early as 1919, the State Department was calling for an open-door policy in Iraq. The reason for this, in turn, was not a commitment to Wilsonian idealism but largely the postwar fear, as unfounded as it has been recurrent, that the United States was running out of domestic crude oil and that its companies — eminently Exxon — needed access to promising new foreign prospects. The State Department pressure was successful within its limits: the other partners to the enterprise, BP, Shell, and CFP, brought in a joint American venture between Exxon and Mobil as a one-quarter partner with them. Indeed, at the outset, IPC did only acquire rights to eight small plots in northeastern Iraq, in accordance with this policy — and British Petroleum received a 6½ percent royalty on any oil produced, in exchange for letting them in. But in the course of the next fifteen years the company gradually, without opposition from any Western government, acquired rights by one means or another to the entire country.

As *The International Petroleum Cartel* and Ralph Hewins's biography of IPC's fifth partner, Calouste Gulbenkian, who had 5 percent of the enterprise, declare, the open door had become a sham. Although they thus achieved a monopoly over the course of oil development in Iraq, the parents of IPC never committed themselves to an ambitious expansion there. They undertook only to produce a minimum of 1¼ million tons a year, or about 25,000 barrels a day — a negligible amount — from one meager area, Mosul, on pain of losing their rights to that part of Iraq. The venture's offtake restrictions were perhaps not as severe as the Consortium's in Iran — once they were relaxed, after World War

II. At that time the four equal partners reached agreement that any one of them could lift, at cost, up to five-sevenths (or about 71 percent) as much as the two lowest lifters together nominated. However, the company made sudden expansion difficult, as it planned its output for five-year periods, five years in advance — which was, in effect, up to ten years in advance.[4] The penalty for overlifting in Iraq, after World War II, was the halfway price between tax-paid cost and the market price. The latter price, which was determined by an outside consultant or "award expert," after a scrutiny of the prices for which Iraqi oil was actually selling on the world markets, came closer and closer to the posted price as time went on.

Naturally, since IPC's output was planned up to ten years in advance, the venture's exports increased at a very deliberate pace. It was easy for the company to draw up an expansion strategy, and in fact it had considerable freedom to choose how it would provide its parents with the oil they requested. A former official with one of IPC's parent companies told this writer that the managing director of IPC was always very secretive with parent-company emissaries who came to Iraq. For one thing, though he always maintained surplus capacity, he kept the location and volume of that capacity secret. This was contrary, for instance, to Aramco policy, at least since 1965.

Then the parent emissaries, with the possible exception of a few top officials in BP, knew virtually nothing about IPC's exploration activities within Iraq. This was partly because they did not want to know, and partly because IPC did not want them to know. Visitors from the American parents, Exxon and Mobil, had a driver, car, and staff member at their disposal when they came to Iraq and were prevented from going places where the managing director did not want them to go, on grounds that there wasn't time or it wasn't safe. It was common knowledge among the parent companies, however, that IPC covered Iraq with seismic surveys, and the former official referred to above did hear of the North Rumaila well when that came in. As for the rest, the official said, "There was no drilling that we knew of."

It is understandable that in this atmosphere of suppressed potential Iraq's fields were almost never overproduced. Some wells in Kirkuk did start yielding water in the 1950's, but IPC promptly corrected this with a water-injection program. Zubair, in the south, did develop salt problems, and IPC commissioned desalting equipment there which cost the company 4 or 5 million dollars — but never was used, because engineers had in the meantime found a way to minimize salt-water production by shutting off certain zones. The one case of overproduction in Iraq occurred at Mosul, where oil wells were going to water because IPC had to sustain a minimum average rate of about 25,000 barrels a day to keep the concession. IPC's managing director in the 1950's constantly replaced managers at Mosul in a frantic quest to find someone who could keep production there up at the minimum level.

IPC had one other obligation to maintain production at a certain level, and this was at Kirkuk, where the company had to produce at least 20¾ million tons a year, or about 415,000 barrels a day; since the company maintained a production rate of about 1 million barrels a day there, it never had trouble meeting this commitment. It will be recalled that Kirkuk was IPC's first, and most prolific, property and that BP enjoyed an overriding royalty there. When IPC extended its operations to other parts of Iraq, it did not grant BP a similar royalty in them (or indeed in other countries such as Qatar, where IPC went as a group). During World War II, BP proceeded to destroy some wells in Iraq and all the ones in Qatar, on the pretext that it wanted to keep oil from the Germans and Japanese. As the historian Stephen Longrigg, a former official of BP, has written, "All but six Kirkuk wells (enough to keep up capacity) and one Qayyara well were plugged so effectively as to preclude all hope of reopening" in 1942.[5] It made Mobil and Exxon furious that they could no longer export oil from IPC ventures without paying an override to BP, but they could do little about it: the areas were under British military occupation.

After World War II, IPC consistently and stubbornly understated the nation's oil reserves, failed to follow up promising geological leads, left the middle third of the nation totally undeveloped (while refusing to relinquish it), and kept the information it had acquired regarding the nation's oil potential very largely secret from the Iraqi government.

This in time led to a bitter series of negotiations with the government, starting in 1958, which eventually cost the companies virtually all of their acreage in Iraq — but did not profit the Iraqis either, as IPC effectively kept any other Western firms from developing these properties for a decade.

The presence of massive undeveloped oil reserves in the southern half of Iraq is a subject which is most vividly apparent from two maps.

The first is the standard one, found in most geological textbooks or surveys of the Persian Gulf, such as a paper entitled "Stratigraphic Distribution of Oilfields in the Iraq-Iran-Arabia Basin," by a British geologist, H. V. Dunnington.[6] It covers the entire Persian Gulf oil province, extending from southern Turkey to the Indian Ocean and showing all fields whose existence had been acknowledged by oil companies to that time, early 1967.

Dunnington, in his paper, makes an elaborate case for the similarity of the crude oils in both the northern segment of this province — Turkey, Syria, northern Iraq — and the rich southern segment, which includes Marun, Agha Jari, Burgan, Ghawar, and all the other known fields of Iran, Saudi Arabia, Kuwait, and the remaining gulf states. Dunnington points out that the northern and southern oils are found in much the same kind of strata and structural environments and are chemically very similar as well. For instance, with a few exceptions, they all contain roughly the same volume of sulphur. Other geologists expert in the area who attended the reading of this paper at the institute's London headquarters, at 61 New Cavendish Street, seemed to accept Dunnington's thesis in large measure to judge by the comments following the paper.

However, as one can see from the map, there lies, in the midst of this homogeneous and contiguous oil province, a great void, roughly 250 to 300 miles in length, between the northern and southern segments. Dunnington's plate shows only one small field in the entire area — Naftkhaneh/Naft-e Shah,* which straddles

---

* This field is, strangely, operated by the national oil companies of the two states, not their guests, because the latter did not think them worth retaining; they were too far from water.

the border between Iran and Iraq. One would expect that there might be some other, larger fields between the two main segments, between the Jambur field due north of Baghdad and the Rumaila field just north of Kuwait.

As it turns out, there are. Little is known about them, thanks to IPC's reticence with geological information — a point to which Dunnington himself alluded when he admitted that his paper might contain "errors attributed to an unknown element of misdirection owing to policies of various companies toward release of information."[7] IPC explored in these areas, though — even in the big southern lake and marsh area, the Hawr al-Hammar, on which the firm conducted seismic tests by motorboat.

One of the most ambitious inventories of the area lies in the November, 1967, and February, 1968, issues of Abdullah Tariki's *Arab Oil and Gas Journal,* which contain a two-part article by an Indiana-trained Iraqi geologist, Abdullah Sayyab, entitled "The Geological Factors Bearing on the Oil Potential of Iraq."

Sayyab places a most different evaluation on the Iraqi portion of Dunnington's hiatus, claiming that it holds at least thirteen big oil fields (see page 119).* Most of the fields he shows on his map may not be producible, but several certainly are; *The Middle East Economic Survey* has written, "There is one discovery well in each of Rachi, Ratawi, Luhais and Dujaila [four of Sayyab's thirteen], oil having been encountered in the Cretaceous zone."[8] Another example — so far, the most obvious — is the pair of structures which Sayyab merely represents by two tentative dotted ovals on the map and labels "Suhain." This pair lies within the extensions and trends of lush Iranian structures, and the French state firm ERAP, after gaining rights to them in 1968, actually proved the existence there of two massive fields, Buzurgan and Abu Ghirab, in 1969–1971. The two fields lay more than two miles below ground and yielded up heavy, sulphurous oil, but there was a lot of it. After conducting initial tests, ERAP claimed that Buzurgan had reserves of 4 billion barrels.[9] Later, ERAP claimed the field would be able to produce about 160,000 barrels

---

* Since this map and Dunnington's were published, the Consortium has discovered at least seven fields in the Iranian segment of this hiatus: Danan, Sarkan, Maleh Kuh, Kabud, Cheshmeh Khosh, Dehloran, and Halush.

a day and the Iraqi government upped the reserves figure to 14 billion barrels.

Then, in the following year, the French declared that the field was "uncommercial" on the terms the Iraqis had granted them, which would have imposed a high investment burden on the French and only given them 15 percent of the field's potential output.[10] However, by 1973, five years after the original grant, the "economic prospects" of the fields improved again, when ERAP brought Sumitomo of Japan into the venture as a 40 percent partner and gained the right to buy 30 percent of the production at a "privileged price."[11]

Among the other fields to which Sayyab referred in his article (from which the map on page 119 is reproduced) were Falluja, Halfaya, al-Kifl, al-Samawa, and Nahr Omar (which also appears on Dunnington's map). In the last of these, IPC had drilled three productive wells, where it found two oil zones.

Some of these fields could turn out to be remarkable. The same could hold true for northern Iraq, too, according to Sayyab. He argued, "There is no doubt that patience, self-discipline and repeated study will elevate the classification of this region, and important parts of it, to the first rank as regards volume of petroleum and mineral reserves. . . . Many geological structures with closure in this area — Makhul, Samarra, Milh Tharthar, Mallan, Sasan, Mashuradagh, Ibrahim and so forth — have been drilled into but the quantities of oil found in them were not sufficient for the commencement of oil production. As far as Iraq is concerned, unless production is at a rate above 5,000 barrels a day, the well is uneconomic."[12]

The orginal letting of rights to the Suhain prospect occasioned a bit of a scandal in 1968. It was the same Abdullah Sayyab who, as executive director of Iraq National Oil Company, contributed to the granting of the concession to the French ERAP, declaring on Iraqi television that this was "virgin territory." Another Iraqi oil expert, Ghanim al-Uqaili, reacted to this award with indignation. He wrote a memorandum to President Aref claiming that Sayyab had known that this was not so all along, and that his article in *The Arab Oil and Gas Journal* proved that he knew this acreage held excellent potential. Al-Uqaili added that the structures discovered to date in Dunnington's hiatus could be the richest un-tapped acreage in the world, containing reserves of over 50 bil-lion barrels. He implied that Sayyab was covering up before the Iraqi people, knowing that there was more to the award than met the eye.[13]

Since those days, references to the undeveloped structures of southern Iraq have appeared often in the Iraqi press. Further-more, no less a personage than Brigadier Stephen H. Longrigg, also formerly with Iraq Petroleum Company, has referred to them in his history *Oil in the Middle East*. He pointed out that the Nahr Omar field had actually yielded up good oil — 43 degrees API (a trade measurement meaning that the oil contains many compounds with a low boiling point) and low sulphur, "the lightest oil yet discovered in the Middle East." However, as he went on to explain, IPC failed to develop it because it had also found another field in the vicinity, Zubair, and developed that rather than Nahr Omar because "the uncertain potentiality of this structure and its greater distance from a sea-outlet determined the company to concentrate at Zubair."[14] Zubair, however, was the deepest field discovered in the area up to that time, and de-veloped serious problems with salt water encroachment.

By mid-1973, Zubair had yielded up over 600 million barrels and was running close to a million barrels a day. The Iraqis de-veloped Nahr Omar on their own and scheduled to bring it on-stream in 1974.

The oil history of Iraq from 1958 on illustrates one truth which pervades the history of oil in the Islamic East: while oil is in-extricably bound up with politics in many complicated ways, the host countries have almost always pressed the serious issues on their own merits. Near Eastern politicians rarely embrace or dis-card issues because of their own personal bias regarding Western capital and influence. Oil development in the Near East is not just a religious invasion, like the Crusades, nor do Arabs generally view it as such. Iraq's 1958 negotiations began, in fact, *before* the revolution; before as well as after, they dealt with the same prob-lems: the timeworn issues of relinquishment of acreage, greater profits for the host country, wastage of gas, and production increases.[15] It is true that Kassem, after the revolution, introduced one new issue into the dialogue, Iraq's wish to acquire 20 percent of the concession; but in the deepest sense, this was the oldest issue of all. It went back to what the Iraqis considered their rights from the old San Remo agreement — before the very creation of their state.

The IPC parents had always given Iraq short shrift relative to Arabia and even Iran. At the Church Subcommittee hearings in March, 1974, Senator Percy asked Howard Page to explain why IPC's rate of production increase in the 1950's and 1960's was so low. Page admitted that Exxon, and the other IPC participants, had been "in on one tough problem." While claiming, "We were taking more than the agreement called for out of Iran," he did admit that IPC would have expanded further in Iraq — if it had had to in order to keep the concession. In other words, Exxon and the other IPC parents took a negative view toward oil development in that country: what they wanted was not so much to take oil from Iraq themselves as to keep others from doing so. They developed it only as much as they had to to retain their monopoly in the country.

Certainly, Kassem did become more and more intractable as the 1958–1961 negotiations wore on, escalating several demands, as oil industry executives have often charged. Industry people, in fact, have privately said that Kassem was crazy. In the end, though, his failure seems to have been loss of patience more than fanaticism or insanity. In October, 1961, when the companies seemed to be caving in on the relinquishment issue, because they were running out of rebuttals to Iraq's position and were anxious to preserve their total ownership of IPC at all costs, Kassem said he wanted this to be "the last round."[16] Had he not been so impatient, had he been willing to prolong the negotiations, and had he drawn back in part on his demand for a 20 percent share of the concession, he might have gained in exchange much which the companies were also reluctant to yield.

For the companies had backtracked, in greater or lesser degree, on the other points but by October were still holding firm on this one. They were afraid of setting a precedent, knowing that other nations would immediately demand 20 percent of the concessions in their territories as well. Furthermore, they had one strong argument: Iraq would actually stand to lose money if it bought into the concession, as they hastened to point out. However, they too handled the negotiations with little grace. They could have made a much greater effort to compensate for obduracy on participation by proving more resilient on other points.

One thinks especially of the relinquishment of acreage. In essence this was the second most important point at issue between IPC and the Iraqis. Other companies in the area had given back great areas which they once worked. By the late 1950's, the Iranian Consortium only held title to about one-fifth the land area of Iran, Aramco by the early 1960's perhaps also one-fifth of Arabia. IPC, though, still had the oil rights to all of onshore Iraq.

In fact, the 1958 negotiations had begun with a display of flexibility on both sides. IPC was reputed to agree to cede some unexplored areas to the government and reached an interim agreement to hike production capacity (though not necessarily production itself) to 1.4 million barrels a day by 1962.[17] It actually did carry out some aggressive development in northern Iraq, for the first time in almost a decade. Although the Iraqi public was putting pressure on the government to take over that portion of IPC which belonged to France's CFP — as an act of solidarity with the Algerian revolutionaries — its relations with IPC itself remained cordial for a time. Kassem did allow the first chief negotiator, the leftist Ibrahim Kubbah, to maintain an intransigent attitude at the negotiating table but commanded him to make mild statements in public, because Kassem was treating the companies with caution, if not deference.* Then, in December, 1959, Kassem made a specific demand: that IPC return 60 percent of its acreage to Iraq.

The demand went unrequited. The relinquishment talks failed the following February and Kubbah was out as negotiator and as minister.

A moderate, Muhammad Salman, took his place but came under pressure, as the year wore on, to adopt a militant stance. The

---

* As David Hirst described the negotiations (*Oil and Public Opinion in the Middle East*, p. 83), this moderation even extended to Kubbah's relations with Communist-bloc newspapers. Leftist though he was, Kubbah refused to reassure them that Iraq would nationalize IPC.

Iraqi government made another effort to acquire greater revenues: it imposed port dues on oil exported from southern Iraq. This, too, backfired. IPC claimed that it was no longer economically feasible for it to produce oil in southern Iraq, and it had a point: it showed that these fees were ten to twenty times greater than in other gulf oil ports, and they were not strictly speaking a tax for real services anyway, since IPC was exporting the oil from its own terminal. So it cut back its production in southern Iraq drastically.

Once again, the talks resumed: the Iraqis enunciated a new stand. The companies had just cut the posted price of crude again and the Near Eastern states were joining forces with the Venezuelans to stop this erosion of revenues. To this end they brought OPEC into being. Iraq incorporated OPEC's demand for price stability into its talks with IPC.*

The fall 1960 talks between Iraq and IPC came to naught also. Further discussions took place, sporadically, through the winter, then broke down in April, 1961, over a relatively small issue, deduction of rents for undeveloped land as an expense, a matter of $2 million or so a year. Kassem was present at these negotiations himself and took the unprecedented step of publishing minutes to them.[18] He also suspended all of IPC's exploration activities until the two sides "came to a just agreement."

By that time, Iraq had come to demand that IPC relinquish all its undeveloped territory.

In June, 1961, Iraq suffered a severe setback in another area. The state of Kuwait, just south, had acquired its full independence from Britain that month. Iraq claimed that Kuwait had formerly been part of its territory, and made an awkward attempt

---

* OPEC was born of a crude-oil price conference the five major states Iran, Iraq, Kuwait, Saudi Arabia, and Venezuela held in Baghdad in September, 1960, and the Second Arab Petroleum Conference the following month in Beirut, where Abdullah Tariki, in rage against the companies, exclaimed, "When the oil companies lose in Germany, they cut the price in the gulf. When the oil companies make money in Germany, they keep the profits." He indicated that when Middle Eastern prices rose, the postings did not — the companies' tanker subsidiaries, based in tax shelters, just pocketed the increase. Tariki also called for a crude oil prorationing system, a concept which has never worked, not even in the partial embargoes of 1967 and 1973. But the price stabilization held.

to invade its neighbor. The British, and other Arab states, came to Kuwait's defense so Kassem's ploy failed utterly. But Kassem's luck with oil was running stronger. IPC agreed to meet his demand for the nondeduction of rents, and asked to resume talking. It offered to send a higher-level contingent than it had before, one which could make decisions of its own accord rather than shuttle back to London for instructions.

This was to be the last round. It basically boiled down to the two big issues: the relinquishment of acreage and the 20 percent share of Iraq Petroleum Company.

IPC's first move was to bring Kassem a memorandum from London, which in essence informed Iraq that it would be pointless for the nation to seek a share of IPC, because Iraq would lose money. It would be better off leaving matters as they were, letting IPC keep title to all the properties and taxing it on the artificially high posted price. This was a cogent argument. However, the memorandum was a sort of confession of weakness: it read more like a sales pitch than an ultimatum.

For instance, it made much of the competitive threat from Russian oil, which may have seemed to be growing at that time but has since faded. It endeavored to show that IPC had been sheltering Iraq from the vicissitudes of the marketplace — which in a sense it had — claimed that the industry's capital requirements were vast, and, what is most significant, declared that if it made less money from oil production, its strength in the international market would be sapped further. "If in any way the share remaining to the companies were reduced further," it concluded, "the future of the companies would be seriously prejudiced. The prosperity of producing countries is closely linked with the prosperity of the companies.[19]

Kassem failed to perceive the companies' defensive tack. He, too, sounded like a suppliant on the participation issue, though maintaining that the memorandum contained "feeble excuses which could not be taken into consideration."[20]

The companies, however, were even weaker on the question of the acreage they should relinquish to Iraq, because, while they obdurately refused to let Iraq select the acreage it wanted, they knew that this stand was not unassailable even on commercial grounds, as their argument against participation had been.* This dialogue between Premier Kassem and the leader of the IPC team, an Exxon director named H. W. Fisher, should help illustrate this edginess:

Kassem: Our discussions dealt with relinquishment on the basis that the government would choose part of the concession area while the companies would take the other part.

Fisher: We did not agree to the government taking the first choice. . . . I wish to comment on this subject. The idea that the government should have the first choice is not a *practical* suggestion because it means *the government will choose the lands which contain oil.* [Italics supplied.]

Kassem: Why not? We are partners and you now have oil-producing wells whilst we do not possess wells.

Fisher: We offer you now a plan which will give you wells in a short time.

Later on, Fisher ceased discussing whether or not Kassem's demand was "practical" and merely said, "I am unaware of any place in the world where the government chooses the lands given up by the oil companies."

Kassem said, "Each side will choose."

Riposted Fisher, "It is the companies which choose the lands they relinquish in all parts of the world."

Now the issue had become one of precedent — the precedent which the companies had set. Toward the end, they discussed the matter further:

Kassem: Do you agree that 75 percent [of the acreage] be taken, on condition that the government selects?

Fisher: The companies cannot carry out exploration and then submit the information to the government to select.

Kassem: Funds expended on exploration are shared by both sides.

Fisher: The funds, like other expenditures, are paid out of the cost.

Kassem: Why should the companies alone benefit from them, and why should not the government benefit from them as well?

* This is assuming that the minutes are to be taken as accurate, which they most probably were. This author has seen no protest against them on IPC's part.

But Kassem did not seem to appreciate that the IPC team had shown that it knew it was on shaky ground by stating that Iraq had no right to determine which of its own acreage it could redeem; rather, it became obvious in the minutes that what he was really after was 20 percent of IPC — which is what the companies were specifically most reluctant to give up.

Kassem: If you are losing [money on your refining and marketing operations in Europe], then why do you not spare us the time which is consumed in negotiations and share with us all the operations?

Fisher: I believe that Iraq does not possess sufficient funds, even if we agreed. [Again, the Exxon man's readiness to speak for the man across the table.]

Kassem: We have enough funds, and we also have the oil. . . .

. . . Fisher: You have a share in kind [that is, the 12½ percent royalty, which they could take in cash or kind].

Kassem: Decide that we should take a share in kind of 20 percent, and let us end the negotiations.

Fisher: You have a share in kind of 12½ percent.

Then later this dialogue took place, after Fisher reviewed the terms of the 1920 San Remo agreement, pointing out that the government had exercised its option, had chosen to take a fixed royalty instead of a 20 percent share (and that three ministers had resigned forthwith) :

Kassem: What is the reason you will not confirm the government's right to share, despite the fact that the San Remo Agreement included this right?

Fisher: Because the possibilities mentioned by Article 34 of the concession did not take place. . . . The agreement provided that if the company became a public company, the government would then have the right to share 20 percent.

Kassem: Were the companies in the areas where sharing by 20 percent was granted private or public companies?

Fisher: To our knowledge, the companies were private.

Kassem: From this it appears that the explanation is always in favor of the companies. With respect to Iraq, you say the company is private and cannot share, while in other countries the companies are private and are given shares.

Fisher: We are talking about Article 34 only. It is not right to compare sharing in 1961 and the situation in 1925. . . .

And still later:

Kassem: No country in the world was wronged in its dealings with the companies as Iraq has been. Have you seen any company in the world taking all the territory of the country, its seas, and its airspace in one concession? You have taken this right from people who were traitors to their country.

Fisher: We did not take this right from anybody. We made an agreement with the government.

Kassem: The government was traitorous.

Fisher: It was the recognized Iraqi government.

Kassem: For this reason it brought woe to other governments and left a great hatred for the [Western] governments which cooperated with it. . . . We came to remove the seeds of hatred and sow the seeds of friendship.

Fisher: We too.

Kassem: Therefore, we must change the previous situation.

So IPC was edgy on this subject too, obviously unsure of its position, though it had a stronger argument for keeping Iraq out of IPC than for holding onto all the lushest undeveloped acreage in Iraq. Kassem's mistake, again, was that he did not appreciate this, did not press where he was strongest, did not demand acreage in exchange for abandoning a claim to 20 percent of IPC.

Still, he made a move in this direction — to which IPC did not respond. Toward the end of the talks Kassem said, "With regard to participation, is it your final opinion that the government cannot participate?"

Fisher fenced around and did not give a clear answer.

Kassem offered him a last-minute proposal: that IPC immediately relinquish 90 percent of its concession acreage, in return for which Iraq would cease asking for the right "to participate in the existing wells."

This was more than he had been offering up to then. Fisher replied, "This is a sudden proposal"; but he did not grasp at it, or even show enthusiasm for it. In a few moments the negotiations collapsed.

In two months' time Kassem passed his famous Law 80 for the year 1961, whereby Iraq expropriated 99.5 percent of the IPC concession — that is, 99.5 percent of the acreage in Iraq, including one known field, North Rumaila, which had not gone onstream but on which three wells had proved to hold great potential.

One can certainly argue that the Iraqis' yearning for a 20 percent share of IPC might have been fabricated, that Kassem and other Iraqi figures pressed so hard for it because they knew the companies were reluctant to grant it. Maybe it was a useful device for embarrassing IPC — thus for making Kassem seem to his people like an illustrious leader, one who could stand up to and defeat the greatest collection of private companies in the world. Certainly it was an excellent bargaining tool. How deeply the loss of the 20 percent share really grieved Kassem, and the extent to which he was cynically manipulating the demand, is hard to establish. Nor can one ignore that the companies had to make a firm stand, to protect themselves against further, stiffer demands.

The fact remained, though, that the Iraqi public discovered that their government, at some point in the past, had been offered the right to share in IPC and had somehow, irrevocably, lost that right — without gaining anything substantial in exchange, such as good acreage. It is this awareness which rankles: the perception of what could have been but was denied, perhaps forever. The company's mistake lay right there: in its stiff refusal to give this gut emotion its due.

As it turned out, although Kassem was overthrown and assassinated a little more than a year after the passage of Law 80, there was logic to his move: over the following decade, many companies tried to gain access to the expropriated acreage.

Had Law 80 come a decade later, when countries started to get away with the expropriation of oil rights, and when the threat of takeover had ceased to jeopardize world peace or the prosperity of the international market, it would have worked; it would have opened up large areas of Iraq to development.

It was no secret, even in 1961, that Iraq had excellent potential. In August, at a crucial stage in the Iraq-IPC negotiations, a rumor circulated that some independent companies had approached Gulbenkian's firm, Partex, which held 5 percent of IPC, with an offer to purchase this share and related interests in Qatar, Abu Dhabi, and Oman for $100 million. The Gulbenkian interests, when asked about this overture, "refused comment."[21] Their reticence leaves us room to speculate that perhaps such an offer had indeed been made and that Partex had considered taking it — perhaps only turning it down in the end under duress.

Then, within a week of the issuance of Law 80, the Syrian-American entrepreneur J. W. Menhall, who had held a concession briefly in eastern Syria, then lost it after Syria united with Egypt in 1958, made overtures for acreage to the Iraqi government.

Following him came many other companies — the Italian ENI, the French ERAP — and CFP — and seven crude-short American enterprises, Sinclair, Union, Standard of Indiana, Continental, Marathon, Pauley, and Phillips.

The IPC parents and the United States State Department successfully quelled the overtures of the American firms. Most of the companies backed off quickly under their pressure, but Union Oil of California proved stubborn: it continued to talk with the Iraqis until it received a "strong cable" from the head of IPC himself.

The very parents of IPC — except for Exxon — tentatively made a deal with the government to get back into much of this territory, but the deal fell through in the end.

In 1967, in the wake of the Arab-Israeli War, when General de Gaulle of France enjoyed a rapprochement with the Arab world for his refusal to continue selling arms to "all combatants" — meaning all Israelis but only some Arabs — it became known that the French state firm ERAP was interested in acquiring some of Iraq's expropriated acreage, North Rumaila in particular. This led to the negotiations described at the beginning of this chapter.

The IPC parents, alarmed because there were few reprisals they could take against the government of France, encouraged their French partner CFP to rush into this acreage before ERAP got it. The Iraqis turned CFP down. ERAP won the excellent plots at Buzurgan and Abu Ghirab but failed to acquire North Rumaila; eventually, with the help of Hungarians and Soviets, the Iraqis developed this themselves.

Throughout the sixties, IPC continued to negotiate a broad range of issues with the government of Iraq, in an effort to regain the acreage it had lost, in particular North Rumaila. As indicated above, the firm came close to reaching agreement, in 1965, with the moderate government of Abdel Salaam Aref and his bright, technologically-minded young oil minister Abdel Aziz al-Wattari.

This round of negotiations was prolix in the extreme, thanks to the royalty-expensing demands which all OPEC countries were bringing forth in one front. This was to gain the countries another dime or so a barrel.* Iraq, for its part, tied the royalty expensing issue to the other matters over which it was at odds with IPC, such as Law 80, but eventually agreed to enter with all IPC parents (except the unyielding Exxon) into an agreement to develop in concert some of the acreage Kassem had expropriated — including North Rumaila.[22]

The government could not quite afford to ratify this agreement. Domestic opposition to it was too strong. In 1967, when war broke out between Israel and its Arab neighbors, the Iraqi government abandoned the agreement entirely and passed another piece of legislation, Law 97 for the year 1967, which signed all the expropriated acreage over to Iraq National Oil Company for once and for all.

Later, not surprisingly, after the accession of Ahmad Hasan al-Bakr, the Iraqi press entered into a campaign against the conciliatory policies of the Aref regime. For instance, the major Baghdad daily, *al-Thawra,* described the early days of the national oil company thus: "A company board of directors was chosen, most of whose members were spies of the oil companies and servants of imperialism. . . . From 1961 onwards, and specifically since 1964, there were frantic attempts to nullify Law 80 and there was coordination between the efforts of government and oil company officials to sabotage the law and strip it of its contents. In addition, there were secret negotiations during which were prepared the two

---

* This demand was for a provision whereby the states would receive the 12½ percent royalty on top of the 50 percent tax, not as a credit against 25 percent of the tax, as had been the case. This was to gain the countries another 23 cents or so a barrel, but countervailing "marketing allowances" would remove some of that, as much as 13 cents.

bad agreements of 1965 which provided for the return of the best discovered fields and oil lands to the companies."[23]

As al-Bakr began to lurch out of the dugout, al-Wattari turned away and trudged off to the distant bullpen of Libya, where he found employment as a consultant. (There are about as many Arab oil experts working as consultants in adopted Arab states as there once were White Russian princes driving taxis in Paris.) Al-Bakr, for his part, waved in a successor, Rashid al-Rifai, from the even more distant bullpen of New Mexico Institute of Mining and Technology. Later, another self-exiled technocrat, Saadoun Hammadi, came in from Libya (and Wisconsin) to take his place.

The events of 1970–1971 — the dramatic increases in oil taxes which occurred first in Libya, then in the Persian Gulf, and once again, thanks to Libya, in the Mediterranean — further exacerbated Iraq's relations with the industry. This story is to unfold later. However, one development in this price escalation was crucial to Iraq: the genesis of "the hinge."

The hinge was the posted price of Iraqi (and indeed Saudi) oil at the eastern Mediterranean terminals. It was the pivot point in an arcane relationship between the prices for crude oil landed in the Mediterranean (especially Libya) and that landed in the Persian Gulf. There was usually an imbalance between these two sets of prices. Furthermore, there was usually an imbalance between the export prices of Iraq's two oils, that from Kirkuk in the north and from Basra in the south. There had been problems with this before: the imbalance was a bone of contention during Kassem's negotiations and a real object of acrimony between Syria and IPC in 1966.

Beginning in 1971 then, since prices rose much higher in the Mediterranean than they did in the gulf, Kirkuk oil suddenly became more costly to the IPC parents than did southern Iraqi oil.

This strange but natural occurrence induced the IPC parents to lower their exports of Kirkuk crude oil from the eastern Mediterranean, drastically, in 1972. It brought a swift showdown. The Iraqi government demanded that the company raise its offtake of

Kirkuk crude to the former level within two weeks, and to sustain that higher level. The IPC parents refused. The Iraqis then expropriated the IPC concession in northern Iraq.

Perhaps the companies had committed a fatal blunder. One journalist, David Hirst, certainly thought so. IPC's explanation that southern Iraqi crude was cheaper to export than that from Kirkuk, "though perhaps commercially justified, is political dynamite," he wrote. "The companies must know it. . . . After the breakdown in company-government talks last February, it seems to be inviting a showdown."[24]

Perhaps. Maybe the companies — and the United States State Department — could have worked to prevent this occurrence had they seriously endeavored to do so. But then perhaps the Iraqi government was bent on such a showdown anyway — and the oil companies had little to do with it. As with the Syria-IPC controversy of 1966–1967, the cause for showdown may have been local politics more than industry policies. This time, the political problem was very serious; it involved the Iraqi government and the Kurds, who had made peace of sorts about two years earlier. The Kurds, however, remained restive; they were not totally satisfied with the agreement. They kept raising the demand for an autonomous local government in those areas of Iraq where they were in the majority. It was not clear what these areas were, precisely, because the Iraqi government refused to take a nation-wide census, but the Kurds kept claiming that the Kirkuk area was one of them. Underlying this claim was the certainty that if the Kurds gained autonomous rule in Kirkuk, they would demand rights to the oil produced at the Kirkuk field. The Kurds claimed that not only did Iraqi authorities refuse to take a census — they were trying to settle Arabs in the area too, to tilt a census should they ever be forced to take one. (The Iraqis charged that the Kurds were moving thousands of their people down from Turkey for the same reason.)

At any rate, one obvious Iraqi government strategy in such a situation would be to make the Kirkuk field a less important property, by expanding oil production in the south; this would lessen the pressure the Kurds could exert on the Iraqis by cutting off, or threatening to cut off, the government's main source of revenue. One French journalist — quoting an unnamed "oil specialist" — wrote that "by 1980 Kirkuk will no longer be so important. . . . The Iraqis need Kirkuk at the present time but that country's future lies in the South." So, by 1980, "the Iraqis could nearly afford to shut off the flow of oil at Kirkuk." The journalist, having answered the question, then asked it: "Does the Baathist regime, which holds all the data of a too little known oil situation, consciously seek to temporize while waiting for the 1980 deadline, a time when the Kurds will no longer be able to use the Kirkuk blackmail?"[25]

Perhaps the Iraqi government, therefore, by nationalizing Kirkuk in 1972, was not punishing IPC so much as attempting to checkmate the Kurds — showing its northern tribal insurgents that the threat to take over Kirkuk was vain. At any rate, its act was the first major expropriation in two decades of Middle Eastern oil history. It was also the only such act to have come to a "happy ending" by this writing. IPC at first tried to stop other Western companies from buying hot Kirkuk oil directly from Iraq, and for a time it looked as if the company would succeed, just as its campaign to keep other companies out of the Law 80 acreage had succeeded for the better part of a decade.

However, Iraq started to sell some of this hot oil. It had already been shipping some North Rumaila crude west; now it allowed CFP to continue lifting the share of Kirkuk oil to which it would have been entitled had the expropriation not occurred, and at tax-paid cost; Czechoslovakia agreed to buy about 10,000 barrels a day, Hungary took a little bit, East Germany probably skimmed some off too.[26] The price of this crude, at the terminal in Baniyas, Syria, dropped more than a dollar below posted price,[27] but in the end, after IPC had threatened action against companies attempting to lift this crude, and placed advertisements in newspapers throughout the Western world to this effect, the company suddenly reversed itself. It now stated that it would take no legal action while it pursued negotiations with al-Bakr's government. President al-Bakr proclaimed a period of "sumoud wa taqashshuf tamm" — perseverance and utter asceticism — and gained financial aid from Kuwait, Libya, and the Soviet Union. By October, Iraq was exporting about 700,000 barrels from Kirkuk each day — more than before nationalization.[28]

By that time, the oil companies had become faced with something new: the demand from all Arab states that they yield up at least 20 percent of the concessions to their hosts.

Month after month, IPC extended its moratorium. Finally, in early March, 1973, the two parties reached full agreement. IPC would accept Law 80 and the nationalization of the Kirkuk concession, would receive over 100 million barrels of Kirkuk oil free of cost and tax, and would pay the Iraqi government an overall settlement of all claims, including royalty-expensing, of 141 million pounds sterling. In addition, it would step up production from the southern fields.

IPC celebrated the accord with a further splash of advertisements in the financial pages of major Western newspapers.[29] It looked as if Iraq's anti-Kurdish strategy was paying off.

Suddenly Western companies wanted to go into Iraq again. Suddenly the country's production, stagnant for years, rose by more than 40 percent. Iraq even upped its production further during the 1973–1974 embargo. Oil circles began to conjecture, through *The Oil and Gas Journal* and other organs, that maybe Iraq's oil reserves were greater than those of any other Persian Gulf state, except Kuwait and of course Saudi Arabia.[30]

This was quite a reversal. Over the years, no one in the industry had publicly admitted that Iraq's reserves amounted to more than 25 billion barrels. Now, to have the third biggest inventory in the gulf, Iraq would have to have 60 billion barrels of recoverable reserves at the very least. Assuming a conservative rate of production, say 4 percent of reserves per year, the country could easily produce at a rate of two billion barrels per year — at the very least. This would allow an increase in production of about 5 million barrels a day.

Iraq, where production had never stayed as high as 2 million barrels a day, had, in a roundabout and expensive way, vindicated itself.

10

A Footnote on the French

Now, something very curious is happening with the United States. . . . It is perfectly true that there has never been a will to political conquest in the United States. There were episodes, but that doesn't count. . . . In America there are some very great powers — and these powers are generally but not merely economic.

— André Malraux

THE INTERNATIONAL OIL INDUSTRY had truly changed — though not quite in the manner the oil companies and the American government have since claimed. The change was long in coming and slow in maturing, in Saudi Arabia and Iran as well as their poor stepsister Iraq. What brought the revolution was a development far to the west, beyond the Suez Canal but still within Arab territory: in the apparently primitive and nouveau-riche state of Libya. In turn the evolution and revolution in that Mediterranean land owe much to the policies of a dynamic but much-neglected element in the international trade, the French.

The 1958 revolution in Iraq, which took place — probably by coincidence — on Bastille Day, was a shocking experience for the United States. Iraq, under the monarchy, had been a staunch member of the American side in the Cold War; it belonged to the Baghdad Pact, was hostile to the international Communist movement, and welcomed foreign capital. The revolution took the State Department — and in all likelihood the CIA — by surprise, undoubtedly provoking an agonizing reappraisal of our nation's entire approach to the Persian Gulf, and ushered in a series of governments which have all been more or less hostile to the West and to America in particular. It was America's biggest setback in the region since the war. Since 1958, Iraq's governments have on many occasions hosted Communists (although they have also persecuted them on occasion) and the nation entertains good relations with the Soviet Union to this day.

The Russians have not penetrated Iraq very deeply, but they have exerted influence there — have helped develop Iraqi ports on the Persian Gulf, finally opening a solitary window for themselves onto the warm waters of this sea. This has been a vexation to our government. In American strategic terms, the Persian Gulf is probably the third most vital foreign area there is, after western Europe and the Caribbean, and for good reason. Now that western Europe (and Japan) has, through the commercial dynamism of American oil interests, become overwhelmingly committed to oil for its energy needs (all within one generation), it is to America at least a matter of economic urgency, and some would say necessity, that these consuming states continue to receive voluminous supplies of oil, guaranteed over the long term, from the Moslem East (the price is a secondary matter). The best guarantee for this is that the Near Eastern states be on good terms with America.

But America is not the only party interested in seeing that oil continues to move west from this region in a secure, voluminous flow. The major importing states feel that they have to enjoy insurance of a more direct, immediate kind than America requires, because they hardly have oil resources of their own.* The British and Dutch have always enjoyed some protection in this sense, through the operations of British Petroleum and Royal Dutch/Shell. The Italians, despite their efforts to develop foreign

* Except in the North Sea, which will be coming onstream in a very big way about the middle of this decade.

sources of oil, have not. In the 1950's and early 1960's the head of Italy's state oil firm, ENI, Enrico Mattei, fought hard to acquire good properties for his company, thus enraging the major firms and incurring the distrust of the United States State Department. Mattei offered such countries as Egypt, Tunisia, and Iran 75 rather than 50 percent of the profits from the oil concessions, and bargained with the Soviets for crude oil. He proceeded to lower natural gas prices in Italy, to prove that his "seven sisters" were overcharging the Italian public, and he built several refineries in Africa.* As a result, ENI was not invited into the Iranian Consortium in 1954.[1] In time his efforts lost momentum and he was killed in an air crash. It is an article of faith in the International Left that French right-wing terrorists fighting the Algerian revolutionaries sabotaged his airplane, fearing that Mattei had been making a deal with the nationalists to develop the Sahara after Algeria won its independence.

Like Mattei and ENI, the French suffered by being outside the Anglo-Saxon center of the international oil industry, but they struggled longer than the Italians, and with greater success, to improve their position. Their efforts, in fact, were motivated more by financial than by political considerations. In most times, the main problem facing major importing states like France has been not so much whether they would have access to the oil they needed, but whether they would have to pay exorbitant prices for it in foreign currency. Only in Algeria and Iraq have the French so far had significant access to crude purchased from French suppliers.

Of course they have always wanted more than they got, and this helps explain their attitudes, often antagonistic toward the oil companies — even as partners — and their attempts to curry favor with the states of the Near East. This was certainly a major element, too, in de Gaulle's hostility toward Britain and America during the 1950's and 1960's.

* For instance, see the testimony of Ambassador George McGhee, former geologist and director of Mobil, before the Church Subcommittee in January, 1974. McGhee expresses criticism of Mattei's flamboyant projects, and speaks even more strongly against the deal to buy crude from Russia. "We were naturally concerned," he said, and claimed that the State Department urged the companies "to supply the Italians oil within the framework of the existing commercial market, so they wouldn't have to buy it from the Soviet Union."

The quest for Saharan oil was one of the main obstacles to resolution of the eight-year war of liberation in Algeria. During this struggle between France and the Algerian FLN, French interests found some oil in the Sahara. Situated some four hundred to five hundred miles from water, and concentrated in only moderately large deposits, this was the most expensive oil exported from the Arab world. To illustrate this fact, several major oil companies, such as Exxon, Gulf, and the Oasis group, found oil only a few scores of miles away from the deposits the French were exploiting in the Fezzan "pocket," but they refused to develop this other oil, which was in Libya, because by their standards it was too costly. Later, in a controversy with the Algerian government, the French state conglomerate ERAP declared that its average production costs were very high — 85 cents a barrel. The other big French firm, CFP, stated that its production and pipeline costs were 43 cents a barrel (quite close to the Libyan average).[2]

The French, at great expense, constructed a pipeline out of the Fezzan pocket and up to Tunisia, though it moved only about 200,000 barrels a day. They followed up this development with somewhat more extensive discoveries in the Hassi Messaoud area of central Algeria, slightly closer to the Mediterranean, but still separated from it by high mountains.

During the long peace talks at Evian which concluded the Algerian war, the future of the virtually uninhabited Sahara was one of the last problems to reach a solution, mainly because of the oil.[3]

The crude-thirsty French ultimately ceded this region to the Algerians. In exchange, their oil interests there gained a few years' peace. At first, after independence in 1962, they enjoyed excellent tax advantages and paid low royalties on their production. In 1965, though, with the downfall of Algeria's first president, Ahmad Ben Bella, and the advent of the financially shrewder Houari Boumedienne to power, the fledgling state pushed through an agreement which, on paper, was stiffer than any other in the Middle East at the time. The French (and minor "Anglo-Saxon" interests, for Shell and several American companies had also acquired rights in Algeria) were obligated to pay tax on a posted price which was above that for similar crude in neighboring Libya. The discrepancy widened still further in 1968 — to almost 40 cents a barrel.

The French, nonetheless, held on to Algeria's oil resources and developed them. In 1970, France was importing about two million barrels of oil a day; of this, 26 percent came from Algeria, and French companies had title to 70 percent of it. France's second-biggest source of oil was Iraq, where CFP's entitlement came to about 250,000 barrels a day. Algeria was thus by far the nation's biggest source of franc-zone oil.

The major international firms refining and marketing products in France — Caltex, Mobil, BP, Shell, and Exxon — had to buy a certain amount of franc-zone oil for their operations as well. Thus the French sheltered Algeria from the potential ferocities of the international market, for the benefit of their own economy.

The natural tension in this relationship notwithstanding, other factors militated in favor of the maintenance of close bonds between the two states. France provided employment for hundreds of thousands of Algerians; Algeria formed a good market for French goods and services and a source of franc-zone agricultural products. For a short while after independence, Algeria allowed France the use of a naval base. It also provided the French with an important area of cultural influence — the sort of privilege the French value very highly. But most vital of all was the oil relationship, because the Algerians wanted to change it and the French, while wanting it to remain just as it was, gave the Algerians unwitting encouragement by their protection and also by their indifference to such inviolable premises of Anglo-Saxon oil as the frozen posted price, the fifty-fifty profit split, and company ownership of the means of distribution. As Le Monde described it, "Algeria considers that cooperation between the two countries can only blossom once oil 'decolonization' has been fulfilled, whereas for France, from the outset, oil relations were to be the cornerstone of this cooperation."[4]

As time went on the Algerians imposed conditions of increasing severity on the companies, and the companies capitulated in most cases. The French, in 1965, had insisted that French contractors obtain awards to drill for joint Franco-Algerian exploration ventures; the Algerians found that the American firm Sedco could do the job cheaper, so formed a joint venture with it.

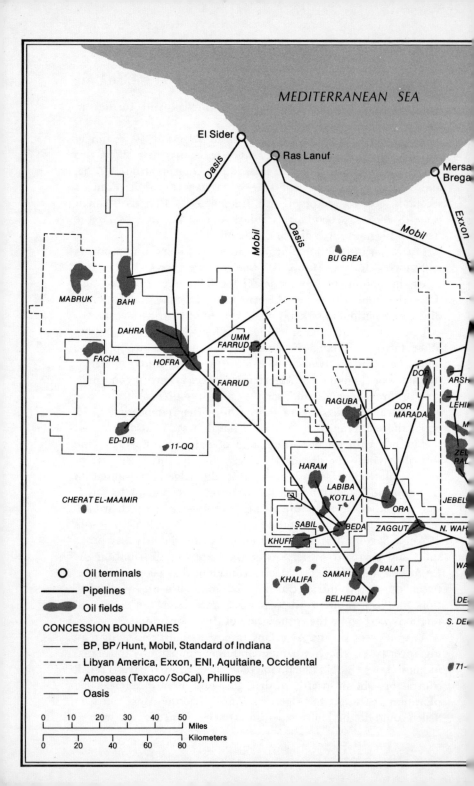

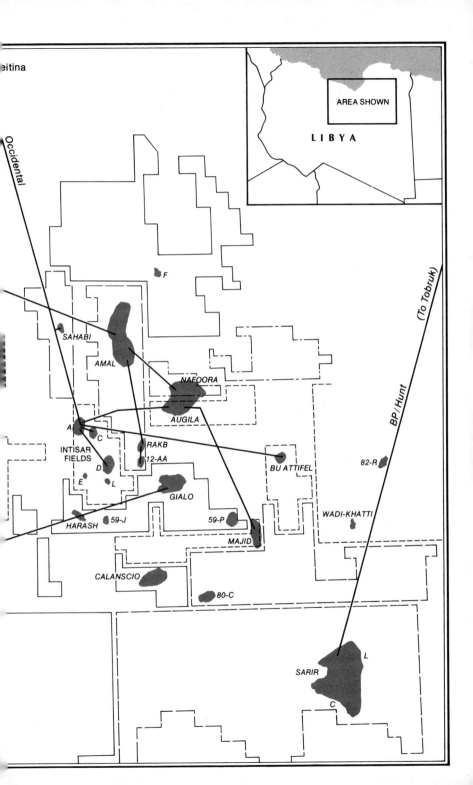

The French protested. The Algerians stood firm. The French started to take a closer, more critical look at the chemical composition of the wines they imported from their former colony. The Algerians nationalized French insurance companies. Expatriate Algerian laborers found themselves standing in line longer to renew their French work permits. Then the Algerians began to impose, on their American guests, the terms which they had gained from the French in 1965, and further terms. Getty, the lone wolf, obliged them, consenting to an agreement which many oilmen thought too generous to be viable, one which "would have difficulty passing the board of directors of most big international companies," as one commentator put it. This included acquiescing to a posted price of $2.635 a barrel, FOB the Algerian port of Bougie, for oil which Getty would be obligated to lift from the national oil company Sonatrach, if Sonatrach elected not to sell the oil itself. It also abrogated the hallowed fifty-fifty profit split: Algeria raised its tax take to 55 percent of net profits. The Algerians thought this agreement so important that President Boumedienne himself entertained the Getty team for dinner the night before it was signed.

As it turned out, this agreement was epochal, but the Algerians had difficulty persuading other companies to accept it. Sinclair, when presented with terms similar to those Getty had agreed to, balked and received an invitation to leave the country. The pretext was that it had failed to ask Algeria's permission before merging with Atlantic Richfield back in the states; one rumor going around Algiers' foreign community had it that a top Sinclair official once offered to throw an Algerian labor leader out his window. In fact, Atlantic Richfield was offered a deal to stay on in Algeria, but found it too costly and declined it.

The Algerians turned to the interests of an American gas firm, El Paso, in a local oilfield; El Paso countered with an offer to find clients, in America, for Algerian gas, if only it were to be spared. The Algerians spared it and El Paso thrashed and wrangled for years, though its plans to import gas into the United States were eventually postponed for the better part of a decade.

What the Algerians were doing in all this was quietly to strive toward total control of their industry. The Americans were actually abetting them by agreeing to somewhat better terms than the French had settled on in 1965.

The Libyan actions of 1970 must have hastened the Algerian drive for autonomy, as they did the Iraqis' drive. This acceleration of the inevitable, in turn, made pioneers of the Algerians. Boumedienne turned to the French and asked for terms which the Americans had granted him — including 51 percent of their oil interests. Lengthy and acrimonious discussions followed, and in February, 1971, President Boumedienne announced that he had nationalized 51 percent of their oil interests anyway — and expropriated all their gas properties.

The maverick French fought back bitterly and the next four months were hard for Algeria. Its oil production fell by two-thirds. At one point Algeria shut down the pipeline leading from the Fezzan pocket to Tunisia and at another point both CFP and ERAP withdrew their technicians from the country — so the Algerians asked that the talks resume. The outcome of the talks was fairly favorable to the French companies; CFP, which settled first, received about $37 million in indemnification. But the nationalizations stuck. The French, who for years had struggled to keep their partners in IPC from going into Saudi Arabia without them; who had taken the secret APQ formula and the Participants' Agreement to the Shah of Iran in frustration at their failure to get the oil they wanted from the Consortium; who had offered Iran, Libya, and Iraq exciting new concession terms (thereby enraging the international majors, though the terms were not always lucrative), finally, in their dependence on Algeria, gave in to the spirit of the February edict by late spring.

On paper, the Algerian achievement was not overwhelming. Since the 1965 agreement had given the fledgling state 49 percent of many French oil properties anyway, including the biggest one, Hassi Messaoud, all they did in 1971 was take over another 2 percent — for which in fact they repaid the French most handsomely. But they had made their point: they had acquired a large degree of right to control the production, and minimum price, of their own oil. It remained for the other countries in the Near East — indeed, all over the world — to do the same.

11

The Near Easterners Look at the Industry

Do you see how you complicated matters? Concerning participation, you said: The company is a private one. Concerning the increase of the share, you said: We are an old company. Concerning the gas which had burnt, you said: This was in the public interest and we cannot give you any compensation. We told you: Give us the gas to dispose of. You said: We have other proposals.
— Abdel Karim Kassem, former premier of Iraq

ONE MIGHT AT THIS JUNCTURE PAUSE to take stock of a tiny incident which occurred several years before, in March, 1967 — just after the resolution of the Syria-IPC controversy. The Sixth Arab Petroleum Congress met then in Baghdad, Iraq, and many colorful personalities contributed to lively debate at this forum on issues central to the Near East. One commentator, a moderate pro-Western expert named Abdel Amir Kubbah, who was publishing a magazine in Iraq, distributed among the participants a supplement to his magazine, in which he presented a sarcastic indictment of the views of the fiery nationalist Sheikh Abdullah Tariki. Since he had left Arabia in exile, in 1964, Tariki, too, had been publishing an oil magazine — *The Arab*

Oil and Gas Journal, out of Beirut. He had been appearing at Arab Petroleum Congresses and other oil colloquia, freely dispensing advice to his fellow Arabs, and calling for the outright nationalization of Western oil interests.

Or had he?

Kubbah, in his supplement, indicated that this militant was being inconsistent in his views. He gave several examples. Once, Tariki had defended a concession he himself had negotiated, with the Japanese off the Neutral Zone, then had severely criticized another concession his successor, Yamani, had drawn up — though its terms were no less stringent. "Why is the Shaikh unable to congratulate Ahmad Zaki Yamani while going overboard in congratulating [Iran's] Dr. Eghbal?" Kubbah asked further, giving another example.

Then he pointed out that Tariki had counseled Kuwait not to nationalize its oil-producing properties and then had attacked Iraq for failing to nationalize IPC: "The foreign oil companies in Iraq are monopolistic and should be got rid of," Kubbah mimicked Tariki, "but in Libya and Kuwait they are commercial enterprises and 'the governments must treat them fairly, so that they remain in the country, and take no measure that might do them harm.' "[1]

Kubbah made several other points, the gist of which was that perhaps Tariki had motives other than simple patriotism; maybe he was not doing the Arab public a service so much as vindicating himself and his career. Indeed, perhaps he was "soft" — hard on those who had insulted him or made him jealous, generous and sentimental with those who had given him, or Arabs in general, ritual concessions. However, Kubbah, by documenting his claims with specific, closely reasoned points, had got himself into trouble. The Iraqi authorities revoked the license to his magazine on grounds that he had "exceeded his prerogatives."

Eventually, five years later, Tariki got into trouble too; Lebanese authorities suspended his license, though they returned it in time. One reason that Tariki's magazine lasted longer than Kubbah's was that it *was* soft and generous, despite its veneer of rancor and militance. While praising Arab initiatives in the industry, such as the Algerians' pipeline from the Sahara to the

Mediterranean or Iraq National Oil Company's new agreements with foreigners, it did not concentrate much on touchy details. Tariki's targets were uncontroversial for their milieu. He lashed out at vague generalities — America, Zionism, imperialism — and called for safely farfetched measures of nationalization of some foreign interests, while declining to attack individual persons or companies for specific acts. Tariki would rarely even criticize a specific foreigner. To be sure, he would say, of the American archaeologist-entrepreneur Wendell Phillips, "He is now considered one of the richest men in the world . . . as a result of his ability to sneer at the brains and beards of those sultans who are content to isolate themselves from Arab affairs and take advisors for themselves from among our country's enemies." He did rail, too, against Calouste Gulbenkian, who had been instrumental in arranging the concession which later became IPC in Iraq. But Gulbenkian has been dead almost twenty years and Phillips, who now lives in Hawaii, has had little working contact with the Middle East or influence over the oil industry.*

This is not because Tariki knows less about concrete, secret acts of malfeasance by local politicians, corrupt acts or malpractices by companies, or even subtle accounting procedures than the citizenry in Cairo, Beirut, Tripoli, or Baghdad — who know a good deal. It is not his lack of knowledge which prevents him from writing about these things but his own ambivalences and the attitude of the society in which he functions toward the publication of such material.

First of all, Near Easterners are not very curious about the inner workings of their major industry. Intellectual curiosity is not the dominant feature of Near Eastern peoples and the oil industry, because of its identification with a dark, unpleasant fluid, is not a very attractive subject for contemplation anyway.

More important, there are laws against criticism of Arab individuals and states, even in such open countries as Lebanon and Kuwait. A law exists on the books in Kuwait which calls for penalties against "besmirching the relations between Kuwait and

---

* One advisor to a sheikh told this writer that Arabs have mixed feelings about Phillips anyway — "like watching your mother-in-law drive over a cliff in a brand-new Cadillac."

fraternal Arab states" and "prejudicing the character of an Arab individual." In 1972, for instance, the Kuwaiti government levied a number of fines against newspapers and magazines for such breaches of etiquette as printing cartoons unflattering to King Hussain, attacking the Saudi foreign minister for being friendly to Iran, or reproducing a letter smuggled out of a Sudanese jail by a convicted Communist.[2] Although the 1972 fines in Kuwait were small — no more than 150 dinars, or about $400 — they carried an implied threat: if a publication went "too far," it could, as Kubbah learned in Iraq, lose its license.

Such laws, then, inhibit Arabs from printing anything controversial against other Arabs — even indirectly, through implication with an American company or governmental agency.

An unwritten law underlies this attitude: no matter how radical one's views might be, one should not rake muck, assuredly not oil industry muck. The Near East's great cash industry must not fall into jeopardy through the exposure of its sensitive features. Even the far left goes easy on the oil industry. The Saudi National Liberation Front, whose radical denunciations of Aramco have been faithfully reproduced by the Marxist press in Aden, has fallen short of demanding the outright nationalization of this giant venture.[3]

There is some investigative reporting in Egypt and Lebanon — rather limited and ephemeral — but the Near Eastern press is quite generally free of exposés and indictments of prominent individuals in all areas. The explanation for this, in turn, lies in public attitudes themselves. In the Near East, freedom of expression is not the most highly cherished of rights. The real objectives, in this day and age, are freedom from poverty, drought, illiteracy, and disease. The current generation of Middle Easterners feels that it bears little responsibility for these problems, which take decades to eliminate. One can always blame the Turks, the British, the Americans for cultivating the environment that fostered them in the past — or that fostered censorship, for that matter. Recently, one writer commenting in the moderate-conservative Lebanese magazine *al-Hawadith* on Arab strategy toward Israel ascribed the dearth of open debate on this subject to "American-Soviet intellectual terrorism."[4] In other words, at least some Arabs do not consider themselves to blame even for the obstructionists and hard-liners who prevent moderates from discussing alternatives to all-out war with Israel.

To the Near Easterner, the dangerous person more often than not is less the emotional firebrand Tariki than the Kubbah, who, though perhaps holding only moderate views, does not observe the unwritten law and makes hard, specific attacks on other persons' records. He poses a threat not only to the individuals he attacks but perhaps also to prominent individuals in many other places.

This pallor of the self-critical spirit has helped dull the hostility many Near Easterners might feel toward the oil industry. On the other hand, one should add that the oil companies can have little said in the Near Eastern press on their behalf unless they pay for it. This is true even in Lebanon. A Near Eastern commentator who might feel some appreciation or sympathy for the companies and might wish to raise points in their favor had best express himself carefully. It is very easy to call such a person an agent for the CIA. For instance, a short while ago the Beirut daily *al-Nahar* carried two articles on the subject of oil and participation.[5] One article, sympathetic to nationalization and the outright expulsion of Western "cartels" from the Arab world, was signed; the other, sympathetic to the moderate oil policies of Saudi Arabia, bore no signature.

Were one to question this state of affairs a Near Easterner would most likely reply, "If the oil companies want to have something said on their behalf, why shouldn't they pay for it? Don't they have the money?"

Another fact of life in the Near East serves the interests of the Western oil companies at least as well. Some Near Eastern leaders are bitterly against them, others are mean by nature, some are aloof and remote and hard for oil representatives to approach, but even these people operate under constraints. In the Middle East, even though one concession would dominate a country, several oil companies usually made up this venture — though on occasion, as in Saudi Arabia, they gathered under one foreign flag. In these conditions, it was easy for the companies'

hosts to feel that they were dealing not just with a group of directors from one corporation but with a broad consensus of Western interests. So the question facing Near Eastern oil policymakers was not "Why do business with this specific company?
Why serve the interests of this specific mercantile hierarchy?" It
shaded into a broader consideration: "Why should we continue
to do business with a specific collection of Western interests,
claiming to serve the consumers of, and seeking the intercession
of diplomats from, a group of powerful Western states?

"Why should we continue to deal with the very West itself?"

The companies conveyed the impression that they enjoyed
powerful backing. The one important instance where oil properties lay under the exclusive control of one foreign firm, British
Petroleum in Iran, the concessionaire, as we have seen, came
to grief.*

In the postwar generation, the United States State Department
interceded on behalf of American oil companies when problems
arose.

The American oil companies — especially the major ones —
have received first-class treatment from the State Department
over the years, and this, on top of Near Eastern reluctance to
bear down hard on the industry, has placed the firms in a very
powerful, enviable position. Yet the firms have squandered their
power.

In part, this is the fault of the State Department, which never
demanded a price for this support. The United States government almost never succeeded in learning truths about the international trade which it could communicate in detail to the
American public. At the Church Subcommittee hearings in early
1974, one panelist, Missouri's Senator Symington, complained
about this; he asked John J. McCloy, a distinguished elder statesman and long-standing lawyer to the industry, "Why should the

* Richard Funkhouser, in his 1953 memorandum to Parker Hart, wrote, "Some
oil executives and economists, for example, believe that British Petroleum
might never have been nationalized if they had had competitors in Iran.
There is a certain safety in numbers. . . . If Exxon, Mobil or Shell and several independent groups of whatever nationality had been producing oil in
Iran . . . British Petroleum would not have been blamed for everything that
went wrong in Iran."

government come in and help these [companies] out when they get in trouble in other countries and then allow them to make high profits and benefit from their support?"

McCloy's answer merely was, "That's quite a philosophical question. The oil companies are very tricky businesses — are very risky businesses."

"I like the way you put it first," replied Symington.[6]

McCloy should have added that the industry, just to prove how tricky it is, has made the business of learning the true nature of its operations off limits to those on the outside, and here is where the industry has let its opportunities slip in the Near East — for two reasons, reticence and secretiveness on the one hand and poor diplomacy on the other.

The oil industry in the Near East has operated in a manner alien to all democratic governments, most dictatorships, and many commercial enterprises. This is not, of course, reprehensible in itself; but as we have said, the international oil industry has been underwritten, and often rescued, by democracies.

The Iranians and Arabs raise the same objections as Americans, from the other side. Ahmad Yamani, petroleum minister of Saudi Arabia, has said, as an example, that he was excluded from a share in key industry decisions. Aramco, which had a board of directors, on which Saudi officials were represented, also had an executive committee, where the Saudis were not represented but which made most of the controversial decisions. Material of a really sensitive nature was taken around by courier to top officials, who would read it without taking notes on it, then return it to the courier. Saudis were probably kept in the dark about most exploratory information, for instance. Then the all-American executive committee would submit its decisions to the Aramco board later as a *fait accompli*. The Saudis were quite aware that this committee existed and were never happy with it. Not until 1973, with the Saudi buy-in, did the American companies let the Saudis into it, though.[7]

An example of what Aramco told the Saudis, and did not tell them, occurred in the summer of 1973, in the midst of a verbal poker game, masquerading as a conversation, between Frank Jungers, the president of Aramco, and oil minister Yamani.

(Jungers reported this conversation to Aramco's treasurer, John-ston, in New York, who then conveyed it to SoCal, who put it in the files, where the Church Subcommittee, in its quest for engi-neering trip reports, unearthed it and dutifully published it as part of their record.) [8]

The conversation dealt with Saudi Arabia's oil reserves and Aramco's production. Yamani, who did not really want to play the game, protested to Jungers that a number of his colleagues in the Saudi government were, for political and technical reasons, opposed to Aramco's recent big production hikes. Aramco had just given Yamani a letter stating that the nation's reserves were no longer 95 billion barrels, but 245 billion. Why, Yamani won-dered, did Aramco give him that letter at just that time? How could he believe this sudden, extraordinary upward revision? Jungers transcribed his response as follows: "True enough, in the past we have given ultraconservative numbers as proven reserves of 90 billion barrels, and there were a number of reasons why we didn't have to worry about what they truly were. They were big enough even at that rate. And in due course of time, when every-body was pushing us for production, this renewed our interest to speculate as to how high they were. But now . . . by the fact that [Yamani] had asked for a depletion study and we attempted to make this study, we found ourselves arguing here in Aramco on what our true reserves were. And we finally came to the position that our true reserves were 245 billion based on the method that is commonly accepted for determining these figures."

When Aramco got into a difficulty of this sort it often fell back on the measure of sending a man called Ingram to a place called Taif. Jungers forthwith told Johnston that he was doing that, "and he is going to explain how we arrived at the 245 number."

The conversation moved on. Jungers "reminded [Yamani] that really we had more oil every year than we produced. He said 'Yep,' they knew that too, and they figured we would probably do this again in 1973, but not in 1974, and so we couldn't use that argument. And I said 'Well, your guess is as good as mine on it.' I told him that we just incidentally found a little oil in Marjan 25, another billion barrels or so, and he said 'Oh you had better get that out in public print fast.' "

Toward the end of the meeting, Yamani asked Jungers what

the current production rate was. "I told him 8.5 million barrels a day," Jungers related, "and he said, 'Wow, wait till the people hear that.'

"It is pretty clear here that we have got to do a number of things on this conservation bit to work with him," Jungers concluded his transcription. "We are going to have to get in there quick with Ingram to not only explain how we got the 245 but also to get this depletion study built up to these various levels and get it out into the open."

In their negotiations with Near Easterners, not only have oilmen been reticent and secretive, they have tenaciously refused to act in a spirit of true compromise. They have given ground, but almost always on terms they found congenial, as these pages have sought to show many times. The oilmen never gave up any significant ability to make money. In Iraq, Saudi Arabia, and Iran, they refused to accept the demands which their organizations found it hard to assimilate, and they got their way.

Negotiation, especially with Near Easterners, can become a form of controlled madness, an act of schizophrenia wherein the negotiator is constantly sensitive to the demands and aspirations of the other side while striving to hold ground against them; yet, for over a generation, the oil industry steadfastly refused to field men who would truly hear what the other side was saying, who would hear more than mere threats.

By the 1950's, the industry rarely advanced anyone in its Near Eastern operations who was not an engineer, preferably a chemical engineer. People with diplomatic or liberal arts backgrounds rarely even had a chance to get jobs in the industry, let alone advance in it. This is understandable if one grants that the industry is an extremely complex technical operation and nothing more, less understandable if one postulates that the industry is not so complex and does not operate in a vacuum.

Thus, the men the oil companies sent to the Near East had a good chance of getting out of their depth, and they often did: men with rigorous training in some aspects of industry operations often were ignorant and unfamiliar with the Middle East and its political and economic problems. As one State Department official involved in Near Eastern oil, Richard Funkhouser, wrote his superior, Parker Hart, in 1953, "Formal discussions and agreements on oil turn out to be defensive and try to insulate the oil industry from trends abroad in the world. Nationalism as applied to the oil industry and interpreted by the industry becomes a scheme of local radicals who 'wish to kill the goose that lays the golden eggs.' Consequently, oil policy discussions tend towards the restrictive, the unrealistic and the unimaginative."[9]

Relations between individuals tended to mirror the tone of these discussions. For instance, it was widely stated that Abdullah Tariki hated Howard Page, yet Exxon continued to send Page out to negotiate with Tariki. Tariki's frustrations turned to real bitterness. We have sought to indicate that Tariki had a soft, generous side. To another key oil industry official — no stranger to these pages — the remark was often ascribed, "Yamani is a lot easier to deal with than Tariki but he's a lot more expensive." Yamani was the moderate, this reasoning went, the pacific financier, while Tariki, indifferent to finances if not ignorant of them, talked only of banishing foreign influence from his land as a matter of principle. The oil executive had as much as said, "Yamani you can at least buy off." Of course there were Americans who could have handled Tariki with finesse, but the industry made little attempt to find them. In the American foreign service, if a Page encountered enduring hostility in Arabia he would sooner or later have been allowed an opportunity to take a break and see if his wits were more compatible in Indonesia, say, or Peru. But then Page was Exxon's man, and he stayed in the center of the stage for years after Tariki departed.

Much the same was true of BP's men in Iran, until Mosaddegh expropriated that firm's holdings out of an inflamed nationalism over which he had lost full control. It was the same in Libya, too, where Exxon kept Hugh Wynne in charge although his relationship with the nation's oil minister, Khalifa Musa, became so notoriously poor that in the end Musa asked to have Wynne relieved (he was not), and in utter frustration refused Exxon permission to put its natural gas liquefaction plant into operation, though it represented an investment of hundreds of millions of dollars. The plant did not go onstream for two years, until 1971.

One might ask what else the companies were supposed to do, then. Didn't they have a diplomatic problem in spite of themselves? The record of ITT in Chile shows what can happen to a company when it ceases to stay aloof and does become involved, one might say. But the companies have always been involved, to some extent. Their spokesmen did keep referring to their "diplomatic" problems, as in the Church hearings. They were faced with diplomatic problems and the obligation to behave like diplomats whether they liked it or not. Diplomacy is a hard business and people who are not very good at it should get out of it — or employ competent diplomats. They should not follow the example of past presidential administrations and use foreign diplomàtic posts as rewards for diligent service in the United States, but this is what they have done, consistently. They were often inept at treading the fine line between pressing their case and becoming ensnared in local politics — and treading this line is precisely the function of diplomats.

Hand in hand with the obduracy and deafness of the industry representatives went a real absence of diplomatic creativity. Almost no interesting diplomacy emerged from the industry in the postwar generation, although industry men have repeatedly stated that their problems were "diplomatic."

One can illustrate this by considering the role of Egypt's President Nasser and the industry's failure to deal with it in intelligent ways. As one can see from Chapter 4, and the story of the 1966 Syria-IPC controversy, Nasser was not just a hated symbol, a figure the industry would like to see gone. He was also eminently placed, as symbolic leader of Arab nationalism, to act as an arbiter with and between other Arab states, although Egypt itself was "oil-poor." Yet to this writer's knowledge the companies never considered him or his successor Anwar Sadat as such.

Certainly the companies did not appreciate Nasser's usefulness in 1967, nor did they apparently ask him or Sadat for intercession in 1970–1971, in Libya. In the ferocious negotiations in that period, one of the key Libyan negotiators was a brash youngster, the prime minister, Abdel Salaam Jalloud. Jalloud could be extremely unpleasant to deal with but he was not without his constraints. The industry men were usually a generation older than he but did not stand up to him as firmly as a social worker would stand up, at knife point, to a delinquent adolescent. Jalloud, after all, could only throw a negotiator out of Libya — and he could not get away with that many times.

Then, a creative diplomat who was thrown out could always try to get back in. He could go to Egypt and ask the mediation of Nasser's men, taking pains to illustrate the sort of climate Jalloud was creating in the name of Arab nationalism. The companies had real leverage with Egypt, as well as the power to complain. They could always promise through-put commitments for the Suez-Mediterranean pipeline Nasser was hoping to build, or offer crude oil and products at discounts. Several major firms, in particular Mobil, were important marketers of petroleum products within Egypt itself and had access to the top oil policymakers in Egypt. In time of real crisis in Libya — or Iraq — Mobil could have been delegated to talk to the highest figures in that key Arab state.

One example will help illustrate the frustrations Western commercial interests could face by not taking pains to acquire access to Nasser. After the 1967 war, the American construction firm Bechtel drew up what it thought was a brilliant scheme, for itself as well as for world peace. It proposed to build a pipeline across the Sinai Peninsula, with a right of way on both sides which would be under international control. The line would serve as a buffer between Egypt and Israel and perhaps also include a desalinization plant or two, a railroad, and satellite cities. The British banker Edmond de Rothschild expressed interest in the scheme, as he had been interested in constructing a desalinization plant in Israel and one in Jordan, and claimed that Jordan's King Hussain said it was "workable," after mutual friends broached the plan to him. The British banker had been interested in defusing the Arab-Israeli struggle, and would help finance the scheme. Top officials in the Ford Foundation expressed interest in the idea — as did Kaiser Industries, which Bechtel was willing to include in a subordinate role. This idea, impractical as it may have been, never even got off the ground because no one could come up with a way to broach it to Nasser. Bechtel did not even have an office in Cairo, let alone a relationship with the Egyptian leader.

Yet others did approach Nasser on other occasions, with some success. One notable example lies in a Spanish government initiative. Spain (a country which has enjoyed good relations with Egypt for years) was suffering from the conflict between Gaddafi of Libya and Exxon over the export price of Libyan natural gas — much of which was to go to a utility in Barcelona, Catalana de Gas. The dispute of course stalled exports, causing gas shortages in Spain. Lopez Bravo, Spain's Foreign Minister, lost no time prevailing upon Nasser to mediate between the two parties, and Nasser, just before his death, did arrange exploratory talks between the Barcelona firm and Libya's Premier Abdel Salaam Jalloud.[10]

Sometimes oil companies operating in the Near East allowed themselves to be abused by Near Easterners because it didn't cost them any money. There were numerous examples of this self-effacement in Libya. In general the companies would hire Near Easterners, rather than Americans, to handle delicate local problems because this was one of the cheapest perquisites to grant of all the ones the hosts requested. However, the companies paid a price for this capitulation. For example, Getty Oil's operations in the Neutral Zone employed as employee relations representatives two Palestinians whom none of the Americans trusted — or dared fire.

Of course this is much the way the Near Eastern oil officials wanted matters. While themselves generally displaying a willingness to rise above popular hysteria in their dealings with oil companies, they dealt with shrewd, careful men, gifted perhaps as poker players, who could keep the whereabouts of a billion barrels up their sleeves for years but very largely lacked in qualities of leadership or the intellectual dynamism and flair which the Near Easterners were naturally glad not to have to contend with in negotiation.

There was little point of conflict between the two parties, except for rigid, specific, mostly financial issues, over which the companies often negotiated quite hard. But to all indications, from Mosaddegh in 1951 to the decade of the seventies, the oilmen almost always made a deal with a country rather than have their production shut down, and as the years passed, the Near Easterners did better and better for themselves financially, always ended up a little ahead of where they started, a little more spoiled and a little more sheltered by the oil companies.

The oil companies were generous to Near Easterners in ways which would have been inconceivable to the powers in Washington. Considering the degree to which oil industry negotiations influenced American interests in the Near East as a whole, considering the stake which the American public has had in the oil industry in the Near East, whether or not it so wished, and considering the insistence and decisiveness with which the American public has been excluded for over a generation from any significant understanding of oil industry behavior in the Near East — usually on the grounds that "oil is a tricky business," "the public can't handle its complexities," "the nontechnical cadre below Level C-1 lacks the analytical tools with which to understand the problems we have to contend with" — this ruthless exclusiveness on the part of the industry, which has become a powerful closed system within the very core and pith of a lax, amorphous open society — the second biggest democracy in world history — has become a serious liability to the American body politic.

Also, a system which could not last, as the Libyan history will demonstrate — though not to the benefit of the Western consumer.

12

Round One in Libya

The aversion against bigness has deeper origins; it derives its strength from the instinctive desire to redress the balance between otherwise unequal forces.
— Paul Frankel, *Mattei: Oil and Power Politics*

By THE 1950's, the major oil companies had asserted to the Arabs and the Iranians that the companies were to remain the dominant force, the superego, of the Near Eastern oil industry. As a reward for accepting a subservient role, the nations would receive very good money, in hard currency, from the Western consumer. The Near Easterners, except for a few renegades like Abdullah Tariki, were disinclined to rebel against this condition for two decades, or felt powerless to do so.

The international oil industry, to judge by the control it had established over the Near East in the 1950's and 1960's, might have remained fossilized in this form for the rest of the century. As the example of Iraq should help illustrate, political changes could only damage the countries which attempted them.

It was Libya that transformed the oil industry. Through the structure the oil industry assumed in that westerly Arab land, the old system which crystallized after the traumatic experience in Iran and passed with barely a ripple through the years of deep nationalist ground swell in Iraq and Kuwait was, in the early 1970's, jolted to its foundations, again, through a fortuitous chain of events which, at no stage following an inevitable sequence, had been rendered inevitable in their main trend by the peculiar structure of the Libyan industry.

In fact, to understand the broad sweep of Near Eastern oil history over the past generation, one really need only appreciate three facts. First: Saudi Arabia has massive oilfields, from which it has been extremely cheap and easy to produce great volumes of oil. Second: Iran and Iraq do also (as, to a lesser extent, do Kuwait and Abu Dhabi), but their fields are not on the scale of Ghawar in Saudi Arabia; furthermore, they are also subject to very conservative British oilfield development practices, so the American majors which participate in Aramco have tended to favor Saudi Arabia over Iran and Iraq even, in general, during the hardest times, since they have found that state to be the most effective low-cost vehicle for maintaining market control and keeping market prices high. And third: Libya, from the outset of its development, offered its territory up as many different small concessions to many different companies. There was no guarantee that the territory would contain oil, but the chances were good; the country was very close to Europe, the world's biggest oil import market; and several different ventures did find oil there, all at once. In time, as anyone would, the Libyans learned to exploit this state of affairs. They then proceeded to shake the entire edifice of the industry, and also ultimately of price, in the Near East.

There is much more to Near Eastern oil history than merely this, but virtually all the rest is embellishment of this basic story line.

Libya covers an immense area — it is the fifth biggest country in Africa. In fact, the land became united into one independent country for the first time only in 1950.

Prior to the long Italian occupation of Libya, which began just before World War One and endured through the era of Mussolini, the country consisted of three separate provinces, host to different dialects of Arabic: to the northwest, Tripolitania; to the northeast, bordering Egypt, Cyrenaica; and in the west central area adjacent to the Algerian Sahara, the Fezzan. The rest of the land was desert, interspersed with small oases. For most of its earlier history, during the 1200 years following the Islamic conquest, major areas of Libya together or severally formed parts of a larger whole under the hegemony of successive foreign dynasties, most recent of which was the Ottoman Empire.

For the earliest history of the oil industry in Libya, we are indebted to a deceased journalist, John Gedeist, who has left behind a manuscript on the subject.

Gedeist wrote that the Italians had discovered some oil in Libya before World War Two, near Tripoli, and that the French found some around 1950, in the far west of the Fezzan near Algeria. Mussolini had, in fact, laid claim to the latter territory in the 1930's, when Libya was an Italian colony. The French, colonizers of Algeria, came into occupation of the Fezzan during World War Two, and an American company, Exxon, also conducted tests in the surrounding area and discovered traces of oil there as well.

In January, 1955, Libya, under its second prime minister, Mustafa Ben Halim, ceded to the French Premier Mendès-France the oil-rich portion of the Fezzan which Mussolini had claimed. The Libyan parliament had never formally relinquished Mussolini's claim. The French promptly discovered oil in this bulge, which hosts the Zaraitine and Edjele fields; these structures, and a few others, have been producing at a modest rate, about 200,000 barrels a day, for a decade. Wrote Gedeist: the January, 1955, treaty "realigned the far southern Fezzan-Algerian border in favor of the French territory, and promised [Libya] financial aid."

For many years afterward, it was a common rumor in Libya that not only had Libya received an immense sum of money from the French for this realignment — so had Ben Halim.

At any rate, the first oil concession awards in Libya itself took place under Ben Halim, also in 1955. As Gedeist narrates it, the process leading up to these awards was complicated in the extreme and fraught with international and domestic maneuvers and quids pro quo.

Under Ben Halim's guidance, the government divided the country into grids, upon which the irregular concession blocks were superimposed. One justification which Ben Halim gave for forming many concessions, rather than one massive award, was that it was not clear whether oil ever would be discovered in them, and anyway, the more companies were operating independently in the country, the more the state would receive in customs fees, surface rents, and other immediate emoluments. Libya was very poor in those days and needed the money badly.

Another justification, used with various local political leaders and chieftains, was that more companies would offer greater scope for patronage — "which the central government could dispense in order to hold together a fragile political structure," as Gedeist wrote.

The companies interested in concessions bid most energetically for rights close to the Mediterranean, reasoning that if these plots yielded up oil, they would be the cheapest to develop, requiring fewer pumping facilities and shorter pipelines. As a result, the Libyan Law of 1955 restricted the size of the plots closest to water to 30,000 square kilometers each — much smaller than the size it specified for the less attractive plots deep in the Sahara. In this manner, the government was able to grant plots close to water to more companies.

In the end, thirteen firms, European as well as American, entered the bidding, and almost all of them won acreage.

The most immediately interesting awards, those nearest water, went, from west to east, from Tunisia to Egypt, to Mobil, the French company CFP, Shell, British Petroleum, Amoseas (a joint venture between Texaco and SoCal), Shell again, Amoseas again, Exxon, Mobil, again CFP and Mobil, Libyan American, Exxon again, Shell, Libyan American, Oasis (a consortium of three American firms, Amerada, Continental, and Marathon), British Petroleum, Nelson Bunker Hunt, and once more Libyan American.[1]

To the south, roughly constituting a second tier — again proceeding from west to east — further awards went to Oasis, Shell,

Gulf, again Oasis, Exxon, Oasis, Libyan American, Oasis, Amoseas, Mobil, yet more Oasis and Amoseas, and again the Texan Hunt.

The most attractive areas, those lying along the Mediterranean in a strip fifty miles wide from the Tunisian to Egyptian border, yielded up very little oil in the end. It was the acreage in the second tier, in central Libya, where the big oil lay — in the Sirtic Basin, host to the petroliferous marine detritus of three succeeding ocean encroachments. However, some of the companies in the northern tier survived this development through blind luck. Since so many of the companies had been vying for acreage near the Mediterranean, and had submitted wide overlapping bids for shallow parcels, the Libyan government, in several instances, granted the companies compromise parcels which were narrow but extended deep into the Sirte Basin. Thus it was, for instance, that Exxon gained rights to the southerly Zelten field, one of the two or three most prolific in Libya as it turned out. In like manner, Amoseas acquired the territory of Nafoora (which means "fountain" in Arabic), Mobil, with the German firm Gelsenberg, obtained rights to the territory which yielded up Amal ("hopes"), and Oasis came upon the rich Gialo.

The Oasis parents, known originally as The Conorada Group, bid independently of one another, gained the best acreage position of all applicants, and subsequently pooled their acquisitions. Many competitors claimed that this was not quite in keeping with the spirit of the Petroleum Law.

Since the Libyan government also felt obligated to ensure that other regions gained access to the new influx of money, it forced applicants to take a good deal of less interesting acreage as well, down in the Fezzan and southern Cyrenaica, where in the end they found only little oil — the times they tried to find any in the first place.

Thus was the shape of the oil industry in Libya cast, from the earliest days, in a unique manner: for in all other countries of the Islamic Near East, oil production has, to this day, been maintained by one large concessionaire which has managed, more or less successfully, to exclude other companies from the most attractive acreage in its domain. As we have seen, this has been the case in Iran, Iraq, Kuwait, and Saudi Arabia; it has also been true of the onshore and offshore areas of Qatar, Abu Dhabi, Bahrain, and Oman.

Granted, other firms have received a competence in some of these countries; one may name ENI, Standard of Indiana, and several others offshore Iran, or various American independents — as well as Getty and some Japanese — in the Neutral Zone between Kuwait and Saudi Arabia. In addition, some smaller companies have staked out dominant positions in the less endowed sheikhdoms of Dubai and Sharja.

However, in none of the major states has production by lesser lights accounted for more than 10 percent of the total. Aramco produces almost 95 percent of Saudi Arabia's oil; Kuwait Oil Company and the Consortium account for roughly 90 percent of the production in Kuwait and Iran, respectively; and Iraq Petroleum Company has very nearly monopolized Iraq's output over the past fifty years.

In Libya, though, many of the parcels became productive in nearly equal degree from the very beginning.

This fragmentation immediately brought another phenomenon in its wake: widespread corruption. It is likely, in fact, that corruption figured in the Libyan government's original strategy of granting concessions to independent companies. Here, the history is replete with much rumor and a few interesting details.

The most famous concession broker to enter this round was Wendell Phillips, holder of valuable interests in the Sultanate of Oman — and later Indonesia and Venezuela. Phillips managed to curry favor with a former secretary of the air force, Harold Talbott, who gave him a letter of introduction to Ben Halim, with whom Talbott had a close relationship in view of the United States air force's important stake in Libya at Wheelus Airbase. (Rumor circulating about Libya in the late 1950's and early 1960's also had it that American officials had given Ben Halim a great deal of money for the use of Wheelus.) Shortly afterwards, President Eisenhower relieved Talbott of his position for an unrelated scandal. Wendell Phillips, at any rate, managed to secure contact with King Idris through Ben Halim, then interested an

American independent, Texas Gulf, in acquiring acreage in Libya. This firm entered Libya under the name Libyan American, in conjunction with other interests, and as we have seen the group subsequently won some rights. One of its plots was later revealed to host the Raguba field, which, by mid 1973, had yielded up 375 million barrels of oil.[2]

Then Al Lager, a representative of the Conorada Group, later rechristened Oasis, also became fast friends with Ben Halim, according to Gedeist's narrative and the recollections of others who were in Libya at the time; as noted, his consortium ended up winning the most diversified acreage in Libya. As will appear subsequently, it became very difficult for almost a decade afterward for a contractor to do work for Oasis without Ben Halim's blessings.

Gedeist phrased Ben Halim's preference for independents such as Oasis gracefully. He quoted Amerada's vice president, Ben Weatherby, as stating that Ben Halim "appeared to be very friendly and understanding of our position." Oasis had a strong claim for special attention from the Libyan government, and Ben Halim undoubtedly used this persuasively with fellow Libyans: the argument that Oasis was hungry for oil, hungrier than the major companies; the latter were "already faced with a surplus of Middle East oil, which would probably mean that they would not be as energetic" as Oasis.[3]

Later, when Ben Halim saw the Petroleum Commission's preliminary concession map, he expressed "considerable concern that so much of the near coastal area of the country was in the hands of the major oil companies, from whom he did not expect as much activity as from the independents."[4]

Competition between foreign companies reached its apogee in 1965, with the second concession round. By then it had become essential for the foreign companies which wanted to prosper in Libya to seek the support of a prominent Libyan, or several Libyans, and the threat was always present that the local figure might desert the company for another which was willing to pay him more. This was almost certainly the fate of Libyan Desert in 1965. This small independent had support within the government, through its representative, but it neglected to insist on specific acreage in the second round and thus acquired rights only to poor properties.

By the late 1960's, this pervasive patronage and corruption had forced Libya down a dead end. Government had turned into an unremitting struggle between individuals for power and influence with the foreign companies, and Libya's octogenarian King Idris was powerless to set matters straight. By then he had probably stopped caring.

But this is pulling ahead of the story. After the 1955 awards, the industry went quickly to work in Libya. Within five years, by late 1961, it had discovered ten good fields.* Oasis and Exxon promptly set about building pipelines. The Libyans, for their part, began to make demands on the companies. First, in accordance with the 1955 Law, they regained title to 25 percent of the companies' acreage. Then, in 1961, they secured a repeal of the 25 percent depletion allowance. Exxon took the lead in relinquishing this benefit — in exchange for Libyan government permission to buy 50 percent of Libyan American's concessions.

Exxon was the first company to go onstream in Libya. It commenced export of Zelten crude from its terminal at Mersa Brega on October 26, 1961. For this oil, it posted a price of $2.23 a barrel, which it considered equivalent to postings for Persian Gulf crude of similar gravity plus a bonus of 40 cents or so to represent freight advantage. Zelten was good oil: it was as light as any in the gulf, about 40 degrees gravity, and sweet, containing only two-tenths of one percent sulphur. It had one drawback, which it shared with almost all Libyan crudes: a very high wax content. This meant that the oil tended to congeal and turn sludgy at fairly high temperatures (about 45 degrees Fahrenheit in the case of Zelten) and therefore had to be heated to flow through the pipeline in all weather.[5]

However, the neighboring oil state of Algeria, which exported the highest-cost oil of any significant volume in the Near East,

---

* These were Oasis's Dahra, Bahi, Defa, Waha, and Gialo; Exxon's Zelten; Libyan American's Raguba and Mabruk; Mobil's Amal and Hofra; and Amoseas's Beda. See *The Oil and Gas Journal,* January 16, 1961, and August 14, 1961, for details. There were also several to the west which had never gone onstream, among them Tiji, Atshan, Essania, Nalut, Emgayet, and Bir Tlacsin.

but was protected by and for the French, had posted a slightly higher price for roughly similar oil from the port of Bougie, about a thousand miles to the northwest. As a result, the Libyan Petroleum Commission protested against Libyan's Zelten posting before exports even began, on grounds that this should have been closer to Algeria's posting.

The posted price for Zelten crude remained at $2.23 for almost a decade, but the Libyan government never abandoned its protest.

Meanwhile, Exxon prospered. Though it had waived its rights to the depletion allowance, one perhaps equally important provision remained from the 1955 Petroleum Law. This was Article 14, a classic in the annals of fine print. This provision made it extremely worthwhile for a producer to make haste in exporting oil from Libya, as it stipulated that a company could deduct all the exploration expenses it incurred, in the year in which they were incurred — *after* the date on which that company started to export oil from Libya. This point in time was known as "the effective date." Prior to it, a company could depreciate exploration costs only at the rate of 10 percent per year. These costs included intangible drilling costs and dry holes.

Exxon reaped a great reward from this provision because it began exporting oil almost one year before Oasis, which was the next company to go onstream. Exxon's exploration activities gained momentum after October, 1961. With the exception of Zelten and Raguba, in which it had only a half-interest anyway, its discoveries — Arshad, Jebel, Ralah, Meghil, and Lehib — came later.

Once Exxon had agreed to waive the 25 percent depletion allowance, the other companies operating in Libya perforce followed. Exxon then obliged the Libyan government in one other respect: it rewrote the country's 1955 Petroleum Law. It had a substantial stake in this endeavor, for Howard Page, as head of an industry negotiating team, had reached an agreement with states belonging to OPEC in 1964 whereby these states would receive an added financial benefit: to wit, the expensing of royalties. As explained earlier on these pages, this was the state's right (softened by a 6½ percent marketing allowance) to receive the 12½ percent royalty in addition to the 50 percent tax, rather than as a credit against it. Page had requested that the OPEC states, in exchange for this benefit, include a "most favored company" clause in their concessions. This would ensure that no concession holder suffer fiscal penalties which did not devolve as well upon other concessionaires within the same nation, and it applied in Libya as well as the gulf, once Libya joined OPEC.

On the face of it this seemed a giveaway. Exxon was still the major exporter of oil from Libya at that time and was paying tax to the Libyan government on the basis of the realized rather than posted price, as were the others. Libya, with Abu Dhabi, was the only major Near Eastern exporting state still to allow taxation on this lower price, and the discount was very valuable, of course. However, Page, as usual, knew what he was doing: the discount was less valuable to Exxon than to its competitors in Libya. Exxon sold much more of its Libyan crude at or near posted price anyway, because, unlike the Oasis parents, it had numerous subsidiaries in Europe which needed to buy at a high price for tax shelter. Even then, it engaged in ferocious price wars with the Libyan independents on the battlefields of Europe. For instance, when it opened Bavaria's first refinery, at Ingolstadt, in 1963, it drastically cut the prices for the heavy fuel oil, diesel oil, and gasoline which the plant produced.[6] Oasis's parents, especially Marathon and Amerada, which had little European refining capacity, had to cut price a great deal to sell their oil in Europe.

Thus Exxon, by securing the revision of the Libyan law, which took effect in 1965, managed to invoke the most favored company clause and impose the higher tax on Oasis, thus inflicting some damage on the only independent oil firms yet to enter the world of Near Eastern oil in significant degree.

In Libya, independents suffered at the hands of the majors not only in this financial respect but also in the development of fields where they had an interest. One example lies in the Mabruk structure, on one of the properties most coveted during the 1955 round. This field came into possession of Libyan American, which, as noted above, took Exxon as its equal partner because it lacked European sales outlets of its own.

Mabruk's first well brought up 600 barrels of oil a day. A subsequent "stepout" hit 800 barrels a day. All in all, in Mabruk, which was one of Libya's first finds, the joint venture drilled thirteen wells, all of roughly the same producibility. Although the field was cursed with low permeability, which was responsible for a relatively low potential per well, it yielded up good low-sulphur oil of 36 and 40 degree gravity from two zones. The field is very close to water, and, more important, it is closer still to Oasis's export pipeline, which passes less than forty miles away. Other companies have put on production wells which were no more prolific. In spite of its favorable situation, however, Mabruk has not gone onstream at the time of this writing; Exxon, unlike some other firms in Libya, was reluctant to use a pipeline belonging to another company, and it did not have complete control over disposition of the oil from the field.* As *Petroleum Intelligence Weekly* reported a few years later, Exxon (or Esso, as it is still known in Libya) "understandably has never been as interested as its partners in jointly-held acreage — not least due to a 'guaranteed halfway price' deal it made with Sinclair and Grace [its partners in Mabruk, along with Wendell Phillips] in 1959." This price would give Sinclair and Grace a profit of about 35 cents a barrel on any oil Exxon took from them.[7] The American major did, however, proceed with the development of Raguba, also in conjunction with the Sinclair-Grace-Phillips combine; Raguba, besides being more prolific, was close to Exxon's Zelten-Brega line.

Time and again, Exxon has displayed reluctance to contribute to the development of oilfields in which other companies have a substantial interest. One example lies in the Iranian Consortium;

* The endpaper map of Libya shows what lengths some companies went to to avoid shipping crude through other companies' lines. Oasis's pipeline system, for instance, began just to the southeast of Mobil's and Exxon's systems, then swung far to the south of them, curved west, and doubled half back to reach the Gulf of Sirte about 25 miles away from Mobil's terminal at Ras Lanuf. Much of Oasis's oil traveled twice as far to reach water as it would have had to had it passed through Mobil's, or Exxon's, lines. Other examples are obvious from the map, too. For its part Mobil, from the outset, made it very clear to Ben Halim that it intended to own and operate all the pipeline systems and marine facilities it used. There were firms, such as Amoseas and later ENI, which "tied into" competitors' systems.

another in Iraq Petroleum Company. A third and equally luminous example lies outside the Near East, in the Prudhoe Bay
field of Alaska's North Slope, where Exxon enjoys a strong but
secondary position. There is no definitive figure, as yet, on the
recoverable reserves in Prudhoe Bay, but these total at the very
least 18.3 billion barrels. One oil executive, Thornton Bradshaw,
president of Atlantic Richfield, told this writer that geologists
with his company had delineated the Sadlerochit formation, one
of the oilfield's three "sands," or oil-bearing reservoirs, and ascer-
tained that it, alone, held 10 to 12 billion barrels of recoverable
oil. A study by the brokerage firm of Dean Witter and Company,
"The North Slope: Key to Atlantic Richfield's Future," dated
December, 1971, states that Exxon has smaller holdings there
than Atlantic Richfield and the British Petroleum/Standard of
Ohio combine, whose shares are conservatively estimated at 4 and
7.5 billion barrels, respectively.

It would manifestly be disadvantageous to Exxon to have such
large volumes of crude outside its control flooding such big Exxon
markets as Japan or the American Midwest. Exxon is not yet
strongly represented on the West Coast, but Standard of California is, as it enjoys about 18 percent of this market — one of the
best in the world. And there is strong evidence that Exxon and
SoCal, while complaining loudly of environmentalist opposition
to all projects to build pipelines down from Alaska, have themselves worked in subtle ways to inhibit the construction of such
pipelines.

In an article in the San Francisco *Chronicle,* the journalist William Moore quoted Walter Hickel — himself an Alaskan — as
stating that when the pipeline was coming up for permits, under
his jurisdiction as Secretary of the Interior, "The Exxon people
were not enthused about the pipeline because they did not have
as much production in the North Slope as Arco and Sohio did.
The Exxon people kept delaying the presentation of an engineering plan on the project to the Interior Department. And they
even delayed making their syndicate a legal entity, something
which was required before we could give them the permit."[8]

Moore went on to quote a source "close to the lawyers representing the environmentalists" as stating that Exxon lawyers de-

liberately mounted a weak fight to build the line, dragged their heels, "acted like creampuffs and really didn't give us much of a fight at all."

Sources within British Petroleum itself apparently raised the same point. *Platt's Oilgram* quoted them as saying that "their partners in the proposed Alaskan pipeline consortium haven't done as much as they could" in pushing for early government approval of the project — specifically in "combatting the 'hysteria of environmentalists.' "[9] BP called for an authorization early in 1972, claiming that otherwise it would not be cleared until after the presidential elections. As it turned out, it was not cleared until more than a year after the elections (though BP's chairman disavowed the statement two days later in *Platt's,* stating "This is complete news to me. BP have made no such criticism.").

Then, a top SoCal executive, in June, 1969, told a top construction entrepreneur, "Building the North-Slope-to-Pacific line would be a tragic mistake from the viewpoint of the oil industry." The SoCal executive went on to state that he would prefer a pipeline from the North Slope across northwestern Canada to Edmonton, and said that he thought BP and Atlantic Richfield were "very naïve" about Alaska pipelining and were "off by about 50 percent" in their cost calculations. SoCal's chairman, Otto Miller, was a bit more specific in a speech before the New York Society of Security Analysts in May, 1969, on the nature of this "tragic mistake." He declared that the North Slope finds would create oversupply in the West Coast petroleum industry, and this would result in "some dislocations." But, Miller added, "Companies with the markets usually fare best in an oversupply situation." In other words, he was serving notice to Arco, and others, that SoCal had "every intention" of holding its dominant share in the lucrative market.

Another executive with another major oil company which has a stake in northern Alaska affirmed this by telling the journalist Moore, "It was very clear at the time that [SoCal] did not want any new crude from competitors coming into their lucrative West Coast market, which would happen under the Alaska pipeline."

More than five years earlier, in March, 1969, at hearings of a subcommittee of the Senate Judiciary Committee, several economists had voiced the suspicion that obstacles of this sort might confront parties to the Alaska bonanza. Morris Adelman of MIT, doyen of America's energy economists, stated that "if Alaskan output were given free rein, it would lower U.S. costs and strengthen the industry's ability to compete," since the oil could sell for less in America than Near Eastern crude. The British economic consultant Paul Newton concurred. Another economist, Paul Homan of Cornell, was even blunter: "It could very well be," he declared, "that [when Alaska goes onstream] you are going to have a flow of oil from within your own borders that will itself be just as deadly to the interests of the southwest oil as a much larger import program would be."[10]

This writer asked Thornton Bradshaw of Atlantic Richfield for his views on the matter. He stated that "nobody's holding back anything" on constructing the line and added that no United States crude was a threat to any other crude from the United States; Alaska crude would "back out all the foreign crude coming into the U.S." He admitted that this would be good for his company but added that "the important thing is the balance on the West Coast for the industry — that will be extremely good."

However, the main thing, in the mind of Bradshaw and other industry spokesmen, is that this would not have a downward effect on crude prices in America. The companies concerned would not let North Slope Alaska onstream until they received ironclad guarantees that its oil would reach the market at a very high price. And this is the way the issue was resolved, in early 1974, in the wake of the 1973 price counterrevolt. Several years before, the Nixon administration's Oil Imports Task Force had after considerable effort determined that it would cost only about 36 cents a barrel to produce North Slope oil, and another 45 cents to pipe it down to warm water in southern Alaska. However, the state of Alaska drew up a severance tax schedule which would virtually sanctify a price for North Slope oil of $3.37 a barrel, at least, at the wellhead.[11] Now it seems that this oil will sell for $10 in southern Alaska.

Another force obstructing oil development in the Libya of the mid-sixties was the same British Petroleum whose efforts to export oil from Alaska were to be so frustrated. BP waived its right to the Libyan depletion allowance and gained a 50 percent interest in Nelson Bunker Hunt's Concession 65 — which turned out to lie over the Sarir field, biggest discovered in Africa to this writing.[12] Due largely to BP's obstructive tactics, this field did not go onstream until 1967, almost six years after it first yielded up oil.

As it turned out, BP let it onstream just in time, because the rest of its production lay east of Suez, and the 1967 embargo and closure of the canal hit it harder than any other major company. But it had delayed putting Sarir on so long because it had a surplus of oil in its Persian Gulf holdings and the agreement it had with Hunt obligated it "to market Hunt's share at a 'tax-paid half-way price' " — later revised to quarter-way, or about $1.68 a barrel.[13]

Hunt, in an endeavor to press British Petroleum to acquiesce in the rapid development of Sarir, was said to have leaked information to *The Oil and Gas Journal* indicating that Sarir had recoverable reserves of 7 to 9 billion barrels and could easily produce at a rate of 400,000 barrels a day, although its line then had a capacity of only 250,000 barrels a day.[14] True to its potential, Sarir's production reached 430,000 barrels a day in early 1970 and stayed at that level all through the year.

One other company, Amoseas, the Texaco-SoCal venture, also discovered substantial reserves in Libya but delayed developing them, except for Beda, a small field near Mobil's line, because its parents also had a surplus of production elsewhere. It spent several years delineating structures and availing itself of its Article 14 benefits before it actually brought on its big holding, Nafoora.

Other companies either developed good properties promptly or wished they had them. Mobil discovered the large but flawed field at Amal and continued to explore aggressively well after Gaddafi's revolution although it shared its concession with an independent, the German Gelsenberg.*

---

* Gulf discovered numerous small fields in the west — as did Oasis, Exxon, and the French CFP — and agonized for a decade over developing them, but never brought them on. Had it discovered these fields in another country — like Algeria — it might well have brought them onstream. Shell, too, spent millions of dollars in Libya, never did find lush oil of its own, finally bought into one-half of Amerada's third-interest in Oasis for $64 million after it had entered into a long-term crude contract with the American independent sim-

Graft grew apace with oil in Libya. The story of this development goes back at least to the premiership of Mustafa Ben Halim, in 1955, and to the Shelhi family which dominated King Idris's court. In time it swept many other Libyans up into its vortex as well.

Ben Halim, a Libyan brought up and educated in Egypt, had begun his career as an engineer within the government bureaucracy. Before he became prime minister he was the supervisor of public works in Benghazi, Libya's second city; it was widely stated in Libya that he took so much graft in that position that he did not dare to go to Benghazi at all after a while, for fear of violence to his person. A short time after he left the premiership — probably under pressure from the Shelhi family, which had already driven out his predecessor Muhammad Muntasser — he was appointed ambassador to Paris, where he resided for several years.

In time he returned to private life in Libya, formed an engineering business there, and through this firm, Libeco, became associated with the American construction company Brown and Root.

It soon became difficult for any foreign contractor to prosper in Libya without Ben Halim's cooperation, as another American construction firm, Bechtel, soon discovered. This enterprise, which had played a major role in the construction of Tapline, had built the line from Kirkuk to the eastern Mediterranean for Iraq Petroleum Company, had helped construct Algeria's first line, from the Fezzan "pocket" to La Skhirra in Tunisia, had performed numerous contracts for Aramco, won, in Libya, the first pipeline award, to build Exxon's line from Zelten to Brega.

However, in its day-to-day operations on the Zelten project, it encountered considerable frustration, because it was not in league with Ben Halim. Exxon had difficulty justifying its award of this contract to the Libyan government. Abdullah Senussi,

---

ilar to the one it enjoyed with Gulf in Kuwait. There is no indication that Shell attempted to slow down Oasis's development in Libya. Two other companies, Phillips and Standard of Indiana, came into Libya in 1961, on acreage which some of the first concession-holders had relinquished, flush in the middle of the Sirte Basin: they spent tens of millions of dollars, only to bring up tricklets. Phillips's find was so unremunerative that it left Libya altogether in the wake of Gaddafi's 1970 squeeze.

the "Black Prince," owner of the Saasco interests, also mounted opposition to Bechtel.* When the Oasis pipeline came up for tender, Bechtel made a strong bid for it and found that Ben Halim's opposition was nearly ruining its position in Libya. Oasis, in turn, abetted Ben Halim in his application of pressure on Bechtel, for reasons which possibly go back to the 1955 concession grants.

Bechtel, unable or unwilling to beat Ben Halim's venture, elected to join it. The three then formed a joint venture, under the aegis of Oasis. As a result, Ben Halim won the job of constructing a residential community at Oasis's Es Sider terminal and gained one-third of the work on the gathering system at Oasis's Dahra field.

Dahra abutted, to the south, on the boundary to Mobil's Concession 11. South of the line, of course, Mobil discovered an extension to the field, which it named Hofra. But Oasis went onstream first, about a year before Mobil, and as the usually reliable, never precise American rumor network of Libya had it in subsequent years, Oasis wasted no time drilling a line of wells along the concession boundary and sucking a great deal of oil from the northern fringe of Hofra before Mobil could tie it in.

Bechtel's senior managers were not happy with their company's marriage. Although their reservations were financial rather than moral, they were aware, too, that Ben Halim was disliked by segments of the Libyan population, and they sought to protect themselves by identifying their venture with the will of the oil companies as much as they could. Bechtel stayed on good terms with Ben Halim, at the same time, and granted his firm a prime position in engineering work for the joint venture. At times, Ben Halim was able to have Bechtel remove personnel from its venture if he did not find them to his liking.

Thus it came about that the second biggest family-owned corporation in America — and one of the nation's richest, least accountable, and most parsimonious institutions — entered into

* Senussi went into exile after Gaddafi's revolution, tried to organize a coup d'état against the new government — with some oil company backing — came to grief, and was nearly kidnapped in 1971 by Gaddafi's men in Rome.

a relationship, soon to prove unnecessary, with an unpopular local entrepreneur and failed politician whereby, for one decade, this figure received $2500 a month merely to refrain from obstructing the foreign venture's operations in Libya.

In 1971 Bechtel did terminate Ben Halim's services, almost two years after the Gaddafi revolution, for a severance fee of 9,000 Libyan pounds, but it still retains his brother Abdel Hamid as counsel — for a very handsome sum, considering his light caseload.

It was this venture, in turn, which accounted for much, if not most, of the construction work performed in Libya between 1960 and 1969. The two American contractors, Bechtel and Brown and Root, and their Libyan mentor Ben Halim, built Mobil's Sirtica pipeline, other branch lines, and a road from the Raguba field to Zelten, as well as the pipeline and ancillary facilities for Oasis, in spite of the fact that their bids were often "not low." Ben Halim continued to perform engineering work for Oasis, too; his justification for requesting this work was that he could not keep his office open without it.

13

To the Gaddafi Revolution

The success or failure of any mass society will depend on
whether or not man so reshapes his personality that he
can modify the society into one where we are not coerced
by technology, but bend it to our human needs.
— Bruno Bettelheim, *The Informed Heart*

BY 1965 THE LIBYAN OIL INDUSTRY, so quick to develop,
had reached a plateau, had started to become stabilized. Notwithstanding Oasis's venture, which had become second to Exxon's
and was producing a little over 300,000 barrels a day by mid-1964,
the international market had very largely absorbed Libyan oil without discomfort. The Oasis parents were selling much of their oil at
heavy discounts — Amerada had already proceeded to sell out half
to Shell — and the following year's concession law, which Exxon's
legal staff helped prepare, was to put an end to the tax break
which encouraged independents in Libya to weather the severe
competition facing them in Europe by cutting price. Libya's initial spectacular growth had flattened out in the mid-1960's.*

* See Appendix 1.

Then in 1965 Libya's second round of bids for concessions took place; this was to usher in the second, and more spectacular, takeoff of oil development and corruption in the nation.

The seeds of the second round of concession awards had been planted over the past few years, after the companies which had entered Libya in 1955 relinquished 25 percent of their acreage — thus freeing this territory for further bids. The Libyan press had been voicing considerable reservations about opening up such a second round, stating that further offerings might lay Libya open to the depredations of concession brokers and to bribery from foreign interests. But by mid-1964 the Libyan government had formed a supreme council of petroleum affairs anyway and gave this the task of arranging a second round of offers. The council proceeded to carry out its mission.

In 1965, when it offered up the properties, the Libyan government went farther than it had in the first round, or in the separate 1961 awards to Phillips and Standard of Indiana (which one might label round 1A). It announced that it was going to favor companies which adhered to one or more of the fourteen "preferential factors" it listed. These supplementary benefits included various commitments which would be very advantageous to Libya: the offer to notify the minister of petroleum in advance of contracts worth more than 200,000 Libyan pounds (or over half a million dollars) and to invite the ministry to open the bids for these contracts; a promise to deposit local funds in local banks; a commitment to grant priority in the shipment of crude to Libyan tankers, should any become available; complete disclosure of technical information regarding the concession; an offer to give the Libyan government a higher percentage of profits; an undertaking to conserve natural gas perforce produced from the oil; a promise to establish refineries and petrochemical plants in Libya; and several other lesser undertakings.[1]

The Libyans also made it clear that they would favor smaller companies over the traditional, established majors such as Exxon — provided, of course, that these smaller firms could demonstrate an ability to develop the properties they received. Some oilmen resident in Libya interpreted this almost as a personal slap in the face at Exxon's resident manager by the Libyan petroleum minister, Khalifa Musa, who was reputed to have been slighted by this representative on occasion. (Regardless of the validity of Musa's grievance, this is a further example of oil industry reluctance to remove those of their personnel who entertain poor relationships with important local figures.)

A number of independent oil firms rushed in to bid in Libya in 1965. Although five of the seven majors put in bids too, they won nothing of importance. The list of successful applicants read, rather, like a list of German conglomerates interspersed with trusts from some obscure strip of sand in the Caribbean. In the former category of applicants stood Elwerath/Wintershall, Union Rheinische Braunkohlen Kraftstoff AG, Deutsche Erdöl, Vertex Oil AG, Scholven Chemie, and Mobil's old partner Gelsenberg Benzin. In the latter category one would likely place such names as Mercury, Lion, Occidental, Circle, and Libyan Desert. Of this group, the one which hit it big and changed the structure of the world industry was Occidental.

Occidental was in fact a little-known California firm whose main concentration had been natural gas and fertilizer production in the San Joaquin Valley and whose most flamboyant asset was its chairman, Dr. Armand Hammer, a famous Russian-speaking entrepreneur with a history of involvement in pencils, Russian art, whiskey, and sterile stud bulls.

Occidental had been preparing assiduously for these awards for two years, however, and it must be stated that the company knew what it was bidding for. One of the two plots it won was acreage Oasis had relinquished: the coveted Concession 102 adjacent to Amoseas's Nafoora field. The desirability of 102 stemmed precisely from its proximity to this prolific structure and the near certainty that it, too, would yield up oil: Nafoora, like Oasis's Dahra, came right up to the straight southern boundary of its concession, and since it is most unusual for an oil field — like tree trunks, tortoise shells, or any other work of nature — to possess a straight edge, fifteen firms besides Occidental made a bid for this field, including Amoseas, the neighbor, and Oasis, the former owner of rights to the plot.[2]

Furthermore, Occidental had been lobbying frenetically among the Libyans. In December, 1963, a Libyan government official told a geologist who was then reviewing the relinquished properties for Occidental that it would be possible for Occidental to arouse Libyan public opinion in its favor and perhaps influence the petroleum council and the king, were it to capitalize on its area of greatest expertise, fertilizer production. Fertilizer can be manufactured from ammonia, and ammonia can be derived from natural gas — a commodity which the oil companies in Libya could not help producing with the oil, and which they had simply been flaring off.

The geologist relayed this information to the home office, which proceeded to reinforce its fertilizer wing by acquiring an international fertilizer marketing corporation, Interore. It perfected a plan to dangle the possibility before the Libyan government that, were it to be awarded a good property on which it would be likely to strike oil, it would seek to build a fertilizer plant in Libya to absorb the natural gas which it would perforce produce — and which another company would most assuredly burn away.

In the end it incorporated into its bid an offer to conduct a feasibility study for such a plant. It made two other major offers as well: to apply an Occidental-patented nitrogen-preservation system to the trucking and storing of perishables within Libya, and to offer 2½ percent of its profits above the 50 percent tax to develop the Kufra Oasis, an area deep in the Sahara which happened to have been the childhood home of King Idris and the burial site of the king's father. It also adhered to many of the fourteen preferential factors — with one conspicuous exception: it would not make the commitment to inform the oil ministry of any contracts it might let out over 200,000 pounds in value, or to allow it to open the bids for these contracts. This enabled the firm to retain an important future mechanism for control and influence within Libya.

Occidental officials have since stated that their company won prime acreage in Libya because its bid was generously laced with these sweeteners and was also pitched to Libyan sensibilities — for instance, it was wrapped in a ribbon striped with the national colors of the kingdom. However, the real weight of the successful effort lies elsewhere, among several Libyans, specifically Taher Ogbi, minister of labor in the Libyan government at the time of the 1966 awards, his two brothers, and Omar Shelhi, the minister of court. One or two prime ministers may have played peripheral roles in the grants as well.

Occidental paid Taher Ogbi to intercede with Shelhi, who was as close to the king as anyone in Libya, persuasively to present the king with Occidental's bids for the good properties. The initial fee which the Ogbis and Shelhi acquired from Hammer's company is not public knowledge — the stories go that this ranged from one to twenty million dollars, along with other payments — but it is a matter of record that these benefactors received an ongoing fee in the form of a commission, or "overriding royalty," of 3 percent of the sales price of every barrel of crude oil Occidental shipped out of the country. This fee was to be deposited in a Swiss bank.

Of course, it was likely that Occidental required other intermediaries as well — someone to introduce the company to Ogbi, for instance. In 1968, a year after Occidental made its discoveries, a Frenchman (or Spaniard) of murky provenance, "General" Pegulu de Rovin, took Occidental to court in Libya with the charge that he had been the one to fulfill this function and that Hammer had not paid him adequately for the service. De Rovin claimed that Hammer had agreed to pay him $100,000 at the outset (he in fact admitted receiving this) and $300,000 from the proceeds of any oil Occidental might subsequently export from Libya. Shortly after Occidental did commence exporting oil, de Rovin requested that Hammer pay him this additional sum; he cabled, "It's through my work you're in Libya, with the excellent business deriving for you and company, and you know better than anyone."

For a short time it seemed as if Occidental might not dispute his claim; but then de Rovin could not document it either, so when the case went to court it was dismissed forthwith.

The New York investment firm Allen and Allen also launched a suit against Occidental in the United States, but this case has not borne fruit either.

After the second round of awards, Occidental embarked on a

period of operations in Libya which, though brief, were without parallel in the modern annals of oil for their success. Even Aramco drilled six poor or unproductive wells in Saudi Arabia before it hit the relatively puny Dammam field, and "Dad" Joiner trekked miles of hill country before pricking through the Austin chalk that overlay the East Texas field. Occidental, though, struck its big oil almost at once. Not in 102; the find in that coveted concession was late in coming and not very prolific. (Though it turned out that this find *was* an extension of Nafoora; the Libyan government acknowledged this formally in late 1971, when it unitized production from both Nafoora and 102 — that is, put one company in charge of injecting water into both areas and maintaining pressure in them, though both companies received their share of the profits.) Occidental's other concession, 103, however, yielded up four commercial oilfields on the first five wildcats.

Considering that the 103 fields, which were on acreage Mobil had relinquished, lay two miles below ground level and that the 103D discovery well came in at an extraordinary 70,000 barrels per day, this was both impressive sleuthing and rare good luck. The discovery transformed Occidental into a major corporation. The firm has since become a sort of nouveau-riche multibillion-dollar grande dame, its appearance sustained by flamboyant press releases and such fantastic schemes as a 300,000-barrel-a-day refinery in Maine (which would have required about 20 percent of all the crude oil the government was letting into the United States at the time) and the offer to operate Exxon's expropriated oilfield on a service contract for the government of Peru. Occidental has made gaudy discoveries in the North Sea, Ghana, Nigeria, and Lake Maracaibo — generally in deep water, at if not beyond the threshold of commercial feasibility — and became purveyor (along with Bechtel Corporation) of oilfield and fertilizer technology to Leonid Brezhnev, by Nixonian fiat. It has been estimated that the contracts which these two corporations from Nixon's home state have been discussing with the Soviets will involve 20 billion dollars. (Hammer donated over $100,000 to Nixon's 1972 presidential campaign, paying $46,000 himself, in cash, and channeling another $54,000 through the former governor of Montana, Tim Babcock, who at the time of the campaign was an Occidental executive based in Washington. In December, 1974, Babcock pleaded guilty to the charges of acting as Hammer's conduit.) [3]

Ogbi, the former minister, himself became the recipient of considerable largesse from Occidental after the company hit. One surveying firm he sponsored, Norlicon, received a contract from Occidental, under his insistence, in preference to another firm, Hunting, although the latter had a work force on tap in Libya and the former did not. Ogbi was the agent for a contracting firm which won a bid to supply pipe to Occidental in spite of its high offer. He was always lobbying with Occidental to get in on oil transportation contracts, crude sales deals, contracts for the Kufra Oasis project, or purchases of asphalt for the road leading to Kufra. He had numerous political allies and relatives working for Occidental in Libya — even a shoeshine boy, at one point. The relationship continued well after it was formally severed in January, 1968, after Occidental had made its big finds.

In turn, Occidental sought the help of Bechtel and Ben Halim on its work of developing the 102 and 103 fields. It gave Bechtel the job of constructing a 42-inch pipeline and Mediterranean terminal in the fall of 1967 on a cost-plus contract without competitive bidding. Although Bechtel had by then largely come into its own in Libya and the fortunes of Mustafa Ben Halim and Brown and Root had waned somewhat, Ben Halim's brother Abdel Hamid was performing a great deal of legal work for Bechtel and Ben Halim, himself, still a consultant to Bechtel, was also receiving ancillary contracts and fees for work in the terminal area around Zueitina and Agedabia through his firm Libeco.

By 1967 Bechtel, in fact, was performing as the engineering service arm for most firms producing oil in Libya. It was engaged in most of these companies' operations above ground, except for the actual drilling of wells and dispatching of crude oil for export. In more than one instance, Bechtel even imported fuel oil for oil companies. Since the oil firms did not want to get involved in local business relationships in Libya any more than they absolutely had to, they paid Bechtel a fee often amounting to 18 percent to handle their affairs. Bechtel, in turn, subcontracted much of its work, such as catering and local labor hiring, to domestic and other Arab firms.

The Occidental pipeline contract was a true plum. Originally priced at $43 million, with terminal, it ended up costing $147 million. This obligated Occidental to make further payoffs, through Bechtel, to Libyan figures, since these extra costs could be in part deducted from tax payments to the local government, and government figures would only approve such deductions in exchange for emoluments; generally, the elements in the government who criticized the award of the contract to Bechtel were granted compensatory subcontracts.

One other firm, Williams Brothers, initially expressed some interest in doing this job too, but it dropped out of the running; it would have needed four months more to complete the line. One will recall that Article 14 of the Petroleum Law made immediate writeoffs of exploration expenditures available to oil companies only after they had started exporting oil, so time was of the essence for Occidental. The company found the cash useful in any case.

Bechtel built the line quickly — perhaps too quickly, as mishaps occurred once Occidental began exporting crude; a vent ruptured in a surge tank and numerous leaks cropped up in the line, due to corrosion.* Occidental began exporting oil at the end of February, 1968. In two months' time its exports rose to 300,000 barrels a day. By the end of the year they had almost doubled.

This volume of oil entering international distribution channels just eight hundred miles off Europe, outside the control of

---

* Probably the line was not properly tested before it went onstream. However, even if the construction had occurred at a more deliberate pace and the line had been built flawlessly, not much more than a year would have elapsed between the time Occidental first discovered oil at the 103A field and the time Occidental got it to market. Considering that this oil was 130 miles from the coast and that exporting it entailed construction of a brand new terminal, this illustrates that one claim oil companies repeatedly made during the 1973 counterrevolt, that it takes a minimum of three years to put a new discovery onstream, must be viewed most skeptically. Money can substitute for time.

the major oil companies, posed one of the first major challenges to a system which had held sway for thirty years. Since the Suez Canal was now closed, Occidental's challenge was far greater than that which Oasis had mounted, for its oil was more valuable in Europe. The newcomer promptly played its part in jolting the system to its foundations.

In this context, two features of Libya's general history at that time are immediately relevant to further understanding of the motive force behind Gaddafi's purgative revolution of 1969.

The first is that Occidental abandoned the preferential factors it had extended to the Libyan government in its drive to win the concessions — with one exception, the Kufra project; this turned out to be a minor expense for Occidental, hardly greater than the 3 percent override.

The story of Occidental's biggest commitment, to consider constructing an ammonia plant for the Libyans, presents an enlightening illustration of company-government relations in that nation. The terms of the supplement to Occidental's 1966 concession agreement were fairly clear on the subject of this plant: the commitment to construct the plant would devolve upon Occidental and the Libyan government "if it seemed to the two parties that the project was of productive utility." The plant would have an initial output of 600 tons of urea a day, would be capable of expansion, and would cost in the neighborhood of thirty million dollars.

The supplement also stated that both parties would bear this cost equally; once they agreed to build the plant, construction would begin in ninety days and be completed within eighteen months. Occidental would guarantee the purchase of all fertilizer produced by the plant, in excess of the Libyan government's requirements.

There were additional details regarding funding and management of the project, and one very important point: the company would pay the going rate for gas which the project used as feedstock, but the Libyan government would supply it.

Some time after Occidental received the concession, a debate arose over the meaning of the phrase "productive utility." To Occidental it meant "lucrative" — repaying the investment in three years or less. However, there is no such term as "feasible" in Arabic — though one could perhaps render the sense of the English term adequately in a lengthy phrase, it would still mean something very different to the Libyans. Since their nation had no important resources beyond oil production, and was very anxious to develop indigenous industries, they might well consider a big ammonia plant a boon even if it did not afford a rapid payout, or even any profit at all.

In April, 1967, at the time Occidental began discovering oil, it was enjoying a period of honeymoon with the Libyan government. It presented the government with a preliminary feasibility study for the facility, declaring that an ammonia plant would be feasible if it had a capacity of 1,000 tons a day at least — since, in the next five years, such a plant would be able to sell ammonia at $42 to $46 a ton. The Libyans did not press Occidental to build the plant at that time and Occidental officials asked them to defer discussion of it till later in 1968 anyway, as the firm was busy with other projects, such as posthaste development of the bonanzas at 103.

The Libyans did not hold off long. By June, they were broaching the plan to Occidental again, and Oil Minister Musa had drawn up a master plan for Mersa Brega — Exxon's terminal — in which Occidental's gas production was to play a vital role.

However, by that time signs of glut had begun to appear on the world ammonia market. The price of fertilizer was dropping sharply; the project to build an ammonia plant had ceased to seem "feasible" to Occidental. Furthermore, by that time, Occidental common stock, which had previously shot up in value and been split three for one, was just beginning to flounder on the New York exchange. It reached fifty by mid-summer 1968, then drifted down to the low forties, then the thirties. Since then, it has been selling for about ten dollars a share. Occidental was not coming up with exciting developments in Libya or anywhere else, and its management's former generosity was starting to pale.

Despite mounting Libyan pressure, Occidental held off giving a definite verdict on the feasibility of the ammonia plant until well into August. The Libyans, in turn, held off entering into negotiations to allow Occidental participation in concessions elsewhere in Libya. Occidental then procured an elaborate study from a British corporation which claimed that, although the plant would not be able to pay for itself unless the market price for ammonia were at least $42 a ton, this commodity, in the foreseeable future, could sell for only about $30 a ton.

Armed with this study, Occidental fertilizer experts and advisors came to Tripoli in late August and informed the Libyans that the plant they wanted would not be feasible.

The Libyans simply kept pressing Occidental to build it anyway. They talked of turning their country into the center for fertilizer manufacture in the southern Mediterranean area and supplying massive quantities of ammonia to Tunisia and Spain (countries whose ability to absorb imported fertilizer is, in fact, quite limited).

Occidental had a strong point, but this verdict disappointed the Libyans. They began to feel that they had let Occidental have a valuable concession for nothing. So Occidental began to think up a number of alternate schemes as consolation. Even one company official who rejected a compensatory prize, a plan to purchase two 50,000-ton tankers for the Libyans, on the grounds that that would set a bad precedent for future dealings with this host country, stated that the Libyans had put great store by the industrial prestige they would gain through the plant, and he forthwith proposed offering them another project: that of taking an old, inefficient 200-ton-a-day ammonia plant which an Occidental subsidiary owned in Plainview, Texas, stripping it down, shipping it to Libya at a cost of about three million dollars, and reassembling it there. It would meet North Africa's needs, he said, and the Libyans could run it.

In fact, such a scheme would not cost Occidental much — perhaps 4 cents a barrel, from one year's production. However, imaginative as this plan sounded, Occidental's top men in Libya rejected it on grounds that it would not be sufficient. From their vantage point in Tripoli, it was clear that Occidental would have to provide the Libyans with a good ammonia plant or a viable substitute. They observed that the third anniversary of the concession award was drawing nigh and the Libyan authorities knew that Occidental had, in the words of one Libyan minister, "been showered with golden luck." If Occidental did not offer some generous bonus, Libyans would accuse them of reneging on their contract.

Occidental's staff then turned to other alternatives to the plant. First was an aluminum smelter, which could absorb much of Occidental's natural gas since it would require a great deal of fuel. For once in his life, in his quest for an aluminum manufacturer who would build and operate a plant using Occidental's gas, Hammer was "used" by a businessman outside the oil industry: Reynolds Aluminum was at that time negotiating with Aristotle Onassis to build an aluminum smelter in Greece, and the company invited Hammer to its headquarters to discuss an alternate plant — with enough fanfare to attract Onassis's attention. In the end Reynolds would not give Occidental a letter of intent on this plant, however.

Occidental officials also proposed facilities to process elemental phosphorus, metallize iron ore, or produce chlorine, alkalis, or noble gases for welding. However, they followed none of these up. By the end of 1968, then, the matter of the ammonia plant had passed through a preliminary feasibility study, a full-dress feasibility study, then a Libyan government evaluation of the feasibility study, which disputed most of Occidental's computations.*

Occidental then riposted with a rebuttal to this evaluation, which in turn disputed all the Libyan answers to Occidental's original figures and stated that the scheme would turn a profit only if it could acquire firm sales guarantees and contracts accounting for at least three-quarters of the plant's output at $40 a ton.†

---

* It stated, for instance, that the ammonia the plant produced would sell in the current market for 40, not 30, dollars a ton; that a 1,000-ton-a-day plant would cost only $30 million, not $40 million as Occidental had said; and that production costs would come to only $24 a ton or so — not Occidental's figure of $27 a ton.

† Occidental had made a similar offer to Saudi Arabia in the recent past and had tried to withdraw it for the same reason. In 1965 Hammer had agreed with the Saudi government that Occidental would study the feasibility of participating with the Saudis in a plant to strip sulphur off some of the gas which the American giant Aramco was producing and then flaring in eastern Arabia. After much haggling from Aramco, which indignantly announced that it had

The Libyan government then used the one real lever it had with Occidental: Occidental's desire to obtain further relinquished acreage. Since it could hardly hope to gain this with such a matter as the ammonia project outstanding between itself and the Libyan government, it announced, in January, 1969, that it had agreed to go ahead with the plant.

However, the supplement to the 1966 concession agreement had stipulated that the Libyan government would provide the gas for the plant, and — a point which Occidental officials had discussed thoroughly among themselves — in early 1969 no supply of gas was readily available to the Libyan government. So Occidental never built the plant.

This ultimate development was significant to at least one Libyan official, Ibrahim Hangari, the undersecretary of petroleum, who held a fruitless meeting on the subject with a lawyer and an agricultural expert with Occidental. He had staked some of his prestige on the successful outcome of these talks, and, through Occidental's rebuffs, had lost some face with other Libyan officials at interministry planning group meetings. This became significant later, in November, when an American worker came to Hangari with the claim that Occidental had been shipping some crude out of the country unmetered.

Occidental's commitment to develop the Kufra Oasis did move forward because in the long run it netted the company a tax windfall. To complicate this matter, Occidental agreed to carry out still another project in Libya: a desalinization system for the town of Agedabia, near which its pipeline passed.

The concession agreement had not included the Agedabia system, of course, but had not made it clear, either, whether Occidental's payments to the Kufra fund should come off its profits on the artificial posted price of the oil it exported ($2.23

---

first rights to the gas it was producing, and a feasibility study which Aramco took a year to prepare, the giant firm decided the plant would not be feasible and gave others permission to produce sulphur from its gas. Again Occidental, after taking a one-third interest in the scheme, decided it was not feasible and tried to reduce its stake in the venture to 5 percent. Its Saudi government partner refused to let it off the hook, but the plant has never been built.

a barrel) or its much lower actual sales price (which averaged about $1.70 a barrel when the 103A field went onstream).

Agedabia's water resources were truly atrocious. The town's water table is about twelve feet below the surface of the adjacent Mediterranean and its well water is often inferior to seawater. Some wells contain a surface film of fresh water about eight inches deep, overlying water so saline that it can be used only to hose down dirt roads. Furthermore, the porous limestone terrain of the area is pocked with cesspools, which further contaminate the water supply.

The Libyans had been anxious to provide Agedabia with good water for a long time. Khalifa Musa, the oil minister, tried to enlist Exxon's help in this endeavor — Exxon's terminal was also near Agedabia — and Exxon's resident manager, Hugh Wynne, managed to excuse himself from it in exchange for a promise to develop potable water resources in western Libya — if Exxon ever built a pipeline from its fields there, which of course it didn't. Furthermore, the Libyans had requested Occidental to build its terminal near Agedabia with a view to helping the town's economy. Somehow, in the course of events, they got an oral commitment from Dr. Hammer to help develop the town's water resources as well.

Naturally, Occidental tried to wriggle out of this venture. It failed to do so, but after considerable argument, the company's lawyers managed to turn this commitment to their advantage. They persuaded Oil Minister Musa to accept payments to the Kufra development fund based on the much lower sales price of the oil, rather than the posted price, and in exchange offered to put $5 million into the Agedabia system. This they got back in two years.

Occidental made much of the Kufra project, which it had thus undertaken to complete on such favorable terms. Hammer claimed, after Occidental drilled a few wells in the oasis, that he had discovered a new Nile under the Sahara — that his drills had tapped a reserve of one quadrillion barrels of water.

However, he was not stating anything new. An oasis is, by definition, an area overlying known water resources; an area where water comes up from the ground because the strata bearing water come to, or near to, the surface. The oasis is a particularly Saharan phenomenon, because many thousands of years ago that desert was an area of substantial rainfall and still has a voluminous "bank" of underground water, much of it deposited almost six thousand years ago. Some water under the Libyan desert is 25,000 years old.

Indeed, water would have to be very accessible for primitive people such as those who inhabit the inner Sahara to know of its existence and draw from it. Occidental knew that Kufra held water in great volume before it ever began drilling there. One Occidental official wrote Hammer several months before these operations commenced that the oasis already contained 2,100 wells, 1,200 of which were not in use at the time, and 950 farms under irrigation.

In June, 1966 — less than three months after it received the concession — Occidental prepared a report which verified these figures and extolled the virtues of the Nubian sandstone — the water-bearing stratum underlying Kufra and most of southeastern Libya — as a most efficient and voluminous reservoir and conductor of water. Occidental's report estimated that the Nubian sandstone had a water storage capacity of six trillion cubic meters — over 40 trillion barrels — and an artesian area of 150,000 square kilometers.

Beginning late in 1967, Occidental proceeded to drill wells which were much more efficient than those which had previously supplied the oasis. Also, drawing on the acumen of American agricultural experts, hydrologists, horticulturalists, and the like, it began feeding these wells into traditional and experimental farming units using up-to-date pumps, corrosion-free pipes, and modern drainage networks, with a view to cultivating fruit, vegetables, livestock, and animal food appropriate to the culture and climate. As part of this project, Occidental also agreed, somewhat against its will, to supervise and help finance the paving of about half the 600-mile road from Kufra to the coast, in places where it tends to be impassable in its natural state. Again, Occidental would supply the raw material — in this case asphalt — through its marketing subsidiary in Europe; again, this project never saw the light of day.

In 1968, Occidental set aside about eight and a half million dollars for the Kufra project. In 1969, company officials estimated, this payment would come to about thirteen million dollars.

Despite the attractiveness of the Kufra project to the king, however, and despite the efficient way in which Occidental drilled prolific wells and established pilot farms to expedite the project, this venture was not free of problems, or without serious limitations.

For one thing, Hammer adamantly insisted — against almost unanimous advice from his staff, and opposition from the Libyan government — that the venture turn a profit, even if the Libyans got most of it. This would mean that produce from Kufra might have to sell at higher prices than from other areas in Libya, in order to compete in markets outside Kufra.

This led to another problem: opposition to the project from Libyan planners and intellectuals. Kufra, these people seemed to suggest, would not benefit Libya if it were to become a profit-making business venture, or even if it were to become an agricultural exporter. One Libyan agricultural economist with a ministry of government insisted that much greater expenditures should be made in the populated areas of Libya, which are along the Mediterranean, and on the development of water resources in those areas, than on developing Kufra beyond the point where it could satisfy the needs of its few residents. After all, an under-developed country concentrates its heaviest investments on projects that will bring the greatest good to the greatest number of people, not on a sweetener which will make the award of an oil concession to a particular company tolerable to the leader of the people.

There was also a limit to which the prolific Nubian sandstone could be safely exploited. The underground Sahara is no Nile. This great river is annually replenished by torrential rains in Central Africa and will be flowing as generously two hundred years hence as it is now. However, Occidental's 1966 report estimated the annual recharge of the Nubian sandstone at only 1.5 billion cubic meters a year, a tiny fraction of the Nile's flow. In other words, once one depleted half the reserves of the Nubian sandstone, one would have to wait hundreds if not thousands of years for it to replenish itself unless another Ice Age dawned in the meantime. The report in fact stated that water moved very slowly through the Nubian sandstone — no faster than half a mile, and sometimes only a yard, per year. Since the water entered the sand hundreds of miles away, it would need as much as fifteen centuries to reach Kufra.

Occidental's 1966 report suggested as much when it stated that strong consideration would have to be given to land resource management as well as to the exploitation of water resources. Furthermore, it stated that Libya could put no more than 4 percent of its land into "economic agricultural use" with the water resources it had at hand. Perhaps the company, too, was seeking ways to limit its investment in this oasis. At any rate, several years later, after the 1970 price hikes, the Libyan government took the project over completely.

Meantime, against this devilishly complicated background, the government of King Idris was also experiencing its frustrations with other companies operating in Libya. Through the decade of the 1960's, it maintained its protest against Exxon's posted price for Zelten crude, and all the other prices which Exxon and subsequent exporters posted. In 1968 one Arab commentator wrote, "The problem created by [Exxon's subsidiary] Esso Standard Libya in 1961 by posting a price for Zelten crude which was demonstrably lower than current postings in the Middle East has poisoned the atmosphere of government-company relationships and provoked a feeling of bitterness among the Libyan people which will eventually prove more costly to Esso than the few cents per barrel it has succeeded in adding to its profit." The commentator admitted that it was not clear why the Libyan government had not taken a firm stand vis-à-vis the company on this issue. "It may have been due to lack of experience or to a desire not to scare foreign investors, or to both," he conjectured, and explained that in practice the Libyan government had no say in determining posted prices: "Esso insisted that decisions relating to prices were a managerial prerogative. It had its way through the anomaly of a 'regulation,' which though issued by the government was actually drafted by the company."[4]

The Libyan government entertained poor relations with Exxon in other respects. The company had constructed a second pipeline from Zelten to Brega, whose purpose was originally to pipe salt water down from the Mediterranean to Zelten, for injection into the field. However, the company discovered, after it had proceeded to build the line, that there was a zone at Zelten which contained adequate water to maintain pressure in the oilfield, so it did not need to pump water down from the coast at all. Exxon then decided to use the line to pump natural gas from Zelten to the coast instead, where it would liquefy the gas and ship it to Europe. The terms it demanded, however, offered such little revenue to Libya that government authorities did not allow it to export gas from Mersa Brega for several years.*

Another episode of this ilk was the attenuated industry-wide negotiation of 1968. Libya had had to curtail oil shipments for about a month the previous year, in the wake of the Arab-Israeli War, because of pressure from its eastern neighbor Egypt and from domestic radicals and malcontents. The government calculated that it had lost 26 million Libyan pounds, or more than $80 million, from this shutdown.

The government also saw a chance to increase its postings as a result of the closure of Suez, which had naturally made Libyan oil even more attractive to European purchasers than it had been, relative to oil from the Persian Gulf. So the government demanded that the companies producing oil on its territory add 80 cents a barrel or more to their crude postings. To compute this additional posting, it proposed to use a monthly determination of tanker rates; it expressed a willingness to allow these postings to fluctuate in accordance with fluctuations in the rates.

The companies, however, stood firm against this demand. The government then set about trying to recover the lost 26 million pounds from them in some other way.

The companies agreed to pay one installment on this sum in May, 1968, but then entered into a series of negotiations with the Libyan authorities on another matter which rapidly became tied in with this prepayment.

* The plant was to receive a 20 percent writeoff per year and its exports were to be taxed at the market price — with a 10 cent marketing allowance on top.

This was the matter of the Libyan tax and royalty payment schedule. By 1968, the Near Eastern countries had begun to realize that different concessionaires paid their taxes at varying rates of procrastination. They also discovered that accelerating these payments would give them increased revenues — for a short time.

The Iranian government had already succeeded in gaining an additional month's payment at the end of March, 1968, the beginning of the Iranian year, as an advance on the following year's taxes. Aramco, in Saudi Arabia, would estimate its taxes for a given year — in the Saudi case, the Moslem lunar year, which is about eleven days shorter than the solar year.* Aramco would make its first payment in the first month of the Saudi lunar year, Muharram, which in 1968 coincided with April. This payment would total one-twelfth the company's estimated payments for the year. Aramco would pay a further one-twelfth of this estimate for each of the remaining months and make up whatever discrepancy arose at the end of the year. In 1967, Aramco also had to make a month's accelerated payment, so it paid thirteen installments in all that year.

In Libya, however, companies made their royalty payments each quarter and their tax payments once a year; both payments were quite delayed. The firms would pay royalties thirty days after the relevant quarter had ended and pay tax the February and March of the following year. This was very disadvantageous to the Libyans, when compared with the systems prevalent in Iran and Saudi Arabia, considering the high rates of return the producing states could earn on their money. Occidental, for instance, was reluctant to make any investment in Libya which did not offer a return of 30 percent a year or more. The Libyans thus set about trying to change the system.

They drew up a five-year budget forecast and asked the companies to provide them with estimates of what their production over the next five years would be. The companies dissembled

---

* The Moslem lunar year thus moves forward, relative to the Western solar calendar, by eleven to twelve days a year; the Iranian calendar, like ours, is solar, and its months begin and end approximately on the same days as the months of the zodiac, beginning with March 21.

lustily. Naturally, the higher their advance estimate, the higher the advance assessment levied against them would be. So Occidental, for instance, said that its production in 1970 was likely to be 570,000 barrels a day — although, as it turned out, it produced 659,000 barrels a day that year. The Libyans, thwarted on this front, moved to demand that the companies accelerate their tax and royalty payments too.

The companies fought hard. First, they made counterdemands: they proposed that the acceleration not occur at once but that it be phased out over five years and that the government in addition accept all existing posted prices and withdraw their demand for the 26-million-pound loan. Some companies also demanded the right to delay acceleration of royalties and surtax until their present crude sales contracts expired (some of them ran for twenty years). Occidental, in addition, demanded that the Libyan government grant it the right to take a half-interest in a promising adjacent concession held by the hapless German newcomer Union Rheinische.

The Libyans then countered with an offer to cancel the 26-million-pound loan in exchange for a three-year phase-in, with monthly royalty payments.

While the United States government looked the other way, or coyly winked (as was to become its wont over the next five years, whenever the oil companies operating in the Middle East got together to formulate joint strategy), representatives of the companies held a meeting in New York on September 24, to formulate a counteroffer to this proposal. The final result was an agreement, in October, which would establish tax payments on a quarterly, but not monthly, basis, and phase out the accelerated payments over four years — by which time the companies would have shifted to the more rapid payment schedule. The companies would therefore pay one quarter of the year's assessments as well as those for the previous year, over a four-year period.

In exchange for this benefit, the Libyans agreed to discontinue the five-year "rollover advance" of 26 million pounds, and Petroleum Minister Musa allowed the 1968 down payment on this sum to be credited to the additional accelerated payment for 1969.*

Occidental, for its part, made one more valuable commitment which came back to haunt the Libyan authorities: it would construct a plant to strip liquid petroleum gas (mainly propane and butane) from the rich natural gas which Occidental was flaring in the field because it had not, at that time, found any other profitable means for disposing of it.† It would also reinject some of its gas into the reservoir at 103D, to maintain pressure in that field. By 1969, Occidental had determined that a plant to export the liquid petroleum gas (as contrasted with liquefied natural gas, a less valuable commodity) would, while costing about 66 million dollars, produce about 68,000 barrels per day of these light fractions for export — or for profitable admixture to the exported crude — and would pay out in two to three years.

Bechtel conducted feasibility studies for this plant and received a commission to proceed with· it. By that time, Occidental had made a great deal of money in Libya, perhaps $60 or $70 million, but it had also put a lot of money into the country and become very dependent on Bechtel. Bechtel had virtually become Occidental's labor relations and contracting arm in Libya and was handling most of Occidental's day-to-day problems with local government officials and employees. King Idris and his government, for their part, had ceased to be effective in taking steps against company malpractices.

At the very least, then, the companies operating in Libya had shown themselves, collectively, to be the match for the government. United, they could doubtlessly have stayed that way for good. During the regime of King Idris, the operating companies scarcely made an agreement which did not, in some way, give them a benefit which they had not previously enjoyed.

---

* According to Henry Schuler, one oil company official familiar with recent Libyan oil history, the government sought in early 1971 to levy these royalties and taxes on a monthly basis (*Petroleum Intelligence Weekly*, April 22, 1974, Supplement, p. 6) .

† Occidental had contemplated exporting natural gas in liquefied form, as Exxon was to do from Brega, but abandoned consideration of the project on grounds that it would take as long as twelve years to pay out.

TO THE GADDAFI REVOLUTION 271

If the Libyans felt outsmarted and humiliated by these acts of commercial legerdemain, one other Occidental practice infuriated them. This was that Occidental had been overproducing from its 103A field at a furious rate. Although, as we have seen, some companies, such as Aramco, have been, and still are, producing from oilfields in the Near East and elsewhere faster than good engineering practice warrants — as much from an automatic desire to maximize profits as from a concern to get their money back before these properties are expropriated — Occidental did so in Libya in an unprecedentedly egregious manner.

It is true that the recoverable reserves at Occidental's 103A and 103D fields are great by American standards, belonging perhaps in the same league as Huntington Beach or Wasson, if not Elk Hills or Prudhoe Bay. However, like most Libyan fields, they are paltry by Near Eastern standards. The ultimate recoverable reserves at 103A (which was originally named Idris A, then renamed Intisar, or "victory," A, after Gaddafi's victorious 1969 revolution), have been variously estimated, but the authoritative and generous figure propounded by the prestigious consulting firm of DeGolyer and McNaughton, which was 1.215 billion barrels, should stand as a good guide.

It is possible to produce certain fields at a peak rate of one-tenth of recoverable reserves per year, although in general companies draw from their reserves at a much slower rate than this. In Iran, for instance, the Consortium produces from its fields at a "planning guide rate" of 5 percent of recoverable reserves per year.* In the case of a carbonate reef such as the structure at 103A, a rate of 10 percent would be hazardous; an annual production rate of 5 to 7 percent per year would be more in order.

Even allowing a production rate of 10 percent per year, however, which would be most generous, the 103A field would still

* One study, "Method of Developing a Newly Discovered Fractured Limestone Field in Iran," by Ali Saidi and R. E. Martin (*National Iranian Oil Company Newsletter*, April, 1966), stated that the upper limit in the Consortium was the production of 75 percent of recoverable reserves over a ten-year period, the lower limit 50 percent over a fifteen-year period: "The maximum allowable rate set in this manner averages about five percent per annum initial depletion rate, but is scaled downwards for fields with poorer well flowing characteristics."

only yield an absolute maximum of 122 million barrels a year, or 340,000 barrels a day.

Within half a year of starting up, though — that is, in July, August, and September, 1968 — Occidental, according to published statistics, was producing better than 500,000 barrels a day from the A field. More than one petroleum engineer raised his eyebrows at this, claiming that Occidental would have to discover at least one more billion-barrel field just to maintain this rate — by producing from all its fields in the aggregate, not just 103A in isolation.*

As a result of this overproduction, pressure in the A field dropped fast. At start it was about 4,500 pounds per square inch at the bottom of the well; by June this had dropped to 3,800 pounds per square inch. Sand and rocks started to come up through some flowlines. Some wells, such as A16, were producing steam, even toward the center of the field, where indiscriminate water-flooding to maintain pressure had cut through the once-integral oil zone. Also as a result of this overproduction, pressure began dropping in water-bearing strata for miles around. The configuration of the oil reservoir was being distorted, and pressure in the field was rapidly approaching the "bubble point" — an engineers' expression for the point at which gas would start to bubble up from the oil before the oil reached the well bore, so that oil would cease flowing up the hole (see Chapter 5). Less than a year later, pressure at A was below 3,000 pounds per square inch.

In short, the field was being ruined.

Not only that — and not only were the companies paying the Libyans 10 or 15 cents per barrel less than the international price structure warranted — some companies were flagrantly abusing their prerogatives. Occidental and Bechtel had already had trouble with sloppy industrial safety systems; for example, at Zueitina one Palestinian had been sent to weld a line without a protective "sniffer" and had been burned to death. Some people

---

* As Appendix 8 shows, production at 103A averaged 336,700 barrels a day in 1968, but the field did not go onstream until the end of February, and about three more months passed before it reached its high; therefore, the first five months drastically lowered 103A's average production rate for the year.

at the work site shrugged this accident off, but it disturbed others. Some people even began to suspect that Occidental had been shipping some of its crude out of the country unmetered. One American working on the job, a Bechtel electrician named John Maguire, was told by a supervisor, after he had been protesting a bit energetically against mismanagement in the field, that if he did not get out of the country he would be killed.

Before he did leave Libya, Maguire went to an Occidental official, who listened to his protests and arranged for him to meet with some Occidental engineers to discuss them. Maguire failed to persuade these engineers to take steps to improve the metering and wiring in the field, so he went on to Ibrahim Hangari, the undersecretary of petroleum, whom Occidental had outwitted on the ammonia proposal.

Hangari listened to his story and at the end asked him if Occidental was stealing the nation's oil. Maguire admitted that he could not prove that it was and claimed that it would be very hard to find out. Libyan authorities would have to swoop down on the field suddenly and take the personnel out there by surprise to catch them at it.

Hangari arranged to have Maguire set everything he knew down in writing, anyway, and a police officer provided him with plainclothes guards for protection. Maguire spent all night writing out his statement in his room at the Uaddan Hotel, then went to court with it, where it was sworn into the record. With some difficulty, Maguire managed to get an Alitalia flight to Rome after that, with a plainclothes escort. Several years later, he died of heart failure.

It was information of this nature which gave the Libyans the added bit of courage they needed to confront the companies with their stiff demands a little over a year later.

The abuses had to stop, but who would put an end to them?

Against this background, a junior army officer, Moammar Gaddafi, launched his successful Revolution of the Beginning of September, 1969.

14

Into the Seventies

You are the luckiest bastards in the world. Whenever I
set out to crack down on you, the wind shifts.
— Air pollution control official
to oil executive

THE DECADE OF THE 1960's was the most prosperous in the
history of the oil industry — perhaps, indeed, in all the annals of
Western commerce. However, as we have seen, it ended with an
accumulation of discontent and frustration in many producing
states. In Iran, the bitter annual struggle for increased revenues
left the government feeling distrustful and cheated; half a generation of revolutionary chaos in Iraq had turned some long-standing
grievances into crusades to regain lost national honor; in Libya,
conditions had become so spoiled and corrupt that a growing
segment of the population was beginning to believe that any
change, even if it brought economic hardship, would be an improvement — would at least arrest the disintegration of their

society. "We have lived without oil for five thousand years," people would say. "We can do it again."

Only Saudi Arabia, Kuwait, and the smaller sheikhdoms of the gulf came into the decade of the seventies on good terms with the oil industry. However, the rulers of these states had a problem of their own: the threat of revolution. Although this was undoubtedly not as vivid as they imagined it to be, it was present nonetheless, and it prompted them sometimes to take rather exaggerated steps to preserve their positions.

By 1972, the government of Saudi Arabia upped its defense spending to 27.8 percent of the national budget; however, it had to inhibit the flow of weaponry to the military, since it could never be sure who might turn the weapons against it.[1] There had been an abortive air force officers' mutiny in 1960 and several waves of arrests subsequently occurred in the army. The Saudi government sent its least trustworthy forces to its most distant posts, where the notion of revolution perhaps worked into their imaginations further. Then one of its southern neighbors, Aden, now the Marxist People's Democratic Republic of South Yemen, had been supporting insurrection in a mutual neighbor to the southeast, Dhofar, and made no secret of its desire to spread the insurrection still farther east, to overthrow all "feudal" and "reactionary" states along the oil-rich Persian Gulf. Aden considered the Saudi monarchy to be the greatest evil in the area. As well as publishing underground material smuggled out of Saudi Arabia, its press used to place the kingdom outside the pale of the Arab world in a symbolic sense by superimposing the star of David on maps of its northern neighbor.

This, coupled with frequent Iraqi propaganda along similar lines, made the Saudi government extremely suspicious of any currents of change in the gulf area, inspiring it to tighten internal security and incidentally planting the seeds of an idea which was to flower with the embargo of 1973: if the Arab states as a whole came to conceive of it as the most prolific, therefore the most potentially powerful, of oil states, Saudi Arabia would then be able to exert a political influence in the world at large, through its use of the oil weapon. Thus, it could prove indispensable to the other Arab states in their quest for leverage against Israel.

Thus, perhaps, other Arab leaders would see to it that the kingdom gained immunity from attacks by radicals and revolutionaries, for a time at least.

Much the same reasoning could have influenced Kuwait, although this country, smaller and less endowed with oil, pursued a more passive policy. There, the drift of events suggested that political militants could largely have their way on foreign issues in the press, and often in the National Assembly, and that the government would generously contribute, and encourage its citizens to contribute, to the Palestinian cause.[2] The understanding was that the peace within Kuwait itself would remain undisturbed. Thus, in the early 1970's, while the government of Kuwait seemed to entertain good relations with Kuwait Oil Company, the National Assembly took militant stands against the firm: it refused to ratify an agreement with Gulf and BP for the export of natural gas and it responded to the government's participation campaign with a much stiffer drive for total nationalization.

The industry's troubles in the Near East, however, began with the revolutionary Libya of Moammar Gaddafi.

The highly-fragmented character of the producing industry in Libya was what made it practicable for a Gaddafi to carry out aggressive oil policies. Nonetheless, it took a Gaddafi, a man of messianic, often destructively fanatic temperament, to pursue them to their logical conclusions. For, although King Idris was not able or inclined to effect a significant change in his nation's relations with the oil companies, Gaddafi found it hard too.

For a while after he staged his revolution in 1969, he bided his time and devoted his initial energies to moral and social reconstruction within the country. The night he came to power, he outlawed liquor. Although the Koran, the holy book of the Moslems, forbids the drinking of alcohol, this kind of prohibition is unusual among Moslem states in this era. The only other such nations to enforce it with much zeal are Saudi Arabia, Afghanistan, and perhaps Yemen and Oman, where liquor has not been allowed for a generation anyway. In the Libya of King Idris, however, liquor was consumed in desert camps and the casinos of the big hotels of Tripoli and Benghazi, so Gaddafi's Libya is the only Moslem nation (and probably the only nation in the world) where a stiffer interdiction is in force against alcohol now than in the recent past. Only the foreigners may drink liquor, and that only in the desert camps. Gaddafi's police have been known to comb the garbage cans of Tripoli for empty whiskey bottles, and Libyans have been sent to jail for possessing liquor on their premises. At this writing, black-market scotch goes for about $35 a bottle in Tripoli. The city's inhabitants, as a result, gladly travel at considerable expense to the neighboring countries of Malta, Tunisia, or Egypt just to drink, and in retaliation, the Libyan press publishes false reports that the casinos in Egypt have all closed down. Nonetheless, the business of ministering to Libyans in the seaside resorts of Hammamet, Mersa Matruh, and Jerba, and along Pyramids Boulevard in Cairo, continues apace, while the collection of confiscated bottles at Tripoli Airport spills over into neighboring warehouses — occasionally to be raided by yet other thirsty Libyans.

Beginning in September, 1969, Gaddafi extended his strict moralistic writ in other directions. For example, he banned the public use of the Latin script and proscribed public use of such non-Arabic words as "taxi," "television," and "helicopter." He sought to remove the influence of Western-derived civil law in Libya by reviving certain old Islamic practices, such as severance of the offending hand for theft, whipping of fornicators, and burning of morally dangerous works.

In September, 1973, he consecrated these domestic measures with a general cultural revolution aimed at removing those whom he considered the economic and social enemies of the people from influence within the country; he had already combined these internal measures with acts of retaliation against the foreign world. He had expelled the Americans and British from their military bases on Libyan soil, then, in 1970, confiscated most of the property of the Italians resident in his country — the several tens of thousands of souls, mostly Sicilian by extraction, who had remained after the war and the long occupation under Mussolini. Then he had converted their cathedrals, whose domes and crosses had dominated the cities of Tripoli and Benghazi, into mosques, in the manner of the great Byzantine churches of Istanbul.

Gaddafi's purpose in doing all this has probably not been simply to torment peoples and nations, and banish the last vestiges of colonialism from his land, but to unite his people as well. In his mind the people are not only Libyans, but also the inhabitants of the eighteen other Arab states. Perhaps the motive behind his actions has been to extirpate a personal and even national inferiority complex and lack of dominant ethnic personality. He has thus taken an aggressive stance toward any figure, inside the Arab world or out, whom he considers to have inflicted harm upon his conception of the Arab ethnic or ideal personality. This has led him to dabble in Palestinian violence, to threaten to invade Jordan, to call for an end to the regime in Morocco, to interfere in the domestic affairs of Chad, the Philippines, and Great Britain, to attempt to force a merger with Egypt on cultural terms congenial to him, and, of course, to cleanse the country of the corruption and division which the oil industry had spawned.

Like Nasser, and other figures of recent Arab history, he has come to some grief in his attempts to unite recalcitrant fellow-Arab states into one nation under his dominance, but his regime has been more successful in the sphere of oil politics. His first move, a modest gambit, came in January, 1970, with a mere continuation of the previous regime's attempts to raise the tax reference price of Libyan crude. The demand was something in the neighborhood of a 10 to 20 percent increase, which Algerian and Venezuelan advice had indicated Libyan crude merited.*

An apparent lull set in for a couple of months, while the companies took the government's request under advisement and in essence rejected it. The Libyan government, by degrees, became very frustrated with industry procrastination. The chronicle of that period — from *Platt's Oilgram,* for instance — shows Libyan

---

* Ambassador James Akins, in his October 11, 1973, testimony before the Church Subcommittee on Multinational Corporations, stated that the Venezuelan and Algerian advice was right. "The Libyans were not particularly well versed in oil matters," he stated, "but they had some people who were trained economists and most importantly they had advisors in other OPEC countries, not only Algeria, but I understand from Venezuela and perhaps from others, people who were able to look at these figures and tell the Libyans that their oil was underpriced. . . . I have the same slide rules that the Libyans have and I could calculate it different with transportation costs. . . . You add these together and get something, according to our calculations, a figure higher than 40 cents [above the prices prevalent then]." Since 1968 at least one company, Getty, had been exporting oil from Algeria at a posted price of $2.65.

emissaries, caught in a situation whose gravity they had not foreseen, conferring frantically with other Arabs, Soviets, and European state companies, east and west, presumably for moral support
and emergency buyers should the Libyans find themselves boxed
into a corner where they had to expropriate the companies to save
face. Meanwhile, recession proceeded apace, as the companies cut
back drastically on their drilling.[3] Whereas they had been operating as many as fifty-two exploration rigs in Libya in 1969, this
number dropped by half, to twenty-six, in early 1970. The Libyans
even opened diplomatic relations with Albania, and consulted
with the Canadians, who, in the province of Alberta, play host to
carbonate reefs quite similar to those in Libya and had developed
strict conservation regulations governing production from them.

Meanwhile, deadlock persisted. The government, after present-
ing its demands to all companies, focused on two, Exxon and
Occidental — especially Occidental, the weakest of its guests. In
May, the Libyans ordered Occidental to cut its oil production
back by 300,000 barrels a day.

This move was unprecedented in Near Eastern oil history, but
it had justification on technical grounds: Occidental had been
producing far more rapidly from its fields than good engineering
practice warranted, as the foregoing chapter pointed out. So,
presumably, had most of the other companies: the Libyans forthwith ordered Amoseas (Texaco and SoCal) to cut its production
back too, by over 25 percent or about 100,000 barrels a day. They
followed with orders to Oasis to cut back by about 17 percent, or
150,000 barrels a day, in July, and in August to Mobil by about
40,000 barrels a day. They never ordered BP/Hunt to follow suit,
though — which is one indication that there was truth to a subsequent Libyan claim, that technical considerations alone motivated this cutback and that it bore no relation to the price negotiations at hand.

Nonetheless, the cutbacks gave a real impetus to the negotiations. Occidental and Exxon quickly offered modest counterpro-
posals: an initial increase of 2½ cents and 10 cents, respectively,
to be followed by further annual increases over the next five years.

Occidental, whose position was becoming untenable as a result
of the cutback, took two other decisive steps to protect itself. First,

its chairman, Armand Hammer, went to New York, visited Exxon's chairman, James Jamieson, and offered to stand firm against Gaddafi if Exxon would supply Occidental with crude oil from non-Libyan sources at an exceptional discount, close to cost.[4] Jamieson, probably motivated by distrust or dislike of Hammer, perhaps smarting from the memory of Hammer's offer to operate Exxon's nationalized La Brea y Parinas field in Peru, on a service contract, for the government there, turned his offer down politely by referring Occidental representatives to Exxon's crude-sales staff, who offered him only Exxon's standard discount to outsiders. Exxon's Libyan management bolstered this rebuff by showing Occidental men the consent decree their firm had signed with the United States Department of Justice some years back, in which it promised to refrain from future actions to fix prices or restrain trade — while falling short of admitting that it had ever taken such actions in the first place. (All over the world, Exxon men reputedly trundled this document out whenever asked to participate in an undertaking they did not find congenial.)

Then Occidental played its second card: it cut back on construction of the liquefied petroleum gas export facilities it had been building at Zueitina and down in the field, at a cost of over $60 million. Work on this series of plants had already fallen back badly, due to labor problems, discriminatory Libyan measures against American and other foreign workers, and a serious fire in a cooling plant. Occidental stopped work altogether on the Zueitina part of the project, which was to provide butane and propane for export, reasoning that Gaddafi would not expropriate the fields at 102 and 103 as long as the export facility remained unfinished.

The Libyans, for their part, refused to think of allowing Occidental to increase its oil production at all until it did finish the plant. Occidental then closed Zueitina down altogether but kept working on the facilities to strip butane and propane from the gas at 103; it assumed that if it managed to inject the stripped gas into the field, it would be allowed to increase production anyway.

The struggle between the Libyan government and the two United States firms came to resemble the relationship between

two partners in an arranged marriage who want desperately to
get a divorce but, fearing that they would become outcast and
destitute if they did so, settle instead for coexistence on a mini-
mal basis. The Libyans terminated the visas of ten key Occidental
personnel at one point, while refusing to let Bechtel's resident
manager leave the country. Relations between Libyan and American workers deteriorated. The two groups did not get along very
well together in this venture anyway; the Americans usually referred to Libyans by their payroll numbers, rather than their
proper names. Now, at one point, Bechtel tried to "surplus" one
of its Libyan employees, who had slugged his Occidental supervisor; the government forced Bechtel to put him back on the
payroll.

Bechtel, as Occidental's engineering arm, refused to bring any
new heavy machinery into Libya — for instance, its heavy-duty
vehicles for desert and tundra transport — and it also tried to lay
off hundreds of Libyan workers. In turn, the Libyans made it
almost impossible for Bechtel or Occidental to bring any trained
American personnel into the country and upped the pressure on
Occidental a notch.

In turn, the Libyans upped the pressure on Occidental a notch.
Police stopped and searched certain key Occidental personnel
virtually every time they ventured to their offices. Then the government forced Occidental to cut back production by another
60,000 barrels a day, so that Occidental, by late August, was producing only 440,000 barrels a day — slightly more than half its
production at its peak.

Other companies held the line against Gaddafi in various ways,
mostly by maintaining their slowdown in drilling for oil. The
government had noted that the companies were now operating
only thirteen rigs — half the low number of earlier in the year.[5]
The exception was one newcomer, a European state company,
which was reported to have hit salt water on one well but was not
permitted to plug and abandon it because Gaddafi did not want
any more dry wells drilled in revolutionary Libya.

As the first anniversary of the revolution approached, it became
vital for Gaddafi to gain an important symbolic victory in his oil
policies, so the negotiations with Occidental intensified. The first

Libyan team, which had called for nationalization, was withdrawn some time before. The second team, under Omar Muntasser, was reputed to have demanded a sixty-cent increase in postings; the government apparently considered that too high, because it withdrew this team also. Third came the team headed by the prime minister himself, Abdel Salaam Jalloud, who called for an immediate hike of 30 cents, a further increase of 10 cents over a five-year period, and an increase in the tax rate from 50 to 57 percent (largely to absorb the payments to the Kufra fund, which the government was taking over).[6] The Libyans then upped the latter demand to 58 percent.

This occasioned further debate, but Occidental finally gave in to this too, on condition that the Libyans permit it to restore its production level to 800,000 barrels a day. Jalloud settled on 700,000 barrels a day, despite objections from technical experts. One petroleum ministry official erupted when he heard this, calling Hammer a crook and threatening to take the story of Occidental's overproduction to the public. But the cutback had become a political matter after all, and it was thus largely rescinded, in exchange for a concession of great political value to Libya: the increased payments Jalloud had demanded.

Radio Libya jubilantly announced the agreement on September 4 and the government turned to the next most vulnerable company, Oasis. The partners to this venture, with the exception of Shell, capitulated on September 18 on terms similar to Occidental's.*

Occidental, and the Oasis parents except Shell, had no production to speak of elsewhere, which meant that they could not make up for any production they might lose through expropriation in Libya. Furthermore, companies operating in the Persian Gulf had frustrated Occidental in its attempt to acquire cheap alternate crude from them. However, the two firms could afford to offer the Libyan government far more generous terms than the other, major companies could, because they had no important concessions elsewhere to jeopardize by acceding to the extreme Libyan demands. This Shell had understood; if the other majors had stood firm too, Gaddafi's campaign might in the end have

* Their tax rate, however, increased only to 54 percent.

been blunted. Hunt and Mobil did resist an accommodation, but then Exxon, BP, Texaco, and Standard of California capitulated in turn.

One explanation for the big companies' failure to hold firm against Gaddafi and Jalloud in late summer 1970 is that the companies would not stand alone — even as a group. They wanted both the United States and the British governments to stand behind them, to explain that any shortages which might arise in Europe were due to Libyan intransigence. The British were willing to do this, but not the State Department. Then, two of the companies, the Amoseas parents, SoCal and Texaco, were poorly represented in Nigeria, the other major source of sweet crude west of Suez, and felt that they could not afford to do without their low-sulphur Libyan oil. Gaddafi, too, was well served by a temporary shortage of oil in the Mediterranean, the result of a lengthy shutdown of Tapline due to a rupture within Syria. So, while Libya's negotiator Jalloud acted at times like a spoiled adolescent, at one point crumpling up a company's offer and flinging it in the face of the negotiator, the Amoseas parents gave him just what he was asking for.

There is another, more sinister explanation for the majors' pusillanimity, which runs as follows: since these big firms were not nearly as dependent on Libya as the independents — which in turn accounted for more than half Libya's production — the big companies, given the choice of holding firm and damaging the Libyans greatly by hurting themselves, or capitulating and perhaps driving the independents to the wall, chose the latter course. In a sense the independents were intimidated by the simple understanding that if they kept quiet and conformed, they would survive. Until the day Suez reopened, they would always find a market for their oil in Europe. The economist John M. Blair, for one, gives at least implicit support to this theory, by stating, "Restrictions by the Libyan government and nationalization in Algeria combined to reduce the output of 'other companies' [besides the seven majors] from 3,573,000 barrels per day in 1970 to 2,253,000 in 1972. . . . Thus far, one effect of the drive toward nationalization would appear to be the removal of a troublesome thorn from the side of the majors."[7]

At any rate, in the later words of *The Oil and Gas Journal,* "the other dominoes fell in quick order."

But the next domino fell in the very birthplace of the theory which bears its name: the United States of America. Effective 7 A.M. November 11, 1970, Gulf Oil Company announced that it was raising the price it paid and charged for domestic crude by 25 cents a barrel, or almost 10 percent. No justification for this hike was asked or given. Gulf, alone among the majors, had no production in Libya so it had not suffered from the Tripoli agreements. But within three weeks virtually every producer and refiner in the United States had raised the prices it paid and charged for domestic crude by an identical amount, 25 cents a barrel.

The federal government was powerless if not reluctant to stop them and unable to force a price rollback. President Nixon voiced concern, but the only action he took to oppose the increase was to lift controls on the rate of production in "undisputed" federal lands and waters. Though the action drew some indignant comments from officials in midcontinent oil-producing states, which exercised firm control over production rates in most of the nation's oilfields, it had little effect in creating a crude oil surplus of a volume sufficient to put downward pressure on prices. As Senator Proxmire observed, accurately but helplessly, President Nixon's action affected production of only about 300,000 barrels a day — little more than 3 percent of America's total crude output.

Within another month, virtually every marketer of oil products in the United States had raised the price it charged for gasoline by seven-tenths of a cent a gallon. This too went unchallenged.

But not unnoticed. Paul McCracken, chairman of the Council of Economic Advisors, maintained that the state of Texas helped the hikes along: the Texas Railroad Commission, which regulates oil production in the state, had cut back on production allowables — an almost inconceivable step, considering the Libyan cutbacks and the 270-day shutdown of Tapline.[8] The Texas Railroad Commission dropped the permissible crude output level again slightly in December.[9] This drew comment from another member of the CEA, Hendrik Houthakker.[10]

Naturally the increases did not stop at this point. Not only was the rise in the export price of Libyan crude dramatic — far greater than any change which the international oil business had witnessed for a generation. It — and the American increases — also encouraged rises elsewhere, perpetuating what Professor Adelman of MIT had called, almost four years earlier, a "major anomaly or disequilibrium in the price structure": after the 1967 war, this had meant that either Libyan prices had to go up sooner or later, or Persian Gulf prices would go down.[11] As it happened, Libyan prices went up *more* than necessary to establish equilibrium, because the tax rate had risen too — from 50 to at least 54 and on one occasion 58 percent. So the demise of the classic structure of the international industry had begun.

Although the Iranian Consortium's annual round of talks with its hosts had passed with relative tranquility — for the first time in half a decade — the Shah still harbored resentment against the Consortium for its slow, reluctant development of Iranian resources and its indifference to the Iran-Turkey pipeline project. As we have seen, he also harbored obscure, barely articulated resentments against "foreign countries" which had "suddenly shown concern for Iran's democracy" about a decade before. Now he saw his chance to redress some of these apparent wrongs. During the Libyan cutback, he had managed to pressure the Consortium to raise its APQ — by almost 3 percent.[12] Then in October the Shah started to talk about matching the terms the Libyans had been gaining from their guests.

The Consortium inched up toward his earlier demands, coming to within $105 million of them. This was not good enough. Now Iran asked for $5.9 billion over the next five years, or an increase of $200 million a year.[13]

Then other states jumped on the carousel. Soon demands for a 55 percent tax base and a 30 percent increase in postings spread all through the world of OPEC. Around Christmas time, at its tenth anniversary celebration in the Catholic land of Venezuela, OPEC codified these demands in a resolution and extended an invitation to the companies to attend a series of meetings in January, to satisfy them.

These negotiations were obviously going to be tough. The rhetoric which preceded them gave little room for illusion on this score.[14] Iran's Finance Minister Jamshid Amouzegar, who was soon to be his country's chief negotiator in the matter, took note of the 25-cent-a-barrel hike in the United States and wasted no effort giving it full publicity: if America is entitled to increases like this, he seemed to be asking, why can't we demand the same?

Nonetheless, the companies were not without resources of their own. One hopes they did not lack the political imagination to sense that the following stage was going to be the crucial one: that they would undoubtedly have to concede to OPEC the terms which Libya had won in Tripoli that September, but that if they stood absolutely firm after that, they could compel all the states — *including Libya* — to accept these terms as final and to acquiesce in them for a number of years.

At the outset, the industry showed that it realized this. The companies concerned in fact made an effort, with United States government sanction, to set up an industry-wide front toward OPEC. In mid-January, 1971, the companies proceeded to set up a coordinating body in New York, the London Policy Group, which met with the blessings of the Justice Department. The assistant attorney general had provided the companies with a Business Review Letter, which stated that the Justice Department would not prosecute them for violating antitrust law by holding these meetings if they stayed off the subject of American prices and markets.

However, this group came into being with a fatal flaw because issuance of the Business Review Letter occurred through the inspiration of the United States State Department, whose subsequent actions were far less deleterious to the majors than to the independents. Also instrumental in setting the style for subsequent negotiations was John J. McCloy — and he had been representing the seven majors before the United States attorney general for a decade. McCloy and State Department representatives did not even insist on attending London Policy Group meetings, but were content to sit in the anteroom of the office where they were held and look over drafts of the agreements which the companies drew up among themselves.

The group, in fact, made its first blunder by refusing to call OPEC's bluff and acquiescing in worldwide negotiations. *Platt's Oilgram* had one State Department official declaring, "What it looks like is that the OPEC governments wanted to use the threat of a common front as a club to scare the companies. But they had no serious intention of negotiating an OPEC-wide agreement and were counting on the companies refusing. They were taken aback when the companies agreed to negotiate a broad agreement."[15]

Furthermore, even at the outset, the company front lacked unanimity. Though the group was international, including German, Spanish, and Japanese companies as well as American independents and the seven majors, it left out two state firms which owed no loyalty to the major privately held concerns. These were France's ERAP and the oft-rebuffed Italian maverick ENI. No less a figure than French President Pompidou declared that while the predominantly private French CFP's alignment with other majors in the negotiations was "natural and inevitable," ERAP had "a different attitude," colored mainly by French government discussions taking place at the time with Algeria, not only on oil but on a number of other subjects as well.[16]

The need for absolute solidarity within the industry during the following negotiations, which took place in Tehran, was especially obvious to the most vulnerable. These were the independents operating in Libya, who had already been singed once. Henry Schuler, a representative of one such firm, Hunt, gave an exhaustive account on January 31, 1974, before the Church Subcommittee, of the ratiocination he and his colleagues went through in early 1971 and their efforts to persuade the industry as a whole in the London Policy Group of the validity of their conclusions. As he illustrated in his statement, which was as long as a small book, the industry — while readily conceding that OPEC states had the right to negotiate as a group — did not hang together in January and February, 1971, as he had predicted it would have to, and this proved catastrophic for the independent producers and the Western consumer alike.

Recently, the major companies have protested that they did manage to hold prices down, at least until late 1973, that they did the best job they could in Tehran and after. McCloy himself has written that "the companies fought tooth and nail against the demands of the producing countries for an increase in the so-called posted price and the increased 'take' of the producing countries. . . . With the cooperation of the government, they spent much time and thought on how best to organize to keep these prices at reasonable levels. And they indeed did achieve a considerable measure of success in reaching some agreements which produced such a result."[17] Representatives of the major companies made such a claim too, as Chapter 2 should indicate. Exxon's George Piercy told the Church Subcommittee in March, 1974, "I can tell you frankly, I think [the current prices] are too high. . . . We usually settled for one-half to two-thirds of what they asked for, in past negotiations. . . . We've fought hard." (Senator Percy of Illinois replied, "Though you fought hard, you're better off than you ever were.")

But the record shows that the joint effort of early 1971 fell short in two main respects. First, although the London Policy Group worked hard, it failed to come up with a defense of great value to the apprehensive independents. The latter, being the most vulnerable of the lot, requested that the industry establish a worldwide crude sharing agreement similar to what Occidental had requested of Exxon in June, 1970. They claimed that any oil-producing company which stood firm against hikes and was cut back or expropriated for so doing anywhere in the realm of OPEC should receive cost crude from other companies. However, the major companies did not endorse this crude-sharing proposal unequivocally; in the "safety net" agreement which they reached with the other companies, they succeeded in inserting two clauses which would enable them only to replace crude with "dimes and quarters" — an option to provide penalized firms with money rather than oil, 10 cents for every barrel of Persian Gulf oil they lost, or 25 cents for every Libyan barrel.[18] The independents fought bitterly against this clause but had no choice but to accept it.

One representative of a smaller company reputedly compared the majors' attitude toward their more vulnerable firms to that of a farmer who lets his barn burn down to get rid of mice — not realizing until too late that his house is attached to the barn. Later, the ease with which the majors could spurn the independents' demand for crude became apparent when Gulf refused to provide Armand Hammer of Occidental with replacement oil on grounds that too large a volume of oil was involved: the September, 1970, hike from 500,000 to 700,000 barrels which the Libyans had granted Occidental was a payment to Occidental for capitulating, claimed Gulf, with reason.

The second dereliction of the London Policy Group is one which the majors share with the United States State Department. This was the decision to break the OPEC-wide negotiations into two segments — to "split the Gulf from the Med." As was obvious to everyone familiar with the geography of the Near East (and as the parents of Iraq Petroleum Company had learned over the past decade, through "the hinge"), as long as the oil states have the right to demand that oil landed by pipeline on the Mediterranean be taxed on the same basis as that landed on the Persian Gulf, a tension and imbalance will always exist within the international market — *unless the prices for the two oils, brought to a neutral third port, in Europe, say, are about the same.* Take the port of Genoa or Rotterdam: if Saudi crude from Ras Tanura is more expensive, landed there, than oil from Mersa Brega in Libya, because Libya is so much closer, the Libyans will always claim that their oil is underpriced in Europe. The same will hold true in opposite circumstances — witness the Shah's protest after the Libyan price hikes of September, 1970. It was to keep up with the Libyans that the Persian Gulf states made their demands in December.

The real complication arises, however, with oil coming out of Iraq and Saudi Arabia by pipe to the eastern Mediterranean. The governments of these two nations have the right to demand that this oil be taxed at a rate corresponding to that prevailing in Libya, a few hundred miles to the west; but if the tax on this oil goes too high, a real discrepancy will arise between it and other Saudi or Iraqi oils exported from the Persian Gulf. The tax reference price on Mediterranean oils — except for Algeria's — had always been based on Persian Gulf prices plus some freight allowance, however outmoded or "phantom." When Gaddafi shifted the pricing of Libyan oil to conform to the money the Algerians were getting from the French for their sheltered crude, he cracked the entire system. The major oil companies exporting from the Persian Gulf, however, failed to mend the crack.

Again, one must concede that once all the other oil-exporting countries in the non-Communist world had sought to bring their prices up to the level which Libya and Algeria enjoyed, the companies had no choice but to accede to this inexorable natural force. However, having done that once, they had an obligation to insist that the pricing they arrived at remain uniform throughout the world and that Saudi and Iraqi crude piped to the Mediterranean also hew to this worldwide pattern. Otherwise, of course, a race, or auction, was bound to start up wherein some countries would try, and perhaps succeed, to push the price up still further, promoting a dizzy escalation which no other country could ignore, any more than any participant at a banquet honoring Stalin could afford to be the first to stop clapping.*

Again, Henry Schuler's opus is the point of reference: as his statement indicates, the London Policy Group did indicate in its letter to OPEC, in mid-January, that it wanted the negotiations to embrace the entire realm of OPEC. The American government seemed to endorse this strategy — though, as we have seen, some State Department officials didn't even believe that OPEC seriously aspired to a worldwide settlement.

Saudi Arabia certainly went along with the London Policy Group's letter, to judge by Petroleum Minister Yamani's public statement before the negotiation began.[19] Libya promptly attempted, in mid-January, to sabotage the OPEC-wide approach. Prime Minister Jalloud proclaimed, "Libya will defeat the consuming countries and also the oil companies," and he put pressure on Hunt and Occidental to dissociate themselves from the industry-wide front and capitulate to a separate peace. But the independents held him off, facing down three consecutive ultimatums from him. This "proved the soundness of the joint approach agreed in New York," Schuler wrote.[20]

Libya was getting support from Algeria, but, as Schuler pointed out, Algeria was behaving carefully with America. It wanted American government support against France and was viewing the United States East Coast as a potentially lucrative market for its natural gas.

In Tehran, in the second half of January, the industry strategy of conducting talks with all OPEC states as a group came up

* The Russian novelist Solzhenitsyn reports that one elderly man who collapsed after clapping for eleven minutes at such a banquet was taken off by the secret police later that night, never to be seen again.

against strong resistance from the Shah of Iran and his negotiator, Amouzegar. This firm stance may have taken the major companies and the United States State Department by surprise. At first, the companies countered with a message on January 16, declaring their readiness to discuss "a revision to the posted prices of all crudes in all member countries of OPEC," with "a further temporary transportation adjustment for Libyan crudes," but no further increase in tax rates and no new obligatory reinvestment or retroactive payments — all to be firm for five years.[21] But then they drew back from this stand for a worldwide settlement and folded without a whimper. Quite probably, if they had held to their strategy with tenacity, they could have got a worldwide settlement. But the Nixon administration showed no guts, simply. The United States government emissary concerned with these negotiations, Ambassador John Irwin, who helped pressure the companies to meet the Shah's demands, turned out to be woefully unprepared for his task. In his testimony to the Church Subcommittee, he stated that he had been in the State Department only since that September; before then he had been a lawyer in New York and had no experience in oil affairs.

"This was three or four months later," observed Senator Clifford Case. "Just a bright young man from a big New York law firm." As it turned out later, Irwin became ambassador to France. He had contributed $50,000 to Nixon's 1972 reelection campaign.[22]

Furthermore, Irwin had had less than one day in Washington to prepare for the trip, did not consult with oil company representatives before he went, and admitted that he did not even seriously endeavor to stop in Libya on his way, to see Gaddafi. A State Department spokesman explained with some embarrassment that Libya was only negotiating with one or two companies and added, "It's not entirely clear that this settlement in the Gulf will then apply elsewhere, whether it's an appropriate adjustment for quality and transportation or not. But certainly that's what they've asked for and it's entirely right to go talk to the people who are immediately going to be engaged."[23]

When Irwin got to Tehran, the American ambassador there, Douglas MacArthur II, whose support for the Iranian position was well known, had no difficulty convincing him to press the companies to agree to "split the Gulf from the Med."

At his January, 1974, hearings, Senator Church wondered why the State Department had abandoned its position — and that of the companies — so quickly. "There must have been some other factor — was there some consideration for the bilateral relations between the United States and Iran?" he asked Irwin.

Irwin responded in the negative. Schuler wasn't so sure; he talked of the likelihood that the Nixon administration's principal aim was to strengthen the Shah in the gulf.

The Shah had been fighting a guerrilla war to the south, in the Sultanate of Oman, where rebels financed by Russia, China, and the People's Democratic Republic of Yemen were trying to blaze a trail from Aden to the oilfields. Nixon, Viet Nam firm in his memory, was providing the Shah with weapons, the Shah was providing the troops — Moslem against Moslem. This kind of service, necessary though it might be, always carries a price.

As it turned out, the major companies had already been considering capitulating to the Shah. In his statement, Schuler quotes a letter from the industry negotiating team to the Libyans, dated January 21, as stating, "We should prefer, and should have thought that it would be beneficial, in the interests of time, that the negotiations should be with a group representing all the OPEC members. *Nevertheless we should not exclude that separate (but necessarily connected) discussions could be held with groups comprising fewer than all OPEC members.*"[24] (Emphasis supplied.) Thus the companies indicated that they would be willing to institute simultaneous negotiations in Libya and the gulf — sanctifying the split even before they agreed to it. Each company had the power of veto over such a decision: no one exercised it. And when the head of the Tripoli half of the industry team, George Piercy of Exxon, arrived in Libya, Oil Minister Mabrouk would not even see him, except as an envoy of Exxon. Mabrouk had just been to Iran, where other OPEC representatives had stiffened his resolve to keep the Libyan negotiations strictly separate from those concerning the gulf.

Meanwhile, as Schuler relates, the Tehran half of the team had gone on to touch home base in London, and drew up a counterproposal — leaving before the Libyan team got back to London. This further alienation of gulf and Mediterranean strategies was flatly contrary to the London Group's ground rules.

One can certainly argue that had the companies stood firm on their demand for OPEC-wide negotiations, they might in the end have failed anyway; the Iranians and other gulf figures would not have tolerated such a stand. First, the Libyan government kept advertising that it had no desire to be seen in the same room as the "reactionaries" and "feudalists" of the gulf — though its representatives were very happy to consult with them. Second, Amouzegar's team did raise the threat of an OPEC-wide shut-down, which OPEC then sanctified with Resolution 131 of Tehran, on February 4, threatening that the member states in the gulf would "legislate" the issues at hand by February 15 and that one week after that they would follow the legislation with "appropriate measures including a total embargo on the shipments of crude oil and petroleum products" should the companies not return to the table by the fifteenth.[25]

However, it is asking for trouble and defeat to take such a threat as an accomplished fact. It is tantamount to giving in to the old argument, propounded by industry and Western government alike, that hellfire and brimstone await the profligate Western consumer, that the producing states are at all times willing to cut off their oil completely and contemptuously in order to force this consumer (who is defenseless as well as wanton) to capitulate to demands of a political as well as economic nature.

As we have seen, the Near Easterners have never cut their oil off from the West completely. They did not do so in 1956, 1967, or 1973. It is insulting to an outsider's intelligence that he be asked to believe, on the basis of no evidence except pro forma rhetoric, that all the producers in the world would have come close to doing so in 1971, when there was no war on with Israel.

Most important of all is the industry's emphasis. As the history of the Iran-Turkey pipeline shows, when the Consortium really wanted to withhold something from Iran, even a 900,000-barrel-a-day through-put commitment, there was no way on earth the Shah could get it from them. If the companies had stubbornly held out for global negotiations too — if they had wanted them as badly as they had wanted to keep production down in Iran — they would have stood an excellent chance of getting them. But the industry, flying in the face of this fact of life and international coexistence, rapidly backed right down from its final efforts to keep the negotiations universal in scope. On January 30, at a meeting in New York, the London Policy Group abandoned its message to OPEC and agreed "to recognize the total separation of the Gulf and Libyan negotiations."[26]

The American government, meantime, had succeeded in convincing western European states to keep out of the negotiations and had persuaded them that the oil companies had taken the right stance in the negotiations. Iran's chief negotiator Amouzegar for his part was "happy to learn" from the companies' negotiating team that the companies understood "the advantages, reason and logic" of confining their discussions to states bordering the gulf.[27] In exchange, the Shah and the gulf states' negotiating team expressed a willingness to make an agreement which would last for five years.

When he heard of this, Schuler noted, "We're trying to kid ourselves — the best assurances aren't worth a damn and these aren't worth anything, even in their terms!! Doesn't it demonstrate that we're facing an effort to get the best of all worlds and that good faith is completely lacking? Doesn't the position of Hammadi and Yamani indicate that we are going to be unsuccessful in isolating Libya on straight commercial grounds?"[28]

The outcome of the negotiations was almost an anticlimax. The opportunity to make a stand which both would have been generous to the producing states and would have protected the vulnerable, the unintegrated, and the state-owned of the Western world's oil companies passed for once and for all. The industry's negotiating team had a chance partially to redeem itself by salvaging "the hinge" — the compatibility of prices for Iraqi and Saudi crude landed on the Mediterranean with that shipped from the Persian Gulf. The gulf states simply refused to allow retention of the hinge and the industry team hardly protested. Schuler quoted BP's representative, Lord Strathalmond, as even describing a formula concocted to protect the hinge as "a nonstarter."[29] The Iraqi negotiator, Saadoun Hammadi, further rusted the hinge by hinting to the parents of IPC that if these negotiations "went well" his government might be disposed to seek a settlement to the decade-old Law 80 dispute.[30] Nor was the ideological animosity between Saudi Arabia on the one hand,

and Iraq and Libya on the other, apparently enough to induce Saudi Arabia to endorse the hinge and discourage Libya's intransigence: refusal to endorse the hinge would simply guarantee an "open-ended" hike for Saudi Arabia's own oil in the Mediterranean. Of course Saudi Arabia sought refuge in the fear that the Libyans would pay Palestinian guerrillas to blow up Tapline.

Anyway, the major companies won a real advantage in the negotiations on the hinge. Members of the OPEC team conceded that they would demand an increase for their Mediterranean-delivered crude which was equal not in percentage but in *volume* to whatever the Libyans subsequently won for themselves. This was known in the jargon as "the total cost concept" — one of those obscure phrases hinting only vaguely at the hundreds of millions of dollars they conceal. Since the money the Libyans won from the majors was relatively small in volume (they did not account for half that country's production), this drastically reduced the penalties which the majors would have to pay for this other Mediterranean crude.

In less than three weeks, in mid-February, 1971, the negotiations ended with an agreement, reproduced as Appendix 10, that the posted price for Persian Gulf oil would rise by 35 to 50 cents a barrel (depending on the quality of the oil). The increases were to cover inflation (at an annual rate of $2\frac{1}{2}$ percent), freight charges, and "escalation," and represented an across-the-board hike of about 25 percent in the tax reference price. The actual payments to governments would increase by about one-third, or another 30 cents a barrel, and would rise by a like percentage in stages over the forthcoming five years. The Shah expressed his satisfaction with the agreement, at a press conference in Zurich on February 16.

As it turned out, the agreements lasted not five years but less than three. The Libyans, in any event, turned around at once, a week after the Tehran agreement, and presented the companies with a new list of terms. SoCal's Dennis Bonney has described one of the episodes which followed this demand (see Chapter 2). In another episode, Jalloud summoned all executives to a meeting at ten in the morning, but kept them waiting all day and into the next night, when he charged in, disheveled from desert maneuvers, submachine gun over shoulder, and demanded that the companies sell him weapons — as some had tried to else-where. "We pay cash for the weapons, unlike Israel," he said. The Libyans acted in a ferocious but scatterbrained manner, constantly making deadlines and forgetting about them. One Libyan was quoted as saying, once, "The deadline was Saturday, Tripoli time, but we Libyans are always a bit late for appointments."[31] Schuler himself reported that two of the strict deadlines which Jalloud gave elapsed without incident: first was for a February 23 meeting with BP, which was cancelled, the second for a meeting on March 7 with BP and Occidental which was postponed to the ninth and took place then, but unconclusively. By mid-April, after more of this, the two sides reached agreement that the posted price of Libyan crude would rise another 80 cents, and the Libyan government's take another 54 to 63 cents. That week, the chairman of British Petroleum, Lord Strathalmond, declared that the industry had become "a tax collecting agency."

Many will dispute the validity of Schuler's account of the events of the preceding three months, on grounds that he was prejudiced against the major companies. He quite possibly confuses rancor and malice, for one thing. He takes the adamant and contemptuous rhetoric of the Libyans at face value, believing these people to be far more destructive and domineering than they have ever been. Nonetheless, he concedes one point: the blame for these disastrous agreements lay not with the majors but with the independents. The small companies should have held together in London at any price; he maintains they didn't. The record affirms his claim. One of his colleagues compared the smaller companies to a couple of skeletons hanging in a closet, one telling the other, "If we had any guts we wouldn't be here." Maybe they were bought off, individually, by bigger companies, though Schuler doesn't come out and say so.

So the oil industry solidarity essential to maintain real price stability was quietly eroded — or perhaps even sabotaged — by the West's main players. Many Arab observers put an interpretation on events which was different from Schuler's. A prominent Egyptian chronicler, Ahmad Baha el-Din, writing in Cairo's *al-*

Ahram, claimed that the companies gave in to the pressure for higher prices "as a result of the [1967] war" and fear of "the atmosphere of Arab hostility towards them as a result of America's support of Israel." He added that "The oil companies were anxious to alleviate the probable effects of this wave of antagonism by meeting the demands of the petroleum producing countries."[32]

Baha el-Din and others, of course, did not distinguish between major and independent companies; nor did they enjoy access to the wealth of official company and government cables and letters with which Schuler bolstered his case. Furthermore, others who do not share Schuler's bias have reached conclusions similar to his. For instance Professor Morris Adelman of MIT, in his book *The World Petroleum Market,* stated, "When the Libyan cutbacks were decreed, the United States could have easily convened the oil companies to work out an insurance scheme whereby any single company forced to shut down would have crude oil supplied by the others at tax-plus-cost from another source. Had that been done, some or most companies might have shut down, but the Libyan government would have faced a loss of production increase. Bank accounts abroad could have been frozen in retaliation for the seizures, but such a step, however helpful, would not have been strictly necessary. OPEC unity would have been severely tested at a time when they were unprepared for conflict. The revenue losses of Libya would have been gains to all others, and all would have realized the danger of trying to pressure the consuming countries." The folly of the episode in Adelman's eyes — as indeed in Schuler's — is clear: "The higher crude oil and product prices have no connection with world supply and demand for crude oil. *They reflect no scarcity* of crude oil present or foreseen."[33] (Emphasis supplied.)

As in all negotiations, both sides faced risks. Although embargo, or even nationalization, threatened the companies, the oil states had to proceed with caution too: they had to consider the possibility that Western countries might sever relations with them and that the Western consumers might heap blame on them. They had to consider the possibility that they might lose for good the moral advantage that some of them have enjoyed over the West's former imperial powers. It could even turn out that Israel would not vanish, even if its Western support did. Schuler (who has left Hunt and now works for another independent) pointed out that there were certainly advantages for the companies in an OPEC *diktat*. "Actual legislation," he wrote, "would leave us no more vulnerable to constant change than the threat of legislation and capitulation does."[34]

It is by no means clear that the major oil companies are better equipped to cope with "constant change" than are the nations from which they have sprung.

15

An Industry of
Tax-Collectors?

The Yugoslav example is extremely significant . . . in
demonstrating that society's master is he who holds the
monopoly on organization and information. Consequently,
ownership of the means of production, which indeed belongs to workers in Yugoslavia, is a secondary matter.
— Mihajlo Mihajlov

IN APRIL, 1971, the chairman of BP raised a point which
observers of the industry had been discussing for some time and
which came into real prominence at the end of 1973: how essential are the companies, anyway? Are they really more effective,
as mediators between consumers and producers, than the governments of consuming nations? Are these middlemen necessary?

Earlier, in the 1960's, the companies were able to make a strong
case for the social utility of their role. Like lawyers or psychia-
trists, they could claim that they provided essential intermediate
services between members of a family who, in a period of world
crisis, needed one another but were not on speaking terms. They
could export oil from nations which wanted cash and sell it to

nations which needed fuel, with little interference from politicians. South Africa could buy Iranian oil, although Iran adhered to a boycott of South Africa. Oil could get to Israel or Rhodesia from the Persian Gulf. Egypt could invite American firms to explore for oil in the Western Desert just as President Nasser was accusing America of mounting an invasion against him.

Furthermore, although the companies talk less about this, they can help spare governments from dealing unpleasantly with their own citizens. In the 1950's and 1960's it was Aramco, of course, not Saudi Arabia, which dealt with restive labor unions of the Eastern Province, just as in Chile it was Anaconda and Kennecott which used to fight the wage demands of copper workers. A socialist leader would hate to arrogate such a function to himself, as the late President Allende no doubt discovered after he nationalized these firms.

In the heyday of the Cold War, few people mentioned the high price the companies charged for these services: autonomy, the right to complete control over investment decision-making and the release of raw data bearing on these decisions. One of their most cherished rights was the power to produce oil where it was most profitable for them, not most reassuring to their customers. The June, 1967, crisis made it obvious for the first time, perhaps, that although the oil companies had been declaring that the Arabs had the ability to create a terrible shortage of oil — and Arabs in fact almost completely shut off their oil for about a week — no drastic shortage of crude actually materialized. For there was far more spare non-Arab oil-producing capacity within reach than the companies had let on.

The same thing happened in 1973 — although then the industry had help from the President of the United States and managed to create the illusion of shortage.

Beginning in 1967, it started to become apparent, too, that it was hard to get "straight" answers from the companies on the details of their operations in general. The difficulties which President Nixon's Oil Imports Task Force encountered, for instance, in its study to determine whether or not the government should allow more oil to be imported into America, will help illustrate this. The task force found it almost impossible to get cost data on oil-producing operations in this country. When the task force requested this data of the National Petroleum Council, the council treated it contemptuously and replied flatly that "it wasn't feasible" for it to give such information out to the government.[1] Oil company spokesmen even made themselves so bold as to complain about the presence of academic experts from out side the industry, whom they labeled "whiz kids," on the task force.[2] In the end the task force did receive a minor amount of confidential material from the industry, but it would not even list this, or its authors, publicly, let alone release any of it.

It was beginning to seem as if the companies had something to hide. If the oil industry was making it a policy to keep its operations very largely secret — allowing the very maintenance of secrecy to become operating procedure, *and not just for competitive reasons* — it was probably doing this for a purpose. If the entire workings of the industry were to become part of the public domain, if there were to be no secrets about any significant phase of its operations, the justification for the industry's very existence might be jeopardized, if not obliterated. One might for example be able to conclude that the major integrated firms could work perfectly well as smaller, weaker, specialized companies, and thus one could raise a powerful argument for breaking these big firms up. It is not just that the big firms, to prosper and dominate, require massive volumes of capital; the dimensions of this capital are public knowledge. To stay in control of their business, the companies must also have a real monopoly on reserve, cost, and opportunity data. They must, in short, have a monopoly on the *knowledge of where to invest.*

The next round between Near Easterner and oil firm following Tehran-Tripoli/1971 — the 1973 drive for participation — helps illustrate this. It was then that the big companies went a step further and began to demonstrate that not only was their survival predicated to some degree on a negative contribution — their ability to obfuscate and conceal — now their survival came to be predicated on their ability to hinder perhaps more efficient and useful competitors and to pose a threat to Western economies. The ordinary citizen in the West now had to appease the oil leviathans, lest they cause him real inconvenience.

The immediate inspiration for the successful participation drive is obscure. Saudi Arabia's oil minister, Ahmad Yamani, first proposed in 1968 that the oil-producing states adopt the measure universally; he was the main motive force behind the subsequent drive. However, the idea itself is an old one. The Iraqis had been pressing it for years. Furthermore, a decade before, some newcomers to the Near East had accepted it.*

It is probable, though not certain, that the history of the option the Iraqis had won at San Remo in 1920, only to lose in Baghdad five years later, inspired Yamani; this is exactly the share in Aramco he was seeking at the beginning of his drive.

Furthermore, when the participation negotiations began in earnest on an OPEC-wide front in early 1972, the Iraqis made it especially clear that they intended to acquire 20 percent of IPC.[3]

At the outset, the companies put up a resistance against this drive. They termed the August, 1971, OPEC resolution which endorsed the participation demand in principle a violation of the five-year stability which the Tehran agreement had guaranteed them earlier in the year.[4] Henry Schuler probably voiced the sentiments of many when he called it "creeping confiscation." Libya, again, while keeping aloof from the OPEC drive, profited from it and strove for more — in this case, a 51 percent share.

The Persian Gulf members of OPEC continued to press; in September, they drafted a general plan, which left vague the percentage of company shares they would demand, and the deadline for the acquisition but insisted that compensation be based on the quite low "net book value" of the assets to be acquired, rather than the companies' much greater "loss of future profits."[5] The OPEC states also rejected the companies' claim that by demanding participation they were violating the Tehran agreement, and went further, coupling their demand with a call for revision of the posted price to conform to changes brought about by devaluation of the dollar.†

* In the early sixties a Japanese enterprise, Arabian Oil Company, gave the Saudi government a 20 percent share in its concession off the Neutral Zone, and Standard of Indiana gave the same share to two small sultanates in Hadhramaut to the south, for barren property in what is now the People's Democratic Republic of Yemen.

† Most gulf states, except Saudi Arabia, were benefiting from devaluation of the dollar, because they received revenues in pounds sterling, at the official

The participation drive lagged through the end of 1971 and into 1972 — then picked up. To this day, it is not clear what caused the companies to change tack on participation. The industry press places weight on a message which King Faisal sent the companies in late February, with its request that the companies "cooperate with us with a view to reaching a satisfactory agreement."[6] Schuler quotes his oil minister, Yamani, as backing this up with a veiled threat: "There is a worldwide trend toward nationalization and the Saudis cannot stand against it alone. The industry should realize this and come to terms so that they can save as much as possible under the circumstances."[7]

But there is another possible interpretation: perhaps the companies changed tack when their accountants discovered that participation could hardly harm them. It might raise prices some, but the companies could simply pass the added burden on to their consumers. This would help raise the posted price of crude oils in America anyway — and this was a long-range industry objective. As long as the companies maintained a near-monopoly over geological and reserves data, they would preserve their monopoly of knowledge on where to invest; as long as they retained at least 40 percent of the companies' shares, they would maintain their privileged position in the great oil-exporting nations of the world and would lose none of the tax advantages which the United States Department of the Treasury had been granting them for twenty years. And prospects outside the Near East were developing rapidly.

One Mobil vice president, Lawrence Woods, asserted as much when he told this writer, in the course of these negotiations in early 1973, "I'm not too concerned with the color of the paper. It doesn't make too much difference to me if it's in English or Arabic." In other words, to him, as an official concerned with oil supply, the essential matter was not title, or provenance, so much

International Monetary Fund rate. Venezuela kept oil diplomatic activity alive by increasing tax prices on oil exports at the end of the year and adjusting the exchange rate between the bolivar and the dollar (*Petroleum Intelligence Weekly*, December 27, 1971). The companies and most OPEC states reached an agreement in Geneva which called for a hike of 8.49 percent in the gulf posted price, to compensate for world monetary changes. The companies in Libya and Gaddafi's government continued separate negotiations on the subject which were not resolved until May.

as it was supply at good prices: "The value of an oil enterprise is what it can produce," he said. "The compensation question, not the admissibility of participation, was the main one. What mattered was the extent to which we'd have crude available to us."

Within a month, the companies accepted the principle of 20 percent state participation in their various producing concessions, thereby, they said, heading off the threat of "unilateral legislation."*

Once it was accepted that the states could buy into the concessions, the negotiations continued a long time. For a while, they remained stalemated. The companies argued for security of financial terms and future supply. The Iraqi expropriation of IPC's northern holdings on June 1 complicated the discussions by creating a rift between some OPEC members and deflecting some public attention from the participation issue. Furthermore, the Shah, in the same month, opted for a separate arrangement with the Consortium, on grounds that Iranian oil had already been nationalized in 1951 and that therefore his government could not acquire a share of what it already owned in full to begin with.† The Consortium did agree to give the Shah greater revenues, however, in exchange for an extension of the concession to the year 1994.

The other gulf states reached final agreement with the companies by October, 1973. The changes which participation brought into the day-to-day operations were quickly seen to be minor: the companies still had nearly full access to the oil at a price close to the one they had been paying already, except that now, in exchange for a large cash sum from their hosts, they were obligated to buy back most or all of the state's share of oil at a price slightly above tax-paid cost — a maximum, in 1972–1973, of 17 cents more.

---

* Aramco's parents did halfheartedly tender an offer akin to that which IPC's team had extended to Iraq in 1961: if the Saudi government would drop its demand for 20 percent of all producing wells, Aramco would give it 50 percent participation in undeveloped properties on Aramco territory. The Saudis rejected the offer.

† In fact, since 1954 the Consortium, on paper, had been producing the oil for the National Iranian Oil Company, not its members; the latter would purchase the oil for export from NIOC.

The share the two parties finally agreed upon was 25 percent of the concessions. Take Saudi Arabia, for example: this nation bought a quarter of Aramco's oil-producing facilities for $510 million — exclusive of Tapline and the Ras Tanura refinery; in exchange it obligated the Aramco parents to pay it a somewhat elevated price for its 25 percent share of all the oil produced, raising the tax-paid cost of each barrel by 8 to 10 cents.[8] There were two components to this share, "phased" and "bridging" crude, which represented buy-back terms of varying duration. But the oil companies were still in charge of marketing almost all the oil.

The immediately important matter was that the companies, in exchange for a slight additional charge per barrel, had received a windfall of $510 million. This helped empower them to maintain dominance in the bidding for offshore leases in America and the United Kingdom.

In comparison with the breakthrough the oil states had achieved in 1970–1971, these negotiations and their immediate outcome seem anticlimactic. Furthermore, it took well over a year to complete them and even then many loose ends remained.* But by that time, the oil industry and its partisans had begun to feel emboldened to state that they had "lost control of the international market," that they had "no" or "almost no" negotiating power left.

Nothing could have been farther from the truth. In reality, what had happened was this: the companies had started to move the center of gravity of their industry's profitability downstream and west. They had relinquished part ownership of the oil-producing facilities and had begun to relax their grip on the ceiling of posted prices — but simple markups on refined product sales reimbursed them for this and they retained their hold over the

---

* Saudi Arabia reached agreement early, but Iraq, due to the dispute over the nationalization of Kirkuk, did not come to terms until March, 1973, when it reached a global settlement with IPC. Kuwait did not ratify the agreement until May, 1974, when it elected to buy 60 percent of KOC — a compromise between 25 percent and an outright takeover. Libya, which had stayed aloof from the OPEC negotiations, demanded 51 percent, and in summer 1973 nationalized those companies which did not agree to surrender this share, over a slow process of bloodletting which finally removed Hunt — but not Occidental — from the Sirte Basin.

international trade. Notwithstanding Mr. John J. McCloy's statement that "the oil companies fought tooth and nail against the
demands of the producing countries for an increase in the so-
called posted price," the record shows that when in the end, in
late 1973, the posted price rose 350 percent, so did Aramco's
profits — and the companies succeeded in raising the price of
gasoline in America by 20 percent in four months as a result.

The Near Eastern states, however, were achieving something
more by participating in the concessions: they were working
themselves into a position where they could run the concessions
themselves.

If the Near Easterners could run the concessions themselves,
they could get their own oil into the tankers that called for it.
Therefore, why should the tankers not buy oil from them directly? Obviously because most tankers belonged to, or were
chartered by, the same companies which had once dominated
the concessions. But what of tankers which did not? Why should
consuming states not send their own tankers to buy the oil directly now? It was access to the very concessions, after all, which
had made the big oil companies indispensable in the first place.
Iraq Petroleum Company had had concession rights to all Iraq,
and even after the Iraqi government had appropriated 99.5 percent of that, no one in the Western world would touch these
seized properties — not that they hadn't wanted to; as we have
seen, they hadn't dared. The acreage was "hot." The same had
been true with Anglo-Iranian's old concession after Mosaddegh
nationalized it, and it still held in 1973 after Gaddafi nationalized 51 percent of Amoseas and SoCal prevented an American
utility, New England Petroleum, from putting its hands on oil
refined from Nafoora crude.[9]

But now, though the companies stopped fighting nationalization, *still* no outsider, no crude-thirsty Western refiner, had direct access to Near Eastern oil to any significant degree. The
history of the 1973–1974 price counterrevolt is filled with tales of
Western brokers, entrepreneurs, and refiners who received overtures from men who claimed to "have an in with a sheikh's
nephew" and promised participation crude which they never
delivered. The meaning of this is plain. The states were still

not operating independently of the majors. Yet the contention that the companies should be rewarded because two generations ago they had taken some risks and invested the capital that had brought this oil forth into the world was no longer so compelling.

The economist Adelman and the executive Strathalmond point out that the companies had become "tax collectors," publicans, "agents of foreign powers," in that it was now to their interest to pay higher taxes if they could pass them on, *en bloc*, to the consumer; in March, 1974, Senator Muskie kept asking "What is the incentive to keep the posted price down?" and no oil company executive could give him a direct and credible response.

The Iranian case provides a good illustration of the proof that the seven major companies still control international oil. In early 1973, the Shah, who had dropped out of the participation talks, abruptly informed the Iranian *majles* that the Consortium had failed to "safeguard Iran's interests" in accordance with the previous summer's agreement. Now, he declared, he was giving the Consortium two options — it could retain its concession until 1979, in which case it would receive no subsequent preferential rights "and would have to stand in a long line for oil, like everyone else," or it could renegotiate the concession at once and in effect turn itself into a group of long-term crude buyers.[10] The Shah's complaint, again, was that the Consortium had been too reluctant to bring up the nation's oil-exporting capacity.

At first, this statement shocked the Consortium. Representatives of the United States, Britain, France, and The Netherlands expressed concern over it to the Shah or otherwise protested to Iranian authorities. But this reaction was short-lived. The companies reached an agreement with Iran in one month whereby, effective the preceding March, the National Iranian Oil Company would simply take over all the Consortium's operations, and hire the Consortium to operate the facilities.

Thus the process of nationalization started in 1951 was to be completed. The press in Iran, as one might imagine, was exuberant over this development; but it seemed to chagrin no one in the West either.

The reason was simple: in effect the Consortium parents had given up only a little — including a promise to increase their offtake to 8 million barrels a day by 1976. In exchange, they maintained virtual control over the disposition of crude from the old Consortium area. The agreement effectively forbade Iran from competing with the Consortium for major foreign markets. The critical Article 2 of the agreement stated that in 1973 the Consortium parents would export all the oil from the area save 200,000 barrels a day (or about 3 percent of the total) — and that Iran's share would rise to 1.5 million barrels a day, or 19 percent, by 1981. In other words, after almost a decade of "nationalization," the Consortium would still control the disposition of 81 percent of the oil it used to export. Iran could lift off more, but on one condition: that it build greater refining capacity.

Another stipulation in the agreement, Article 16, obligated National Iranian Oil Company to consult with the Consortium members each year to draw up a provisional five-year exploration and capacity development plan. This plan would undoubtedly take the same form as the Consortium's old plans, and the Iranians and the Consortium parents would polish it up over the forthcoming six months and review their finished document the following spring. NIOC, the Iranian state firm, would then "establish the basis" for the next year's plan and budget — "after taking into consideration the views of the Consortium members." In other words consensus, not an Iranian *diktat,* was to govern the exploitation of the "nationalized" properties.[11]

This preservation by the major companies of their control over "nationalized" concessions — known in the trade as "tying up the crude" — has spread beyond Iran, with the buyout of other concessions. Saudi Arabia is the most luminous example: in early 1975, the government of that country bought up all of Aramco's production facilities for about $1.5 billion cash, on top of what it had paid for its initial 25 percent share, and yet the old owners have virtually the same rights the Consortium parents enjoy in Iran.

From the time participation first went into effect in Saudi Arabia, the main concern of Aramco's American parents was not to resist the total buyout of their shares but to keep hold over the oil to which the Saudis had title and very little of which they wished to lift themselves or sell directly. "Participation deal won't stand," President Frank Jungers cabled Aramco's New York office just after the October, 1973, war. The Saudis were no longer content with 25 percent ownership of the concession — or politically able to afford to be content with it; they now had to buy out the entire concession. Nonetheless, Jungers said he was "convinced could tie up crude if deal was right." This was simply because "Saudis not really interested in big crude volumes especially if we could fuzz up [sic] deal somehow." As Jerome Levinson of the Church Subcommittee declared at a later hearing on the subject, Aramco's American parents were "willing to trade off price for this preferential access."[12]

There are two ways of looking at Articles 2 and 16 of the Iranian crude sales agreement — or indeed of agreements the Saudis, and others, have reached with their guests. One is to say, "The Consortium [or Aramco, or IPC, or ADMA] is still lucky; no matter what happens, it is sure to obtain a large but not unmanageable quantity of oil for years to come." The other is to say, "The Iranian [or Saudi, or Iraqi, or Abu Dhabi] government is still unlucky; it is still dependent on the largesse of the Consortium [or other guest] for development of this area, although the guest is still indifferent to it."

One important oil executive told me — while declining to confirm these terms — "if it's the way you say it is, it's a lousy deal."

In brief, the social utility of the agreement is suspect. The companies which make up the Consortium — overwhelmingly majors — need not expand in Iran beyond a certain modest foreordained rate. They thus maintain the power to keep production below the level they *could* reach if they developed other good properties in southwestern Iran. So far they have failed to develop these good properties. They can thus no longer claim that they are indispensable to the thirsty consumer.

Are they indispensable to Iran?

To answer this question, we must consider two further points: would other companies, outside the Consortium, be willing directly to lift any Iranian oil above what the Consortium has committed itself to take? Can any other party find and export the oil which the Consortium will not commit itself to extract?

The answer to both questions is yes. There are now, in the world, many private and state-owned companies which would take oil from Iran at tax-paid cost if they could get it. There are numerous American firms — certainly Hunt, probably the Oasis parents cut back in Libya, undoubtedly others currently spending pounds, guilders, and kroner by the million to explore in the North Sea, the Amazon, and offshore Indonesia, such as Union, Atlantic Richfield, Phillips, Continental, Standard of Indiana, Mesa, Seagram Distillers, Sun, Tenneco, Pennzoil, Ashland, Citgo, Texas Gas Transmission, Murphy, Occidental even — unquestionably Mobil, which has gone in with Japanese firms on a separate concession in the Zagros adjacent to the old Consortium's acreage. Then there are various crude-short Japanese refiners such as Mitsubishi and Sumitomo. There is the British Burmah and the Canadian Dome and Scurry-Rainbow, the less identifiable Blackfriars and Boadicea. There is the Italian ENI, which tried unsuccessfully to get into the Consortium twenty years before, then Belgium's Petrofina with its pittance in Angola, and France's ERAP and Aquitaine, Spain's Hispanoil — which took up relinquished acreage in Kuwait and found nothing there — and a group of German firms, such as those which won acreage in the second round in Libya but came up only with dust and those which have contracted to build large refineries in Iran in exchange for direct access to Iranian oil.

The answer to the second question is affirmative too. Chapter 6 listed, at the end of 1973, seventeen undeveloped fields in the Consortium's acreage. In the aggregate they could produce at least one and perhaps two million barrels a day. These are the fields which the Consortium has discovered but not put onstream because the cost of doing so is not attractive to its parents.

The list includes several fields which were so cheap to develop that the Consortium at one point or another planned to put them onstream, then deferred its plans because it decided that it could get away with not developing them. The Consortium's own plans list these — Sarkan, Maleh Kuh, Cheshmeh Khosh, Mansuri, Ab

Teymur, Kilur Karim, and Karun: the old names. In the aggregate these fields could easily produce one million barrels a day and more; each of them has at least one well so far, capable of yielding up at least 5,000 barrels a day. Wells in Kilur Karim can produce 7,000 barrels a day, those in Karun 10,000, those in Ab Teymur 12,000, and those in Cheshmeh Khosh 15,000.

Some of these fields looked more attractive to the Consortium in 1970 or 1971 than they do today. For instance the Consortium, in 1971, had planned to put Cheshmeh Khosh onstream at 125,000 barrels a day by 1976 but since then has put its plans to develop the field in abeyance — although it would cost only 60 pounds, or about $150, per daily barrel to put it onstream (exclusive of terminal costs). This is less than what it would cost to develop a field in Libya, far less than the costs in Algeria, a mere fraction of American rates.

Then there are other fields of lesser potential than these, which the Consortium has not even considered putting onstream but which would also be attractive to oil-poor independents: as a whole, these, too, could easily produce a million barrels a day.*

Thus, the area which the Iranian government has nationalized, over which it holds full title, contains seventeen fields which the Consortium seems scarcely interested in developing. In addition of course there are nine fields which the Consortium is producing far below ultimate maximum productive capacity (Bibi Hakimeh, Kharg, Pazanan, Kupal, Binak, Lab-e Safid, Par-e Siah, Ramin, and Ramshir).† Supposing the Iranian government allowed the Consortium to retain access only to these, then the old declining central fields, and the "Big Seven": the Consortium would not have to worry about reaching its stated maximum objective of 8 million barrels a day and sustaining that rate for another decade.

Meantime, the Iranians could let the other seventeen fields out to the truly thirsty firms which do not belong to the Consortium, and these outsiders would be sure to develop them.

---

* More of the old names: Gorangan, Dehloran, Bushgan, Golkhari, Susangerd, Halush, Danan, Kabud, Sulabedar, and Shadegan.
† See Appendix 3 for the maximum productive capacities, and production rates, of these and other Consortium fields.

When one contemplates an inventory such as this, one is at a loss to see where the international oil companies could still be fulfilling an indispensable international role, a service to producing state or consuming public. Certainly these companies do not lack the will or the ability to produce at rates their various publics might expect of them. Therefore they must view their mission not as one of satisfying their larger publics but of satisfying the smaller interests of their own companies. Some executives say as much, claiming that if the rate of return on their operations dropped below 7 or 8 percent of equity, say, they would be happy to get out of oil and into something else, just as Mobil considered buying out Montgomery Ward — and did so, with impunity, despite the public outcry.

If the oil is not forthcoming to the consumer in sufficient volume and at reasonable prices at most times, this cannot be to the consumer's profit. Nor, if the oil remains unproduced, can it be to the profit of the nations themselves, although in the main they have not suffered financially in recent years. Therefore, the profit which the companies are seeking to maximize is that which accrues to the companies themselves, and those who stand behind them.

Who does stand behind them? The American government, which, in its foreign policy, is committed, above all, to contribute to the prosperity and goodwill of the nations it considers vital to its own peace — those of Europe, Latin America, the Mediterranean, the Moslem world, Asia?

If this is too broad a group for a collection of multinational companies to render prosperous and happy, what then of the company's stockholders? Hardly anyone knows who the stockholders in a given corporation are — institutions or individuals — although oil executives generally state that it is on behalf of this anonymous group that they labor. Nor are these stockholders generally acquainted with one another, able to form a united front, or, in time of rampant inflation, able to call for shifts in investment strategy or demand handsomely increased dividends. In fact, one wonders what one could gain by owning stock in an oil company at this time, since they are declining in value and paying out less than ordinary bank savings accounts — let alone real estate, say, which has appreciated by 25 percent in many areas of America during the latter half of 1973.

If the stockholders of a company do not profit, indeed are tolerated by a company's management and not much more, there is no one left but the executives who control the companies. No one else remains to enjoy a vested interest in the continued prosperity of these specific companies. They are very prone to become vehicles for the egocentric designs of a handful of largely autonomous individuals.

The events which took place in the last quarter of 1973 and early 1974 forced the public, at least — in America, Europe, Japan, and even the less industrialized of the world's oil-poor nations — to awaken to this range of considerations.

16

The 1973 Counterrevolt

U.S. consumers aren't going back to the bargain-basement prices we have so long been accustomed to paying for energy. Not this year or next. Not ever.
— Hollis Dole, Assistant Secretary, United States Department of the Interior, 1970

IN THE AFTERMATH OF THE ARAB-ISRAELI WAR of 1967, the Israelis occupied much Arab land — western Jordan, southwestern Syria, the Sinai Peninsula, and the east bank of Suez. The oil price counterrevolt of 1973 found its first impetus in this fact. For the Egyptians and other Arabs struggled for six years afterward to dislodge the Israelis from this conquered territory; they conducted artillery duels across the canal, commando raids across the Jordan River, overtures, diplomatic campaigns, espionage capers and counterpranks in Europe, the wholesale recruitment of Soviet advisors and pilots — even, in Jordan, civil war. Yet nothing worked. By 1969, as one Egyptian wrote a British friend, the novelist Desmond Stewart: "Every discussion in Cairo, at home, in the cafes, with our children, centers on one topic: what caused the disaster? Who will lead us out of it, and in what manner?"[1]

Who indeed? If the Arabs could not complete the task themselves, by arms, they might have to use other means, or enlist the aid of outsiders. By 1973 it had become obvious that the Russians could not help them by force. In August, 1970, they lost five pilots to Israeli Phantoms in one brief dogfight alone, over the Gulf of Suez. The Russians could not help by peaceful means either: they had no diplomatic relations with Israel and had been calling its representatives international murderers and gangsters at the United Nations for so long that these provisional occupants of Arab territory would probably no longer listen to any ideas they offered, however sensible. The only efficient way to put pressure on the Israelis to withdraw was through the superpower which was talking to both sides: the United States.

The American government, in its Near Eastern policies, was manifestly partial to Israel; but the real depth of this commitment was questionable. Many people in the United States favored an *apertura agli Arabi:* large groups in the State Department, a few legislators like Senator Fulbright, perhaps even President Nixon and Secretary Kissinger: men who knew what damage to its name the nation's partisan Near East policies were wreaking in the Arab world.

Under ordinary circumstances, it would be hard for an American President or Secretary of State to summon a press conference out of thin air and state, "I have just decided, as the result of a nightmare, that our Near Eastern policy is terribly wrong, and from this day I will work to shift American public and official sentiment toward the Arabs." However, the "ordinary circumstances" — those which had governed the generation since Harry Truman got out of bed at one in the morning to recognize the newly proclaimed state of Israel — were ceasing to obtain. The Arabs and Iranians, for better or worse, had driven a wedge deep into the international oil industry.

The old established companies in the industry — the Red Line partners, Gulf of Kuwait, SoCal, Texaco — had not managed to destroy the new independents and they could no longer stop the

flow of "hot" oil across international boundaries, as they had with
Mosaddegh in 1951. But they were as strong as ever in other respects. They still possessed the bulk of refining and distribution
facilities in the West.[2] They had a good many friends, and few
enemies, in America's Congress and State Department. Since they
had maintained a very tight interdiction over public disclosure
of their operations in the course of the past seventy years, the
people of America and Europe had virtually no notion of how to
cope with them.

There thus developed, during the years 1972 and 1973, three
parallel trends whose outcome was to be the realignment of international relationships in America's favor, on terms most congenial to the major oil companies.

First, in a year when the major oil companies were discovering
thirteen giant oilfields in the North Sea, opening up Ecuador and
the western Amazon basin, spreading out to offshore Indonesia,
and expanding output in Australia, Nigeria, and Gabon, the belief gained currency that the world was running out of oil — at
least non-Arab oil.

Second came the revelation that the Arabs were beginning to
realize, under encouragement from the State Department and
the Aramco parents, how powerful the weapon they possessed
could be. If the United States government could convince the
American public that the Arabs meant to use their weapon and
meant to cut their oil off from the West, it could convince the
public to accept a shift to a foreign policy more favorable to
the Arabs.

Third, the oil industry began to spread the warning that, as
the world ran out of non-Arab oil, so might it run out of gasoline
and fuel too — unless prices rose drastically and made it worth the
companies' while to continue refining and selling these products.
A partial cutoff of some product — explained, if not explicable,
in terms of the Arab cutoff — and the subsequent restoration of
this product to the market, would induce the American public
to bear the hike in silence. The American public had lost some of
the toughness it had acquired during the Depression and World
War II. Anyway, it was enduring inflation in several other areas
where raw materials were in potential surplus, such as paper, lum-
ber, beef, and grain. One more encumbrance might not matter.

By October 6, 1973, fear that the Arabs might put their oil weapon to use had begun to sweep the West. Then, on that day, Egyptian and Syrian forces attacked Israeli-held territory. They mounted well-coordinated, full-scale invasions of the Bar-Lev Line down the east bank of Suez and the Allon Line athwart the Golan plateau which sloped gently down to Damascus, and inflicted temporary reversals on the Israelis.

In time the invasions lost momentum. The Israelis recouped their losses and took the offensive, drawing toward Damascus and staging a counterattack across the Suez Canal. After this process had matured, about two weeks after the start of hostilities, what many commentators had been fearing the Arab states might do came to pass: King Faisal, in belated protest against Western, particularly American, support of Israel, announced an immediate 10 percent cutback in Aramco's oil production and an additional embargo on all shipments of Saudi crude to the United States military. This lowered Aramco's output to about 6.5 million barrels a day.* Abu Dhabi and Qatar followed suit, as did Kuwait, which ultimately cut its production by 22 percent — again, from an abnormally high September level.

In time, Saudi Arabia forced Aramco to cut back even further — ultimately, to its normal level of about 6 million barrels a day, which brought Aramco's 1973 production to within less than one percent of its original forecast for the year. Saudi Arabia also embargoed all shipments of oil to South Africa and its archenemy, the neighboring Arab Marxist state of South Yemen, "for other reasons," and the various embargoes languished into the following March.

But by the end of November, they had become selective; the Saudis and Kuwaitis were embargoing only the United States, The Netherlands, and Denmark. Strangely, though, the other Arab countries — Abu Dhabi, Libya, Algeria, and the poor stepsister Iraq — taken as a whole did not cut back production. Libya did not even join the embargo until the following month. Premier Gaddafi, snubbed by the belligerents, his status as most revolutionary Arab threatened by the prospect that the outcome of the other leaders' war might be successful, stayed completely aloof

---

* This was not far below the average of 7.3 million barrels a day which Aramco had projected for the year 1973 as a whole; see Chapter 5.

from the fray. Iraq's December production actually increased by 7 percent over that in September. As we have seen — and as the history of OAPEC confirms — Iraq has rarely entertained good relations with the conservative producing states. This time, the government of Iraq contended that it had not even been officially notified of the preparations for war. Algeria's production dipped slightly in November and December, but only by 100,000 barrels a day. Abu Dhabi's production — also at a very high level, 30 percent above the previous year's rate, in September — fell back too, but, like Algeria's, it was not as voluminous as output in the other four Arab states. Finally, the international majors permitted production in non-Arab Iran to inch up by 7 percent during the last quarter of 1973.

Much has been said and written about the Arab embargo of October 1973–March 1974 and its scope and effectiveness. The gist of most statements is that this stratagem was eminently successful, well-coordinated, decisive — indeed, a turning point in world history. Some called it a unique event in the history of man. In several respects, however, the claims are erroneous if not misleading — for evidence shows that the embargo was not the product of a unified Arab effort so much as it was the offspring of political tensions within the Arab world, that the oil companies themselves obeyed the embargo to the letter, painted it to be more serious than it was, and profited as much from it in the short term as the Arabs did.

Indeed, what the consuming publics in the West and Japan had been treated to, through all this, was, as it turned out, a triple smokescreen. The screen, whether a magnificent natural occurence, like a long cool misty rain in the midsummer Sahara, or the work of man, or a combination of both, achieved a foreign-policy breakthrough for President Nixon; a major act of self-development — and a major realignment — within the Arab world; and, off to one side, little noted at the outset, a staggering increase in oil prices which allowed the petroleum industry to shift its profitability out of the Near East and into the West.

The foreign-policy breakthrough came when Mr. Nixon, empowered by the Arab action, forced Israel to accept a cease-fire as it started to get the upper hand against its adversaries. This was pressure of a kind which American public opinion would not have let him apply had there been no Arab boycott or threat of one. Now, overnight, it had become a commonplace among Americans that one could no longer antagonize the Arabs for such peripheral considerations as the voting allegiance of a small, vocal Zionist minority.

The Arabs' process of self-development of course came about through the initial, cathartic act of penetrating the Israeli defense lines. Although the Israelis pushed most of the Arab forces back in time, these forces had shown their people at home that they could stand up in battle against the Israelis: the Arabs had erased the humiliating defeat of 1967, when the Israeli blitz demolished their air armada before it got off the ground.

The restoration of Arab self-confidence was an essential contribution toward peace. Egypt's President Sadat, in fact, had had almost no choice but to launch the attack. Over the three years of his tenure, since the death of Nasser, he had been making repeated pronouncements which he could not back up, "postponing" the "battle of destiny"; for a generation, Egyptian leaders had been giving their people promises on which they had never delivered. Of late the Egyptian *rayyes* had been getting deeper and deeper in debt to Libya's militant Gaddafi, becoming the butt of cruel jokes throughout the Arab world, and worse. He was facing sedition from within. A series of unsolved fires broke out in Cairo, obviously arson; most serious of these was the destruction of the historic Opera House, where Verdi's *Aida* received its maiden performance; this was probably the act of Sadat's personal enemies. The crossing of Suez was Sadat's answer to all this: his assertion of his place among his own people as much as an act of aggression against outsiders speaking a different language and practicing a different religion.

But in this context two further points about the embargo are relevant. First, it is vital to remember the timing of this embargo. It was not coordinated with the war but came virtually at the end of it. Indeed, Bernard and Marvin Kalb, in their recent biography of Henry Kissinger, relate that the Secretary of State first learned of it when he was flying to Moscow, at the urgent invitation of the

Soviet government, to prepare a cease-fire in the Arab-Israeli War; this was six days before the actual end of the fighting. As it happened, those states which applied the embargo most assiduously were the moderate, or conservative, pro-Western states, whose regimes were viewed coolly if not with hostility by Arab progressives and radicals. In order to gain protection from pressure and subversion, the moderate and conservative states had to work harder to demonstrate their fealty to the overriding Arab cause than did the "radical" exporting states of Algeria, Libya, and Iraq, which could claim that they had already performed yeoman service on behalf of the cause by their acts of hostility toward the United States government and multinational American firms, as well as by their intransigent stand on the Palestine question.

Second, as we have seen, many Arabs did not view the war, and the process by which it started and ended, with Sadat's euphoric vision. Many pointed out that it did not represent a military victory for the Arabs. Perhaps the most comprehensive indictment of this war has come from Iraq, from an official Baath party broadcast over Baghdad Radio, dated June 13, 1974, some time after the war. The broadcast consisted of a report, approved by the Eighth Baath Regional Congress, which attacked the joint Egyptian-Syrian campaign.[3] It claimed that the Egyptians planned the canal crossing poorly and prepared only for a short conflict; it labeled the Israeli counterattack "a plot in which influential quarters in the Egyptian regime participated." The report's criticism of the war on the Syrian front was equally scathing; again, the planning had been a disaster, the Syrians soon found themselves surrounded by enemy antiarmor missiles, and the Israelis pushed on to the outskirts of Damascus. Fortunately, the report observed, "at a time when Damascus was threatened with imminent occupation and when official circles and a large section of the people were preparing to leave Damascus," the Iraqi government sent forces which managed to push the enemy back and produced "results of an historic and decisive nature." Reminding its listeners that "neither the Egyptian nor the Syrian governments informed us about the war," the Iraqi Baath leadership considered that the very motive which impelled the regimes of Egypt and Syria to war was suspect: the two countries wanted only to take token military action with a view to furthering a peaceful solution with Israel and did not "want to follow the path of the liberation war and shoulder its burdens."

In short, in the view of the Iraqi leadership, the objective of this "war of activation" was "to contain the sweeping revolutionary current by seeking to bring about a cease-fire and to return to bargaining with the Zionist enemy and United States imperialism." The basic course of Arab oil strategy was to conform to this objective; the report contended that the conservative oil states had expected the war to end quickly, before they would have to take any measures, but the government of Iraq foiled this by nationalizing the American share of Basra Oil Company — a "firm decision" which "placed the oil-producing regimes in an extremely embarrassing position." Then the unexpected prolongation of the war and the escalation of anti-Americanism forced the conservative states "to search for a way in which they could try to contain the call for nationalization and deprive the popular pressure of its strong thrust." The oil states' first measure, to reduce production by a mere 5 percent, was "received with disapproval and rejection by the Arab masses," and the continuation of the war forced a slightly bigger cutback.

However, these criticisms notwithstanding, the crossing of Suez did give Arabs greater self-confidence than they had enjoyed for a long time. It emboldened them to begin moving toward what, for a generation, they had considered simple treason — the notion of talking face to face with Israelis in order to arrive at some measure of coexistence with them. Jordan's King Hussain had, in fact, been making the move for a while, though covertly. Now the Egyptians took the step openly. By Thanksgiving 1973, Egyptian and Israeli generals were poring over cease-fire maps together and drinking scotch out of one bottle. Very slowly, the Syrians too approached the position where, at Geneva the following June, they would allow themselves to be seen in one room with Israelis. Well into the summer, word began leaking out of Syria that Hafez al-Asad's government was closing up the Palestine guerrilla training camps and arresting the extremists and terrorists. Then, by mid-1974, some moderate Palestinian nationalists began to indicate that they too might follow Egypt's and Syria's moves to the table, under honorable conditions.

Since then, this process has continued — fitfully. The Arab states have started to give the Palestine Liberation Organization the autonomy it needs to deal directly with the Israeli government, and someday the Israelis will no doubt abandon their refusal to negotiate with this broad, relatively middle-of-the-road coalition, as its leaders renounce certain forms of violence against the Israeli public. Perhaps the negotiations have been going on for some time, but in secret.

In whatever probes they may make toward peace, the Arabs and Israelis will have to move in very gradual, almost imperceptible stages, through secret diplomacy and tight bargaining camouflaged by an atmosphere of bellicosity, gloom, and frenzy — whose purpose will, in part, be to blunt the opposition of such parties who want no settlement as the Iraqi and Libyan governments. Hence, presumably, Dr. Kissinger's tireless and frustrating, if not futile, quest for gradual de-escalation of the conflict. Indeed, the only consolation the Iraqi Baath leadership seems to have drawn from the war is this, in its own words: "Though the Egyptian and Syrian regimes are prepared to make numerous concessions, covering all fields, to the United States and the Arab reactionaries, there are limits beyond which they cannot go, particularly in Syria." Nonetheless, even the radicals of the Arab world agree that the outcome of the war, and the conservatives' oil strategy, enabled the conservative states — foremost Saudi Arabia — to gain political control of events, "in accordance with the basic malicious trends of their policy of colluding with United States imperialism."

The oil price hike, spectacular as it was — moving from about $3.01 a barrel for Arabian Light in October to $11.65 in January — was almost a secondary achievement in the eyes of the Arabs. Some commentators, such as Muhammad Heykal, doyen of Egypt's fourth estate, said as much right after the war — and lost his job in the end, partly as a result of this. The Arabs and Iranians could have gone without these hikes — indeed most of them had committed themselves at Tehran, in February, 1971, to a five-year moratorium on all increases. But the major oil companies did not fight to hold them to their word.

On this subject, the Shah of Iran, at one of his periodic press conferences, in late 1974, made a statement which he was sure none of the reporters present would write down. In December, 1973, he said, he had asked "for seven dollars government take" for Arabian Light, FOB the Persian Gulf. "Later on," he continued, "the oil companies, in their negotiations for participation agreements with other countries of the Persian Gulf . . . raised the price of oil to what it is now, that is, $9.74. I did not do it. The oil companies did." He concluded, "Even if you do not print it, it does not matter," and published the conference transcript as a full-page advertisement in the New York *Times*.[4]

It is unlikely that anyone will ever succeed in proving that the Nixon administration and the American oil companies were looking forward to such a hike and encouraged it. If they ever reached such an arrangement, they could have done so orally, in private, without witnesses. Still, the companies made no serious effort to oppose the hike; they had almost everything to gain from it, and nothing to lose; they seriously overdramatized the effects of the embargo into which they claim they had unwittingly wandered; they made very inaccurate pronouncements about supplies in the West, and the embargo itself; and they worked hard to foster an illusion of scarcity. The Nixon administration — which had received at least $5 million in donations from the oil industry in the 1972 presidential campaign, some illegal — backed the industry to the hilt in these efforts.

What leads one to suspect the motives of the oil industry during the embargo of late 1973 is, first and most compelling, this: it is incredible to consider that the major American oil companies, in particular Exxon, Texaco, Mobil, and SoCal, the Aramco parents, should not have realized that some sort of Arab oil cutoff might occur during 1973 or 1974, whether or not it would be combined with an attack against Israeli armed forces. Aramco had always made it its business to know what was occurring not only in Saudi Arabia but also in the Arab world at large. It had usually been successful in its endeavors, and in the years 1972–1973 the Arabs had not been working to keep it in ignorance of their overall intentions.

The Arabs had been talking for years — for decades, in fact —

about the use of oil as an indirect weapon against Israel. Although they had never used the weapon very decisively, they had been showing more and more enthusiasm to wield it of late. Ambassador James Akins, in his article "The Oil Crisis: This Time the Wolf is Here" (*Foreign Affairs,* April, 1973), stated that influential Arabs had made "no less than fifteen different threats to use oil as a weapon against their 'enemies.' Almost all of them singled out the United States as their prime enemy."

Certainly Gaddafi's rise to power in Libya heightened Arab enthusiasm to test the weapon. Gaddafi made it no secret that he was willing to cut off oil for political reasons. He expropriated British Petroleum's Libyan assets in December, 1971, because the United Kingdom had apparently helped Iran occupy three small Arab islands in the Persian Gulf; he also talked of cutting off oil to force a change in American attitudes toward Israel. The opinion Henry Schuler voiced in early 1974 — that Gaddafi was following "a policy of unhesitant confrontation" to "utilize oil and the revenues derived therefrom in 'the battle to liberate Palestine' " — was common among oilmen in Libya, who did not know what to make of this brash, intransigent youngster's public utterances.

Furthermore, brash and flamboyant though Gaddafi's rhetoric seemed, there was substance to it. The Libyan Three-Year Development Plan for 1972–1975, which appeared in the Libyan *Official Gazette* of June 26, 1972, stated that the Libyan government intended to spend 38 million pounds — over $100 million — on oil production and exploration in this period. This was a very large figure, much bigger than anything Libya had expended on the oil industry so far and almost rivaling the investments of the Consortium and Aramco. Furthermore, most of it, or 33 million pounds, would be invested in the last two years of the plan. Therefore, to anyone who took the trouble to read the plan — or English translations of it, which were available — it was obvious that Libya was giving fair warning that beginning about mid-1973 it would be entering the oil business in a big way: an entry which it could make only at the expense of the companies already present in Libya.[5]

For the Libyan government to do so would, inevitably, require an aggressive campaign against the established Western companies, or the West itself. If the oil companies did not reach this conclusion sooner, the eventual success of Gaddafi's drives to raise oil taxes in 1970 and 1971, and the spread of aggressive oil policies to other Arab states, must have made it apparent that they were going to meet with more dramatic moves from the Arab world, which, after all, had discovered genuine divisions within the international industry. Certainly, after Gaddafi had put a twenty-four-hour stoppage on oil loadings in Libya on May 15, 1973, and Iraq, Kuwait, and Algeria had followed with a one-hour halt in sympathy, it must have become apparent to the oil companies that the oil states were sharpening their weapon still further.[6] Sheikh Yamani began hinting, and Faisal endorsed him later, that Saudi Arabia would use the weapon too — perhaps with sorrow — to save its position among the Arab states. "Saudi Arabia is in danger of being isolated among its Arab friends," the king declared before various representatives from Aramco parent companies,[7] at a courtesy visit they had paid to him in May at his hotel suite in Geneva. Faisal was mulling over use of the oil weapon. One Aramco cable released by the Church Subcommittee, from a Mr. Ellas in Dhahran to New York, dated August 28, said that King Faisal had been starting to ask his oil minister Yamani for detailed reports on Aramco's production plans and "expected impact of curtailed production by Aramco on consumers and on the United States in particular" — wondering, for instance, what would happen if Aramco were to be cut back by 2 million barrels a day. The cable added that King Faisal had never preoccupied himself with such details before.[8]

One influential person who showed that he had heard the Saudis was Senator Fulbright, who called on the television show *Face the Nation* that April for a more evenhanded American Near East policy; another was Otto Miller, chairman of the redoubtable SoCal, who, on July 26, mailed a letter to stockholders in which he said, "There is now a growing feeling in much of the Arab world that the United States has turned its back on the Arab people." For this, militant Zionist groups staged demonstrations before the company's headquarters on Bush Street in San Francisco, splashing animal blood on its venerable gray walls. This reaction helped Aramco's cause. "Arrests of Jewish Defense League activists [following their attempts to disrupt a speech by Miller] was played up by radios Riyadh and Jiddah," cabled one Aramco executive exultantly. "In our opinion the reaction here has been most encouraging."

But this is not to state that Miller's SoCal and the other American giants feared they would lose their position in the Arab world. They continued to pour money into it. Aramco kept working feverishly to expand production in Saudi Arabia all through 1973. At the beginning of the year, this venture was producing about 5.8 million barrels a day. From the beginning of the year to April, output rose by 1.5 million barrels a day, then, between April, when President Nixon declared an end to America's long-standing oil import quota system, and July, Aramco boosted production by another million barrels a day. Although, as we have seen, it began to harm some of its fields by doing this, by failing to make sufficiently large investments in water injections, its overall capital investments rose from $163 million in 1971 to $413 million in 1972 to about $835 million in 1973. For 1974, the company forecast a budget of $2.6 billion — $1 billion of which, however, would be for various gas projects.

All through the year 1973, Aramco increased capacity at a rate of about 200,000 barrels a day each month — or a total of at least 2.5 million barrels a day for the year, a capacity increase of about 40 percent in one year. What is especially remarkable is that the firm awarded the American constructors J. Ray McDermott a $100 million contract, in April, to build it a second export terminal on the Persian Gulf, at Ju'ayma. It was necessary to build this terminal to increase Aramco's export potential, and it added $83 to the cost of every barrel of new capacity. As Jerome Levinson, chief counsel to the Church Subcommittee, summed up his investigations into the matter, "The problems and the magnitude of investment required [to expand above 9.2 million barrels a day] are of an order of magnitude that is quite different from what Aramco has been faced with in the past. In other words, contrary to the popular myth, it is not just a matter of turning on the taps to get additional production in Saudi Arabia."

Again, since the Iranian Consortium could have increased its capacity to lift non-Arab oil by 3 million barrels a day in the same year, but didn't, one can only conclude that Aramco's actions in 1973 marked the behavior of a very stupid or a very clever investor, but certainly not one riddled with suspicions about the continuing good will of its hosts.

Furthermore, since July is a time of slack fuel demand in almost all the industrialized world, such an increase must be considered anomalous for such a time of year, regardless of the depth of Arab hostility toward the West; especially when the non-Arab oil-rich state of Iran lay right across the gulf. Indeed, the Aramco parents found themselves hard-pressed to dispose of this volume of new Saudi oil and sent much of it to America. Three-quarters of America's spectacular increase in oil imports from the Near East during the summer of 1973 came from Saudi Arabia.

By September, Saudi Arabia was still producing 8.5 million barrels a day, and Kuwait's production had shot up too — to 3.5 million barrels a day, or half a million more than the absolute limit the Kuwaiti government had set for conservation purposes over a year earlier. Aramco actually had a production capacity of 9.2 million barrels a day and had been preparing to produce 8.76 million barrels a day in October and 9.1 million in November.

This investment decision seems mad on the surface, and it was far more ambitious than Aramco's earlier plan, in 1970, to double production — that is, to raise it to 8 million barrels a day — by 1976. But it was, in reality, not mad. The Aramco parents were not seriously afraid that they would be forced out of Saudi Arabia and denied preferential access to Aramco oil in future, even if they were bought out. We have seen much evidence of this, and this study has endeavored to put much of it on the record. No less a personage than Otto Miller, SoCal's chairman, declared as much under questioning by the Church Subcommittee in summer, 1974, when he stated, "I never really did think that the Saudi government would nationalize Aramco." One must be careful to stay on good terms with one's hosts, to be sure; Miller understood this and acted accordingly. But Miller also claimed that the Saudis could not continue to run the operation, and expand it, by themselves even if they hired outside help. He implied that that was because of Aramco's engineering and technical ability. Aramco's president, Jungers, had stated on an earlier occasion that the Saudis "were not interested" — hence perhaps unwilling or unable — to dispose of big crude volumes themselves, and perhaps this strikes closer to the truth. In either event, as Miller pointed out, "we have a lot of leverage."[9]

But the embargo did seem, briefly, to have exposed Aramco's lavish investments as folly. Production in Saudi Arabia — and in Kuwait — dropped 20 percent or more by Christmas.

But Aramco cooperated *molto con brio,* if not *fortissimo,* in implementing the will of its hosts. Since Saudi Arabia did not possess the ability to administer the embargo effectively, it largely consigned this task to Aramco; the company performed it well — even preventing indirect sales to the United States or the American military. The president of Aramco, Frank Jungers, declared, in a cable that his contact with SAG (the Saudi government) indicated "great satisfaction with Aramco, and Americans, in taking pro-Arab stand." Jungers did protest to his contact that the cutback was "not good for our business," but the contact set his apprehensions to rest. "We hope to reward you," he replied laconically.[10]

The reward took the form of increased production. It is still not exactly known when production in Saudi Arabia picked up again, and by how much. Industry sources such as *The Oil and Gas Journal* had the Arab embargo running at about 20 percent as a whole by mid-December, but other observers were more conservative. The president of Atlantic Richfield, Thornton Bradshaw, told this writer that the embargo was "certainly not as successful as anticipated" and might have been running at 2.5 to 3 million barrels a day — far less than 20 percent of Arab production in September. Then the International Longshoremen's Association demonstrated through a study of tanker movements that the Persian Gulf must have been exporting over one million barrels more than the *Oil and Gas Journal*'s figure, or over 20.7 million barrels a day, in December.[11] *The Economist* of London, in its December 15 issue, pointed out that shipments from the Persian Gulf in late November and early December were 39 percent above the level for the corresponding period of the previous year. Two investigative journalists for the Philadelphia *Inquirer,* Donald Bartlett and James Steele, showed through a perusal of shipping records in Europe, beginning with their paper's December 9 issue, that postembargo sailings from the six main terminals in the Persian Gulf were up 31 percent from the previous year.

Normally, Persian Gulf exports of crude oil have been increasing at a rate of about 10.5 to 11 percent per year. If one gives credence to the dissident reports, gulf shipments in December, 1973, had increased over those in December, 1972 (which incidentally was a much harsher month in Europe), by at least one million barrels a day, or 5 percent. Thus the cutoff, at that time, was only in the neighborhood of 5 percent.

In February, when Aramco was still claiming that its production was running about 6 million barrels a day, the Washington investigative reporter Jack Anderson went to Saudi Arabia, and, in his column of February 25, stated that Sheikh Yamani, the Saudi oil minister, had said that his country's oil production was already back up to 8.6 million barrels a day.

The Shah of non-Arab Iran, too, had been casting doubts on the severity of the Arab embargo for some time, in the presence of anyone who would listen to him. On January 4, for instance, the German magazine *Der Spiegel* published an interview with the Iranian monarch, and the Manchester *Guardian Weekly* carried an English translation of it two weeks later, on January 19.

Der Spiegel — or the *Guardian,* in its secondhand version of the interview — neglected to publish three passages from the version which the Iranian government itself released at the time.[12] The longest of the three omitted passages included this exchange:

Spiegel: . . . Gaddafi called for a "revolution against the crime of peace with Israel."
Shah: I heard that on the radio. But you should not take seriously everything Mr. Gaddafi says.
Spiegel: We must take him seriously because he supplies a large share of the oil we need in Germany.
Shah: In that sense, yes. *But he is still going to sell his oil and say those things. He has never stopped.* (Emphasis supplied.)

Der Spiegel asked the Shah how he would explain this contradictory position, then, and the monarch made a lengthy statement on the importance of Jerusalem to all Moslems, King Faisal in particular.

Spiegel: But you don't accept to use oil as a weapon for such a political or religious goal as the possession of Jerusalem?
Shah: No, only if I were in a war myself, for my country. But now that we are talking of peace, to use that weapon could be superfluous because if you get used to that it can't be used any more.

The Shah was not an Arab, of course, but as a Middle Easterner he was familiar with the way Arab leaders thought. He probably thought much the same way himself, on similar matters. What is most significant here is that he was giving some Western media valuable advice free of charge, and these media, for some reason, refused to pass it on to their publics.* Here, the Shah had cut to the heart of the matter: the *threat* of an embargo is an excellent weapon; the actual use of it can be fraught with danger.

And the Shah's skepticism grew more intense as winter wore on. On CBS's television program *Sixty Minutes* of February 24, he declared that America's imports of crude oil were as high as they had ever been. Technically this was correct, but it drew an instant and angry response from William Simon, head of the United States Federal Energy Administration. He labeled the Shah "reckless and irresponsible." President Nixon toned that statement down a bit the following day, conveying the impression that his lieutenant was perhaps expressing himself a bit enthusiastically. But Simon did not retract it — within three months, in fact, he became Secretary of the Treasury.

One reason for Simon's outburst undoubtedly was that Arab states *were* shipping more oil out of the Persian Gulf than they were willing to admit, and were perhaps even permitting some of this to find its way to America — on the strict understanding that no responsible figure confirm this, for fear of enraging mili-

---

* A news director for America's third television network went so far as to tell this writer, during a recess between oil hearings, "You can't tell the real story [about oil] on TV anyway. They'll cut off the advertising."

tant anti-Western Arabs, who would charge that they were being deceived or sold out (as the Baath Party leadership in Iraq indeed did) and might set a wave of demonstrations, or perhaps even sabotage, in motion throughout oilfields on the Arab side of the gulf. This is fair enough; but to compensate for their silence, Messrs. Simon and Nixon should have done everything in their power to ensure that the major oil companies decline to reap benefits from the illusion of shortage, and in this they failed.

During the 1973–1974 price counterrevolt, in fact, the administration's representatives performed a real service for the industry, which wished to keep out of the public eye as much as possible, as it had, for instance, during the abortive gasoline crisis of the previous summer.* The oil industry, contrary to the democratic ideal, is woefully unprepared and unwilling to defend its ideas and principles in open debate with hard facts, at every challenge. This goes back to the industry's innate weakness in communication and diplomacy: there are, in fact, people within the industry who can see in advance that certain tactics or a given strategy will be wrong, but they have been conditioned not to speak out, and dare not do so.

The government officials, then, helped the industry plead its case before the public. They called mostly for price rises. John Love, former head of Nixon's Energy Policy Office, appealed several times for the deregulation of natural gas prices at the wellhead — once, in early October, 1973, before the Senate Commerce Committee in conjunction with Interior Secretary Morton. Duke Ligon, head of Interior's Office of Oil and Gas and now an assistant FEA administrator, called for natural gas deregulation in September. Mr. Love, at Finance Energy Subcommittee hearings, stressed that the oil industry needed economic incentives for capital investment and called for a relaxation of price controls, just before he resigned in late November. On November 29, at a news conference, Counselor Melvin Laird proposed a compromise two-year plan for natural gas deregulation. The

---

* One instance of this was when the Oakland, California, television station KTVU invited SoCal and Pacific Gas and Electric to send representatives to a panel discussion on energy problems and the two companies informed the panel's host, Gary Park, that they were "unable to attend."

Interstate Oil Compact Commission recommended deregulation at its annual convention in December. President Nixon himself, in his November 25 energy address to the American people, said nothing of imposing sanctions on the industry, but his talk was full of the sacrifices he expected the consumer to make for the purposes of conserving fuel.

These protestations and claims are especially strange coming from an administration which had been rebuffed for four years in its efforts to get meaningful data from oil companies on the workings of the industry.

In time, the protestations went beyond simple calls for price hikes. By the end of winter, officials were stating that there were shortages in natural gas and crude oil which only generous price breaks and sweeping legislation could remedy, but they still were not backing up their claims with hard statistics. Energy chief Simon, for his part, passed the entire winter insisting almost arrogantly that there was a crisis, while refusing to flesh out the real dimensions of this crisis with hard facts. He once complained before Congress, "The American public wants us to dipstick every tank in the country."

There, he was correct. However, he would assign only a token force to this task. Meanwhile, his bureau was literally riddled with oil company executives. The previous fall, the Department of the Interior had taken on two hundred and fifty oil executives to help with fuel allocation, and now the FEA gave important positions to fifty-eight others, including a top Phillips executive, Robert C. Bowen, who soon became embroiled in a classic conflict-of-interest case involving regulations extremely favorable to oil importers, where even Simon admitted that Bowen came close to violating his mandate as a consultant. Another executive, Melvin Conant of Exxon, received $90,000 from his employer to ensure that he did not "suffer an economic pain" on going to take a two-year post with the Federal Energy Administration.[13] This too became a bit of a *cause célèbre* later in the year, when the sum became public knowledge. Conant angrily refused at one point to return the money and stated, "What is at stake is my integrity. If someone says return the money, he is saying, 'There is something about you that makes us suspicious.' And I won't accept that."[14]

Mr. Conant ignored the only real point at issue, which has nothing to do with money: that is that oil executives, retired or still active, can with impunity walk into high-paying and influential government jobs, which give the industry decisive control over public energy policy — in effect making democracy safe for oil — while only a few handpicked citizens can ever find employment in the oil industry to begin with, and even then only at a young age and under strenuous conditions of surveillance — a weeding-out process which is long-term and ruthless and which, once called into play, ensures that the rejects will most likely never find employment elsewhere in the industry. At the end of 1974, Conant still occupied his post as an assistant to the FEA administrator; in essence, he was still a vice president of the FEA.

By March, 1974, the FEA had two thousand employees and 10 percent of them were public relations staffers, "necessary," one bureaucrat said, "to inform the public about the oil crisis."[15] But there still was not a single critic of the industry in the ranks of the FEA — no one from academia such as Fred Allvine, a professor of economics at Georgia Tech, or from the ranks of the law and legislature, such as Martin Lobel, a former legislative assistant to Senator Proxmire, or from the outspoken wing of the consumer movement, such as Ralph Nader or one of his aides. The FEA's director of consumer affairs, Lee Richardson, left in high dudgeon in mid-August, 1974, claiming that the energy chief, John Sawhill, never responded to his recommendations and that the office had no influence over energy decision-making.[16] Sawhill himself was squeezed out by the end of October: even he was too independent for the administration's tastes. President Ford nominated as his successor Andrew Gibson, a man who was forthwith discovered to be receiving severance pay of $1 million, in annual installments of $88,000, from his former employer — a big oil shipping firm. In time, with reluctance, Ford dropped this nomination and eventually replaced it with another assistant to the FEA administrator, Frank Zarb, who had no background in the oil industry. Nonetheless, the FEA remained in the pocket of the industry. There was still no way for an outsider to gain access to meaningful information on how the industry worked.

What influence did the embargo have in America? Not only did the United States government resolutely refuse to discuss the ambiguities — if not the tensions — which underlay the Arab embargo, and the defensive purpose behind it (which was to give the conservative oil states protection from Arab radicals and progressives), it also refused to give the American consumer an honest appraisal of the extent to which the embargo, big or small, threatened or catastrophic, was really affecting the supply of petroleum and products within the United States.

The story actually goes back to 1971, after the domestic price hikes, when the United States government had a chance, by following the recommendations of President Nixon's Oil Imports Task Force, to reform one mainstay of domestic energy policy, which was the imports quota system, and perhaps replace it with a tariff system. On an ABC television special on energy, on March 20, 1974, David Freeman, one energy expert who worked on the Task Force study, sardonically declared that "something happened to the report on its way to the White House." Former presidential aide John Ehrlichman agreed.

Thus the government failed to work to increase the supply of crude oil in the United States; in conjunction with this, a shortage of crude oil products began to appear in the United States in the winter of 1972–1973. In this period, as Professor Fred Allvine of Georgia Tech has stated, America's major oil companies began both to run their refineries abnormally below capacity and to slow down refinery construction. Allvine has stated that it would have been impossible for a shortage to develop in this country without the inaction of the Nixon administration, which failed to obtain an increase in imports — and thus starved America's refineries of crude oil. Even then, Wisconsin's Congressman Aspin has stated that "the oil companies in the fall of 1972 could have made a profit by producing fuel oil, but they felt that the size of the profit and profit margin were unsatisfactory."[17] A special New York State grand jury, conducting an autopsy on the "crisis," concurred with the statement that the majors knew in advance that products shortages would develop in 1973, but fell short of providing the necessary amount "even though the industry at that time possessed the overall capability."[18]

The large firms have on occasion admitted this, by declaring that they did not increase refinery construction because it was not economically feasible for them to do so. This does not rebut the fundamental charge of critics, which is that America's major oil firms have the power to force increases in product prices simply by their failure to invest — a failure, moreover, which government has very largely neglected to challenge.

President Nixon, as we have seen, finally did rescind the oil import quota system, but at a much later date — April, 1973 — and, as we have seen, the consequences, if not the intent, of this act were quite remote from that of providing America with abundant crude oil when it was most needed.

In the meantime, as a result of the administration's dereliction in working meaningfully to expand America's potential crude oil supply (coupled, as we have seen, with resistance to the construction of the Alaska pipeline not only by environmentalists but also by Exxon and Standard of California), America came into 1973 headed for a real shortage of products.

The first serious alarm came in late spring. For a brief period it seemed as if the nation might be caught in a gasoline shortage. This passed. Then came the October embargo.

Oil industry officials have made much of this embargo's effect on America, playing it for all it was worth, and more. They claimed that the Arabs had put America's access to oil in real jeopardy. By the third week of December, for instance, Mobil Oil was running television commercials which claimed that the world was now running out of crude oil. Then the industry sounded ferocious alarms of shortages in products — fuel oil, gasoline, kerosene for jet aircraft, and other materials. In late November and early December, Continental Oil was running advertisements, in newspapers whose total circulations ran to 15.7 million, stating that "the overall reduction of crude oil and products in the United States is estimated [by anonymous sages] at some 2,700,000 barrels per day, or 15 percent of total requirements." Not even half such a shortage ever materialized. The preceding summer, Shell Oil Company had made very pessimistic predictions about shortages of distillates and gasoline by the end of 1973 which actual developments utterly belied — America's distillate inventory turned out to be half again as big as Shell had said it would be.[19] No less a figure than Bob Dorsey, the chairman of Gulf Oil, stated in November that America's inventory of products would be down to 400 million barrels by the end of December unless consumption was sharply curtailed; with very mild curtailment, this inventory came to 550 million barrels, or 37 percent more than Dorsey's prediction, by New Year's. Consumer abstinence could account for only a tiny fragment of this discrepancy.

Most important, the embargo did not affect American imports directly; though the Liberian vessel *Sidney Spiro* steamed into San Francisco harbor with America's last consignment of pre-embargo Arab crude at Thanksgiving, crude oil imports into the United States kept running at a high level through December and into January. December's imports ran 7 percent above those for the preceding year, or almost 2.9 million barrels a day, according to figures from within the industry itself.

In addition, the Arabs did not succeed, through the embargo, in rewarding "friends" and punishing nations "hostile" to their cause. One student of the embargo, Professor Robert Stobaugh of Harvard Business School, demonstrated this in a statement which he delivered before the Church Subcommittee on July 25, 1974. He pointed out that the companies circumvented the apparent objective of the Arab embargo by shipping oil from non-Arab sources to the "hostile" states.[20] Stobaugh pointed out that the supply of crude oil and natural gas liquids available to the most "hostile" state, the United States, had been reduced by a slightly greater percentage than that going to the rest of the world — according to primarily industry sources of information — but that the supply never dropped more than 7.4 percent, in the worst month, from September's artificially high level. This is in spite of the fact that Aramco's American parents policed the embargo on America, and on the United States military, most effectively according to Aramco's own cables.[21]

Almost as crucial, in casting doubt on the genuineness and effectiveness of the embargo, was the "new Motown sound" which blared forth from Detroit: the near silence with which America's three big automobile manufacturers greeted the gasoline shortage. Although it seemed, for a while, as if these three manufacturers, who had stubbornly clung to the production of big vehicles in recent years because they afforded much greater profits than compacts, would be hit hard by the gasoline "shortage," they scarcely complained about it. This helps to convey the impression that they, like Roy Ash, knew that the shortage was ephemeral and superficial, if not artificial, though, unlike Ash, they did not impart any such knowledge to the public.

In January, United States oil imports settled down to a level of about 2.4 million barrels a day. This was substantially below the January-March, 1973, level. But was it the 1973 level, or that for the current year, which was unusual? Imports in winter of 1973 had been 20 percent greater than those for winter 1972 — yet this increase did not reflect a corresponding increase in demand for products. The demand for petroleum products, with the exception of residual fuel for heating and electricity, has been rising only by 4 to 6 percent a year within the United States.

There was a real drop in the rate of imports between mid-January and mid-February, 1974; in this period the figure fell from 2.4 to 1.8 million barrels a day. But this, too, could have had nothing to do with the Arab embargo, since no Arab oil had reportedly come to the United States for a month and a half. In fact, Stobaugh's 1974 statement before the Church Subcommittee declared that Arab oil was coming into the United States during January and February at a rate of only 19,000 barrels a day.[22]

Perhaps these reduced imports were, rather, the result of oil company initiatives. The federal government, faced with insurrection from lesser refiners who were dependent on the major companies for crude, had set up a program to allocate crude to them from major companies which were importing more than enough to keep their refineries running at 76 percent of capacity. So the majors, in turn, staged, or at least threatened, a counterrevolt on this score by deliberately reducing imports. One executive, Z. D. Bonner of Gulf Oil, went so far as to state publicly that the allocation program was "a major disincentive for anyone who has access to foreign crude oil to import it." One administration source concurred that other major importers shared this attitude: "They said, 'the hell with it. It is not worth it.' "[23] Only later did it come to light that such once and future oil executives as Phillips's Bowen had played a substantial part in drawing up and running the allocation program to begin with.

As it turned out, although prices had risen catastrophically, the nation's refineries could not have used up more than 3 percent, or 8 million barrels, of the nation's crude oil stocks in the period between December 7 and March 1, to go by statistics of the American Petroleum Institute. In March, America still had 237 million barrels, or about twenty days' supply, of crude oil on hand — more than it had had a year before. This is especially significant when one considers that over the past decade America's crude and products stocks have increased very little, year by year.

In addition — and even more significantly — a greater volume of raw feedstock was coming into the domestic refining industry than the industry was actually processing. In other words, America's refineries were dragging their feet. United States refining capacity was 13.4 million barrels a day at the time, and as a rule of thumb refineries normally run at 93 percent of capacity, or about 12.5 million barrels a day.[24] Yet in the winter of 1973–1974, these plants were running at only about 83 percent of capacity, or 11 to 11.2 million barrels a day — *although they were receiving raw material at a faster rate.* Domestic crude oil production in early February averaged 9.2 million barrels a day, crude imports were still at 1.8 million barrels a day (which was the low for the entire winter), and natural gas liquids production for gasoline manufacture was running at 800,000 barrels a day on top of that — a total, therefore, of 11.8 million barrels a day, above and beyond the crude petroleum already in stock.

If the nation's refineries had been running at even the level of 11.8 million barrels a day, which is only 88 percent of capacity, and if they had been putting out about 53 percent of their yield as gasoline, they would have been furnishing the nation with about 6.25 million barrels of gasoline per day, which was about what the nation would normally have consumed at that time of year anyway.

In other words, if the nation's refineries had been running

just at a level which they could have attained without eating into stocks, there would have been no cause for cutbacks, gasless weekends, damped thermostats, talk of rationing, or zany price hikes. In other words, the American oil industry had combined the Arab embargo with a true act of deception at the expense of the American consumer.

The same conditions prevailed in America's petroleum products inventory: at March 1, 1974, America had about 550 million barrels of refined and finished oils on stock — more than it had had at the end of the preceding winter. America's supplies of middle distillates — home heating oil and kerosene, one range of products which oil industry spokesmen had predicted would all but fade from the nation's markets — were up, at the end of winter, the peak consuming season, by 21 percent over the preceding year's level. Motor gasoline stocks stood at 222.4 million barrels — several million more than the previous March, and over a month's supply.[25]

Yet it was gasoline which the industry, and the administration, had withheld from the public in some measure. This is probably because government and industry would not have dared withhold the other major products, fuel oils, from America's cold northeastern quadrant in January and February. That would have been politically dangerous. A gasoline shortage would be, and no doubt was, less controversial.

One could protest that it was only prudent of the government and industry to keep a large inventory of products in reserve, for fear of the unlikely — a really long embargo, say. That point would have been defensible, if debatable — but no one in government raised it. To do so would have meant conceding that America's products inventory was sound.

The companies, as it turned out, gained superb profits — for all but four of America's eighteen biggest oil firms, these were on the order of 60 to 130 percent for the first quarter of 1974 compared with the same period a year earlier, and 30 to 100 percent for the year 1973 as a whole, compared with 1972.*

* See Appendix 2 for a rundown.

Much or most of these profits came from the increased value of inventories, but some could also be attributed to the fact that income, and profits, per unit sold had risen dramatically.

Standard of California, in its December, 1972, *Financial Forecast,* had hinted that such was going to be the case. On page 17 of this document, it predicted that its refining, marketing, and pipeline profits in the Western Hemisphere would rise by 85 percent, or from $75 to $139 million, from 1971 to 1974, while the volume of products it sold remained almost the same. The company predicted that Western Operations, running at a loss in 1971, would register a profit, by 1974, of $39 million.

Then, about the end of winter, the Arabs declared an almost total end to the embargo. Only Denmark and The Netherlands remained on their blacklist — small countries consuming a small amount which could easily be brought in from Nigeria or Iran, and largely was.

In America, the long lines of cars waiting for hours to receive five- or ten-gallon tricklets from gas pumps had literally dissolved. Within a week or two there were no more shortages; no more gasless weekends; attendants even started to wash windshields again. Virtually overnight, the struggle had ended. The Arab states had moved toward a genuine cease-fire with Israel.

Not a trace of animosity and panic remained from the preceding winter. In June, President Nixon traveled to the Middle East. Signs of protest greeted him in Israel, but not in Cairo, Riyadh, Damascus, or Amman, where the crowds gave him a genuinely warm if carefully structured welcome. Almost everyone of importance outside the non-Communist world — and many in it too — endorsed his moves in the Middle East.

Still, the incredibly high prices remained. Somehow those would not wash off. The public would have to learn to live with them. This was because they would not drop. The managers of the oil industry would not allow them to drop.

Some oil executives were direct about this. For example Thornton Bradshaw, president of Atlantic Richfield, told this writer flatly that the government's former energy policy had been "a tragedy of catastrophic proportions." He claimed that it cost his company eight to ten dollars to get a barrel of oil products — gasoline, jet fuel, heating oil, and so forth — to the public and that crude oil should sell for ten dollars a barrel in this country. He would recommend stiff import controls to help assure this and implied that it wouldn't be worth the oil industry's while staying in business for less. "There is a total lack of any understanding of the industry's economics in government," he claimed, and gave an example of academic consultants and economists whom he once took up to look at Arco's properties in the North Slope of Alaska. They seemed amazed when he told them that he expected to get a return of 35 percent per year on the Prudhoe Bay field. He told them, "We can't stay in business without it. We need two fields returning 35 percent."

Nonetheless, there is much evidence that the 1973 price increase, in the United States, was an artificial act — the product of arbitrary government decision. Chapter 3 has shown evidence that it cost one major company, SoCal, no more than $6.45 to get a barrel of products before the public — *all costs and investments included* — before this increase. In those days, crude was selling for $3.28 a barrel on the average in America. The Cost of Living Council distributed memoranda in December, 1973, which cast real doubt on the justification for any price rise. On the basis of material which Ralph Nader has had released to the public, one can almost imagine a group of bureaucrats, some totally ignorant about oil, sitting around and flipping a coin over the rise, or hitting on numbers in accordance with prejudices in favor of business and against the consumer. John Dunlop, Director of the Cost of Living Council, wanted an increase to no more than $5 a barrel; Simon wanted an increase to $7 — or $8, a figure which Ted Eck of Standard of Indiana, a member of Simon's "Evaluation Panel," preferred; Treasury Department aide William Johnson wanted the price to go up to $10, economic advisor Herbert Stein wanted it to rise to $12. Simon's successor John Sawhill, at his confirmation hearings, was asked what he was doing to lower the price of $5.25, by Senator Jackson. Sawhill said, without enthusiasm, that he would "take a new look" at it — but the price, to this writing, remains where it is.[26]

The oil price and supply troubles which have been visited upon the Western consumer in the 1970's owe much, in their distant inspiration, to the industry's failure to take uniform measures in the 1950's which would update and upgrade agreements which prevailed in the 1930's. Even then, it is not the Arab or Moslem world which has visited these troubles upon us so much as it is a Nixon administration desperate for survival at almost any cost — including the cost of an artificial crisis within America — and an international oil industry determined to raise prices in the Western world to make up for its mistakes in the East.

But, alas, there are no pure villains in this narrative. And, just as there is no pure market on earth, so is there no pure oil monopoly or cartel either. It is in the nature of the international oil business that the producing states cannot work together as closely as the major companies could. The time for joining in the debate between the international industry and the United States Department of Justice has passed, apparently but not really leaving anarchy in its wake because the consumer, the ultimate buyer of the oil, has begun to free himself of the old stricture that the companies control prices and regulate production; he will soon begin to discover, instead, that the oil states do not control prices and regulate production nearly so effectively as the big firms do. Their geographic situations do not coincide and their political views are not congruent.

In other words, if the consumer is looking for bargain prices, he would be better off appealing to the producing countries than to the firms. The firms hold together better than Norway, the Moslem states, Ecuador, Canada, the United Kingdom, Nigeria, and Venezuela. This book has brought forth some examples — actual written contracts and agreements, mostly labeled "confidential" — of the control mechanism by which the companies colluded; but we know of no oil control treaties between producing states — just OPEC resolutions. Iran, Iraq, and Saudi Arabia, generally at loggerheads, almost certainly have never drawn up an APQ system or quarter-way price mechanism between themselves, but the independent companies in the Moslem East were never able to open up production and operate at the volume they desired if they worked in concert with any of the seven majors — with one exception, Gelsenberg, which teamed up with the crude-anxious Mobil in Libya. The nations, by comparison, have been much more lenient in allowing the companies to expand at the rate they wished. Compare Gaddafi's willingness to sell oil to New England Petroleum Company during the Arab boycott of America with the Consortium's refusal to let Iran bring products refined from its own oil in eastern Europe back onto Iranian territory.

In addition, the oil states and their leaders have been jealous of one another to a degree almost unknown in the cold-headed environment dominating the international oil industry, where hatchets have been most quickly and effectively buried over the decades in the name of "market stability." One example of the states' unwillingness to be bested by one another in wresting advantageous terms from their respective guests lies in the documents unearthed by the Church Subcommittee, in Saudi Arabia's statements to Aramco, Telexed by Frank Jungers and others to the firm's American parents:

"[Yamani wanted to know] what was the Iranian deal and he was particularly concerned about the 8 cents that the Iranians are now talking about. . . . That was becoming loud and serious and he wanted to know all the details."

"[Yamani] warned that it was most important that the companies carefully measure their position in Kuwait because the Saudis would not give up their predominant position in this matter and that the general agreements would not stand if there were any serious changes made here."

"There was a big change in prices. [Yamani] mentioned that Qatar had made a deal at above posted price."

"[Yamani] pooh-poohed remarks in San Francisco which suggested something like Indonesian deal. They must have unique deal that cannot be copied by other countries."

"[Yamani] asked what I knew of Kuwait. I related all I knew including postponement of assembly discussion scheduled for Saturday. He said we must act before then."

[Yamani said] " 'If Libyans take drastic action, I will have to renegotiate participation. I hope to live with participation, but you must realize there is a limit.' "[27]

Nonetheless, the OPEC states did hold their fragile coalition together in the year following the 1973–1974 embargo, and a great deal of argument, or speculation, or speculative argument, some as enlightening as medieval controversies on the nature of Satan continues to swirl about as to whether or not a Persian Gulf "producers' cartel" has or will come into being and whether or not the posted prices for Persian Gulf crude will drop in the middle-near future. Professor Adelman and most other academic observers are on opposite sides here.

The latter believe, and often state, that prices will stay high; they often claim that energy has been underpriced for a generation, or more, and that the OPEC "cartel" is impregnable. Like small-town priests from the Middle Ages, they think that the ordinary citizen should be subjected to terrible mortification of the flesh (perhaps even for an eternity) in payment for his sins, or misdemeanors, such as driving to work without a car pool (on freeways built by massive appropriations from Congress, often acting under pressure from oil and automobile lobbyists, and maintained by gasoline taxes). Adelman, however — though he might have modified his thinking somewhat in the wake of the 1973 price riots — has for a long time been pointing out that pressures to bring down the prices of crude oil are quite strong. For one thing, he demonstrates that the actual cost of bringing oil out of the Middle East is very low, as we have seen, and that it will rise only slowly, or even decline, over the next twenty years. (It may rise faster than he thought, but from a very low base.) He testified in March, 1969, before a Senate Judiciary Subcommittee, "The basic fact about the world oil industry is that there will be ample supply at less than current prices for fifteen or more years" and declared that "host governments would lower taxes to let companies cut prices" if the United States increased oil imports.[28] Then he wrote, in 1971, "Governments are avowedly out to take everything over and above the [companies'] minimum necessary return, and *also* firmly committed to actions that will tend to depress prices." At that juncture he gave several instances when Near Eastern states — Iran, Iraq, Saudi Arabia, and Libya — entered into new kinds of agreements with the French state firm ERAP, which Near Eastern states touted highly at the time but which the Harvard economist Thomas

Stauffer proved would eliminate the floor to prices. Adelman also pointed out that Kuwait and Iran waived royalties and taxes to buy crude oil from Kuwait Oil Company and the Consortium, on occasion.[29]

It is the view of this writer that the evidence of the past twenty or thirty years will demonstrate that Adelman is right and will be proved right for the wrong reasons. (That is, not by the inexorable force of economic logic, necessarily; just by the unfolding of a political scenario.)

As one consultant to the oil industry, James Jensen, points out in a recent paper, different oil states have different investment policies as well as different interests.[30] Saudi Arabia's policy may well become — as Kuwait's has, at times — to treat the oil *itself* as a kind of investment, and to save it as if it were money, gold, or fine art. Yamani once confided his dilemma to Jungers: "If [you] allowed production to increase, of course [you would have] too much money; and if you curtailed production, the prices would go up again and [you] would still have too much money." Iran, on the other hand, is likely, given the pressure of population, to elect to "take the money and run." It is certainly open to argument whether Iran would run faster or more slowly if its reserves were likely to be depleted faster; possibly the consideration that its reserves are finite would induce it to move even faster out of oil and into steel, copper, petrochemicals, cement, paper, and other processing industries for which it has the requisite materials and in which it would tend to suffer less competition from its southern neighbors than it has suffered in the extraction of oil, or even gas.

This question is largely academic because Iran has very great petroleum reserves — far greater than the Consortium which it hosts has indicated. For nearly a decade, Iran has been dissatisfied with the rate at which the Consortium produces its oil. The twenty-year sales and purchase agreement which the Consortium parents concluded with the Iranian government in 1973 will not go far toward alleviating Iran's dissatisfaction, because it restricts very severely the Iranian government's right to sell oil abroad. Probably, the Iranians will one day seek to modify or replace the agreement, perhaps removing the offtake restrictions and giving itself the right which true independence would give it, namely, that of producing the old Consortium oil directly, for anyone who asked for it.[31]

Once it earned this right, it could pass it on to third parties — France's ERAP, Italy's ENI, or even Japanese independents. Should these third parties succeed in gaining direct access to Iranian oilfields, and should Iran elect to receive assistance from them in paying for the facilities such added production would require, these parties would be very likely to insist on cheaper crude oil as a reward. It may turn out that the Iranian government would not actually lose money through such an arrangement.

A dramatic increase in output could mean an increase in gross revenues, even in the event of a price drop. Then the outsiders could grant the Iranians low interest rates, or no interest at all, on the capital they provided for such expansion. The Japanese government, or the ministry of trade and industry, or a group of Japanese refiners, could for example state, "We will provide $100 million for the facilities, interest-free, on condition that Japanese constructors build these facilities, using Japanese steel and equipment, and we will take the $100 million back in the form of a $3.00 discount off the posted price for 100 million barrels of crude oil over a five-year period." They could vary the numbers, of course — request a $1.50 discount, for instance, for 200 million barrels over seven years.

Should the Iranian government accept these terms, or analogous ones — or further terms from other state firms, perhaps entailing crude from only two or three of the Consortium's seventeen virgin fields — it is conceivable that Iraq, viewing this development with alarm, could elect to offer even better terms. There is nothing to prevent Japanese — or Britishers, or even independent American refiners, or such foreign investors as Onassis who have been seeking to invest in America — from exploring similar opportunities with such other countries as Iraq or Saudi Arabia, even while they are in the process of bargaining with Iran. It could be that these or other countries would see fit to offer competitive terms, if only on a limited scale, just as a hedge to protect their shares in the market. The reopening of

Suez, for instance, would probably make the Libyans less hostile as well to deals of this type.

Such a development would certainly help drive down prices. Once the outside companies constructed facilities to accommodate independent buyers, surplus capacity might then come into being; other independent buyers could use this on a spot basis to meet their short-term requirements. Prices would then drop still further; the truly independent consumer would just buy from the cheapest source of supply.

The United States government, which has also publicly expressed dissatisfaction with the high prices, can do its part to help reduce them — not by threatening or cajoling the exporting states, but by eliminating or restructuring the foreign tax credits which benefit the major companies producing the bulk of the oil abroad (especially in the Persian Gulf, where they lift off 90 percent of the crude).

There is no guarantee that the actions outlined in the last few paragraphs will ever take place, but then there is no reason why they shouldn't, either. This study has consistently doubted that a "cartel" of oil states exists and has maintained that eight or ten countries with diverse political interests and cultural traditions ranging halfway around the world cannot have anything near the singleness of purpose and solidarity which the seven big Anglo-Saxon oil companies possess. And indeed the OPEC states maintain what solidarity they have more through mutual suspicion and fear than through consensus. By their June, 1974, meeting in Ecuador, the OPEC states had started to disagree on whether or not to raise the posted price further. Publicly, Iran was in favor of such a rise, but it could always excuse by its "Saudi opposition" its failure to attain it.[32] And of course this internal dissension widened with time. At another OPEC meeting in September, the Saudi government made it quite clear that it thought prices should go down and indicated that it might well bring them down — though not in isolation. On September 20, Saudi Oil Minister Yamani told a press conference in New York, "The oil price increases of 1973 accounted for all the inflation of the last ten years and probably six years into the future as well." On October 5, on a televised panel discussion hosted by the American Enterprise Institute in Washington, he was even bolder: "I hope that the price of oil will go down," he said, "but in a very quiet manner — not with so many headlines." Even officials from Venezuela and Iran, which adopted a harder position on price, hinted that even if the prices should not go down they considered the oil company practice of passing all tax hikes on to consumers nothing short of outrageous — thereby conceding, after a fashion, that the consumers have the right to be angry about the prices they are paying.

The *Oil and Gas Journal,* in its international editorial of January 13, 1975, agreed with the thrust of these arguments. It stated that 1975 would see "some interesting changes" in international oil. It predicted that nine, and probably eleven, of the twelve OPEC states would take over the concessions on their territories completely and hand them over to their respective national oil companies. "We will see them competing for the world oil market in an atmosphere of surging surplus and sagging demand," declared this magazine, whose bite is sometimes worse than its bark. It went on to say that the national oil companies of the OPEC states "probably will fall victim to the forces of a normal market this year," and observed: "Of the twelve OPEC states, eight [sic] are hungry and four are rich. And if the hungry ones cut prices to sell their oil, we can't see the rich ones standing aside just to save face." So, concluded the journal, "the competition is coming, and with it, lower crude prices — not at the lows of 1960, but lower."

Real skepticism must remain whether the Arabs seriously want to embroil the Western consumer in a campaign to regain Jerusalem or establish an independent state in the Gaza Strip or on the west bank. The Israeli problem is just about the only one which unites more than two or three oil-producing states in one political cause, but there is no real unanimity among Arabs even on that issue.

Arab diplomats have often said, "But there is nothing for us to negotiate with Israel." In a way, they are right: much of the negotiating from now on will take place between Arabs. Though many Arab leaders would favor the creation of a Palestinian state on the west bank, some might not. King Hussain even now might not. King Faisal might defer to him, though he did the opposite at the Rabat Summit in October, 1974. Some Palestinians view the creation of such a state as a half-measure, or even a sellout of their cause. There is also a debate whether the Palestinians should hold out for a full-scale repatriation or should accept the alternative of financial compensation — especially those tens of thousands living between San Francisco and Buenos Aires who have found a living in new societies, many of whose children no longer even know Arabic. The government of Kuwait has always said that it believes every last Palestinian has a duty to go back to his homeland; Iraq sounds the same way; but then there are people inside Israel and out who believe all Jews have the same obligation to the Jewish state, no matter where on earth they might live, and many Jews disagree with this doctrine — only about 10 percent of the world's Jews live in Israel. Some Arab states might counsel dispossessed Palestinians simply to take cash and stay where they are if that is what they want to do.

Past differences between Saudi Arabia and Iraq, say, or between Libya and Iran, have been real differences of belief, not just of marketing strategy, unlike the quarrels which might arise between a Gulf and a Shell, and most serious students of international oil do not believe that a cartel has existed even among the seven major oil companies. Truly, it is harder for sovereign states to act in concert than it is for powerful international oil companies to do so.

In the meantime, the Western consumer will continue to be aware that the international oil firms possess great power and will realize more and more that this power is not an economic necessity but an end in itself; then he will continue contemplating measures to reduce this power. In America, a powerful elite has grown up around the international oil industry, far too powerful, too isolated, and too unaccountable to have become another typical American meritocracy.

To reduce the power of this elite, the American public needs understanding of, and control over, its inner workings. There are at least two ways to achieve this. One is through broad, sweeping legislation — the passage of laws ordering the companies to bare geological, accounting, engineering, and other information to the public at large. Another is to develop a cadre of experts in government who are not on loan from oil companies, at generous salaries, but who owe no debts, or even loyalty, to the industry itself or people within it. Perhaps through such disclosures, perhaps through a training ground within government itself, such as a federal oil and gas company competing, and taking its blows, with the rest of the industry, can such a diffusion of knowledge and control come about. If the public does not make substantial progress in acquiring this knowledge by these means, it should start to consider broader measures, such as a breakup of the integrated industry into smaller, hungrier, more specialized firms. It should certainly force oil companies to divest themselves of all coal and nonassociated gas properties.

The American public — or its representatives, delegated or not — has committed mistakes in the past in the Near East. The public knows well enough not to let them happen again, not to let its spokesmen make them again. Now that the Arab world is opening up to America once more, after a decade of isolation, the people of the United States have a chance to stay on reasonable terms with it for a long time to come.

One final question, almost lost in the turmoil: what has become of Gaddafi, the militant, since the 1973–1974 counter-revolt?

He wandered away from his objective too. He ceased to concentrate on righting injustices against Libya and fell under a compulsion to maintain his status as the most revolutionary figure in the post-Nasser Arab world. Since he was running out of other areas in which to excel, he felt driven to turn to expropriation — an action which no oil state had taken on a serious scale since the days of Mosaddegh. A little over a year after his nationalization of BP's substantial Libyan holdings in 1971, Gaddafi proceeded to expropriate 51 percent of the assets of eight major oil companies operating on Libyan soil.

There could have been political motives behind this action, since most of these companies were American. Gaddafi admitted as much some time before he embarked on this course, when he talked with a newspaperman about the longer-range objectives of his policies, which converged mostly on the struggle against Israel. He stated, as others had, that America was the evil power behind the very existence of Israel: coerce America to withdraw its support from Israel, by putting pressure on its companies in the Near East, and Israel would simply crumble. The survival of Israel, he suggested, depended on American connivance.

Then Egypt invaded Israeli-held territory without obtaining clearance from Gaddafi first — but after consulting, rather, with the arch-conservative oil monarch Faisal for support and money. Then, too, the companies Gaddafi had nationalized fought back.

The Libyan premier maintained total silence about the war until it was almost over, on October 19. Even then he spoke up only to announce that he was cutting off his nation's rather minor oil shipments to the United States. By contrast, some of his arch-enemies had made actual contributions to this war. Two Arab kings, Hasan of Morocco and Hussain of Jordan, had dispatched arms and troops to the fray, and the third king, Faisal, had announced a significant cutback of oil production. As for Gaddafi, his anti-Israeli rhetoric had vanished for the duration of the war.

A few months later, once the Near East had regained a measure of tranquility, some of the oil companies, such as Exxon, Mobil, and Shell, accepted Libya's 51 percent nationalization, but others, such as Texaco and SoCal, held out. It looked very much as if Suez would be open in a year's time, by mid-1975. Much of the advantage which Libyan oil had been enjoying in Europe relative to that from the Persian Gulf was fated to disappear.

Gaddafi's very reputation was in jeopardy, along with his base of support and power, and in fact, by mid-1974, his colleagues on the Revolutionary Command Council ruling Libya stripped him of his ceremonial powers, at least, and he ceased making public pronouncements. In May, Egypt's President Sadat wrote what might well be the epitaph to the young revolutionary's career, or at least its most militant phase. He all but told the British Broadcasting Corporation that Gaddafi, in April, 1973, had ordered an Egyptian submarine out to torpedo a passenger liner headed for Israel. Then he published a letter he had written to the Libyan government in which he accused Gaddafi of holding back money and spare parts for armaments which Egypt needed in its struggle with Israel. Sadat wrote, "Your skepticism — and I can almost say sabotage — reached a strange point when the colonel [Gaddafi], who should at least have respected the secrecy of the communication, delivered a public speech a few weeks before the war, announcing that he was washing his hands of the Egyptian-Syrian battle plans and predicting disaster."[33] At this writing, though, Gaddafi still seems to be on good terms with Occidental and Dr. Hammer.

Perhaps analogous to Gaddafi's stand has been that of another old militant, Sheikh Abdullah Tariki, the apostle of nationalization. His tone has mellowed too. Shortly after the massive 1973 price hikes, he told a Kuwaiti newspaper that there was no need for the states to nationalize the remainder of the concessions; the nations had at last attained their rights and had achieved a just price. He added another point, which is virtually identical to the official Saudi position: it will not be possible to complete the process of nationalization until Arabs are trained to take over all phases of the concession operations; this will not be until the end of the decade, at the earliest.

"Nationalization has been practically achieved," Tariki declared, neglecting to add that the nations could not continue to receive the high price without the cooperation of the major oil companies.[34]

We may never know if the conservative oil-producing states, Saudi Arabia, Kuwait, and Abu Dhabi, would have mounted their embargo in 1973 had the Arab forces maintained the upper hand over Israel in the second week of the war, or had the war ended sooner than it did. The embargo could well have been just a signal to the United States that if the war went on, that if America did not prevent the Israelis from scoring greater victories than they already had, the conservative states would lose whatever power and influence they still possessed in Arab-wide deliberations and that hence America itself would lose whatever influence it still enjoyed in the Arab world.

Gaddafi, for all intents and purposes, was gone; so was the old reaction against the imperialist past. In a sense, the industry had come full circle; its center of gravity had returned to the Persian

Gulf, where it had been during all but six of the last thirty years. But, in a deeper sense, the industry had changed for good. The system which once dominated in the gulf had been shattered, and the architects of this demolition were Gaddafi, Occidental, and the hubris of the unyielding Exxon, the redoubtable SoCal, and the other five majors. The heyday of the independents in Libya — like an accident on a freeway — has left its trace on the industry, long after its debris has been cleaned up.

Notes

CHAPTER 1

1. Kazem Zarnegar in Middle East Institute, *The Present Situation in Iran*, pp. 125–126.
2. See *Platt's Oilgram*, April 15, 1969, for a description of this offer.
3. See New York *Times*, February 14, 1974.

CHAPTER 2

1. United States Department of Justice, *Plaintiff's Statement of Claims, United States of America vs. Exxon, Mobil, SoCal, Texaco and Gulf*, 1961.

CHAPTER 3

1. Penrose, *The International Petroleum Industry*, pp. 29–31.
2. See New York *Times*, Sept. 24, 1974, for these figures.
3. Ikard's statement appears in *Platt's Oilgram*, January 29, 1971; Aspin's in "The Oil Company Blues," *New York Review of Books*, March 7, 1974.
4. All these figures appear on p. 17 of Standard of California's 1972 *Forecast*.
5. Eleanore Carruth, "The New Oil Rush in Our Own Backyard," *Fortune*, June 1974; U.S. Senate Government Operations Committee, Subcommittee on Investigations, *Current Energy Shortages Oversight Series*, Part 3.
6. U.S. Senate Foreign Relations Committee, Subcommittee on Multinational Corporations (Church Subcommittee), *Multinational Corporation and United States Foreign Policy*, Part 7, p. 591.
7. See Saidi and Martin, "Method of Developing a Newly Discovered Fractured Limestone Field in Iran," and Paran and Crichton, "Highlights of Exploration in Iran 1956–1965," for details regarding the Asmari and Bangestan zones.
8. This is set forth in Iranian Oil Exploration and Producing Company, N.V. [the Consortium], *Look-Ahead Plans for Crude Capacity Development*, February 1967, p. 12.
9. See documents distributed by Standard Oil Company of California at the Church Subcommittee hearings, March 27, 1974.
10. New York *Times*, April 27, 1974, p. 1.
11. The Medreco refinery case is discussed in the magazine *al-Hawadith*, Beirut, Lebanon, August 10, 1973, quoted by Joint Publications Research Service, *Translations on Near East*.
12. New York *Times*, May 28, 1974, p. 55.
13. Garland and Dietzman, *Engineering Cost Study of Development Wells and Profitability Analysis of Crude Oil Production*, p. 25.
14. From a tabulation of daily runs in all the company's United States refineries, *Oil and Gas Journal*, April 2, 1973.
15. This phenomenon is described in *Wall Street Journal*, September 13, 1974.

CHAPTER 4

1. Adelman, *The World Petroleum Market*, p. 159. Since he wrote this, of course, we have witnessed the 1973–1974 peak.

2. *Ibid.*, p. 181.
3. *Platt's Oilgram*, September 26, 1960.
4. Penrose, *The International Petroleum Industry*, p. 196.
5. *Al-Ahram*, March 23, 1972, quoted by Joint Publications Research Service, *Translations on Near East.*
6. *The Economist*, September 3, 1966.
7. See quotations from the Lebanese press in *Middle East Economic Survey*, February 17, 1967.
8. *Platt's Oilgram*, January 5, 1967.
9. *Middle East Economic Survey*, January 13, 1967.
10. *Ibid.*, March 10, 1967.
11. *Wall Street Journal*, March 3, 1967.
12. *Petroleum Intelligence Weekly*, June 12, 1967.
13. *Middle East Economic Survey*, August 25, 1967.
14. *Platt's Oilgram*, September 6, 1967.
15. *Al-Ahram*, reproduced in *Middle East Economic Survey*, July 7 and 14, 1967.

CHAPTER 5

1. Gulbenkian, the concession-broker who had managed to acquire and keep 5 percent of the IPC concession, claimed credit for drawing this boundary, as he was familiar with the reach of the old Ottoman Empire. See Hewins, *Mr. Five Per Cent*, p. 141.
2. *Arabian Oil Ventures*, p. 81.
3. Penrose, *The International Petroleum Industry*, p. 179.
4. Statement of Barbara J. Svedberg in Church Subcommittee, *Multinational Corporations and United States Foreign Policy*, Part 7, p. 80.
5. See also testimony by F. A. Davies, Joint Hearings of the U.S. Senate, *Emergency Oil Lift Program and Related Oil Problems*, 1957.
6. The Federal Trade Commission staff study, *The International Petroleum Cartel*, p. 104.
7. *Platt's Oilgram*, October 20, 1961.
8. See Anwar Abdel Malik, *Egypt: Military Society*, pp. 273–274.
9. See 1954 Agreement between the Iranian Consortium and Iranian Government, Article 20B.
10. This is covered in considerable detail in *Petroleum Intelligence Weekly*, April 8, 1974.
11. William Rugh, "Emergence of a New Middle Class in Saudi Arabia," *Middle East Journal*, Winter 1973.
12. Church Subcommittee, *Multinational Corporations and United States Foreign Policy*, Part 7, p. 222, shows the history of Aramco's production forecasts since 1963.
13. *Platt's Oilgram*, December 29, 1960, stated that this totaled $2.75 million for 25,000 barrels a day, or about $110 per barrel per day.
14. *Ibid.*, September 11, 1959.
15. See *Aramco World*, June–July 1963, for a full discussion of this point.
16. *Petroleum Intelligence Weekly*, April 2, 1973.
17. *Washington Post*, January 11, 1974.

18. Church Subcommittee, *Multinational Corporations and United States Foreign Policy,* Part 7, p. 3.
19. *Ibid.,* p. 540.
20. *Ibid.,* pp. 409–411, 483.
21. *Ibid.,* pp. 550–554.

CHAPTER 6

1. See article by Clyde H. Farnsworth, the New York *Times,* March 17, 1974, p. 1.
2. From an article by Ania Francos, *Jeune Afrique,* March 24, 1973.
3. Eghtedari, "Some Financial Aspects of the Anglo-Iranian Oil Dispute," p. 52.
4. *Ibid.,* p. 29.
5. See Bayne, *Persian Kingship in Transition,* p. 150, and Richard Funkhouser's State Department memorandum to Parker T. Hart, 1953 (released by Church Subcommittee).
6. See Zabih, *Mosaddegh's Era: A Study of Domestic Political Forces of Iran.*
7. For some of the many different interpretations, see Miles Copeland, *The Game of Nations,* p. 62; Malcolm Kerr, editorial in the UCLA newspaper, *The Daily Bruin,* on the occasion of the award of an honorary degree to the Shah, May 21, 1964; books by E. A. Bayne, Richard Cottam and Bahman Nirumand; reports by the left-wing organization MERIP (Washington, D.C.).
8. See, for instance, a book review by Richard Cottam, *Middle East Journal,* Autumn 1972.
9. For a discussion of this point, see Funkhouser's 1953 State Department memorandum to Parker T. Hart.
10. Reproduced in Church Subcommittee, *Multinational Corporations and United States Foreign Policy,* Part 6, p. 86.

CHAPTER 7

1. Mosley, *Power Play,* pp. 232–233.
2. Robert Engler, *The Politics of Oil,* 207–208. The Church Subcommittee has published Davies' letters on the subject to Secretary of State Dulles and Attorney General Brownell in *Multinational Corporations and United States Foreign Policy,* Part 7, pp. 249–252.
3. This is set forth in the Consortium's document *Look-Ahead Plans for Crude Production Capacity, 1965–69,* June 1964, Appendices I–III.
4. *Middle East Economic Survey,* January 27, 1967, p. 10.
5. *Ibid.,* May 5, 1967. It is interesting that Mr. Warder should have had such exact knowledge of Saudi production costs, although he came from British Petroleum, which had no interest in the purely American venture Aramco.
6. See text of question period following Mr. Shafer's testimony before the Church Subcommittee, March 1974, *Multinational Corporations and United States Foreign Policy,* Part 7, pp. 269–270.
7. Tillman Durdin, New York *Times,* May 12, 1969.

8. New York *Times*, May 16, 1969.
9. *Petroleum Intelligence Weekly*, August 18, 1969.
10. J. H. Carmichal, New York *Times*, November 6, 1966.
11. *Wall Street Journal*, article by Jerry Landauer, March 27, 1974.
12. Daniel C. Ion of British Petroleum, *Petroleum Intelligence Weekly*, March 9, 1970, p. 7.
13. *Petroleum Intelligence Weekly*, April 13, 1970.
14. Chicago *Sun-Times*, January 27, 1974.
15. *Chicago Journalism Review*, February 1974, p. 6.
16. Consortium, *Look-Ahead Plans for Crude Production Capacity, 1965–69*, Appendix III. Standard of Indiana's lack of foreign crude has also been a factor in its drive to take over Occidental, starting November, 1974.

CHAPTER 8

1. Ragaei el Mallakh, economics professor at the University of Colorado and advisor to some Arab gulf states, offered the figures on Kuwait's GNP and aid at a lecture at the University of California in March 1974.
2. Kuwait, *al-Ra'y al-ʿAmm*, April 6, 1974, through *Translations from Near East*.
3. Federal Trade Commission staff study, *The International Petroleum Cartel*, describes this history in detail on pp. 129–134.
4. See U.S. Senate, Emergency Oil Lift Hearings, pp. 2690–2709.
5. *Petroleum Intelligence Weekly*, August 6, 1973, records that Gulf's net crude oil production in 1972 was 3.214 million barrels per day; its refinery runs 1.945 million barrels per day; its worldwide crude oil production, therefore, 165.2 percent of runs worldwide. Furthermore, Gulf's refinery runs were 116 percent of its product sales that year.
6. *Platt's Oilgram*, April 27, 1960, describes the 1960 shareholders' meeting for details on the gradual termination of the Gulf-Shell offtake agreement. See New York *Times*, January 4, 1975, and *Wall Street Journal*, January 6, 1975.
7. Memorandum, *Gulf-Shell Offtake Agreement*, November 3, 1953, p. 30. As it turned out, according to Adelman (*The World Petroleum Market*, pp. 152, 154), Kuwaiti oil did threaten the stability of price in the American market during the 1950's, perhaps more than any other Near Eastern crude.
8. *Ibid.*, p. 29.
9. *International Petroleum Cartel*, p. 133.
10. *Middle East Economic Survey*, February 7, 1969.
11. *Petroleum Intelligence Weekly*, March 28, 1966.
12. *The World Petroleum Market*, pp. 209–210.
13. *Ibid.*, p. 214.
14. *Al-Taliʿa*, July 3, 1971, through *Translations on Near East*.

CHAPTER 9

1. *New York Review of Books*, March 21, 1974.
2. Review by Elie Kedourie, *Encounter*, November 1972.
3. *Platt's Oilgram*, January 15, 1968; June 16, 1971.

4. Penrose, *The International Petroleum Industry*, pp. 157–159.
5. See Penrose, p. 70, and Longrigg, *Oil in the Middle East*, p. 121.
6. *Journal of the Institute of Petroleum*, April 1967.
7. *Ibid.*, p. 144.
8. *Middle East Economic Survey*, August 1, 1969.
9. *Petroleum Intelligence Weekly*, November 30, 1970.
10. *Ibid.*, August 2 and October 18, 1971, and September 11, 1972.
11. *Petroleum Intelligence Weekly*, May 14, 1973.
12. *Arab Oil and Gas Journal*, February 1968, p. 28.
13. *Middle East Economic Survey*, January 17, 1968.
14. Longrigg, *Oil in the Middle East*, p. 186.
15. Hirst, *Oil and Public Opinion in the Middle East*, pp. 76ff.
16. *Platt's Oilgram*, October 11, 1961.
17. *Ibid.*, April 28, 1959.
18. *Ibid.*, April 24, 1961.
19. Iraq Petroleum Company, unpublished memorandum to the Government of Iraq, September 18, 1961.
20. *Platt's Oilgram*, November 24, 1961.
21. *Ibid.*, August 24, 1961.
22. Dr. Penrose discusses this episode lucidly in *The International Petroleum Industry*, pp. 72–73.
23. *Al-Thawra*, December 12, 1971, from *Translations on Near East.*
24. *Manchester Guardian Weekly*, June 3, 1972.
25. Chris Kutschera, "Iraq: a Strong Smell of Oil," *Jeune Afrique*, July 3, 1971.
26. *Petroleum Intelligence Weekly*, August 21, 1972.
27. *Ibid.*, October 2, 1972.
28. *Ibid.*, November 13, 1972.
29. See, for example, San Francisco *Chronicle*, March 12, 1973.
30. See *Oil and Gas Journal*, August 6, 1973, p. 3.

CHAPTER 10

1. Mosley, *Power Play*, p. 230, quotes Exxon's Page as stating, "At no time did Mattei ever approach me, nor did I ever hear that he had approached others, to get into the Consortium. I'm sure I would have known if there had been a confidential approach." According to a footnote on the same page, Mattei had had a meeting with BP's Lord Strathalmond during the Mosaddegh era. Page, furthermore, did not say that *no one* from ENI had made an approach.
2. *Platt's Oilgram*, August 3 and September 24, 1970. But this average includes very high depreciation and amortization.
3. See Kraft, *The Struggle for Algeria*, pp. 249–252.
4. *Le Monde*, May 4, 1971.

CHAPTER 11

1. *Middle East Economic Survey*, March 3, 1967.
2. See article by Kamal Darwish, *al-Siyasa* (Kuwait), May 10, 1973, through *Translations on Near East*.

3. Aden, *al-Thawri,* "Draft of the National Program of the Saudi National Liberation Front," September 20, 1973, through *Translations on Near East.*
4. See article by Salim al-Lawzi, *al-Hawadith* (Beirut), November 17, 1972, through *Translations on Near East.*
5. *Al-Nahar,* Supplement, September 3, 1972.
6. San Francisco *Chronicle,* February 7, 1974, and Church Subcommittee, *Multinational Corporations and United States Foreign Policy,* Part 5, p. 276.
7. Leonard Mosley, New York *Times Magazine,* March 10, 1974.
8. *Church Subcommittee, Multinational Corporations and United States Foreign Policy,* Part 4, pp. 539–541.
9. Richard Funkhouser, State Department memorandum to Parker T. Hart, 1953. Released by Church Subcommittee.
10. *Platt's Oilgram,* September 21, 1970.

CHAPTER 12

1. See "Thirteen Firms to Start Libyan Search," *Oil and Gas Journal,* January 16, 1956.
2. See Solow, "The Drillings and Diggings of Dr. Phillips." Adequate but not precise figures on the output of individual fields such as Raguba appear annually in the *Oil and Gas Journal's* last issue of the year.
3. Gedeist Manuscript, Chapter IV.
4. *Ibid.,* Chapter V.
5. *Platt's Oilgram,* August 11, 1961.
6. Occidental's chairman, Armand Hammer, leveled this charge in a statement quoted by *Platt's Oilgram,* September 16, 1968.
7. *Petroleum Intelligence Weekly,* August 11, 1969, and May 23, 1970.
8. San Francisco *Chronicle,* April 30, 1974.
9. *Platt's Oilgram,* November 16, 1971.
10. U.S. Senate, Committee on the Judiciary, Subcommittee on Antitrust and Monopoly, *Governmental Intervention in the Market Mechanism,* March–April 1969. Miller's remarks before the New York Society of Security Analysts appeared in an article by Thomas W. Bush, Los Angeles *Times,* May 13, 1969.
11. See, for example, the *Oil and Gas Journal,* November 19, 1973, p. 35, which states that through several bills, "which generally follow the lines of a compromise agreement reached between the oil industry and Governor William A. Egan [of Alaska]," the state drew up a severance tax schedule which was dependent on wellhead prices. The tax would be 8 percent of the wellhead price on wells producing 1,000 barrels or more per day (meaning all the wells in the North Slope) — but it could not be less than 27 cents a barrel. This virtually sanctified a price of $3.37 a barrel (of which 27 cents would be 8 percent) — for 36-cent oil! As long as Alaska's revenues were dependent on price, not volume, the Alaskan government could not oppose a high price, and this is where the Alaskan government blundered. *Platt's Oilgram,* August 8, 1969, details the man-

ner by which the Oil Imports Tax Force reached its production and transportation cost figures.

12. *Platt's Oilgram,* January 23, 1961.
13. *Petroleum Intelligence Weekly,* February 23, 1970.
14. *Oil and Gas Journal,* March 27, 1967.

CHAPTER 13

1. *Middle East Economic Survey,* Supplement, July 22, 1966.
2. *Ibid.,* August 12, 1965.
3. See Associated Press dispatch in the San Francisco *Chronicle,* June 29, 1974, which quoted American business sources as saying the Russian oil-fertilizer deal was "the largest single transaction ever concluded between a nation and a private company." Hammer's contributions to Nixon's 1972 campaign, and his use of Babcock as a conduit, appear in the New York *Times,* and dispatches of the Associated Press, dated December 11, 1974.
4. "Is Libyan Crude Underposted?" *Review of Arab Petroleum and Economics,* September–October 1968.

CHAPTER 14

1. For the Saudi Arabian budget, see *al-Madina* (Jidda), August 10, 1972, through *Translations on Near East.*
2. See Ali Hashim's dispatches from the Persian Gulf in *al-Nahar* (Beirut), Summer 1972 (also reproduced in *Translations on Near East*).
3. *Platt's Oilgram,* June 8, 1970.
4. New York *Times,* February 1, 1974, p. 47. Church Subcommittee, *Report to the Committee on Foreign Relations, United States Senate,* January 2, 1975.
5. Church Subcommittee, *Chronology of the Libyan Oil Negotiations,* 1974.
6. See Church Subcommittee, testimony of Ambassador James Akins and Henry Schuler.
7. Statement before the Church Subcommittee, July 25, 1974.
8. *Platt's Oilgram,* December 2, 1970.
9. *Ibid.,* December 17, 1970.
10. *Ibid.,* February 2, 1971.
11. *Ibid.,* February 23, 1967.
12. *Petroleum Intelligence Weekly,* September 7, 1970.
13. *Ibid.,* November 2, 1970.
14. See "Arab Music in Caracas," *The Economist,* December 19, 1970.
15. *Platt's Oilgram,* January 28, 1971.
16. *Ibid.,* January 25, 1971.
17. Letter to the New York *Times,* June 21, 1974.
18. See *Petroleum Intelligence Weekly,* May 6, 1974, for full text of the Libyan Producers' agreement. The "dimes and quarters" provisions were Articles 4 and 9.
19. *Wall Street Journal,* January 20, 1971.
20. *Petroleum Intelligence Weekly,* Supplement, April 22, 1974, p. 8.

21. *Platt's Oilgram*, January 19, 1971.
22. San Francisco *Chronicle*, June 28, 1974.
23. *Platt's Oilgram*, January 19, 1971.
24. *Petroleum Intelligence Weekly*, April 22, 1974, supplement, p. 8. Italics supplied.
25. *Platt's Oilgram*, February 9, 1971.
26. *Petroleum Intelligence Weekly*, Supplement, April 22, 1974, p. 14.
27. *Ibid.*, February 1, 1971.
28. *Ibid.*, Supplement, April 22, 1974, p. 16.
29. *Ibid.*, p. 20.
30. *Ibid.*, p. 18.
31. *Wall Street Journal*, March 15, 1971.
32. *Al-Ahram*, October 1, 1972, through *Translations on Near East.*
33. Adelman, *The World Petroleum Market*, pp. 253, 254.
34. *Petroleum Intelligence Weekly*, Supplement, April 22, 1974, p. 19.

CHAPTER 15

1. *Platt's Oilgram*, July 17, 1969.
2. *Ibid.*, April 22, 1969.
3. *Petroleum Intelligence Weekly*, January 17, 1972.
4. *Ibid.*, September 13, 1971.
5. *Ibid.*, September 27, 1971.
6. *Ibid.*, February 28, 1972.
7. *Ibid.*, Supplement, April 22, 1974, p. 32.
8. *Ibid.*, January 15, 1973.
9. *Wall Street Journal*, February 15, 1974.
10. *Petroleum Intelligence Weekly*, January 29, 1973.
11. *Ibid.*, Supplement, July 23, 1973, for a copy of this agreement.
12. Church Subcommittee, *Multinational Corporations and United States Foreign Policy*, Part 7, pp. 403, 514.

CHAPTER 16

1. *Encounter*, June 1969.
2. Furthermore, they still dominated oil production. The economist John M. Blair, in a statement before the Church Subcommittee, on July 25, 1974, stated that the seven international majors accounted for 90.9 percent of crude production in the Near East and 70.6 percent of that in the Free World as a whole, in 1972. The First National City Bank gave figures which would indicate a smaller share (see *Petroleum Intelligence Weekly*, August 6, 1973) : net crude production of the seven majors in 1972, being about 25.113 million barrels a day, would be about 60.9 percent of non-Communist production of 41.214 million barrels a day. As for refinery runs and product sales of the seven majors, First National City Bank gives 20.887 and 21.751 million barrels a day, respectively — or about 50.7 and 52.8 percent of total non-Communist crude production.
3. Radio Baghdad, June 13, 1964, 11:30 GMT, through *Translations on Near East.*

4. New York *Times,* November 11, 1974.
5. Law No. 56 for the year 1972, Authorizing the Three-Year Development Plan for the Years 1972–75, from the Libyan *Official Gazette,* through *Translations on Near East.*
6. *Petroleum Intelligence Weekly,* May 21, 1973.
7. Church Subcommittee, *Multinational Corporations and United States Foreign Policy,* Part 7, p. 504, and carried in an article by Jerry Landauer, *Wall Street Journal,* August 7, 1974.
8. *Ibid.,* Part 7, p. 542.
9. *Ibid.,* Part 7, pp. 446–453.
10. *Ibid.,* Part 7, p. 514.
11. New York *Times,* February 6, 1974.
12. Government of Iran, Ministry of Foreign Affairs, Department of Press and Information, January 19, 1974.
13. See *Wall Street Journal,* June 17 and July 1, 1974.
14. New York *Times,* August 31, 1974.
15. See New York *Times,* May 4, June 13, 1974; *Wall Street Journal,* June 17 and July 1, 1974; and "Merry-Go-Round," December 4, 1973, and March 10, 1974.
16. San Francisco *Chronicle,* August 13, 1974, from the Washington *Post.*
17. Aspin, "The Oil Company Blues," *New York Review of Books,* March 7, 1974.
18. New York *Times,* October 8, 1974.
19. Shell Oil Company, *The National Energy Problem: the Short-Term Supply Prospect,* 1973.
20. *Oil and Gas Journal,* August 5, 1974, p. 103.
21. San Francisco *Chronicle,* August 7, 1974.
22. New York *Times,* July 26, 1974.
23. *Ibid.,* February 22, 1974, p. 1.
24. *Ibid.,* January 28, 1974.
25. See the *Oil and Gas Journal*'s weekly statistical roundup; for example, issue of April 1, 1974, p. 151.
26. New York *Times* and Washington *Post,* June 8, 1974.
27. Church Subcommittee, *Multinational Corporations and United States Foreign Policy,* Part 7, pp. 504–505, 514, 533, 538.
28. U.S. Senate Committee on the Judiciary, Subcommittee on Antitrust and Monopoly, *Governmental Intervention in the Market Mechanism,* pp. 7, 10.
29. *The World Petroleum Market,* pp. 8, 77, 218–19. Stauffer first made his case in a paper before the Sixth Arab Petroleum Congress, "The [NIOC-] ERAP Agreement: a Study in Marginal Taxation Pricing," reprinted in various publications, such as *Platt's Oilgram* (issue of March 27, 1967).
30. Jensen, "International Oil — Shortage, Cartel, or Emerging Natural Monopoly?" *Vanderbilt Journal of Transnational Law,* Spring 1974.
31. See numerous articles in the New York *Times,* January and February 1974, passim, on the desire of such firms and states to acquire direct access to Iranian oil.
32. "Decisions of OPEC Experts on Raising Oil Prices," *Ettelaat,* June 2, 1974. See also New York *Times,* June 13, 1974.
33. New York *Times,* May 25, 1974.
34. Kuwait, *al-Siyasa,* February 20, 1974, from *Translations on Near East.*

Appendices

Appendix 1

Annual Production (Millions of Barrels per Day) and Production Growth Rates (Percentages of Increase over Previous Year) in the Major Oil States of the Islamic Near East, 1945–1973

Year	Saudi Arabia (Aramco)		Iran (BP/Consortium)		Kuwait (KOC)		Iraq (IPC)		Libya (all)		Abu Dhabi (all)	
	mb/d	%	mb/d	%	mb/d	%	mb/d	%	mb/d	%	mb/d	%
1945	.0584	174.2	.3576	28.3			.0961	13.7				
1946	.1642	181.2	.4022	12.5	.0162		.0977	1.7				
1947	.2462	49.9	.4246	5.6	.0444	174.0	.0981	.4				
1948	.3903	58.5	.5201	22.5	.1270	186.0	.0713	−27.3				
1949	.4767	22.1	.5608	7.8	.2465	94.1	.0848	18.9				
1950	.5467	14.7	.665	18.6	.3444	39.7	.1362	60.6				
1951	.7615	39.3	.3883	−49.1	.5613	63.0	.1784	31.0				
1952	.8248	8.3	.0213	−93.7	.7470	33.1	.3855	116.1				
1953	.8446	2.4	.026	22.1	.8618	15.4	.5760	49.4				
1954	.9530	12.8	.059	126.9	.952	9.0	.6258	8.7				
1955	.9650	1.3	.329	457.6	1.092	14.7	.6882	9.9				
1956	.9861	2.2	.538	63.5	1.093	.1	.638	−7.3				
1957	.9921	.6	.716	33.1	1.143	4.6	.449	−29.6				
1958	1.0151	2.3	.822	14.8	1.401	22.6	.730	62.6				
1959	1.0954	7.9	.925	12.5	1.383	−1.3	.851	16.6				

Appendix 1 (continued)

Year	Saudi Arabia (Aramco)		Iran (BP/Consortium)		Kuwait (KOC)		Iraq (IPC)		Libya (all)		Abu Dhabi (all)	
	mb/d	%	mb/d	%	mb/d	%	mb/d	%	mb/d	%	mb/d	%
1960	1.2471	13.9	1.048	13.3	1.624	17.4	.967	13.6				
1961	1.3925	11.7	1.171	11.7	1.644	1.2	1.000	3.4	.018			
1962	1.5207	9.2	1.3016	11.2	1.834	11.6	.997	—.3	.181	905.6	.015	
1963	1.6290	7.1	1.4443	11.0	1.933	5.4	1.155	15.8	.459	153.6	.050	233.3
1964	1.7161	5.3	1.6554	14.6	2.125	9.9	1.252	8.4	.855	86.3	.189	278.0
1965	2.0249	18.0	1.8079	9.2	2.171	2.2	1.315	5.0	1.223	43.0	.284	50.3
1966	2.3927	18.2	*2.0169	11.5	2.275	4.8	1.386	5.4	1.504	23.0	.363	27.8
1967	2.5976	8.6	2.4665	22.3	2.2924	.1	1.2207	—11.9	1.7406	15.7	.3820	5.2
1968	2.8299	8.9	2.704	9.6	2.4211	5.6	1.5000	22.9	2.5998	49.4	.5013	31.2
1969	2.9927	5.6	3.1065	14.9	2.5755	6.4	1.5184	1.2	3.1007	19.3	.6006	19.8
1970	3.5489	18.6	3.5157	13.4	2.7845	6.2	1.5584	2.6	3.3213	7.1	.6909	15.0
1971	4.4976	26.7	4.1705	18.7	2.9255	7.0	1.7066	14.8	2.7584	—16.9	.9344	35.2
1972	5.7334	28.4	4.5693	9.6	2.9993	2.5	1.4460	—15.3	2.247	—19.7	1.0545	12.4
1973	7.310	27.5	5.406	18.3	2.8334a	—5.9	1.964	35.8	2.187	—1.3	1.298	23.6
1974b	8.065		5.656		2.578				1.937		1.753	

a January–October only.
b First half only.

SOURCES: Annual reports, Platt's Oilgram, Petroleum Intelligence Weekly.

Appendix 2

Annual Net Profit Figures (Millions of Dollars) and Growth Rates of the Fifteen Biggest United States Oil Companies, 1967–1973

Company	1967	1968	1969	1970	1971	1972	1973	1973 over 1967 volume %	Annual growth %
Exxon	1155	1275	1240	1308	1515	1530	2440	111.3	13.3
Texaco	754	820	770	822	904	889	1290	71.1	9.5
Standard of California	409	452	454	455	511	547	844	106.4	12.8
Mobil	385	428	457	483	541	574	843	118.9	14.0
Gulf	568	626	611	550	561	447	800	40.8	5.9
Standard of Indiana	282	309	321	314	342	375	511	81.2	10.3
U.S. Shell	285	312	291	237	245	261	333	16.8	2.7
Atlantic Rich-field/Sinclair	225	226	231	206	210	193	270	20.0	3.1
Continental	136	150	146	161	140	170	243	78.7	10.1
Sun	156	164	152	139	152	155	230	47.4	6.5
Amerada Hess				114	133	26	218		
Phillips	164	130	128	117	132	148	230	40.2	5.8
Union/Pure	145	151	139	115	115	122	180	24.1	3.6
Cities Service	128	121	127	117	105	99	136	6.3	1.0
Getty		98	106	102	120	76	135	37.8	6.6ᵃ
Marathon	74	83	90	85	89	80	129	74.3	9.8

ᵃ From 1968 to 1973.

SOURCES: *Petroleum Intelligence Weekly, Wall Street Journal, New York Times, The Oil and Gas Journal,* annual reports.

Appendix 3

Production of Fields Developed by Iranian Consortium, 1964–1974, with Ultimate Maximum Productive Capacities (Thousands of Barrels per Day)

Year	Ahvaz (Asmari and Bangestan)	Marun (Asmari and Bangestan)	Agha Jari	Gach-saran	Paza-nan	Paris	Karanj	Central Fields
1964	134	. . .[a]	863	448	14	. . .[a]	5	187
1965	160	. . .	800	456	64	. . .	40	183
1966	171	45	781	645	57	5	72	154
1967	163	157	919	665	56	25	75	134
1968	203	427	1025	562	46	25	75	113
1969	240	586	1045	724	41	18	112	104
1970	260	739	1045	842	30	68	175	94
1971	409	1070	1036	940	24	462	200	89
1972	808	1060	1052	924	28	450	262	88
1973	853	1058	1023	887	24	451	270	82
1974[b]	956	1054	1010	912	34	423	316	80
UMPC	1817	1860	1052	940	175	680	600	88

Year	Kharg Island	Bibi Haki-meh	Rag-e Safid	Ram-shir	Kupal	Binak	Par-e Siah	Lab-e Safid	Man-suri
1964	1	. . .	. . .[a]	. . .	. . .	. . .	. . .	. . .	. . .
1965	5	3	. . .	. . .	. . .[a]	. . .	. . .	. . .	. . .
1966	9	70	. . .	. . .	. . .	. . .	. . .	. . .	. . .
1967	13	230	22	8	. . .	. . .	. . .[a]	. . .	. . .
1968	20	445	47	4	. . .	12	. . .	. . .	. . .
1969	20	369	23	5	4	36	. . .	. . .[a]	. . .
1970	20	436	38	1	7	44	2	. . .	. . .
1971	58	456	75	2	7	54	12	2	. . .
1972	75	453	181	16	20	57	10	30	. . .
1973	73	366	198	15	18	55	7	26	. . .
1974[b]	66	362	313	19	21	56	7	22	5
UMPC	175	650	325	20	165	58	12	110	50

[a] Discovery well.
[b] First six months only.

SOURCE: Consortium annual reports, capital development and look-ahead plans. In the author's opinion the figures for UMPC are very conservative; for example, Bibi Hakimeh, with recoverable reserves of over 5 billion barrels, could easily produce 850,000 barrels a day. Figures for 1968–1972 reflect productive capacity, which was 10 to 15 percent greater than actual production.

Production of Fields Developed by Aramco, 1960–1974
(Thousands of Barrels per Day)

Year	Dammam	Abqaiq	Qatif	Ghawar	Safaniya	Khursaniya
1960	34.6	299.7	16.2	714.3	181.0	1.4
1961	32.3	350.3	20.4	705.5	241.3	42.7
1962	32.4	370.9	28.0	715.9	293.4	79.8
1963	31.8	383.4	25.5	769.9	305.3	71.3
1964	33.5	376.5	28.3	733.5	388.5	106.9
1965	25.8	409.6	32.5	889.9	472.2	129.5
1966	26.1	482.0	72.8	961.6	544.4	130.2
1967	23.8	515.3	60.5	1244.0	439.2	89.3
1968	22.6	534.9	54.4	1519.6	407.9	31.1
1969[a]	22.7	567.5	77.6	1427.1	407.4	81.1
1970[a]	19.7	761.6	93.4	1484.7	728.6	54.2
1971	21.3	903.0	105.8	2163.0	771.4	86.1
1972	23.5	1009.3	128.7	2725.9	955.1	122.9
1973	25.7	1057.2	103.0	4038.2	908.3	102.2
1974[a]	17.8	870.7	93.6	4653.5	1019.1	115.4

Year	Abu Hadriya	Fadhili	Manifa	Abu Sa'fa	Berri	Zuluf	Al-Harma-liya	Marjan
1960	...	...	...	...	...	...	...	...
1961	...	...	...	...	...	...	...	...
1962	.3	...	...	...	...	...	...	...
1963	41.5	.03	...	...	...	...	...	...
1964	24.9	22.4	.9	...	...	...	...	...
1965	45.0	19.6	...	...	...	...	...	...
1966	60.2	31.0	50.9	32.2	...	...	...	...
1967	65.4	40.8	54.4	40.1	23.2	...	...	...
1968	81.6	50.7	44.9	60.4	19.4	...	...	...
1969[a]	67.5	32.6	32.8	65.7	29.9	...	...	...
1970[a]	55.3	41.6	38.9	75.3	18.9	...	...	...
1971	105.8	52.1	22.2	86.9	185.6	...	...	...
1972	98.1	53.5	49.2	91.9	446.6	...	...	...
1973	86.3	48.1	36.6	188.5	606.6	143.7	41.8	.8
1974[a]	102.1	49.3	34.9	121.5	639.5	193.4	129.9	1.9

[a] First six months.

SOURCES: Aramco annual reports, *The Oil and Gas Journal*.

Joint Communiqué and Resolutions of the Khartoum Summit Conference, September 1, 1967

The Joint Communiqué

In response to the invitation extended by the Government of the Republic of the Sudan for holding a conference of their Majesties and Excellencies the Arab Kings and Presidents during the period August 29 — September 1, 1967 to study the present Arab situation and consider the drawing up of a joint Arab plan to eliminate the effects of the [June Israeli] aggression, the following met in the city of Khartoum: His Majesty King Hussein ibn Talal, King of the Hashemite Kingdom of Jordan; His Excellency Isma'il al-Azhari, the President of the Sudanese Sovereignty Council; His Excellency General 'Abd al-Rahman 'Arif, President of the Republic of Iraq; His Majesty King Faisal 'Abd al-'Aziz, King of the Kingdom of Saudi Arabia; His Excellency President Gamal 'Abd al-Nasser, President of the United Arab Republic; His Excellency President 'Abd Allah al-Sallal, President of the Arab Yemeni Republic; His Highness Amir Sabah al-Salim Al Sabah, the Amir of Kuwait; His Excellency President Charles Helou, President of the Republic of Lebanon; His Highness Amir al-Hassan al-Rida, Crown Prince of the Kingdom of Libya; His Excellency al-Bahi al-Adgham, Secretary of State for the Presidency representing His Excellency Habib Bourguiba, President of the Tunisian Republic; His Excellency Mr. Abdelaziz Bouteflika, Minister of Foreign Affairs and member of the Revolutionary Council, representing President Houari Boumedienne, President of the Popular Democratic Republic of Algeria; His Excellency Dr. Mohamed Benhima, Prime Minister of the Kingdom of Morocco, representing His Majesty King Hassan II, King of the Kingdom of Morocco.

Their meeting was characterized by a common realization of the weight of the historic responsibility facing the Arab people at this decisive and delicate stage of our struggle; and they reaffirmed their determination to stand united in facing the fateful provocations and the responsibilities thereby placed upon the Arab peoples.

Their Majesties and Excellencies the Kings and Presidents and their representatives discussed the implications of the aggression to which the Arab states were exposed on last 5 June, and decided that the elimination of the effects of the aggression from Arab territory is the joint responsibility of all the Arab states and necessitates the mobilization of all Arab capabilities. They are fully confident that these capabilities will ensure the elimination of the effects of the aggression, and that the setback experienced by the Arab peoples should provide a strong incentive for the unity of Arab ranks and for consolidating joint Arab action.

Within the framework of this appraisal, their Majesties and Excellencies the Kings and Presidents and their representatives agreed on effective means to ensure the elimination of the effects of the aggression, including support for those states whose economic resources were directly affected as a result of the aggression so as to enable the states in question to stand steadfast in the face of economic pressure.

Their Majesties and Excellencies the Kings and Presidents and their representatives expressed their firm conviction and unwavering determination regarding the necessity of maintaining united Arab action to safeguard the sacred right of the people of Palestine to their homeland. The assembled Arab leaders appeal to the peoples and governments of the world to strive to uphold this just cause so that a positive stand may be adopted vis-à-vis the Zionist-Imperialist states which have obstructed the exercise of this right by the people of Palestine.

The Arab Kings and Presidents and their representatives reviewed all aspects of the relations between their respective states and agreed to take steps calculated to consolidate and cement relations between them and to strengthen the Arab Solidarity Pact for the purpose of fulfilling the aspirations of the Arab people for prosperity and progress.

Their Majesties and Excellencies the Kings and Presidents and their representatives express their utmost appreciation for the initiative taken by the Government of the Republic of the Sudan in calling this historic meeting. They also express their overwhelming appreciation for the warm reception accorded them by the noble Sudanese people.

The Summit Resolutions
1. The conference reaffirms the unity of Arab ranks and collective action, the way having been cleared of all obstacles thereto. The Kings, Presidents and their representatives further reaffirm the adherence of their countries to the Arab Solidarity Pact — concluded at the Third Arab Summit Conference in Casablanca — and its implementation.

2. The Conference decided upon the necessity to consolidate all efforts to eliminate the effects of the aggression on the basis that the occupied territories are Arab territories whose recovery is a charge incumbent upon all the Arab states.

3. The Kings and Presidents agreed to unify their efforts as regards political action on the international and diplomatic levels in order to eliminate the effects of the aggression and ensure the withdrawal of Israeli forces from Arab territory which they occupied after June 5. This initiative is to take place within the general framework of the political principles to which the Arab states adhere, namely: no peace with Israel; no recognition of Israel; no negotiation with Israel; insistence on the rights of the Palestinian people to their homeland.

4. The Conference of Arab Ministers of Finance, Economy and Oil had recommended the possibility of employing the stoppage of the flow of oil as a weapon in the battle. However, after careful study of the matter, the Summit Conference concluded that the oil flow could itself be used as a positive weapon in that Arab oil represents an Arab asset which could be used to strengthen the economies of those Arab states which were directly affected by the aggression, thereby enabling them to stand firm in the battle. The Conference thereby decided to resume oil pumping operations on the grounds that this is an Arab asset which can be put to use in the service of Arab aims and in contributing towards enabling those Arab states which were subjected to aggression and a consequent loss of economic resources to stand firm in their resolve to eliminate the effects of the aggression.

The oil producing states have in fact already made a positive contribution towards enabling the countries affected by the aggression to stand their ground in the face of any economic pressure.

5. The conferees approved the proposal presented by the Kuwait government for establishing an Arab economic and social development fund, in line with the recommendation of the Conference of Ministers of Finance, Economy and Oil which was held in Baghdad.

6. The conferees decided upon the need to take all the required steps to promote the military build-up in order to face up to all eventualities.

7. The conference decided to speed up the liquidation of foreign bases in the Arab world.

The Conference issued a separate decision the text of which was as follows: "The Kingdom of Saudi Arabia, the State of Kuwait and the Kingdom of Libya have decided to commit themselves to the payment of the following annual sums, in quarterly installments in advance starting in mid-October and continuing until the effects of the aggression are eliminated: the Kingdom of Saudi Arabia, £ 50 million; the State of Kuwait, £ 55 million; the Kingdom of Libya, £ 30 million. In this way the Arab nation will guarantee its ability to continue the battle until the effects of the aggression are eliminated."

Appendix 6

APQ Nominations of Iranian Consortium Partners, 1957–1973 (Thousands of Barrels per Day)

	Partner	Nomination			Partner	Nomination
1957	BP	750		1961	SoCal	973
	CFP	750			Gulf	940
	Shell	714		1962	Iricon	1370
	Iricon	700			BP	1370
	EXXON[a]	*690*			Shell	1370
	SoCal	603			CFP	1370
	Gulf	574			*MOBIL*	*1342*
	Texaco	528			Texaco	1195
	Mobil	528			SoCal	1170
1958	CFP	827			Exxon	1115
	Iricon	826			Gulf	1000
	Shell	822		1963	BP	1575
	Mobil	814			CFP	1575
	BP	*787*			Iricon	1535
	Exxon	759			Shell	1534
	SoCal	724			*MOBIL*	*1521*
	Texaco	700			SoCal	1360
	Gulf	655			Texaco	1299
1959	Iricon	912			Exxon	1200
	Mobil	890			Gulf	1068
	BP	850		1964	Iricon	1740
	Shell	850			Mobil	1721
	SOCAL	*850*			Shell	1708
	Exxon	841			BP	1680
	CFP	822			*CFP*	*1680*
	Texaco	805			Texaco	1470
	Gulf	680			Exxon	1400
1960	Mobil	1111			Gulf	1314
	Iricon	1023			SoCal	1214
	BP	984		1965	CFP	1863
	Shell	960			Iricon	1860
	CFP	*911*			BP	1836
	Exxon	900			Shell	1836
	Gulf	880			*MOBIL*	*1836*
	Texaco	875			Gulf	1685
	SoCal	874			Texaco	1589
1961	Mobil	1213			Exxon	1575
	Iricon	1201			SoCal	1370
	BP	1192		1966	Iricon	2030
	Shell	1192			BP	2027
	CFP	*1192*			Shell	2027
	Exxon	980			Mobil	1964
	Texaco	980			*CFP*	*1945*

	Partner	Nomination		Partner	Nomination
1966	Exxon	1890		BP	3329
	Texaco	1712		*CFP*	*3329*
	Gulf	1700		Exxon	3205
	SoCal	1644		Gulf	3200
1967	CFP	2274		SoCal	3164
	Shell	2233		Texaco	3134
	BP	2219	1971	Iricon	4054
	Mobil	2178		Mobil	3986
	IRICON	*2178*		BP	3973
	Exxon	2100		Shell	3973
	Texaco	2005		*CFP*	*3973*
	SoCal	1973		Exxon	3973
	Gulf	1871		SoCal	3767
1968	Iricon	2698		Texaco	3562
	Shell	2678		Gulf	3286
	Gulf	2571	1972	Iricon	4678
	BP	2568		CFP	4645
	CFP	*2568*		Exxon	4638
	Mobil	2568		Shell	4590
	SoCal	2391		Mobil	4516
	Exxon	2363		SoCal	4500
	Texaco	2363		*BP*	*4372*
1969	Iricon	3062		Gulf	4257
	BP	3014		Texaco	4200
	Shell	3014	1973	Gulf	5428
	Mobil	3014		Iricon	5342
	CFP	*3014*		CFP	5297
	Gulf	2900		Exxon	5250
	Exxon	2849		BP	5137
	SoCal	2795		*MOBIL*	*5068*
	Texaco	2679		Shell	5055
1970	Iricon	3547		Texaco	5043
	Shell	3346		SoCal	4857
	Mobil	3342			

The name of the company whose nomination set APQ for each year is in capital letters and, along with its nomination, italics. Note that nominated volumes are for production, *not* export, which is always slightly less.

Source: U.S. Senate Foreign Relations Committee, Subcommittee on Multinational Corporations.

Aramco Partners' Liftings of Crude Oil from Saudi Arabia, 1963–1973

Year	MOBIL				SOCAL			
	Liftings (thousands of barrels per day)	Percentage of Total	of Over-lift	Dividend per barrel (dollars)	Liftings (thousands of barrels per day)	Percentage of Total	of Over-lift	Dividend per barrel (dollars)
1963	159.8	10.2	0.2	.921	408.6	26.0	— 4.0	.955
1964	189.8	11.3	1.3	.733	449.9	26.8	— 3.2	.798
1965	263.9	13.4	3.4	.565	490.1	24.8	— 5.2	.662
1966	280.9	12.0	2.0	.645	492.6	21.0	— 9.0	.856
1967	354.6	14.0	4.0	.586	483.3	19.1	—10.9	.748
1968	389.4	14.1	4.1	.595	535.4	19.4	—10.6	.825
1969	411.1	14.1	4.1	.594	565.3	19.4	—10.6	.792
1970	475.1	13.6	3.6	.545	713.5	20.5	— 9.5	.553
1971	541.1	12.3	2.3	.518	1099.8	25.1	— 4.9	.461
1972	630.5	11.3	1.3	.731	1537.1	27.5	— 2.5	.751
1973	772.4	11.1	1.1	.988	2007.3	28.7	— 1.3	1.04

Year	TEXACO				EXXON			
	Liftings (thousands of barrels per day)	Percentage of Total	of Over-lift	Dividend per barrel (dollars)	Liftings (thousands of barrels per day)	Percentage of Total	of Over-lift	Dividend per barrel (dollars)
1963	533.4	33.9	3.9	.842	471.7	30.0	. . .	.937
1964	531.6	31.7	1.7	.730	504.8	30.1	0.1	.777
1965	614.9	31.1	1.1	.578	606.8	30.7	0.7	.600
1966	695.5	19.7	—0.3	.699	875.4	37.3	7.3	.585
1967	821.0	32.4	2.4	.603	878.1	34.6	4.6	.635
1968	899.9	32.5	2.5	.680	941.9	34.0	4.0	.627
1969	914.7	31.3	1.3	.658	1029.4	35.2	5.2	.622
1970	1005.6	28.9	—1.1	.524	1290.9	37.0	7.0	.500
1971	1228.4	29.4	—0.6	.499	1458.5	33.2	3.2	.542
1972	1688.1	30.2	0.2	.766	1729.9	31.0	1.0	.756
1973	2062.4	29.5	—0.5	1.02	2147.9	30.7	0.7	1.01

Note that total liftings of the four companies are somewhat less than total Aramco production for the year.

Source: U.S. Senate Foreign Relations Committee, Subcommittee on Multinational Corporations.

Appendix 8

Important Fields Developed by Companies Operating in Libya, 1961–1973, with Company Totals (Thousands of Barrels per Day)

	Exxon				Oasis							Mobil/Gelsenberg			
Year	Zelten	Jebel	Ragu-ba[a]	Total	Dahra	Samah/Belhe-dan	Waha	Gialo	Defa	Bahi	Total	Hofra	Ora	Amal	Total
1961	ca 10	⋮	⋮	⋮	ca 120	⋮	⋮	⋮	⋮	⋮	⋮	⋮	⋮	⋮	⋮
1962	ca 120	⋮	⋮	⋮	ca 120	⋮	⋮	⋮	⋮	⋮	⋮	⋮	⋮	⋮	⋮
1963	250.3	⋮	43.8	⋮	118.5	5.7	42.2	⋮	⋮	⋮	⋮	2.9	⋮	⋮	⋮
1964	407.8	⋮	72.8	⋮	124.8	38.5	127.1	26.4	⋮	⋮	⋮	45.5	⋮	⋮	⋮
1965	433.1	38.3	95.7	⋮	128.9	51.2	122.4	194.3	1.9	⋮	⋮	68.6	29.3	⋮	⋮
1966	439.9	48.3	95.8	⋮	98.9	69.9	134.4	266.2	3.1	⋮	⋮	34.7	43.3	84.5	⋮
1967	447.5	40.0	107.2	603.0	99.4	86.6	135.6	303.5	⋮	⋮	630.0	27.0	23.9	153.2	204.2
1968	552.4	41.9	117.2	740.6	87.0	90.7	145.2	357.2	⋮	⋮	686.0	22.3	18.6	196.2	235.5
1969	569.9	32.6	125.0	746.2	76.6	75.9	125.7	333.4	12.5	na	789.7	12.4	15.9	204.4	264.5
1970	528.2	22.2	121.3	692.0	58.6	84.8	141.1	380.9	173.0	108.1	948.6	6.1	12.8	199.1	253.3
1971	314.8	16.4	98.6	445.6	35.6	56.4	124.9	341.0	160.3	103.5	827.0	.8	10.8	150.8	186.4
1972	225.5	13.8	93.7	354.0	37.4	57.9	118.4	321.3	156.8	104.7	798.8	⋮	7.4	102.5	162.8
1973	187.5	23.1	82.7	311.2	31.2	46.5	130.2	292.9	173.3	91.2	768.3	⋮	6.2	118.5	144.3
1974[b]	163.9	23.4	70.4	260.0	30.7	25.2	118.2	203.1	156.8	84.3	620.8	⋮	5.1	104.2	n.a.

[a] Exxon has a 50 percent interest in this field, Atlantic Richfield and Grace another 50 percent.
[b] First six months only.

SOURCES: *The Oil and Gas Journal*, annual reports, *Middle East Economic Survey*, *Petroleum Intelligence Weekly*.
NOTE: Individual fields do not add up to exact totals, owing to exclusion of minor or recent fields and discrepancies among various independent sources.

Year	Amoseas				Phillips	BP/Hunt[a]	Pan Am	Occidental					Aquitaine Group	ENI
	Beda	Kotla	Nafoora	Total	Umm Farrud Only	Sarir Only	Khuff, then Sahabi	103A	103D	103C	Augila	Total		Bu Attifel Only
1961														
1962														
1963														
1964	13.1													
1965	43.7	7.6			2.4									
1966	43.8	13.6	25.3		8.2	4.0	8.3							
1967	32.5	11.2	84.0	129.0	4.7	168.5	4.4							
1968	24.9	11.5	202.0	243.5	7.4	304.1	1.1	336.7	44.3		0.2	381.6		
1969	17.6	12.9	330.0	368.9	6.0	321.3	0.5	346.6	232.2		51.9	608.1	5.5	
1970	12.4	13.4	290.9	323.0	4.2	408.0	7.7	240.9	302.9	31.3	84.4	659.6	20.1	
1971	7.8	11.4	236.2	261.2		405.9	14.7	187.3	281.0	30.8	61.1	586.7	17.0	
1972	6.8	9.4	b	234.0		215.8	9.4	100.6	201.2	38.0	b	424.0	16.3	24.0
1973	6.5	8.7	b	234.7		235.9	5.8	71.5	196.4	39.4	b	349.9	13.0	145.6
1974+	9.7	6.7	b	191.9		162.6	4.3	73.6	203.7	36.7	b	n.a.	n.a.	126.2

[a] BP's 50 percent interest was nationalized in late 1971, that of Hunt in 1973.

[b] Nafoora and Augila fields were unitized, and their production figures combined, in late 1971.

Appendix 9

Estimated Comparative Development Costs of Some Iranian Consortium Fields in Recent Years (In Pounds Sterling Per Daily Barrel)

Field and Area	Volume (b/d)	Well Productivity (b/d)	Months Needed to Drill Well (Rig Months)	Cost of Drilling Well	Cost of Oil Line From Field
1. Paris 1 and Expansion	300,000	36,000	1.25	5.63	. . .
2. Marun 2	150,000	25,000	2.25	5.3	4.37
3. Bibi Hakimeh 2	150,000	20,000	1.25	7.2	3.33
4. Gachsaran 3	100,000	40,000	1.0	3.7	. .
5. Karanj 2	50,000	40,000	1.5	4.53	2.36/1.11
6. Bibi Hakimeh 1	150,000	20,000	1.25	7.2	4.73
7. Paris 2	150,000	36,000	1.25	5.63	3.70
8. Paris 2 Expansion	180,000	36,000	1.25	6.1	. . .
9. Karanj 2 Expansion	55,000	40,000	1.5	6.62	. . .
10. Marun 1 Expansion	150,000	25-30,000	2.5	13.18	2.93
11. Ahvaz 4	220,000	26,000	1.25	8.4	. . .
12. Rag-e Safid 1 Expansion	100,000	13,000	1.75	16.36	2.7
13. Lab-e Safid Test and Expansion	100,000	20,000	1.75	14.88	5.3
14. Rag-e Safid 2	100,000	13,000	1.75	22.9	1.45
15. Marun 4	300,000	30,000	2.25	12.3	5.42
16. Rag-e Safid 2 Expansion	50,000	8,300	1.75	27.77	. . .
17. Ahvaz 1 Expansion	220,000	27,500	1.25	7.47	. . .
18. Ahvaz/Bangestan	150,000	20,000	3.25	27.66	. . .
19. Marun 5	375,000	25,000	3.25	22.7	2.25
20. Ahvaz 3 and Expansion	165,000	15,000	1.75	19.9	15.21
21. Kupal Test and Expansion	70,000	11,000	2.25	36.1	3.0
22. Sarkan	25,000	15,000	1.5	11.74	24.08/8.4
23. Kupal/Bangestan	90,000	15,000	3.5	38.5	3.0
24. Ramin	75,000	10,000	3.5	46.2	3.27
25. Cheshmeh Khosh	105,000	15,000	2.25	24.8	21.33
26. Marun/Bangestan	60,000	15,000	4.5	51.05	2.44
27. Mansuri	50,000	5,000	1.5	51.05	6.0
28. Kharg Expansion[a]	50,000	7,000	2.75	66.86	. . .
29. Ab Teymour	50,000	12,000	4.75	67.35	6.25
30. Ramshir/Bangestan	N.A.	12,000	6.0	88.29	nil
31. Binak/Bangestan	N.A.	35,000	6.5	32.73	nil
32. Par-e Siah	N.A.	9,000	1.5	29.4	14.0
33. Kilur Karim/ Bangestan	N.A.	5,000	3.5	123.5	nil

Field and Area	Cost of Pumps From Field	Cost of Intermediate Down-Stream Lines and Pumps	Total Cost per Daily Barrel (£)	Total Cost per Daily Barrel ($)	Production Startup Date
1. Paris 1 and Expansion	.76	3.14	9.53	22.87	1970
2. Marun 2	. . .	. . .	9.67	23.20	1968
3. Bibi Hakimeh 2	. . .	. . .	10.53	25.24	1968
4. Gachsaran 3	7.5	. . .	11.2	26.88	1966
5. Karanj 2	1.71/.48	2.14	12.33	29.59	1971
6. Bibi Hakimeh 1	1.16	. . .	13.09	31.41	1967–68
7. Paris 2	.48	1.71/2.14	13.66	32.78	1971
8. Paris 2 Expansion	.9	9.37	16.37	39.28	1975
9. Karanj 2 Expansion	.9	9.37	16.89	40.53	1975
10. Marun 1 Expansion	.66	.92	17.69	42.45	1970
11. Ahvaz 4	10.18	. . .	18.58	44.59	1974
12. Rag-e Safid 1 Expansion	1.08	. . .	20.14	48.33	1972
13. Lab-e Safid Test and Expansion	.68	. . .	20.86	50.06	1972–76
14. Rag-e Safid 2	2.0	. . .	26.35	63.24	1973
15. Marun 4	3.13	6.46	27.31	65.54	1974 (Oct)
16. Rag-e Safid 2 Expansion	. . .	. . .	27.72	66.52	1974
17. Ahvaz 1 Expansion	2.41	19.64	29.52	70.84	1972
18. Ahvaz/Bangestan	3.83	. . .	31.49	75.57	1973
19. Marun 5	.49	6.46	31.90	76.56	1975
20. Ahvaz 3 and Expansion	2.15	. . .	37.26	89.42	1972–74
21. Kupal Test and Expansion	4.66	. . .	43.76	105.02	1975
22. Sarkan	. . .	. . .	44.22	106.12	undecided
23. Kupal/Bangestan	4.66	. . .	46.16	110.78	undecided
24. Ramin	. . .	. . .	49.47	118.72	1975
25. Cheshmeh Khosh	5.98	. . .	52.11	125.06	undecided
26. Marun/Bangestan	.57	. . .	54.06	129.74	1974
27. Mansuri	.34	. . .	57.39	137.73	1974
28. Kharg Expansion[a]	. . .	. . .	66.86	160.46	1972
29. Ab Teymour	.71	. . .	74.26	178.22	undecided
30. Ramshir/Bangestan	N.A.	N.A.	88.29+	211.89+	no prospect
31. Binak/Bangestan	N.A.	. . .	N.A.	N.A.	1977?
32. Par-e Siah	. . .	. . .	N.A.	N.A.	no prospect
33. Kilur Karim/ Bangestan	N.A.	. . .	123.5+	296.40+	no prospect

SOURCES: Various Consortium documents, primarily Capital Development Plan and Program (1971–75, 1972–76, 1973–75).

NOTE: Rig-month costs ranged from £120,800 in 1970 to £176,600 in 1974–75. £ = $2.40.

This table makes it possible to see the extent to which the depth and productivity of the individual well, and the proximity of the field to the coast, determine whether or not to invest in a prospect, and how soon to invest in it. However, some costs, mostly downstream, are adventitious; since they were postponed as long as possible, they do not reflect only the development of a particular field, they also reflect the development of other fields which went onstream earlier. For instance, the table shows that it was cheaper to develop Bibi Hakimeh 2 than Bibi Hakimeh 1, because the requisite pumps had already been installed; the expansion of Ahvaz 1 appears expensive because it was accompanied by heavy investment in downstream lines and pumps which were already on the verge of being overtaxed by earlier development. So it is not entirely fair to lay the cost for these facilities entirely upon one prospect.

Note that this table does not include all development costs of Iranian fields. It contains the significant variable costs but leaves out two other elements. First is costs for production facilities, which in fact vary only slightly, from about £7.14 to £11.6 (or $17 to $28) per daily barrel, except for small test facilities, which naturally are more expensive since they handle small volumes.
[a] Second is the cost for all facilities at the Gorreh booster station on the coast, the pipelines from there to Kharg Island, and the facilities on the island itself. These devolve about equally on all fields (except Kharg itself) and ranged from about £27.4 per daily barrel in 1971 to £38 in 1974.

Text of Agreement Between Oil Companies
and Persian Gulf Members of OPEC
Tehran, February 14, 1971

Abu Dhabi, Iran, Iraq, Kuwait, Qatar and Saudi Arabia (the said six States being hereinafter known as "the Gulf States" insofar as their exports from the Gulf are concerned) and the Companies listed in Annex 1 and their affiliates (hereinafter known as "the Companies"), to establish security of supply and stability in financial arrangements agree:

1. The existing arrangements between each of the Gulf States and each of the Companies to which this agreement is an overall amendment, will continue to be valid in accordance with their terms.

2. The following provisions constitute a settlement of the terms relating to government take and other financial obligations of the Companies operating in the Gulf States as to the subject matters referred to in OPEC Resolutions and as regards oil exported from the Gulf, for a period from 15th February 1971 through 31st December 1975. These provisions shall be binding on both the Gulf States and the Companies for the said period.

3. These provisions are: —

  (a) NO LEAPFROGGING: During this Agreement no Gulf State will seek any increase in government take or other financial obligations over that now agreed regarding Gulf production, as a result of: —

    (1) The application of different terms in:

      (i) any Gulf States as a Mediterranean exporter; or

      (ii) any Mediterranean producer; or

      (iii) any producer from any other area; or

    (2) The breach of contract through unilateral action by any Government in the Gulf; or

    (3) The elimination of existing disparities in the Gulf under paragraph (c) (2) (iv) or any settlement under paragraph (c) (3) THIRDLY; or

    (4) The application of different terms to any future agreement in any country bordering on the Gulf.

  (b) NO EMBARGO: The requirements of the six Member Countries of OPEC bordering the Gulf under OPEC Resolutions XXI.120 and XXII.131 are satisfied by the terms of this Agreement. During the period of this Agreement the Gulf states shall not take any action in the Gulf to support any OPEC member which may demand either any increase in government take above the terms now agreed, or any increase in government take or any other matter not covered by Resolution XXI.120.

  (c) FINANCIAL TERMS TO MEET OPEC RESOLUTION XXI.120, PARAGRAPH 1:

    (1) Total tax rates on income shall be stabilized in accordance with existing arrangements, except that insofar as present tax laws provide for total rates lower than 55 percent, the Companies concerned will submit to an amendment to the relevant income tax laws raising the total rates to 55 percent.

(2) In satisfaction of the several claims arising out of paragraphs 2 and 3 of OPEC Resolution XXI.120:

(i)   Each of the companies shall uniformly increase as from the effective date its crude posted prices at the Gulf terminals of the Gulf States by 33¢ per barrel.

(ii) (aa) Each of the companies shall make further upward adjustments to its crude posted prices to the nearest tenth of a cent per barrel by increasing on 1st June 1971 each of such posted prices by an amount equal to 2½% of such posted price on the day following the effective date. On 1st January of each of the years 1973 through 1975 a further increase to the nearest tenth of a cent shall be made in each such posted price equivalent to 2½% of the posted price prevailing on 31st December of the preceding year.

(ii) (bb) Each of the companies shall increase its crude posted prices on 1st June 1971 by 5¢ per barrel and by a further increase of 5¢ per barrel on 1st January in each of the years 1973–1975.

(ii) (cc) Each of the companies shall further increase its crude posted prices as from the effective date by 2¢ per barrel which, together with paragraph 3 (d) is in satisfaction of claims related to freight disparities.

(iii)   The increases included in (ii) above shall be in satisfaction of claims in respect of freight, escalation and of inflation under both OPEC Resolution XXI.120 and OPEC Resolution XXI.122, and also in satisfaction of certain other economic considerations raised by the Gulf States.

(iv)   Each of the Gulf States having an existing claim under negotiation based on posted price disparity has discussed and resolved such claim with the Companies exporting the crude grade concerned as follows:
In the case of Iranian Heavy, Saudi Arabian Medium and Kuwait, the posted prices shall each be increased by the Companies concerned by one cent with effect from the effective date. In the case of Basrah after the adjustment provided for in (3) firstly the posted price will be $1.805 for 35° API.

(3) OPEC 120 PARAGRAPH 4:
Firstly For crude oil API gravity 30.0° to 39.9° with effect from the effective date each posted price shall be further increased by the Companies by ½¢ per barrel for each degree such crude is less than API° 40. A table showing the resulting increases before taking into account the settlement of disparities under (c) (2) (iv) is attached (Annex 2) and forms part of this Agreement.
Secondly Posted prices shall apply to shipments falling within the range of .0 to .09 degrees of any full degree of API gravity and shall be subject to a gravity differential on the basis of 0.15¢ per barrel for each full 0.1 degree API.

Thirdly In the case of crudes under 30° API the Governments and Companies shall agree on a basis for adjusting the posted price. However, if no such agreement is reached the same principles applied in firstly and secondly above shall apply.
The existing percent allowance, the gravity allowance and the ½¢ per barrel marketing allowance shall be eliminated as from the effective date of this Agreement.

(d) If Libya is receiving a premium for short haul crude which premium is to fluctuate according to freight conditions in accordance with a freight formula and if in respect of any period the premium applied by any major oil company which has production in Libya and the Gulf States exceeds for any reason the lowest level permitted by such formula for such period the Gulf States shall be entitled to additional payments as set out in Annex 3.

4. "Affiliate" shall mean in relation to any Company, any company which is wholly or partly owned directly or indirectly by that Company.

5. Each of the Gulf States accepts that the Companies' undertakings hereunder constitute a fair appropriate and final settlement between each of them, and those of the Companies operating within their respective jurisdictions, of all matters related to the applicable bases of taxation and the levels of posted prices up to the effective date.

6. The effective date of this Agreement shall be 15th February 1971.

Done this 14th Day of February, 1971 at Tehran, Iran.

For the Gulf States: Mana Saeed Otaiba, Abu Dhabi; Jamshid Amouzegar, Iran; Saadoun Hammadi, Iraq; Abdul-Rahman Al-Ateeqy, Kuwait; Hassan Kamel, Qatar; Ahmad Zaki Yamani, Saudi Arabia.

For the Companies: Strathalmond; George T. Piercy; A. C. DeCrane, Jr.; John E. Kircher; W. P. Tavoulareas.

Annex 1

The British Petroleum Company Limited
Compagnie Française Des Pétroles
Gulf Oil Corporation
Mobil Oil Corporation
The Shell Petroleum Company Limited and
   Shell Petroleum N.V.
Standard Oil Company of California
Standard Oil Company (New Jersey) [now known as Exxon]
Texaco Inc.
Continental Oil Company
Standard Oil Company (Ohio)
Hispanica de Petróleos S.A.
American Independent Oil Company of Iran
Signal (Iran) Petroleum Company

Annex 2

Crude	Deg. API	Present Posting $/Barrel	½¢ Per Barrel × Degrees of Gravity Under 40	Adjusted Posted Price* $/Barrel
Qatar	40	1.93	0	1.93
Abu Dhabi	39	1.88	.005	1.885
Abu Dhabi Marine	37	1.86	.015	1.875
Qatar Marine	36	1.83	.02	1.85
Basrah	35	1.72	.025	1.745
Arabian Light	34	1.80	.03	1.830
Iran Light	34	1.79	.03	1.820
Iran Heavy	31	1.72	.045	1.765
Kuwait	31	1.68	.045	1.725
Arab Medium	31	1.68	.045	1.725

The crude below API Gravity 30 deg. is not covered by this table.

* Subject to paragraph 3 (c) (2) (IV)

Annex 3
Short Haul Freight

The following provisions shall apply with respect to the implementation of paragraph 3 (d) of the Agreement to which this Annex 3 is attached.

(1) Any major oil company concerned shall pay to each Gulf State (as a supplemental payment) that proportion of a "balancing amount" as such company's crude production exported from Gulf terminals (including Arabia/Bahrain pipeline) in such Gulf State bear to the total of such Company's crude exports in such period from all Gulf States in the Gulf.

(2) The "balancing amount" will be equal to the monetary amount by which the Company's payments to Libya for the period exceed the monetary amount which the company would have paid to Libya for the period if it had effected the full reduction of premium permitted by its agreement with Libya or if it had effected a reduction in premium equal to 21½¢/B which is agreed with the Gulf States to be the short haul premium, whichever reduction is smaller.

(3) "Major Oil Company" for the above purpose means any of Esso, Texaco, SoCal, Gulf, Mobil, BP, Shell and CFP.

(4) Illustrative examples of the implementation of the terms of this annex are shown in Exhibit A, following.

Exhibit A
Illustrative Example of "Balancing Amount"

	Cents/BBL			
Shorthaul Premium agreed with the Gulf States:	21.5	21.5	21.5	21.5
Libyan "Premium" for illustrative purposes:	18.0	21.5	24.0	30.0
Lesser of Under-Reduction of Libyan Freight Premium or 21½¢/B:				
1. Libyan Premium should be reduced by 25% but is not	4.5	5.375	6.0	7.5
2. Libyan Premium should be reduced by 50% but is not	9.0	10.75	12.0	15.0
3. Libyan Premium should be reduced by 100% but is not	18.0	21.5	21.5	21.5
4. Libyan Premium should be reduced by 100% but was only reduced to 50%	9.0	10.75	12.0	15.0
5. Libyan Premium should be reduced by 100% but was only reduced by 25%	13.5	16.125	18.0	21.5

To obtain balancing amount:
(a) Multiply figure given under 1–5 by the total Libyan tax rate on income plus (100 percent minus such rate) applied to the royalty, all as applicable to the producer concerned.
(b) Multiply resultant dollar/B figure in (a) by the barrels of the major company's crude production exported from Libya.

Bibliography

1. GENERAL WORKS ON OIL

Adelman, Morris A., *The World Petroleum Market,* Baltimore: Johns Hopkins University Press, 1972.
———, "Efficiency of Resource Use in Crude Petroleum," *Southern Economic Journal,* October 1964.
Aspin, Les, Congressman, "The Oil Company Blues," *New York Review of Books,* March 7, 1974.
Dugger, Ronald, "Oil and Politics," *Atlantic,* September 1969.
Engler, Robert, *The Politics of Oil,* New York: Macmillan, 1961.
Frankel, Paul, *Mattei: Oil and Power Politics,* London: Faber & Faber, 1966.
Garland, T. M., and W. D. Dietzmann, *Engineering Cost Study of Development Wells and Profitability Analysis of Crude Oil Production,* United States Department of the Interior, Bureau of Mines, 1972.
Hartshorne, J. E., *Politics and World Oil Economics,* New York: Praeger, 1962.
Kaufman, Gordon, *Statistical Decision and Related Techniques in Oil and Gas Exploration,* Englewood Cliffs: Prentice-Hall, 1963.
Odell, Peter, *Oil and World Power, a Geographical Interpretation,* New York: Penguin Books, 1970.
Penrose, Edith, *The International Petroleum Industry,* London: Allen & Unwin, 1968.
———, "Opec and the Changing Structure of the International Petroleum Industry," *Middle East Economic Survey,* March 7, 1967.
Rothschild, Emma, "What is the Energy Crisis?" "Illusions About Energy," *New York Review of Books,* July 19, August 9, 1973.
United States Congress, House of Representatives, Permanent Select Committee on Small Business, Subcommittee on Activities of Regulatory Agencies, *Energy Data Requirements of the Federal Government,* Parts I–III, January–May 1974.
United States Congress, Senate, Foreign Relations Committee, Subcommittee on Multinational Corporations, *Multinational Corporations and United States Foreign Policy,* Parts 4–7, 1974.
United States Congress, Senate Committee on Government Operations, Permanent Subcommittee on Investigations, *Current Energy Shortages Oversight Series,* Parts 1–4, 1974.
United States Congress, Senate, Committee on the Judiciary, Committee on Antitrust and Monopoly, *Governmental Intervention in the Market Mechanism: The Petroleum Industry,* Parts I–V, March–April 1969.
United States Congress, Senate, Select Committee on Small Business, *Role of Giant Corporations,* November 1971.
United States Department of Justice, International Petroleum Cartel Case, *Plaintiff's Statement of Claims,* Washington, D.C., 1961.
United States Federal Trade Commission, *The International Petroleum Cartel,* Staff Report by United States Senate, Subcommittee on Monopoly and Select Committee on Small Business, 1952.

2. WORKS ON OIL IN THE MIDDLE EAST

Barger, Thomas, "Middle Eastern Oil Since the Second World War," *Annals of the American Academy of Political and Social Science,* May 1972.

Breckenfeld, Gurney, "How the Arabs Changed the Oil Business," *Fortune*, August 1971.

Brown, Robert W., "Geographic Factors in the Construction and Operation of Libyan Petroleum Ports," *The Libyan Economic and Business Review*, Benghazi, Autumn 1966.

Brown, Stanley H., "Dr. Hammer's Magic Tingle," *Fortune*, July 1968.

Demaree, Allan T., "Aramco Is a Lesson in the Management of Chaos," *Fortune*, February 1974.

Dunnington, H. V., "Stratigraphical Distribution of Oilfields in the Iran-Iraq-Arabia Basin," London, *Journal of the Institute of Petroleum*, April 1967.

Eghtedari, Ali Mohammad, "Some Financial Aspects of the Anglo-Iranian Oil Dispute," unpublished M.A. thesis, University of California, Berkeley, 1952.

Fatemi, Nasrollah Saifpour, *Oil Diplomacy: Powderkeg in Iran*, New York: Whittier Books, 1954.

Froozan, M., "Problems of the Oil Industry in the Middle East," National Iranian Oil Company, *Newsletter*, Tehran, June 1966.

Funkhouser, Richard, "Memorandum to Ambassador Parker Hart," 1953 released by U.S. Senate Committee on Foreign Relations, Subcommittee on Multinational Corporations.

Gedeist, John, untitled manuscript on the origins of the oil industry in Libya.

Heard, Don T., "Production of High Volume, Low Energy Crude Oil," Libyan Association of Petroleum Technologists, Tripoli, Libya, January 1966.

Hester, Richard L., "Persian Gulf: A Geological Picture that Promises Much," *Oil and Gas Journal*, November 1, 1965.

Hewins, Ralph, *Mr. Five Per Cent, the Story of Calouste Gulbenkian*, New York, Rinehart, 1958.

Hirst, David, *Oil and Public Opinion in the Middle East*, London: Faber & Faber, 1966.

Iraq National Oil Company, "Dawr Sharikat al-Naft al-Wataniya al-'Iraqiya fi Tatwir Naft al-Iraq," (Role of Iraq National Oil Company in Developing the Oil of Iraq), Baghdad: al-Nujum Press, 1965.

Iskandar, Marwan, "Economic Development Planning in Oil Exporting Countries and their Implications for Oil Production Targets," *Middle East Economic Survey*, March 7, 1969.

———, "Arab Oil After the Summit," *Middle East Economic Survey*, September 15, 1967.

Issawi, Charles, and Mohammad Yeganeh, *The Economics of Middle Eastern Oil*, New York: Praeger, 1963.

Jensen, James T., "International Oil — Shortage, Cartel, or Emerging Natural Monopoly?" *Vanderbilt Journal of Transnational Law*, Spring 1974.

Lenczowski, George, *Oil and State in the Middle East*, Ithaca: Cornell University Press, 1960.

Lichtblau, John H., "The Politics of Petroleum," *The Reporter*, July 13, 1967.

Longrigg, Stephen, *Oil in the Middle East: Its Discovery and Development*, New York: Oxford University Press, 1962.

El Mallakh, Ragaei, "The Economics of a Reopened Suez Canal," Middle East Institute, Problem Paper No. 4, Washington, D.C., 1974.

Middle East Institute, "How Will We Pay for Oil?" Problem Papers No. 1, No. 1 Revised Edition, Washington, D.C., 1974.

Mosley, Leonard, *Power Play: Oil in the Middle East,* New York: Random House, 1973.

———, "The Richest Oil Company in the World," New York *Times Magazine,* March 10, 1974.

Naghavi, Said, and Manoochehri, Nasser, "Iranian Gas Trunkline Project," National Iranian Oil Company, *Newsletter,* Tehran, June 1967.

Nahai, Lotfollah, and Charles L. Kimbell, *The Petroleum Industry of Iran,* Washington, D.C., U.S. Department of the Interior, Bureau of Mines, 1963.

National Iranian Oil Company, *San'at-e Naft-e Iran dar Dowre-ye Shahanshahi-ye Selsele-ye Pahlavi* (Iran's Oil Industry in the Imperial Era of the Pahlavi Dynasty), Tehran, 1971.

———, *Taghvim-e San'at-e Naft-e Iran* (Chronology of the Iranian Oil Industry), Tehran, n.d. (post-1969).

O'Brien, William D., "Libya's Revenue From Petroleum," *The Libyan Economic and Business Review,* Benghazi, Spring 1968.

Pachachi, Nadim, "The Development of Concession Arrangements and Taxation in the Middle East," *Middle East Economic Survey,* Supplement, March 29, 1968.

Paran, Y., and J. G. Crichton, "Highlights of Exploration in Iran 1956–1965," National Iranian Oil Company, *Newsletter,* Tehran, July 1966.

Penrose, Edith, "The International Oil Industry in the Middle East," National Bank of Egypt, Fiftieth Anniversary Commemoration Lectures, Cairo, 1968.

Philby, H. St. J. B., *Arabian Oil Ventures,* The Middle East Institute, Washington, D.C., 1964.

Platt's Oilgram, "Texts of Minutes of Kassem-Herridge Talks in Baghdad on IPC Agreement," April 24, 1961.

———, "Texts of Minutes on Negotiations in Baghdad on IPC Agreement," November 24, 1961.

al-Qaysi, Hameed A., *An Economic Appraisal of Iraq Petroleum Concessions,* Columbia University Press, 1961.

Rand, Christopher T., "The Arabian Fantasy," *Harper's,* January, 1974.

———, "U.S. Tax Law and the Price of Oil," *Worldview,* December, 1974.

Saidi, Ali and R. E. Martin, "Method of Developing a Newly-Discovered Fractured Limestone Field in Iran," National Iranian Oil Company, *Newsletter,* Tehran, April 1966.

Sayyab, Abdullah S., "Al-ʿAwamil al-Jiyulujiya lil-Ihtimalat al-Naftiya fil-ʿIraq" (Geological Elements in the Oil Potential of Iraq), Beirut, *Arab Oil and Gas Journal,* November 1966, February 1967.

Sheehan, Edward R. F., "Unradical Shieks Who Shake the World," New York *Times Magazine,* March 24, 1974.

Solow, Herbert, "The Drillings and Diggings of Dr. Phillips," *Fortune,* February 1957.

Stauffer, Thomas R., "The ERAP Agreement, A Study in Marginal Taxation Pricing," Baghdad, Sixth Arab Petroleum Congress, 1967; reprinted in *Platt's Oilgram,* March 27, 1967.

———, "Impact of Middle East Petroleum Operations Upon the U.S. and U.K. Balance of Payments," *Middle East Economic Survey,* May 30, 1969.

————, "The Economics of Petroleum Taxation in the Eastern Hemisphere," *Middle East Economic Survey*, October 17, 1969.

Stocking, George W., "National Oil Companies and OPEC's Aims," *Middle East Economic Survey*, May 19, 1967.

Tanzer, Michael, *The Political Economy of International Oil and the Underdeveloped Countries*, Boston: Beacon Press, 1970.

Tariki, Abdullah, *Al-Bitrul al-ʿArabi: Silah fil-Maʿraka* (Arab Oil: a Weapon in the Struggle) , Beirut, Palestine Liberation Organization Research Center, 1967.

United States Congress, Senate, Committee on Foreign Relations, Subcommittee on Multinational Corporations, *The International Petroleum Cartel, the Iranian Consortium and U.S. National Security*, Washington, 1974.

United States Congress, Senate, Committees on the Judiciary and Interior and Insular Affairs, *Emergency Oil Lift Program and Related Oil Problems*, 1957.

3. GENERAL WORKS ON RECENT NEAR EASTERN HISTORY

Abdel-Malek, Anouar, *Egypt: Military Society*, New York: Vintage Books, 1968.

Ambroggi, Robert P., "Water Under the Sahara," *Scientific American*, May 1966.

Aramco World, a publication of Arabian American Oil Company which appears once every two months.

Bayne, E. A., *Persian Kingship in Transition*, New York: American Universities Field Staff, 1968.

Cottam, Richard W., *Nationalism in Iran*, Pittsburgh: University of Pittsburgh Press, 1967.

Copeland, Miles, *The Game of Nations*, New York: Simon and Schuster, 1969.

Draper, Theodore, "Israel and World Politics," *Commentary*, August 1967.

Elwell-Sutton, L. P., "Nationalism and Neutralism in Iran," *The Middle East Journal*, Winter 1958.

Ford, Alan W., *The Anglo-Iranian Oil Dispute of 1951–52*, Berkeley: University of California Press, 1954.

Head, Simon, "The Monarchs of the Persian Gulf," *New York Review of Books*, March 21, 1974.

Hurewitz, J. C., "The Persian Gulf: British Withdrawal and Western Security," *Annals of the American Academy of Political and Social Science*, May 1972.

Iran, Government of, Interviews Granted by His Imperial Majesty Mohammad Reza Pahlavi Aryamehr, Shahanshah of Iran, to: the magazine *Der Spiegel* (January 4, 1974) , Peter Snow, Independent Television News, England (January 28, 1974) , Ian Colvin, *London Daily Telegraph* (February 5, 1974) .

Kedourie, Elie, "Arab Political Memoirs," London, *Encounter*, November 1972.

Kerr, Malcolm, *The Arab Cold War 1958–1967*, New York: Oxford University Press, 1967.

Kraft, Joseph, *The Struggle for Algeria*, Garden City: Doubleday, 1961.

Lacouture, Jean, *Nasser, a Biography*, New York: Alfred A. Knopf, 1973.

Laqueur, Walter Z., *The Arab-Israeli Reader,* New York: Bantam Books, 1969.
———, *The Road to War,* Baltimore: Penguin Books, 1969.
Lenczowski, George, "United States Support for Iran's Independence and Integrity," *Annals of the American Academy of Political and Social Science,* May 1972.
———, *Russia and the West in Iran 1918–1948,* Ithaca: Cornell University Press, 1949.
Middle East Institute, *The Present Situation in Iran,* Washington, D.C.: December 1953.
Nirumand, Bahman, *Iran, the New Imperialism in Action,* New York: Monthly Review Press, 1969.
Rodinson, Maxime, *Israel and the Arabs,* Penguin Books, 1969.
Rouleau, Eric, "Crisis in Jordan," *The World Today,* February 1967.
Seale, Patrick, and Maureen McConville, *The Hilton Assignment,* New York: Praeger, 1973.
United States Congress, House of Representatives, *New Perspectives on the Persian Gulf,* Hearings before the Committee on Foreign Affairs, Subcommittee on the Near East and South Asia, June–November 1973.
Upton, Joseph M., *The History of Modern Iran, an Interpretation,* Cambridge: Harvard University Press, 1960.
Zabih, Sepehr, *The Communist Movement in Iran,* Berkeley: University of California Press, 1966.
———, "Mosaddegh's Era: a Study of Domestic Political Forces of Iran," unpublished M.A. thesis, University of California, 1958.

4. PERIODICALS AND GENERAL REFERENCE WORKS

American Enterprise Institute, *United States Interests in the Middle East,* Washington, D.C., 1968.
Arabian American Oil Company, *Aramco Handbook,* Dhahran, Saudi Arabia, 1968.
Annual reports: Iranian Oil Exploration and Production Company, Arabian American Oil Company, National Iranian Oil Company, Exxon Corporation, Texaco, Inc., Mobil Oil Corporation, Gulf Oil Corporation, Standard Oil Company of California, and others.
The British Petroleum Company Ltd., *Annual Statistical Review of the World Petroleum Industry,* London.
Iranian Oil Producing and Exploration Company, *Capital Development Plan and Program; Look-Ahead Plans for Crude Production Capacity,* 1964–1972.
Iranian Petroleum Institute/Anjoman-e Naft-e Iran, publications.
Joint Publications Research Service, Department of Commerce, Washington, D.C., *Translations on Near East,* including regular economic, political and legal items from major Near Eastern periodicals, principally *al-Nahar* (Beirut), *al-Ahram* (Cairo), *al-Ahram al-Iqtisadi* (Cairo), *al-Ba'th* (Damascus), *al-Thawra* (Baghdad), *al-Anwar* (Beirut), *al-Fajr al-Jadid* (Tripoli, Libya), *al-Tali'a* (Kuwait), *al-Ray' al-'Amm* (Kuwait), *Ettelaat* (Tehran), *Keyhan* (Tehran).
Majallat al-Bitrul wal-Ghaz al-'Arabi (Arab Oil and Gas Journal), Beirut.

Middle East Economic Survey, Beirut, Lebanon.

The Middle East Journal.

National Iranian Oil Company, *Newsletter,* Tehran; superseded by *Iran Oil Journal.*

The Oil and Gas Journal, Tulsa, Oklahoma.

Petroleum Intelligence Weekly, New York.

Petroleum and Petrochemical International, London.

Petroleum Press Service, London.

The Petroleum Publishing Company, *International Petroleum Encyclopedia,* Tulsa, Oklahoma, 1968, 1970.

Platt's Oilgram, New York.

Index

C